"Because so much discussion of work and how it is changing across the world involves analysts and policy makers employing work categories to understand what is happening, this book offers a vital contribution to ongoing and emerging debates. Those wanting a critical perspective on the various fashionable discussions that abound in analysis of work and its future will find this volume of especially notable interest."

Tony Watson, Professor of Sociology, University of Nottingham

"The key question in this exciting volume is one that has become extra important during our post-pandemic times: How do we look at work, and what consequences does this view have – for the people who work, for the rest of us, for society? The answers to this question turn out to be both complex and surprising. Highly recommended."

Richard Swedberg, Professor of Sociology, Cornell University

"This book offers an original perspective on the contemporary transformations of work. It proposes ingeniously to start from the categories used by social actors to talk about work, to organize it, to regulate its forms (such as remote work, dirty work, emotional labor, platform work . . .). Through the 18 proposed entries, all of which are equally fascinating, a kaleidoscope of tensions and tendencies affecting our social world takes shape."

Eve Chiapello, Research Director at EHESS, Paris

SHIFTING CATEGORIES OF WORK

What do human beings do when they work, how is work organized, and what are its multidimensional – economic, social, political, biographical, ecological – effects? We cannot answer these questions without drawing on the numerous categories that we use to describe work, such as "skilled" or "unskilled" work, "domestic work" or "wage labor," "gig work" or "platform work." Such categories are not merely theoretical labels as they also have practical effects. But where do these categories come from, what are their histories, how do they differ between countries, and how are they evolving? *Shifting Categories of Work* asks these questions, illuminating the many ways in which our societies categorize work. Written by sociologists, philosophers, historians and anthropologists as well as management and legal scholars, the contributions in this volume contrast different cultural practices and frameworks of categorizing work across different countries.

Organized around the three axes of (un)organized work, (in)visible work and (in)valuable work, this book shows how ways of categorizing work express, but also recreate, lines of privilege and disadvantage – challenging our preconceived notions of what work is and what it could be, as it invites us to rethink the categories we use for understanding the work we do, and hence, to some extent, ourselves.

Lisa Herzog is professor of political philosophy and works at the intersection of political philosophy and economic thought. Since 2019 she has worked in the Faculty of Philosophy and the Center for Philosophy, Politics and Economics at the University of Groningen. She holds a master's degree in economics from LMU Munich and a Master of Studies in philosophy and a Ph.D. degree in political theory from the University of Oxford. She has worked at or been invited to lecture at the universities of St. Gallen, Leuven, Frankfurt/Main, Utrecht and Stanford. She was a Rhodes Scholar (2007–2011) and in 2019 she received the Tractatus-Preis and the German Award for Philosophy and Social Ethics; in 2021 she received the Ammodo Science Award for her groundbreaking research. Herzog has published on the philosophical dimensions of markets (both historically and systemically), liberalism and social justice, ethics in organizations and the future of work. She is currently focusing on workplace democracy, professional ethics and the role of knowledge in democracies. Her publications include *Inventing the Market: Smith, Hegel, and Political Theory* (2013); and *Reclaiming the System: Moral Responsibility, Divided Labour, and the Role of Organizations in Society* (2018).

Bénédicte Zimmermann is professor of sociology at L'École des hautes études en sciences sociales in Paris and a Permanent Fellow at the Wissenschaftskolleg zu Berlin. She holds a master's degree in history from University Panthéon-Sorbonne in Paris, another one in political sciences and a Ph.D. degree in political science from Sciences Po Paris. Her main research interests are in the social history of categories of public action; the sociology of work, organizations and workers' life courses; and epistemologies and methodologies of the social sciences. Her publications include *La constitution du chômage en Allemagne. Entre professions et territoires* (2001), *Ce que travailler veut dire. Une sociologie des parcours et des capacités* (2014).

SHIFTING CATEGORIES OF WORK

Unsettling the Ways We Think about Jobs, Labor, and Activities

Edited by Lisa Herzog and Bénédicte Zimmermann

Routledge
Taylor & Francis Group
NEW YORK AND LONDON

Cover image: © Shutterstock

First published 2023
by Routledge
605 Third Avenue, New York, NY 10158

and by Routledge
2 Park Square, Milton Park, Abingdon, Oxon, OX14 4RN

Routledge is an imprint of the Taylor & Francis Group, an informa business

ISBN: 978-1-032-37673-8 (hbk)
ISBN: 978-1-032-37662-2 (pbk)
ISBN: 978-1-003-34132-1 (ebk)

DOI: 10.4324/9781003341321

Typeset in Bembo
by Apex CoVantage, LLC

CONTENTS

CONTRIBUTORS

Bernard, Sophie (University PSL-Paris Dauphine, France)

Sophie Bernard is Professor of Sociology at PSL-Paris Dauphine University, France, and a researcher at IRISSO (Institut de Recherche Interdisciplinaire en Sciences Sociales). Her work focuses on the porosity of employment statuses, between self-employment and salaried work, namely in the context of platform capitalism.

Braig, Marianne (Free University Berlin, Germany)

Marianne Braig is Professor of Political Science at the Institute for Latin American Studies at Freie Universität Berlin, Germany. Questions of transregional and global interdependencies and inequalities, the relation between state and society, political culture and gender studies are part of her research. She forms part of the DFG-Project "Forced Labour as a Shifting Global Category."

Credland, Nicki (University of Hull, UK)

Nicki Credland is Reader at the University of Hull, UK. Her background is in intensive care and latterly critical care outreach, with research spanning incivility, patient deterioration, recognition and response. Nicki is Chair of the British Association of Critical Care Nurses (BACCN).

De Verdalle, Laure (Printemps, CNRS and University Paris Saclay-UVSQ, France)

Laure de Verdalle is a senior researcher at the French National Center for Scientific Research (CNRS), member of the Laboratoire Printemps (CNRS/Université Paris Saclay-UVSQ) and associate researcher at the Centre Marc Bloch (Berlin). Her research focuses on creative work and entrepreneurial dynamics in the cultural field.

Dirringer, Josépha (University Rennes 1, France)

Josépha Dirringer is a lecturer at the University of Rennes 1, France, member of the IODE laboratory, currently leading the TransSEN project (Social Transformations and the Digital Economy). She is a specialist in social law studying the transformations of social law, social norms, the social state and the effectiveness of workers' social rights.

Disko, Sasha (Deutsches Museum, Verkehrszentrum, Munich, Germany)

Sasha Disko is a social and cultural historian of technology who views economic imperatives as central to understanding modern societies and individual motives. She currently holds a position at the Deutsches Museum, Verkehrszentrum in Munich, researching the past, present and future of transportation and mobility.

Dougnon, Isaie (Fordham University, New York City, USA)

Isaie Dougnon is Associate Professor of francophone humanitarian studies at Fordham University in New York City, USA. He advocates a historical and anthropological approach so as to offer a local perspective on labor and migration in colonial and post-colonial Africa.

Frega, Roberto (CEMS, CNRS, France)

Roberto Frega holds a Ph.D. degree from Paris 8 University. He is a permanent senior researcher at the CNRS (French National Center for Scientific Research) in Paris. He has published several books and articles on democratic theory. His latest book is *Pragmatism and the wide view of democracy* (Palgrave Macmillan, 2019).

Game, Annilee M. (University of East Anglia, UK)

Annilee M. Game is Associate Professor of Organisational Behaviour and Business Ethics at Norwich Business School, University of East Anglia, UK. Her research draws on perspectives from psychology, organization studies and sociology and currently focuses on workplace emotions and relational understandings of work, organizations and well-being, particularly the nature and effects of social dynamics in the workplace.

Greb, Maximilian (WZB Social Science Center Berlin, Germany)

Maximilian Greb is a research assistant at WZB Social Science Center Berlin. His research focuses on the relationship between political economy, technological change and culture.

Griffin, Martyn (Sheffield University, UK)

Martyn Griffin is Senior Lecturer at Sheffield University, UK. His research focuses on workplace democracy and cultural perceptions of work and organization. This currently includes writing on counter-hegemonic histories, organizational readiness, as well as power and resistance in organizations.

Grollmann, Philipp (Federal Institute for Vocational Education and Training, Bonn, Germany)

Philipp Grollmann is deputy head of the section "International Vocational Education and Training (VET) – Comparison, Research and Monitoring" at the Federal Institute for Vocational Education and Training (BIBB). His fields of interest are the international comparison of VET systems, the education of teachers and trainers in VET, and work-based learning.

Hamilton, Peter (Durham University, UK)

Peter Hamilton is Associate Professor of Human Resource Management at Durham University, UK. His main research interests are in discourse and rhetoric within the processes and practices of employment relations and human resource management.

Harness, Oonagh (Northumbria University, UK)

Oonagh Harness is Lecturer at Northumbria University, UK. Oonagh's main research interests are in the intersection of emotional labor, temporality, relations and embodiment at work, with a particular focus on the co-creation of service encounters.

He, Linxin (University Paris 1, France)

Linxin He is Lecturer at University Paris 1 Panthéon-Sorbonne. He is also a research fellow at the Max Planck Institute for social law and social policy in Germany. His research interests focus on fundamental rights theories and the transformation of the welfare state.

Herzog, Lisa (University of Groningen, Netherlands)

Lisa Herzog is Professor of Political Philosophy at the University of Groningen, NL, and works at the intersection of political philosophy and economic thought. Herzog has published on the philosophical dimensions of markets (both historically and systemically), liberalism and social justice, ethics in organizations and the future of work.

Hoffmann, Maja (Vienna University of Economics and Business, Austria)

Maja Hoffmann is a Ph.D. candidate at the Vienna University of Economics and Business. Her research in environmental social science focuses on work and critiques of work in the context of social-ecological transformation, degrowth and post-development theory. Her background is in political science, Nordic philology, environmental studies and sustainability science.

Jamie, Kimberly (Durham University, UK)

Kimberly Jamie is Associate Professor of Sociology at Durham University, UK. She is a medical sociologist with particular interests in the work of healthcare practitioners and scientists, health and medicine in everyday life, the body (particularly women's bodies) and the politics of reproduction.

Kogut, Bruce (Columbia University, New York, USA)

Bruce Kogut is a social scientist working on the future of work and the application of machine learning to social science and the humanities. He is currently a professor of sociology in the business school at Columbia University. He is currently on the advisory board of the Institut Polytechnique de Paris and the Columbia University Global Center in Paris.

Krzywdzinski, Martin (Helmut Schmidt University, Hamburg, Germany)

Martin Krzywdzinski is Professor of International Labor Relations at the Helmut Schmidt University in Hamburg, Germany, director at the Weizenbaum Institute for the Networked Society and head of the research group "Globalization, Work and Production" at the WZB Social Science Center Berlin. His research focuses on the globalization of work and technological change in the workplace.

Kuhlmann, Martin (Sociological Research Institute Göttingen, Germany)

Martin Kuhlmann is director of the Soziologisches Forschungsinstitut (SOFI) at Georg-August-Universität Göttingen, Germany. His research is covering the fields of sociology of work and industrial relations, working on issues like work and new technologies (digitalization), work and new management concepts, working conditions and innovative work policies.

Lallement, Michel (Conservatoire national des arts et métiers, Paris, France)

Michel Lallement is Professor of Sociology at the Conservatoire national des arts et métiers (CNAM), Paris, France. His research affiliations are with the Lise-CNRS. He has written numerous articles on work, employment, industrial relations and international comparisons, utopian communities, and the history of sociology and is currently member of the editorial board of *L'Année sociologique*.

Letourneux, Frédérique (Nantes University, France)

Frédérique Letourneux has a doctorate in sociology and teaches in higher education (Nantes University, CNAM Pays de la Loire, France). Her main fields of research are the sociology of employment and work with a special focus on distance working and the reconfiguration of the relationship to time and space.

Li, Hanyu (Hertz Corporation, USA)

Hanyu (Evelyn) Li received her bachelor's degree in Economics from Sun Yat-sen University and a Master of Science in Business Analytics at Columbia University in 2021. She is currently a data scientist for the blockchain company CertiK.

McMurray, Robert (RCSI Graduate School of Healthcare Management, Dublin, Ireland)

Robert McMurray is Professor of Organization and Management at RCSI Graduate School of Healthcare Management, Ireland. His research focuses on emotion at work, dirt, collaboration and health care organization. A qualitative researcher, McMurray employs visual and immersive methods.

Perrin-Joly, Constance (University Sorbonne Paris Nord, Paris, France)

Constance Perrin-Joly is Associate Professor of Sociology, a researcher at the Interdisciplinary Institute of Social Issues (IRIS) and associate researcher at the French Centre for Ethiopian Studies (CFEE). Her research focuses on sociology of economy and work, particularly on moral economies in companies.

Renard, Léa (Free University Berlin, Germany)

Léa Renard is a postdoctoral researcher at the Freie Universität Berlin, Germany, Lateinamerika-Institut. She is a member of the DFG project "Forced Labour as a Shifting Global Category." Her research interests are in the historical sociology of statistical categories, especially with regard to the fields of work and migration.

Schalkowski, Nicola (Free University Berlin, Germany)

Nicola Schalkowski is a Ph.D. candidate at Freie Universität Berlin, Germany, and member of the DFG-Project "Forced Labour as a Shifting Global Category." Her research in the fields of gender and feminist labor studies focuses on (un)paid domestic work.

Schütz, Gabrielle (University Versailles Saint-Quentin-en-Yvelines – Paris Saclay, France)

Gabrielle Schütz is Associate Professor of Sociology at University Versailles St Quentin-en-Yvelines – Paris Saclay (Laboratory Printemps, CNRS/UVSQ), France. She is interested in work transformations in organizations, development of subcontracting, outsourcing, transformation of wage relations and changes in the work environment, with gender being a transversal axe that irrigates all her research.

Segrestin, Blanche (MINES Paris-Tech, France)

Blanche Segrestin is Professor at MINES Paris-Tech, France, and head of the Center of Management Sciences. She holds the Chair of "Theory of the Enterprise. Models of governance and Collective creation." Her work focuses on the new theories of the enterprise, responsible innovation and new legal models for corporate responsibility.

Simonet, Maud (IDHES, CNRS and University Paris Nanterre, France)

Maud Simonet is a sociologist and senior researcher at the research centre "Institutions et Dynamiques Historiques de l'Economie et de la Société" (IDHES), France, and director of that research-center unit at the University of Nanterre. Her research focuses on volunteer work, civic service and the non-profit world, workfare, and on digital labor in France and the United States.

Slutskaya, Natalia (University of Sussex, UK)

Natalia Slutskaya, Ph.D., is a reader in Work and Organization Studies at the University of Sussex. Her current research focuses on issues of recognition at work and stigma management. Her co-authored paper "Beyond the Symbolic:

A Relational Approach to Dirty Work through a Study of Refuse Collectors and Street Cleaners" won the SAGE Prize for Innovation/Excellence.

Sold, Katrin (Wissenschaftskolleg zu Berlin, Germany)

Katrin Sold is a political scientist and Research Associate at the Wissenschaftskolleg zu Berlin and the Merian Centre for Advanced Studies in the Maghreb (MECAM) in Tunis. Her research focuses on socio-economic and political transformation processes in the region of North Africa, with a particular focus on the transformation of work and its social implications.

Tiemann, Michael (Federal Institute for Vocational Education and Training, Bonn, Germany)

Michael Tiemann is a senior researcher and deputy head of the division for research on "qualifications, occupational integration and employment" at the Federal Institute for Vocational Education and Training (BIBB). He holds a doctoral degree in sociology from Cologne University. His main fields of interest are changes in occupational content and knowledge and learning at the workplace.

Wobbe, Theresa (University of Potsdam, Germany)

Theresa Wobbe is a professor emerita of sociology and gender sociology at the University of Potsdam, Germany. She is one of the founders of the DFG project "Forced Labour as a Shifting Global Category." The focus of her research is on the historical sociology of work, institutional arrangements of gender relations, the sociology of classification and world society studies.

Zhang, Jennifer (School of Engineering, Columbia University, USA)

Jennifer (Yujia) Zhang received her BA from UCLA and a Master of Science in Operations Research from Columbia University in 2021. At UCLA she was a data analyst for the project "Economics of Crime." She is currently a data scientist at Ernest & Young.

Zimmermann, Bénédicte (Ecole des Hautes Études en Sciences Sociales, Paris, France and Wissenschaftskolleg zu Berlin, Germany)

Bénédicte Zimmermann is Professor of Sociology at L'École des hautes études en sciences sociales in Paris and a Permanent Fellow at the Wissenschaftskolleg zu Berlin. Her main research interests are in the social history of categories of public action, the sociology of work, organizations and workers' life courses, and epistemologies and methodologies of the social sciences.

INTRODUCTION

Lisa Herzog and Bénédicte Zimmermann

Imagine a person cycling past you and wearing a big backpack that seems to contain food items. What kind of work is she doing? She might be bringing home groceries for her family, which is a form of unpaid domestic but arguably essential work. Or she might be transporting food in exchange for money, either as an employee or as a self-employed worker, but in both cases akin to platform work organized via online mediation. In some countries there is a great likelihood that she does this work in the informal sector, maybe even as a form of more or less coerced labor, perhaps because she is indebted to a trafficker who brought her into the country. But maybe she is also working under happier circumstances, say, as a member of a democratic delivery cooperative that is jointly owned by the members and aims to make delivery services more sustainable. We cannot make sense of the simple activity – transporting a bag of food items by bike – without drawing on concepts and categories of work that help to fully compass the situation.

We cannot even begin to raise such questions without employing various concepts and categories of work, some of which are widely used in public and academic discussions. Work is described as "skilled" or "unskilled," "formal" or "informal," "paid" or "unpaid," "efficient" or "essential," etc. It is through such concepts and categories that we make sense of human activities. Work-related categories are not simply theoretical constructs or mere descriptions of what a person does but are embodied in laws, social norms and practices, formal and informal institutions, and thereby shape the realities with which employers and workers must deal. Providing a basis for public policies, these categories help to delineate companies' organization of work and serve to define workers' experiences. They often also influence the social order through wage classification or social insurance schemes. As such, they are intertwined with questions of power,

DOI: 10.4324/9781003341321-1

prestige and the distribution of material and non-material benefits. They vary widely across periods and places. For example, what counts as "informal" work is shaped by social and economic practices as well as the existing legal regulation of work.

Questions about categories of work are all the more important because discussion about the "future of work" has made a lively comeback in public debates. With the arrival of new digital technologies, advanced forms of artificial intelligence (AI) and growing concerns about ecological sustainability, questions are being raised as to just how human activities will be organized and value created in the future. While some commentators predict a massive replacement of human beings by robots and software (e.g., Frey and Osborne, 2013), others expect a more gradual process of change (e.g., Autor, 2015; Benanav, 2020). This process raises fundamental questions as to the kind of work that will be available in the future and for whom – as well as how it will be categorized and for whose benefit.

The aim of this volume is to bring together essays that analyze various ways in which work is conceptualized and categorized. In highlighting some of the changes and shifts in concepts and categories that we can observe across historical periods and in different countries, it seeks to map out the currently shifting boundaries of work.

Historical Legacies and Current Challenges

Most authors in the volume come from the North Atlantic realm, and while a number of chapters take on the perspective of other countries or international organizations, our vision cannot but be shaped by this certain positionality and a number of longer-term trends that have their focus in North America and Europe.

One long-term trend in this part of the world is the tendency to organize many forms of work along the logic of markets, a form of "disembedding" (Polanyi, 1944) that has been going on at least since the nineteenth century but that has accelerated in the "neoliberal" era ever since the 1980s. Many forms of institutional protection and counterpower, for example, through unions, have been cut back and replaced by a single-minded search for corporate profits (Harvey, 2005). This trend has often been criticized and questioned, even with calls from an organization such as the Business Roundtable for firms to have a "purpose" beyond profit-making (Business Roundtable, 2021). In practice, however, it continues to prevail in many countries, leading to a polarization between better and worse forms of work (Goos and Manning, 2007).

Secondly, there is the welfare state and labor law regulation (Supiot, 2001, 2012) which have played an important role in categorizing work ever since the late nineteenth century. Welfare provisions and the legal codification of labor made wage labor and subordinated work core categories of work, and for a long time, they tended to obscure other forms of work. Yet in earlier times, work was often centered around households and done to satisfy basic needs – often a combination of "free" and "unfree" work, for example, by slaves or serfs. It was through successive waves of professionalization and industrialization that many forms of work moved into offices, factories and other workplaces outside the household (on the history of work, see most recently Lucassen, 2021). An important effect of this development was that the "home," as we understand it today, was created as a private place. "Domestic work" was relegated to the realm of unpaid work, with women continuing to shoulder a greater share of the burden than men.

Thirdly, there is the international division of labor, sometimes described as the "globalization" of work, with certain forms of work being outsourced to other countries in order to benefit from lower wages but with highly problematic conditions for the workers there. Western countries thereby externalize many forms of low-qualified and poorly paid work (Lessenich, 2016) while at the same time putting pressure on their internal labor markets and individuals fearing that their jobs might be moved abroad.

Fourth, there is a plethora of developments that come under the label of "technological change," which occurred in historical waves and modified the content of work and the way we categorize it. In recent years these technological changes have mostly consisted of new applications of artificial intelligence and digitally mediated forms of work and thus giving rise to new categories such as platform work (e.g., Gray and Suri, 2019). The use of these technologies also challenges existing legal categories, like once more raising the question as to who exactly is an "employee" in the context of subordinate work.

Partly related to these historical trends is the ecological transformation, which raises fundamental questions as to which forms of work should continue to exist at all in view of the need to decarbonize within the next two to three decades. More broadly speaking it forces us to ask what "sustainable work," as a category in the making, should in fact look like. It raises questions regarding the continuity of many forms of work in productive sectors, while also creating opportunities for new jobs, whether in the conversion of sectors such as transportation or building or in new forms of service work.

The Corona crisis has served to catalyze many of these changes, while also bringing to light underlying issues that have hitherto received little attention, such as the "essentiality" of many forms of work that are poorly paid and receive little societal recognition. For a short time, the spotlight was on care work in its most diverse expressions (health care, cleaning, provision of food and basic necessities, etc.) and forms (paid or unpaid work in domestic or subordinate contexts) and thus challenging the established hierarchies of work. At the same time, there has been a wave of resignations in what has been appropriately dubbed the "Great Resignation" (Thompson, 2021). For reasons yet to be explored in more detail, the willingness to stay in unfulfilling or badly paid jobs seems to have reached a breaking point.

During the pandemic and the accompanying lockdowns, working from home became mandatory for many office jobs, thus raising new questions as to the future geography of work. The geographies of cities, including their transportation infrastructures, have until now been very much divided between zones for "living" and those for "working." Whether this will remain the case in the future is an open question; after all, the "commute" has also been identified as a major source of discomfort and one of the reasons why individuals are less engaged in communal activities (Putnam, 2000). Many people wish to retain certain aspects of working from home, but there seems also to be a widespread yearning for that sociability outside the home which the traditional workplace offers.

What was considered "normal" work before the pandemic might have reached its historical peak, but the crisis of "normal work" – if there is such a thing – creates both challenges and opportunities. One of the big questions it raises is whether the workplace will continue to play its historic role of a place where social integration takes place, a meeting point for people from different backgrounds and with a variety of political views (Estlund, 2003; Mutz and Mondak, 2006). And yet new ways of organizing work, both geographically and in terms of the human element, could also offer opportunities for addressing unresolved problems such as the uneasy relation between domestic work and paid employment and questions of gender justice (Barca, 2020).

Hence the public discussion on work creates an opportunity to reprioritize and reorder different forms of work in ways that go beyond the mere logic of the marketplace. But doing so requires an awareness of just where the concepts and categories that we use to think about work come from and how they evolve. This is the contribution that our volume seeks to make by focusing on the origins, transformations and effects of categories of work.

Concept, Categories and Categorizations Processes

Categories are not only knowledge-based constructs but used by institutions as vehicles for normative activities that go to shaping social reality and people's behavior. Moreover, they are used by individuals to categorize their own experiences and orient their conduct. While being the result of a cognitive and social construction (Berger and Luckmann, 1966), categories also provide an operative basis for collective and individual action. Fueling public policies and determining which types of work are considered worthy of economic support or public recognition, categories are necessarily endowed with a certain performative power by placing labels on the individuals engaged in these activities and sometimes reinforcing existing social hierarchies or creating new ones.

This practical orientation is what distinguishes a category from a concept. Albert Ogien (1994) stated that a concept defines "a list of empirical elements which, in various combinations, form the spectrum of meanings that can be given to a word in the natural language," whereas a category also involves concrete practical criteria that allow us to assess whether a given individual or element pertains to this definition or not (Ogien, 1994, p. 245). A category goes beyond the general definition provided by a concept to draw boundaries between "insiders" and "outsiders" who are situated in time and space and rooted in specific socio-economic and political configurations. A category, therefore, has both an integrative and exclusionary effect – for instance with respect to a person's entitlement to welfare benefits and/or the stigmatization involved in certain categories such as unemployment.

Drawing a line between insiders and outsiders requires defining some criteria of equivalence (Desrosières, 2010) so as to identify in both concrete and practical terms, the features shared by insiders. Moving the focus from a concept to a category thus means shifting our analysis from mere semantical considerations (Koselleck and Presner, 2002) to a pragmatic of action. Going from platform work as a concept to a category, for instance, involves moving beyond the general definition of an activity mediated by online devices and addressing concrete issues such as the legal status of those who perform the work, that is, as employees or self-employed, which may vary according to national labor laws.

In order to understand how categories evolve and change, it is not enough to just look at existing ones. Instead, we need to dig deeper into processes of categorization. This requires adopting a socio-historical perspective from which several analytic implications will follow. One of these is the need to identify those events and moments (Abbott, 2016) that trigger shifts and changes in the process. Another is the need to identify the drivers and brakes of the categorization process, starting with the actors involved. Just *who* is categorizing and against which background is as important an issue as the question of which *actors* – public institutions, employees, union representatives, employers, scholars – are using certain categories and in which ways over time.

Categories are developed, taken up and changed within fields of social power. They affect the rights and interests of different groups – empowering some while disadvantaging others – and may contain implicit or explicit hierarchizations (e.g., in "skilled" vs. "unskilled" work). They raise issues that involve those forms of power, benefits and domination which are associated with their implementation. It is for these reasons that categories are almost never uncontroversial. A variety of groups will often challenge them; as a consequence, they are not always clear-cut and never completely stabilized.

In fact "work" itself is a contested category. The principle of equivalence, which is called upon to delineate work from other kinds of activities, is far from being consensual. While the dominant inherited view sees this principle as the commodified feature of an activity, critical feminist thinkers object to this perspective (Plumwood, 1993; Salleh, 1997; Barca, 2020) and regard caring for one's own family members to also be a form of work. Such dissent can be observed in many other instances, for example, "entrepreneurial work." Is it indeed "work" when I present my entrepreneurial self on social media in order to attract job offers and other opportunities?

In viewing categories as social constructs that result from a process of categorization, we must also examine the cognitive arrangements, procedures and forms of expertise (statistical, legal, etc.) involved in delineating their boundaries as well as the conflicts that might result from competing forms of expertise (Zimmermann, 2001). Looking at categorization processes thus allows us to question the underlying rationales that nurture the controversies about work and to trace how the latter manifest themselves in public and political discussions, and academic ones as well.

Indeed the plurality of concepts and categories of work also permeates academia, with contrasting disciplinary perspectives throwing light on different types and dimensions of work. The authors who contributed to this book come from a range of academic disciplines – sociology, philosophy, history, anthropology, management, law – and from an equally wide range of countries. By bringing together these various perspectives, we hope not only to entertain a cross-disciplinary dialogue but to show the historical contingency and development of certain concepts and categories of work, and in so doing, we seek to demonstrate the potential for conceptualizing and categorizing and ultimately organizing work *differently*.

Structure of the Book

Section I: (Un)organized Work

A first way of looking at work is to ask how it is organized. Even though Western economies are often described as "market economies," economic activities and in particular many forms of work are not only structured through markets. The way in which work is organized immediately raises questions as to power and hierarchies. Who determines what work is done, where it is done and how it is executed? The "normal" case for many jobs was the bureaucratic organization, either as a public administration or as a private company, which, despite their many differences, share a number of features when it comes to internal organization (Weber, 1968; Downs, 1967). Work was and often continues to be structured hierarchically – within chains of command. This "normality" is currently being challenged in various ways, and the chapters in this section throw light on some of the concepts and categories that reflect these challenges.[1]

In the chapter "Subordinate Work: How Does the Law Categorize Modern Labor Relationships?," legal scholar Linxin He contrasts two readings of the widespread work configuration where one person is subordinated to another. This dynamic is a matter of material subordination based on unequal standing, or a matter of relational subordination between parties that are essentially equal, and thus it requires mutual consent to a system of divided labor with different roles. Linxin He traces the category of "subordinate work" through the nineteenth and twentieth centuries in French, German and British legal thinking, describing the gradual shift toward a more egalitarian understanding of the relation between employees and employers. But he also warns that new forms of atypical work and bogus self-employment pose the real risk of regressing toward material forms of subordination.

In the chapter "Corporate Work: A Category That Has Lost Its Managerial Foundations?," management scholar Blanche Segrestin describes how the "corporation" as dominant legal category arose in the nineteenth century. Back then managers played a critical role in not only supervising workers but developing new skills and production processes. Their authority was often seen as delegated by the shareholders of corporations, but this is a misconception. Legally speaking, the shareholders are not the owners of a corporation, which is a legal entity all its own. In recent years new legal categories for corporations have developed that explicitly stipulate social and environmental agendas. They therefore also challenge what is meant by "corporate work" by going beyond the goal of profit maximization.

Before the widespread advent of digital technologies, it was often taken for granted that "workers" had to be situated at "workplaces." But as sociologists Frédérique Letourneux and Gabrielle Schütz show in their chapter "Remote Work: From Employee Telework to Self-Employed Home-Based Work?," there are now more varied forms of "remote work." At different points in time, and for different types of employees, it might have been understood very differently: as a way to combine work with family obligations for parents with young children (mostly women) or as a sign of privilege for highly sought-after managers or other experts. The legal and managerial structures of remote work are also evolving, offering people hope for more autonomous work but also raising fears of a return to home-based forms of work at low wages and with workers being isolated from each other, as was the case in the nineteenth century.

Sociologist Sophie Bernard and legal scholar Josépha Dirringer zoom in on one particular form of remote work: work mediated by digital platforms such as transportation services. In their chapter "Platform Work: New Workers, New Rights?," they show how difficult it is to provide a typology of such work, which can take place digitally or in real life and with workers being employed or self-employed. This new form of work raises numerous questions as to how one can secure the legal protection of workers against abuse without undermining the advantages that many workers, such as Uber drivers, appreciate about this form of work, namely flexibility and autonomy (or at least the appearance thereof). Together with the chapter on "Remote Work," this chapter raises fundamental questions as to the boundaries of organizations and the legal situation of workers who are no longer physically present at a "workplace."

The last two chapters in this section address internal questions pertaining to the organization of work. Who has the say in how work gets done with regard to concrete day-to-day tasks but also more far-reaching strategic concerns? In their chapter on "Teamwork: From Self-Managed to Lean and Agile Teams," labor sociologists Martin Krzywdzinski and Maximilian Greb trace the history of the concept of "teamwork," which first arose in the human-relations approach as a response and counterpoint to the Taylorist understanding of work. After a revival in the 1970s, especially in Scandinavia, interest in this approach receded but then made a comeback in the form of management concepts such as "lean production" or more recently "agile work" in which employees, especially in software development, are expected to organize workflows between themselves. This also raises a fundamental question as to the purpose of teamwork. Is it meant to emancipate workers or increase the rationalization of work?

Philosopher Roberto Frega and sociologist Martin Kuhlmann, in their chapter on "Democratized Work: Concepts and Practices," discuss forms of work that promote democratic interaction between individuals. Such democratic work can be achieved in various ways and at various levels – through direct participation or worker representation, taking into account not only formal structures but actual workflows, patterns of behavior, and social relations at work. Especially in Scandinavia and Germany, there have been various experiments done with such forms of democratic work. The involvement of workers is of particular importance in processes of digital transformation because it allows for a nuanced evaluation of the usefulness of new technologies.

Section II: (In)visible Work

In this section, we gather concepts and categories of work which, in different ways, deal with forms of work that are precisely *not* seen when the standard category of "work" is evoked in the sense of full-time employment within clearly defined legal structures. Many such forms of work are performed by socially disadvantaged groups, whether they be women, migrants or indigenous people. From the perspective of capitalist labor markets, these individuals are hardly visible and yet their work is often crucial to keeping societal processes going and quite literally keeping people alive.

In their chapter "Forced Versus Free Labor: Challenging Their Boundaries," sociologists Léa Renard and Theresa Wobbe trace the history of the concept of "forced labor" and in so doing they question the assumption that there is a strict dichotomy between "forced" and "free" labor. While this dichotomy has taken on different forms throughout history – for example, in the anti-slavery movement of the late eighteenth and early nineteenth centuries – this dual category also informed the actions of the International Labor Organization (ILO). In the course of the twentieth century, the discussion shifted from a (post)colonial context to more recent concerns about human rights and decent work, but the boundaries between "forced" and "free" labor remain contested and this in the research as well.

Political scientists Nicola Schalkowski and Marianne Braig trace the history of another category of work often associated with the "Global South," namely "Informal Work." Within those narratives on modernization and development that prioritized formality, informal work was often understood as the "other" of "normal" labor markets with formal employment. The ILO played an important role in its attempts to define a new statistical category through its Bureau of Statistics and especially in its research on the so-called Third World. But it failed to cover many labor practices through its strict division between formal and informal work, overlooking the many ways in which the two are in fact intertwined. While statistical definitions thus helped to create this category of work, they also obscured certain of its aspects.

Based on his own field research in West Africa, anthropologist Isaie Dougnon highlights diverse forms of migrant work, which has very different legal constellations and demarcations between privilege and disadvantage. In his chapter "Migrants' Work: An Anthropological Perspective From West Africa," he analyzes three dimensions of how migrant workers are understood: material, social and symbolic. Despite their being subject to very different material and social conditions, West African youths as a whole have long viewed migration as a form of self-realization through work. But the way in which they make sense of their work is tied to its impact on their village or city of origin, and its material, social and symbolic impacts there. Moreover, migrants from different cultural backgrounds have chosen different strategies, for example, of self-employment or dependent work, in line with their conception of what kind of work is fitting for them and their community. What is striking is how much the categories in which migrant workers think about their own work differ from those used by the societies of the host countries, which is why taking their voices into account is crucial.

In the chapter "Domestic Work: The Invention of a Gendered Relationship," sociologist Michel Lallement discusses a category of work that was often not officially recognized as such, namely "domestic work," which is unpaid and therefore not included in economic conceptualizations of work. This category arose together with the gendered division of labor in the nineteenth century, the "home" sphere being assigned to the "housewife" and the category of "domestic work" defining what a good housewife entailed in terms of her efficiency. Since then, various attempts have been made to measure the contribution made by domestic work. Although approaches vary, the research has made quite clear that the material and non-material contributions of domestic work are enormous – along with "care work," a category that has gained greater prominence in the recent public discourse on work.

Sociologist Maud Simonet broadens the focus to that more general notion of "Unpaid Work: Expansion and Mobilization of a Feminist Category." Even during the COVID lockdowns, when much light was shed on various forms of previously invisibilized work, the work of women within the household was rarely mentioned. The same holds true for those many forms of unpaid voluntary work outside the house that are overwhelmingly done by women. Drawing on feminist literature, Simonet analyzes the discourse over "unpaid work" of the last decades. Beyond the unresolved questions about family work, she points to new phenomena such as striking (unpaid) interns or class-action lawsuits by (unpaid) bloggers, which show that the category of "unpaid work" has a far greater scope than is often assumed.

In the chapter "Emotional Labor: Concept and Practical Categorizations in Light of COVID Critical Care Nursing," health-management expert Robert McMurray and his co-authors take the recent COVID crisis as an occasion to explore the role of emotions in work. In research on management and organization, emotions have often been sidelined by a specific understanding of formal rationality. But emotions are necessarily part of organizational life, where they are often coded as "right" or "wrong" emotions. This issue is illustrated by drawing upon research on critical-care nurses for whom the management of emotions is a crucial part of their work.

Section III: (In)valuable Work

Almost all concepts and categories of work contain valuations – some carry positive associations, others less so; some designate higher positions in social hierarchies, others lower ones. But certain concepts and categories are more explicit in their evaluations of work: they entail praise or blame, or they point to other valuable principles or features. To be sure, all kinds of evaluative adjectives – "creative," "interesting," "meaningful" – can be applied to "work." But some concepts and categories have become either commonly used stock phrases or scholarly or practical categories that aim to specifically express certain socially shared evaluations. This section brings together a number of such concepts and categories of work, including ones that are currently raising the need for reform of the world of work for ecological reasons.

In her account of "Dirty Work: Physical, Social and Moral Taint," organizational scholars Natalia Slutskaya and Annilee M. Game discuss the ways in which certain jobs have been characterized as "dirty" – always carrying a physical, social and moral taint, but in ways that are socially and historically contingent. They trace the history of research on "dirty" work and the ways in which workers in "dirty jobs" themselves conceptualize their own work. It is noteworthy that the same jobs which have "dirty" features (bad smell, filth, etc.) often make a real contribution to society, which in itself can be a source of self-esteem for the worker who performs these jobs.

In their chapter "Efficient Work: Exploring Algorithmic Approaches to Categorization," historian Sasha Disko and management scholar Bruce Kogut, together with their co-authors, trace the history of the concept of "efficiency" with regard to work. In addition to traditional historical methods, they also use an automated textual analysis of articles published in the *Harvard Business Review* and the *International Labour Review* – two outlets that operate with different evaluative frameworks while yet showing comparable trends in how work is to be judged as "efficient."

In their chapter "Skilled and Unskilled Work: From Theoretical Concepts to Social Practices," educational specialists Philipp Grollmann and Michael Tiemann throw light – and doubt – on the widely used distinction between "skilled" and "unskilled" work. They show that according to various national contexts different semantic fields are employed to delineate these two categories, both of which show unmistakable connections to the educational system. What counts as "skilled" mainly depends on the concrete task at hand, which different international classification systems order in widely different ways. Thus, while a distinction between "skilled" and "unskilled" seems to cut across cultural lines, what exactly counts as "skill" is context-dependent, which also raises the issue of a future in which much work is performed by robots, yet human skills will probably remain indispensable.

Sociologists Laure de Verdalle and Constance Perrin-Joly analyze a category that has often been praised in recent years: "Entrepreneurship: Moral Categorizations Across Three Countries." Comparing the French, German and Ethiopian contexts, they show how the positive image of the "entrepreneur" as an innovative creator of social wealth, which always coexisted with a more negative one as a greedy exploiter, traveled from context to context not least through the work of international organizations. Public policies, for example, funding for training measures, often follow such a category but take on different aspects in different economic and cultural contexts.

The chapter "Essential Work: A Category in the Making?," by philosopher Lisa Herzog, political scientist Katrin Sold and sociologist Bénédicte Zimmermann, starts from the observation that "essential workers" were suddenly receiving public praise during the Corona lockdowns. An analysis of newspaper articles from the United Kingdom, France and Germany during that period shows how similar groups of workers – for example, care workers, supermarket cashiers – were singled out as "essential workers" but contextualized in somewhat different ways. Drawing on economic and philosophical research, the authors suggest that a promising way of determining what the "essentiality" of certain jobs entails is to draw upon the capability approach of Martha Nussbaum and Amartya Sen (1993). But they also argue that the question of "essentiality" cannot ultimately be answered without taking a broader perspective that also takes into account the ecological bases of human life.

In her chapter "Sustainable Work: Foundations and Challenges of a Contested Category," social scientist Maja Hoffmann explores the possibilities of categorizing work as more or less sustainable in an ecological sense. Various related concepts such as "green jobs" have been suggested, but there is a risk of such categories being used for "greenwashing" purposes. Hoffmann suggests that we also need to ask the opposite question: What is unsustainable work? In other words, what is work which cannot be sustained given the urgent imperative to mitigate climate change? This question, however, is still largely of a theoretical nature because the real-life implications – furthering forms of sustainable work and discontinuing forms of unsustainable work – are still not to be realized in any practicable manner.

Acknowledgments

We would like to thank all authors as well as other members of the research network "Working Future" for embarking with us on the adventure of exploring work and its future across disciplinary and national boundaries. We also acknowledge the support provided by the Wissenschaftskolleg zu Berlin for the "Working Futures" research network from which this book emerged, and particularly for the three workshops in which we discussed the chapter drafts. Special thanks are due to Katrin Sold and Sandra Engelbrecht, who worked as coordinators of the network. Without their support, at both logistical and substantive levels, this book project could not have been brought to fruition. Finally, we thank Kevin McAleer for his thorough proofreading of the texts in this book.

Note

1 Other categories that could have been included in this section include "permanent full-time employment" or "unionized work" among others, but were omitted for reasons of limited book length.

References

Abbott, A. (2016) *Processual Sociology*. Chicago, IL and London: The University of Chicago Press.

Autor, D. (2015) 'Why Are There Still So Many Jobs? The History and Future of Workplace Automation', *Journal of Economic Perspectives*, 29(3), pp. 3–30.

Barca, S. (2020) *Forces of Reproduction*. Cambridge: Cambridge University Press.

Benanav, A. (2020) *Automation and the Future of Work*. London: Verso.

Berger, P.L. and Luckmann, T. (1966) *The Social Construction of Reality: A Treatise in the Sociology of Knowledge*. New York: Anchor Books.

Business Roundtable (2021) 'Statement on the Purpose of a Corporation', July 2021. https://s3.amazonaws.com/brt.org/BRT-StatementonthePurposeofaCorporation-July2021.pdf.

Desrosières, A. (2010) *The Politics of Large Numbers: A History of Statistical Reasoning*. Cambridge, MA and London: Harvard University Press.

Downs, A. (1967) *Inside Bureaucracy*. Boston, MA: Little, Brown and Company.

Estlund, C. (2003) *Working Together: How Workplace Bonds Strengthen a Diverse Democracy*. New York: Oxford University Press.

Frey, C.B. and Osborne, M. (2013) 'The Future of Employment', Working Paper, Oxford Martin Programme on Technology and Employment. www.oxfordmartin.ox.ac.uk/downloads/academic/future-of-employment.pdf.

Goos, M. and Manning, A. (2007) 'Lousy and Lovely Jobs: The Rising Polarization of Work in Britain', *The Review of Economics and Statistics*, 89(1), pp. 118–133.

Gray, M.L. and Suri, S. (2019) *Ghost Work: How to Stop Silicon Valley From Building a New Global Underclass*. Boston, MA and New York: Houghton Mifflin Harcourt.

Harvey, D. (2005) *A Brief History of Neoliberalism*. Oxford: Oxford University Press.

Koselleck, R. and Presner, T.S. (2002) *The Practice of Conceptual History*. Stanford: Stanford University Press.

Lessenich, S. (2016) *Neben uns die Sintflut. Die Externalisierungsgesellschaft und ihr Preis*. Berlin: Hanser.
Lucassen, J. (2021) *The Story of Work: A New History of Humankind*. Yale: Yale University Press.
Mutz, D.C. and Mondak, J.C. (2006) 'The Workplace as a Context for Cross-Cutting Political Discourse', *Journal of Politics*, 68(1), pp. 140–155.
Nussbaum, M. and Sen, A. (1993) (eds.) *The Quality of Life*. Oxford: Oxford University Press.
Ogien, A. (1994) 'Les propriétés sociologiques du concept', in Fradin, B., Quéré, L. and Widmer, J. (eds.) *L'enquête sur les catégories. De Durkheim à Sacks*. Paris: Editions EHESS, pp. 243–269.
Plumwood, V. (1993) *Feminism and the Mastery of Nature*. London: Routledge.
Polanyi, K. (1944) *The Great Transformation*. New York: Farrar & Rinehart.
Putnam, R.D. (2000) *Bowling Alone: The Collapse and Revival of American Community*. New York: Simon & Schuster.
Salleh, A. (1997) *Ecofeminism as Politics: Nature, Marx and the Postmodern*. London: Zed Books.
Supiot, A. (2001) *Beyond Employment: Changes in Work and the Future of Labour Law in Europe*. Oxford: Oxford University Press.
Supiot, A. (2012) *The Spirit of Philadelphia: Social Justice vs. the Total Market*. London: Verso.
Thompson, D. (2021) 'The Great Resignation Is Accelerating', *The Atlantic*, 15 October. www.theatlantic.com/ideas/archive/2021/10/great-resignation-accelerating/620382/
Weber, M. (1968) *Economy and Society: An Outline of Interpretive Sociology* (ed. Guenther Roth). New York: Bedminster Press.
Zimmermann, B. (2001) *La constitution du chômage en Allemagne. Entre professions et territoires*. Paris: Maison des Sciences de l'Homme.

PART 1

(Un)organized Work

1

SUBORDINATE WORK

How Does the Law Categorize Modern Labor Relationships?

Linxin He

Introduction: The Relational and Material Aspects of Subordinate Work

In his classic work *Labour and the Law*, British labor law scholar Otto Kahn-Freund wrote that "[t]here can be no employment relationship without a power to command and a duty to obey, that is without this element of subordination in which lawyers rightly see the hallmark of the 'contract of employment'" (Kahn-Freund, 1983, p. 18). Hierarchical order, depicted here as necessary within the economic realm, is in effect a much broader social phenomenon visible in every culture. In this sense, subordinate work – the work accomplished by a person subordinated to some kind of control by another person – has a history as long as the existence of human society. Its foundation is precisely "a power to command and a duty to obey." All manner of power (political, social, spiritual, etc.) implies the subordination of its subjects (Supiot, 2000) and the work of these subjects is subordinate work. The nature or the content of the work matters little here. Let us call this approach the "relational aspect" based on the relationship among the involved subjects of subordinate work. From this perspective, while relationships can be harmonious, they can also be permeated by conflicts and domination.[1]

At the same time, subordinate work can be the result of the division of labor, another common phenomenon in human societies. The famous Confucian philosopher Mencius (circa fourth century B.C.) wrote that "[s]ome labor with their minds, while others labor with their strength. Those who labor with their minds govern others, while those who labor with their strength are governed by others" (Ivanhoe et al., 2009, p. 56).[2] The more or less contemporary Greek philosophers adopted similar distinctions in their theories concerning the division of labor. For example, slaves were said to be the ideal force for the cultivation of

DOI: 10.4324/9781003341321-3

the soil since the work itself was deemed to be servile.[3] It is clear that the subordination here was based on the *nature* of work executed by the workers. This understanding might be called the "material aspect" based on the objective content of the subordinate work.

This basic distinction does not mean that the relational and material aspects are mutually exclusive or reflect separate social realities. On the contrary, they are closely intertwined and can reciprocally constitute the cause of one another: power holders can assign the subordinated population to a particular type of activity, and (socially acknowledged) competencies can also lead to a justification of the distribution of powers. For a translation of this dialectical relationship into concrete terms, we can take the Indian caste system as an example. Professional activity strongly affects the affiliation to a particular caste: "In the general scale of relative purity, features which are deemed professional carry great weight compared with features not connected with profession" (Dumont, 1988, p. 93). More fundamentally, however, "this view of an ordered whole, in which each is assigned his place, is fundamentally religious" (ibid., p. 107). The "dominant" caste thus has the religious and inherited power to impose subordinate work on the lower castes. In other words, the material and relational aspects are not separated in the caste system, even though the latter (constituting religious and traditional power) weighs more heavily in the balance.

Even if they are closely intertwined, it is important to distinguish the two aspects because they imply two kinds of differentiation. The relational dimension involves a differentiation in functions or roles, whereas the material dimension of the division of labor relates to the differentiation in capacities (based on assets, abilities, competencies, etc.). The inequalities resulting from the first differentiation can be temporary and functional, while those originating from the second differentiation are entrenched and real. This article puts forward the thesis that the categorization process for subordinate work should aim at the reduction and ultimately the elimination of the material aspect of subordination and strive for a purely relational form of subordination as based on a fair distribution of powers (Anderson, 2012). This thesis is to be fundamentally understood as a normative claim: human society *should* embrace subordinate work at a purely relational level (Frega et al., 2019). At the same time, this normative pursuit is reflected to a certain degree in history, since it has guided numerous social movements and legal debates in the past. Kahn-Freund implied this idea when he wrote: "The power to command and the duty to obey can be regulated. An element of co-ordination can be infused into the employment relationship. Co-ordination and subordination are matters of degree" (Kahn-Freund, 1983, p. 18). Kahn-Freund clearly opposed coordination to subordination and defined the domain of coordination as the relationship between the management side (the employer) and organized labor (trade unions). However, it might not be contrary to his spirit if we interpret this coordination as a fair distribution of roles (and the related powers) in an employment relationship, and if we were to understand just such an infusion of coordination as the ultimate form of subordinate work.

The rest of this article presents subordinate work in a dynamic way and draws lessons mainly from the legal resources of several industrialized countries while focusing on France and Germany. It first briefly recalls the abolition of material subordination in work based on the principle of equality; it then deals with the legal recognition of relational subordination before explaining the legal constructions that limit relational subordination; finally it provides a brief account of the revival of material subordination in current economies. It is necessary to remark here that we should not neglect the fact that despite its centrality in the private economy, subordinate work is also a common form of work in the public sector. Civil servants carry out subordinate work every day under the control of their supervisors. Nevertheless, as Alain Supiot clearly points out, administrative law legally recognizes the existence of hierarchy – differentiation of identities in principle – due to the preeminence of public interest (Supiot, 2011, p. 119) and the requirement of democratic legitimacy. This article therefore principally examines subordinate work in the private sector.

Abolition of Material Subordinate Work in Law: The Principle of Equality

Western feudal societies were well-known for the central place occupied by the vassalage and the personal bond of dependence (Supiot, 2017, p. 210). In those societies, the population was divided into estates and the lowest estate had to execute the most arduous work, which was imposed on them by the privileged estates. Believing that "all men are created equal," advocates of the Enlightenment were fundamentally opposed to this kind of division of labor which produced what we can define as material subordinate work. According to these advocates, freemen were also expected to be able to engage in arduous work in society. As Montesquieu wrote, "working in the mines was judged too toilsome for any but slaves or malefactors; at present, there are men employed in them who are known to live comfortably" (*The Spirit of Laws*, book XV, chapter 9). Abbé Sieyes explained most vigorously the necessity to abolish privilege in the division of labor when he wrote (albeit mainly regarding public services):

> [the higher posts] ought to be the natural prize and reward for recognized ability and service; [and] if the privileged have succeeded in usurping all well-paid and honorific posts, this is both a hateful iniquity toward the generality of citizens and an act of treason to the commonwealth.
>
> *(What is the Third Estate?, chapter 1)*

In other words, no citizen was obliged to perform a particular kind of (subordinate) work due to her objective (inferior) status.

On the basis of equal citizenship, which was realized in the revolutionary period of the late eighteenth century, work was then frequently considered as an agreement of services concluded between free and equal persons. This conception was especially visible in the French Civil Code of 1804, which was almost completely silent on industrial relationships (Stocquart, 1895). Working relationships were generally framed as "the hiring of work," that is, the temporary use of one person's labor by another. Article 1710 stated that "[t]he hiring of work is a contract by which one of the parties engages to do something for another for a price agreed upon between them." It showed no concern for the subordinate character of certain kinds of work. The more precise definition of the hiring of labor and industry in Article 1779 did better in distinguishing "workmen who engage themselves in the service of anyone" (*locatio operarum, louage de services*) from "persons who undertake a work by estimate or by contracts" (*locatio operis, louage d'oeuvre*). The only provision concerning "workmen" is the prohibition of perpetual service (Article 1780) aiming at the protection of the freedom of contract. Eager to promote equality between the parties of the contract, the Code was blind to all kinds of inequality between them (the factual inequality of capacities and the inequality of powers). Another debate at the beginning of the nineteenth century confirmed the eagerness of the French legislator to ignore all differentiations between the two parties: it addressed work as belonging to either the domain of "things" or that of "persons." Legal scholars were firmly opposed to the definition of work as a thing since it had to be performed in person by the worker. A famous commentator on the Napoleonic Code in the nineteenth century, Troplong, explained that the hiring of work was different from the hiring of things since there could be no forced work, whereas the hired thing might be transferred by force (*manu militari*) to the leasee (Xifaras, 2004). Moreover, the conceptualization of work as a thing would have led to a complete and objective domination of the employer in the employment relationship based on ownership. This would have been in direct contradiction to the principle of equality. German legislation was similar to its French counterpart in this regard since the German Civil Code of 1900 regulated the employment relationship through a general article on the "contract of services" (*Dienstvertrag*; see article 611). Only in 2017 did the legislator finally decide to create a specific provision recognizing the peculiarity of the employment contract in the text of the Civil Code (article 611a).

However, this negligence of all subordinate aspects of work after the revolutionary period only belied the emerging tension between the formally equalized social status and the long-lasting factual inequality of appertaining conditions. For example, in his 1894 *Traité élémentaire de législation industrielle*, Paul Pic noted that factory workers were in a clear relationship of dependence vis-à-vis their employer (Pic, 1894, p. 315). This tension and its social effects, which led to the formulation of the "social question" (Case, 2016), have served to place subordinate work at the center of the debate on the foundation of industrial legislations, dealing again with the reduction of the subordinate character of work.

Recognition of Relational Subordinate Work: Legal Subordination

If the recognition by law of equality among all citizens does not prevent the material inequality of conditions, how should one conceive the relationship between an employee and his employer? In other words, the equalization of social identities, as perceived by law, and the inequality of working conditions raise the question of the legal nature of subordination in work. Analyses more sensitive to the abiding material inequalities would tend to recognize factual dependence (mostly in economic terms) as the regulatory object of labor law, whereas authors upholding the equalized social status would be only ready to accept the relational subordinate work instituted by legal means. More concretely, the question became a doctrinal debate about the criterion of subordinate work. Is it the economic dependence of the worker vis-à-vis the employer, or is it the legal tie that subjects the worker to the employer?

At the end of the nineteenth century, German legal scholar Heinrich Rosin first tried to define the "worker" by the criterion of economic dependency. In his study on the newly established social insurance in Germany, he stated that

> workers in the narrowest sense are people who are in the position of economic dependent employment on the basis of a private-law employment contract, without belonging to the family or household, and are employed by an employer to carry out work of a material nature, namely in trade and industry, agriculture and forestry or construction.
>
> *(Rosin, 1893, p. 145)*

Three elements stand out in this definition: the factual position, the existence of an employment contract, and the execution of material work. Thus, this definition is complex and not free of ambiguity. Rosin emphasized the importance of economic inequality among those elements to the extent that it constituted the foundation of the industrial legislation (ibid., p. 152). But how should one recognize the economic dependence of a worker? It seems that this dependence was proven by the social class to which the person belonged (and which determined, for example, the (non-)existence of other income sources for the worker) and less by the personal relationship between the employer and the employee. Therefore this position did not remain uncontested. Philipp Lotmar, for example, criticized this conception and thought the analysis of social class was irrelevant (Lotmar, 1902, p. 63). Lotmar felt that there should be greater concern shown for the regulatory needs of all particular forms of work and that subordination could only be of a legal nature (ibid., p. 93). However, the thesis of Rosin clearly demonstrates that scholars were no longer able to pretend that the abolition of material subordination was completely accomplished by the revolutions. They had only succeeded in eliminating this aspect of subordinate work in *law*. The *economic* development of the western countries had instead promoted the formation of a working class, if not a proletariat, which represented the return and entrenchment of material subordinate work.

A similar debate took place around the same time in France. Legal scholars such as Paul Cuche argued that one could distinguish two types of subordination: technical subordination and economic dependence. Technical subordination was characterized by the power of employers to use the force and knowledge of the subordinate person for their own purposes. Cuche considered this element insufficient in identifying the scope of the social legislation's application (e.g., home workers would be excluded) and proposed economic dependence as the criterion of subordinate work. According to him, a worker was economically dependent on his or her employer when the means of existence were mainly or exclusively obtained by the work and when the worker had no other employers (Cuche, 1913). This conception was nevertheless criticized by other scholars such as Paul Pic and rejected by the *Cour de cassation* in a famous decision of 1931 (Pélissier et al., 2008, p. 3). Only the "technical" sense of subordination was admitted in law (the "technical subordination" became "a bond of legal subordination" in French terminology).

Finally, economic dependence was also rejected by German courts as the definition of subordinate work (Heuberger, 1982, p. 29). Furthermore, there is a convergence of French and German definitions of legal subordination (*lien de subordination juridique, persönliche Abhängigkeit*). Both of them emphasize the employer's power to command and the integration of the worker into an organization.[4] The reasons for this judicial solution were complicated. Some scholars tried to explain it by citing the practical difficulties of applying "economic dependence" as a clear-cut criterion for the recognition of an employment relationship, especially when social security gained increasing importance in both countries (Auzero et al., 2020, p. 262). Others pointed out that not only blue-collar but white-collar workers were included in the scope of social legislation (Heuberger, 1982, p. 30). In other words, the advantages provided by social legislation were becoming more and more important; and the extension of their scope of application, often demanded by potential beneficiaries, required the recognition of a category of "legal subordination" that included both workers and office employees. This circumstance is interesting for our purposes because it indicates the progressive shift of the legislator's focus to the relational dimension of subordination: the normative ideal of labor law is to take relational subordinate work as its central case and to marginalize the persistent economic dependence when the law does not conflict with the social reality to any great degree. It is important to note, however, that the criterion of economic dependence has not been completely abandoned. German law recognizes, for example, the so-called quasi-subordinate workers or employee-like persons (*arbeitnehmerähnliche Personen*) with the help of this characteristic (Zöllner et al., 2015, p. 56). But the central problem regarding subordinate work is finally the relational one – that is, the use of the power by the employer in an organization.

The traditional way of dealing with relational subordination is to build on the restrictions contained in the employment contract and the collective power of organized labor. However, some authors have recently tried to analyze the question from the standpoint of republicanism as conceptualized by Philip Pettit or Frank Lovett. Indeed, central to republican thought is the idea that freedom consists in the avoidance of dependence on the arbitrary will of another, with all citizens having equal legal and social standing vis-à-vis one another. For instance, Cabrelli and Zahn think that changing economic conditions have rendered the traditional employment relationship obsolete and that republican political theory provides a better basis for limiting the employer's power (Cabrelli and Zahn, 2018). The invocation of this particular branch of political philosophy is indeed interesting, as this analysis does not rely on the employment contract. Pettit famously defines freedom as "non-domination" (as opposed to "non-interference"). Non-domination refers to the absence of *arbitrary* interference. This interference need not be an actual one: the "vulnerability to someone with the capacity for an arbitrary interference" suffices to define a situation of domination. That is why the employee who "lives under the thumb of an employer" cannot count as fully free under the construal of freedom as non-domination, at least as long as there are no mechanisms of counter-power which can ensure that the employee's rights are secured (Pettit, 1997, p. 118). With regard to non-arbitrariness, Pettit asserts that "an act of interference is non-arbitrary to the extent that it is forced to track the interests and ideas of the person suffering the interference" (Pettit, 1999, p. 55). Freedom as non-domination is also characterized as the ability to "look others in the eye, without having to defer to them or fear them." Non-domination, which is different from the liberal conception of non-interference, calls for public redistribution and social legislations (examples of this redistribution are unemployment benefits, health and safety regulations). This idea (especially the "eyeball test") can be traced back to equal citizenship in ancient Greece (Ober, 2014). It thus primarily concerns the abolition of material subordination (in a much broader context than industrial relations); however, due to its emphasis on the exercise of power between individuals, it also clearly defines the limits of legitimate relational subordination. As Alan Bogg (2017) points out, "[i]t is a great strength of Pettit's account of 'basic liberties' that it is rooted in a concern to ameliorate private domination between citizens." In other words, Pettit has the merit of framing the question of subordinate work on the basis of the personal relation between the employee and the employer as such, though the methods he proposes for achieving non-domination are akin to what we can learn from positive law.

Lovett holds a similar conception of "non-domination" in his theory and states that "persons or groups are subject to domination to the extent that they are dependent on a social relationship in which some other person or group wields arbitrary power over them" (2010, p. 119). While both authors place emphasis on the arbitrary exercise of power, the difference between Pettit and Lovett lies mainly in the critique by Lovett of the social relationship. As regards the employment relationship, Lovett writes specifically that

> if employers had to compete for workers as much as workers had to compete for jobs, the latter would not be dependent on the former. . . . Since at least some degree of dependency is a necessary condition for domination, in a perfectly free market there would be none.
>
> *(ibid., p. 53)*

This position leads Lovett to adopt remedies for domination which are very similar to neo-liberal policies bent on a frictionless market. One major proposal is the creation of a universal basic income. One can be skeptical with regard to these remedies, but a more fundamental critique would be Lovett's negative attitude toward social relationships. Through the dismantling of social relationships, Lovett could certainly attain the goal of eliminating domination, but this would also deconstruct all socialization and ultimately produce an atomized society. The conception of relational subordination in this article does not require its complete abolition (contrary to the case of material subordination) but questions its legitimacy in a way that has greater resonance with Pettit's theory. The evolution of the positive law in several countries also tends in this direction.

Legally Constructing Relational Subordination

The acceptance of relational subordination indicates a deep paradox of social legislation: it is criticized for being a tool to maintain the capitalist regime by making arrangements that address the "social question." Regardless of our own opinion about this critique, the dialectical relation is true: labor law institutes relational subordination and restricts it at the same time. In addition to all the legislation pertaining to those objective standards of the labor organization (e.g., working time, safe and healthy working conditions), four mechanisms can be briefly mentioned here: contract of employment, collective autonomy, social protection and fundamental social rights.

The contract of employment is said to be the cornerstone of labor law. However, this particular significance was not uncontested at the beginning. The problematic free consent of the worker rendered the contract suspicious, especially regarding the justification of the subordination, and it was also unclear just how protective the terms of a contract could be. For this reason, lawyers in Germany and France tried first to regulate subordinate work by recruiting the so-called institutional or community theory. This theory bases subordination of the employee not on her consent expressed in the contract but on her entering into the working community (Camerlynck, 1982; Wiedemann, 1966). The community is characterized by solidarity between the employer and the employees whose interests are deemed convergent. The employer is said to possess three kinds of power in the enterprise: the legislative power, the power of direction and the disciplinary power. However, this attempt finally failed because the solidarity of interests was very much a fictional construct. The assimilation of the employer's power to the power of a public authority is equally problematic. The contract of employment finally remains an act that both institutes and restricts subordination in work. It exists "in a mixed domain of voluntarily agreed arrangements and imposed norms" (Freedland et al., 2016, p. 12). The incorporation of standardized implied terms in the contracts of employment in the United Kingdom is a famous example. These terms, which are identified by the common-law judges in order to impose obligations on the employer, are justified as a matter of policy, in particular as mandatory norms which shall limit the powers of the employer (Cabrelli, 2020, p. 169). For instance, it is the employer's duty to exercise reasonable care for the well-being of the employee as well as a duty of trust and confidence. In France, the distinction between contractual elements and working conditions reveals another way of restricting the power of the employer. The elements of the contract – such as the nature of the work, working time and place, and wages – cannot be modified unilaterally by the employer. The consent of the employee is required and her refusal does not constitute a legitimate reason for dismissal.

The protection offered by the contract is nevertheless insufficient and workers have tried since the very beginning to unite their powers, even in a period when this coalition was illegal. Indeed, collective labor organizations might have different histories and cultures in different countries, but freely organized labor is always a power that stands against the power of the employer: workers may collectively attain the autonomy that they do not enjoy at the individual level (Supiot, 2011, p. 124). By elaborating collective labor norms, collective bargaining also takes over the important responsibility of labor regulation. Kahn-Freund famously presented the British industrial relations as "collective laissez-faire" (1983, p. 2) through which the management side seeks to protect its legitimate expectations of industrial peace, while organized labor finds its guarantee for stable and safe employment (ibid., p. 69). The importance of collective bargaining in equalizing social powers and organizing the regulation of labor has also been recognized at the European level ever since the Single European Act in 1986.[5] The practice of collective bargaining is impossible without the well-known triad constituting collective labor rights: freedom of association, the right to collective negotiations and the right to collective actions (especially the right to strike) (Supiot, 2001). It is neither possible nor necessary in this article to go into the particular functions of these rights in leveling subordinated labor. It suffices to note that there is a constant tendency to recognize them as fundamental social rights of the workers, which shows their cardinal place in the organization of workers (see also later).

Another way of organizing collective solidarity and security is the establishment of social protection schemes. However, it would certainly be wrong to state that social security systems were constructed to meet the challenges of relational subordination. One might argue that the Bismarckian welfare state was closely related to employment status. Nevertheless, not only can the welfare state be organized according to a more universal principle (covering all residents, thus beyond the employment relationship as is the case with the Beveridgean model) but the Bismarckian type is also concerned with the minimization of inequalities in welfare (Zacher, 2004). It has thus mainly functioned, following the revolutionary period, as an institution for the promotion of substantial equality (or the elimination of material subordination in the society). It remains the case that, as mentioned by Pettit and Lovett, schemes such as unemployment benefits and minimum income can reduce the "exit costs" for workers and thus their degree of subordination when facing their employer.

Finally, a more recent invention for the protection of subordinated workers is the recognition of fundamental social rights. Initially recognized by such national constitutions as that of Mexico in 1917 and of Germany in 1919, the issue of fundamental social rights received international attention after the Second World War. The Universal Declaration of Human Rights of 1948 recognized traditional political and civil rights as well as social rights. The principle of the indivisibility of human rights was thus adopted by the United Nations, even though in 1966 the UN separately adopted the International Covenant on Civil and Political Rights on the one hand and the International Covenant on Economic, Social and Cultural Rights on the other.

In Europe, the best example for the recognition of social rights and their indivisibility with traditional human rights is the Charter of Fundamental Rights of the EU. This recognition was the fruit of the hard negotiations of national actors together with the pressure of trade unions. Reporting on his personal experience during the drafting of the Charter, Guy Braibant, the French executive's representative at the convention, explained that after the abandonment of a first proposal by the council, a new outline of the Charter was adopted on the proposal of convention president Roman Herzog, which included a chapter on "solidarity." However, the adoption of social rights was fraught with difficulties. Braibant described two types of arguments against their adoption. One was a political argument and concerned the choice of social model: a declaration of social rights would clearly be seen as a challenge to the liberal market. The other was a legal argument and concerned the justiciable character of social rights: some legal scholars held that social rights differed from civil and political rights since they could only be effective in tandem with concrete statutes made by the legislator. Until the last moments of the convention, social rights were still the subject of negotiations, with certain Christian Democrat deputies wanting to insert Europe's "religious heritage" into the Charter. It was thanks to the strong support of trade unions and a German socialist that Braibant finally managed to introduce social rights into the Charter (Braibant, 2001, pp. 38 and 50). Social rights as human rights are now able to provide a direct judicial remedy for any violation of a worker's basic interests and thus restricting the relational subordination to a well-determined space.

The Revival of Material Subordination: Work in a Changing World

Most of the classic constructions of legal subordination seem to have entered a crisis long ago (the fundamental-rights approach might be the sole exception) for the employment contract's classic form is in sharp competition with so-called atypical or non-standard contracts (ILO, 2020). In addition, the decline of trade unionism is becoming a transnational phenomenon (Bernaciak et al., 2014) and the basic principle of the welfare state is being questioned and replaced in practice by a regulatory state of sorts (Majone, 1994). The reasons for these transformations are complex but they include multiple economic crises, an increasingly globalized economy, deregulation and privatization in the social domain, and technological development.

Focusing on the employment relationship, the feature of this long-term development would be the precarization of the working population (Alberti et al., 2018). Robert Castel (2011) clearly shows in one study how the problem of "non-employment" came into being after the "golden age" of full employment and led to the institutionalization of the precariat. In this process, the standard employment relationship is destabilized and "new figures of subordination" progressively emerge. To a certain extent, the frontier between subordinate work and independent self-employment has been blurred through this transformation. According to Alain Supiot (2000), the social-power relations have undergone two important changes, namely the diminution of discretionary power (the employer has more obligations to justify his decisions) and the distribution of previously highly centralized power (the structure of management becomes more complex). This transformation, combined with theories of management exposing the benefits of autonomous work, serves to increase the autonomy of subordinated employees and render them more similar to self-employed persons. Reciprocally, self-employed persons are gradually assimilated with employees in different domains, such as that of social protection.

Examining the situation once again today, it is even more obvious that the process of precarization not only drives one important part of the active population into unemployment but also incites them to work in bogus self-employment arrangements, especially through online platforms (Becker and Chesalina, 2021). Covered by a legally independent status, they are de facto subordinate to platforms that have the power to program their work and sanction their mistakes. It is thus plausible to speak of the revival or return of material subordination due to the development of another kind of capacity: artificial intelligence. The unemployed population is forming a new social class that some have called the "precariat" (Standing, 2014).

It has already been mentioned that economic dependence did not completely disappear from the issue of subordinate work, even though the law tended to marginalize its importance. More generally, material subordination is a social phenomenon that conserves all its potential to make a comeback. Supiot also attributes great importance to such and analyzes it as the revival of the bond of allegiance (2017, p. 269).

Against this background of converging analyses, two attempts have been made to readjust the legal framework of subordinate work. First, judges have tried to adapt the traditional criterion of legal subordination to the specific situation of bogus self-employment. Second, it has been suggested that it be moved beyond employment, a notion that is not entirely new.

As regards the adaptation of the definition of legal subordination, judges in France have been the most audacious in recent years. Redefinition is not uncommon in French jurisprudence. In the decision *Formacad* of 2016,[6] self-employed teachers were redefined by the judges as subordinate employees and thus became subject to social-security legislation. The *Cour de cassation* used a body of evidence to characterize the bond of subordination (e.g., a program fixed by the company or courses given on the premises of the company) which is a typical method in the recognition of real subordinate work. Two recent decisions demonstrated the will of the court to extend this jurisprudence to platform workers. In the first case, as related to delivery workers,[7] the court insisted on the power of the platform to trace and locate the workers and sanction them. These were sufficient indicators for the recognition of subordinate work. In the second case, concerning Uber drivers,[8] the court also focused on the fact that the platform imposed a predetermined path to the driver who cannot freely decide how to choose, and on the fact that the platform can also suspend the account of the driver after three refusals to take the task assigned by the system. Judges in other countries are beginning to adopt the same arguments. Most recently in Germany, the Federal Labor Court recognized a self-employed "clickworker" as an employee and guaranteed him protection against unfair dismissal.[9] For the judges, the worker was integrated in an organized service and executed his tasks in a legally subordinate relationship.

As concerns the idea of moving beyond the notion of employment, this had already been suggested in the Supiot Report for the European Commission (Supiot, 2001). "Beyond employment" no longer means taking the employment relation – a particular type of industrial work – as the object of regulation but rather the work itself. One particular idea is to abandon the strong tie between professional status and the rights of the worker: since careers today are far less stable than before, it would be more reasonable to link the social rights to the working person. From the perspective of this article, we can add that these social rights, saved in a personal account, should not only protect the living standards of the person but create sufficient possibilities to develop her own competences (or capabilities, in the capability approach). It is the only way to avoid social exclusion (e.g., workers in the coal industry who are today facing a major transition of their industry that might soon leave them jobless) and subsequent material subordination to all kinds of capitalist forces (whether exercised via digital platforms or not). Some social-reform processes in recent years were conceived in this fashion, such as through the creation of the individual-activity account in France in 2017.

Conclusion

This article proposes an analysis of subordinate work under two aspects, namely the relational (or subjective) one and the material (or objective) one. If the thesis of a normative evolution toward a relational subordination free from domination is correct, one might be tempted to ask: Ideally, what would be the ultimate form of subordinate work? A possible answer might be drawn from a decision of the Italian Constitutional Court.[10] In this decision, the court defined work performed within the framework of a cooperative as subordinate work and applied the relevant protection of labor law. One could ask further: What is then the dominating power in a cooperative (which normally functions according to principles such as democracy, equality and solidarity)? The Constitutional Court used the criterion of "double alienness," namely alienness of the result of the work and alienness of the productive organization. In other words, it suffices that the worker is integrated into an organization with a distribution of roles, even if there is no predominant commanding power. Would this constitute the complete infusion of coordination in subordination and be a realization of the normative ideal of subordinate work?

Notes

1 Without returning to the famous master-slave dialectic as analyzed by Hegel, a relationship is fundamentally conditioned by the problem of recognition, which determines the freedom enjoyed by each subject.
2 The context of this saying was a debate with the "agricultural school" represented by Xu Xing, whose major idea was that every person should live on his or her own agricultural production. In China this division between (roughly speaking) intellectual work and manual work goes back much further than Mencius. It is equally important to note that Mencius himself did not present this difference in terms of human nature. The distinction between the two categories of people was instead a social one.
3 Most prominently, Aristotle, *Politics*, 1330a 26. However, this theoretical analysis does not fully represent the real value of slave work in ancient societies. But we are mainly concerned here with the principle of division of labor. See also the division of labor in Plato, *The Republic*, 369b et seq.
4 For France see Cour de cassation, Chambre sociale, 13 November 1996, *Société générale*, No. de pourvoi: 94–13.187 (private teachers); for Germany, see Bundesarbeitsgericht, 30 November 1994, 5 AZR 704/93, BAGE 78, 343–356 (radio-station staff).
5 Then article 118B (see the current article 154 of the Treaty on the Functioning of the EU).
6 Cour de cassation, 2e Chambre civile, 7 July 2016, *Société Formacad*, pourvoi no 15–16.110.
7 Cour de cassation, Chambre sociale, 28 November 2018, *Take eat easy*, no. 17–20.079.
8 Cour de cassation, Chambre sociale, 4 March 2020, no. 19–13.316.
9 Bundesarbeitsgericht, 1 December 2020, 9 AZR 102/20.
10 12 February 1996, no. 30/1996, as cited by Pietrogiovanni (2020).

References

Alberti, G., Bessa, I. and Hardy, K. (2018) 'In, Against and Beyond Precarity: Work in Insecure Times', *Work, Employment and Society*, Vol. 32(3), pp. 447–457.

Anderson, E. (2012) 'Equality', in Estlund, D. (ed.) *The Oxford Handbook of Political Philosophy*. Oxford: Oxford University Press, pp. 40–57.

Auzero, G., Baugard, D. and Dockès, E. (2020) *Droit du travail*, 34th ed. Paris: Dalloz.

Becker, U. and Chesalina, O. (eds.) (2021) *Social Law 4.0*. Baden-Baden: Nomos.

Bernaciak, M., Gumbrell-McCormick, R. and Hyman, R. (2014) 'European Trade Unionism: From Crisis to Renewal?', *The European Trade Union Institute (ETUI)*, 18 February 2021. www.etui.org/publications/reports/european-trade-unionism-from-crisis-to-renewal.

Bogg, A. (2017) 'Republican Non-Domination and Labour Law: New Normativity or Trojan Horse?' *International Journal of Comparative Labour Law*, 33(3), pp. 394–417.

Braibant, G. (2001) *La Charte des droits fondamentaux de l'Union européenne, Témoignage et commentaires*. Paris: Seuil.

Cabrelli, D. (2020) *Employment Law in Context*, 4th ed. Oxford: Oxford University Press.

Cabrelli, D. and Zahn, R. (2018) 'Civic Republican Political Theory and Labour Law', in Collins, H., Lester, G. and Mantouvalou, V. (eds.) *Philosophical Foundations of Labour Law*. Oxford: Oxford University Press, pp. 104–121.

Camerlynck, G. (1982) *Le contrat de travail*, 2nd ed. Paris: Dalloz.

Case, H. (2016) 'The "Social Question," 1820–1920', *Modern Intellectual History*, pp. 747–775.

Castel, R. (2011) 'Au-delà du salariat ou en deçà de l'emploi ? L'institutionnalisation du précariat', in Paugam, S. (ed.) *Repenser la solidarité*. Paris: Presses universitaires de France, pp. 415–433.

Cuche, P. (1913) 'Du rapport de dépendance, élément constitutif du contrat de travail', *Revue critique de législation et de jurisprudence*, pp. 412–427.

Dumont, L. (1988) *Homo Hierarchicus: The Caste System and Its Implications*. Oxford: Oxford University Press.

Freedland, M., Bogg, B., Cabrelli, D., Collins, H., Countouris, N., Davies, A.C.L., Deakin, S. and Prassl, J. (eds.) (2016) *The Contract of Employment*. Oxford: Oxford University Press.

Frega, R., Herzog, L. and Neuhäuser, Ch. (2019) 'Workplace Democracy – The Recent Debate', *Philosophy Compass*, 62, p. e12574.

Heuberger, G. (1982) *Sachliche Abhängigkeit als Kriterium des Arbeitsverhältnisses*. Königstein: Athenäum.

ILO (2020) 'Non-Standard Forms of Employment', *ILO*, 18 February 2021. www.ilo.org/global/topics/non-standard-employment/lang – en/index.htm.

Ivanhoe, P. (ed.) (2009) *Mencius: Translations From the Asian Classics* (trans. Bloom I). New York: Columbia University Press.

Kahn-Freund, O. (1983) *Kahn-Freund's Labour and the Law*. London: Stevens.

Lotmar, P. (1902) *Der Arbeitsvertrag nach dem Privatrecht des Deutschen Reiches*. Berlin: Duncker & Humblot.

Lovett, F. (2010) *A General Theory of Domination and Justice*. Oxford: Oxford University Press.

Majone, G. (1994) 'The Rise of the Regulatory State in Europe', *West European Politics*, 17(3), pp. 77–101.

Ober, J. (2014) 'Meritocratic and Civic Dignity in Greco-Roman Antiquity', in Düwell, M., Braarvig, J., Brownsword, R. and Mieth, D. (eds.) *The Cambridge Handbook of Human Dignity*. Cambridge: Cambridge University Press, pp. 53–63.

Pélissier, J., Lyon-Caen, A., Jeammaud, A. and Dockès, E. (2008) *Les grands arrêts du droit du travail*. Paris: Dalloz.

Pettit, Ph. (1997) 'Republican Political Theory', in Vincent, A. (ed.) *Political Theory: Tradition and Diversity*. Cambridge: Cambridge University Press, pp. 112–131.

Pettit, Ph. (1999) *Republicanism: A Theory of Freedom and Government*. Oxford: Oxford University Press.

Pic, P. (1894) *Traité élementaire de législation industrielle: les lois ouvrières*. Paris: Rousseau.

Pietrogiovanni, V. (2020) 'Between Sein and Sollen of Labour Law: Civil (and Constitutional) Law Perspectives on Platform Workers', *King's Law Journal*, pp. 313–323.

Rosin, H. (1893) *Die reichsrechtlichen Grundlagen der Arbeiterversicherung*. Berlin: Guttentag.

Standing, G. (2014) *The Precariat: The New Dangerous Class*. London: Bloomsbury.

Stocquart, E. (1895) *Le contrat de travail: étude de droit social et de législation comparée*. Brussels and Paris: Bruylant-Christophe, Alcan.

Supiot, A. (2000) 'Les nouveaux visages de la subordination', *Droit Social*, 2, pp. 131–145.

Supiot, A. (2001) *Beyond Employment: Changes in Work and the Future of Labour Law in Europe*. Oxford: Oxford University Press.

Supiot, A. (2011) *Critique du droit du travail*. Paris: Presses universitaires de France.

Supiot, A. (2017) *Governance by Numbers: The Making of a Legal Model of Allegiance*. Oxford: Hart Publishing.

Wiedemann, H. (1966) *Das Arbeitsverhältnis als Austausch- und Gemeinschaftsverhältnis*. Karlsruhe: C. F. Müller.

Xifaras, M. (2004) *La propriété: étude de philosophie du droit*. Paris: Presses universitaires de France.

Zacher, H.F. (2004) 'Das soziale Staatsziel', in Isensee, J. and Kirchhof, P. (eds.) *Handbuch des Staatsrechts der Bundesrepublik Deutschland*, Vol. II. Heidelberg: C. F. Müller, §28.

Zöllner, W., Loritz, K.-G. and Hergenröder, C.W. (2015) *Arbeitsrecht: ein Studienbuch*, 7th ed. Munich: Beck.

2

CORPORATE WORK

A Category That Has Lost Its Managerial Foundations?

Blanche Segrestin

Introduction

In recent years the debates over employment relationships and wage employment have been revived. On the one hand, commentators fear that the wage-earning system and its protections may disappear with the advent of "platformization" and the transformation of subordinated wage-earners[1] into independent workers.[2] On the other hand, the meaning of work in large business corporations has been thrown into question. As corporations have become transnational and sometimes much more powerful than states in terms of their capacity to act, their activities affect the fate of entire populations and the environment. Corporations are generally expected to serve as levers for social and economic progress, as in the case of pharmaceutical corporations in the pandemic crisis, but there are growing concerns about inequalities and sustainability (Aubry et al., 2018; Davis, 2021). In addition to historical debates over the balance between capital and work at corporations, questions are increasingly being posed as to the meaning of corporate work and what such work is doing to the world – and more specifically, how it makes a contribution to progress or, on the contrary, further exacerbates social and environmental problems.

These growing concerns regarding the impact of corporations on the planet serve to highlight the ubiquitous but under-conceptualized category of "corporate work," that is, the work of those employed by a corporation. In this chapter, we review the categorization process, which has shaped the contemporary representation of work at the corporation, to emphasize some of its shortcomings and inconsistencies. Our core argument is that to understand the origins of corporate work, we need to disentangle the rise of the corporation in the nineteenth century from the birth of modern management and labor law in the early twentieth century.

DOI: 10.4324/9781003341321-4

On the one hand, the development and liberalization of corporations in the mid-nineteenth century made it possible to raise capital by guaranteeing the limited liability of the shareholders (Djelic, 2013). The corporation became a legal tool as provided by the state ("incorporation") and ruled by corporate law. A corporation could then be formed by contract between various shareholders. In a corporation, the directors who represent the corporation are appointed by corporate members, otherwise known as the shareholders.

On the other hand labor law emerged at the start of the twentieth century, by which time the nature of employment relationships had profoundly changed. Traditionally the wage-earner was the one who rented out his or her services. The hiring contract was thus assimilated into a market relationship where "labor is objectified into a thing sold" (Supiot, 1994, p. 60). Marxist analysis has conceptualized this relationship by regarding what the worker sells as being labor to the capitalist. In this view, the wage is the price paid for a quantity of labor, and the "thing worked upon" (Supiot, 1994, p. 60) as well as the economic results belong to the employer, which explains why the wage-earner has no right to the product of his work or to the product of its sale. Yet, with the birth of labor law in the twentieth century, the employment relationship was no longer a contractual market relationship but one based on subordination. Paradoxically, the recognition in law of this subordination was seen as social progress. This can be understood only if we consider the emergence of a new figure – the manager – who was neither an entrepreneur nor a capital investor but a professional in charge of conceiving and organizing new collective processes. The nature of work was deeply transformed at that time, shifting from a regime of routine production, in which employees were responsible for their own methods, to a regime of innovation in which they were trained and methods were designed by the new category of managerial staff. To put it briefly, the recognition in law of the labor contract was a *coup de force* that can only be understood if we take into account the radical changes in the nature of work: modern work was organized in a collective way to be not only productive but creative (Segrestin and Hatchuel, 2012).

These two transformations are constitutive of modern business organizations in the early twentieth century. And yet, in the thinking and practice of corporate governance, the foundation and role of management was sidelined at the end of the twentieth century. Legally speaking, today's corporate workers are employed by a corporation that is formed by shareholders; practically speaking, business activities are governed by the rule of corporate law. Shareholders appoint directors who themselves can delegate managers or corporate officers to run the business on behalf of the shareholders. And corporate officers supervise employees' work. The chain of agency relationships between shareholders, directors, corporate officers and employees has become the prevalent form of governance of business organizations in the twentieth century. This view radically overlooks the managerial function and it ignores the historical and theoretical foundations of managerial authority. We argue that the category of "corporate work" obscures the conditions under which employee subordination can be legitimate, and for this reason, it creates today major imbalances. It therefore calls for a reappraisal.

This chapter[3] is divided into three sections. The first section shows how two different categories – the corporation and the labor contract – emerged in the late nineteenth century, in parallel and rather disconnected ways. The second section develops how in the late twentieth century the two categories were conflated to form the category of corporate work and why certain problems of corporate governance are related to it. Lastly, the third section discusses the prospects of recategorizing corporate work. Interestingly, this recategorization is already underway with a new type of corporation introduced recently into corporate law: the "purpose-driven corporation." Such a corporation stipulates binding social and environmental objectives in its corporate charter, and it is through such commitments that corporate law restores the role of management. Purpose-driven corporations specify the mandate given to managers and thus clarify the purpose of work, which is no more reducible to the corporation's or the shareholders' interests. The meaning of work as well as its governance are therefore also likely to be revised; however, this chapter suggests that further efforts are needed to recategorize modern corporate work.

Corporate Law and Labor Law: Two Distinct Processes of Categorization

The category of corporate work has become widely institutionalized. It is typically considered from the angle of the employment relationship which, as we know, is a highly singular one. As Freeland noted:

> There are three defining characteristics of the employee, each of which stands in stark contrast to the legal definition of the independent contractor in the market. The first is her status as a servant who is legally required to obey the orders of her employer. The second is her classification as an agent who acts on behalf of her employer rather than for herself. The third – itself a result of the employee's categorization as an agent – is her position as a fiduciary who is obligated to put the employer's interests ahead of her own.
>
> *(Freeland, 2009)*

Despite its institutionalization, this categorization remains highly problematic because it lacks justification. How and on what basis can we agree that workers act under the control and on behalf of the corporate employer? Even if we acknowledge that workers freely consent to submit to their employer's will due to economic dependence, this does not provide any acceptable basis for subordination. Likewise, the ownership of assets cannot justify a right to issue instructions to individuals even if they use these assets (Chaigneau and Vernac, 2012). As McMahon (2013) pointed out, when someone is in your house, it is not because you own the house that you are justified in giving them directives. Thus, the legal grounds for employment relationships are all but obvious (McMahon, 2013).

Corporate work cannot actually be considered separately from the context in which it is embedded, namely the corporation. It is therefore useful to disentangle the historical threads that led to the construction of this category. By so doing, we discover not only successive layers of different rationales in the law but also the fact that theoretical representations have sometimes retained certain elements while disregarding others. This is why we need to revisit the various intersecting categorization processes that constitute the current legal framework, which is generally taken to be necessary or even natural. Here we will analyze French historical development as our main though hardly exclusive case.

Nineteenth Century: Contractualism and the Rise of the Modern Corporation

In the nineteenth century, contractualism constituted a major socio-historical development comparable to the emergence of serfdom or historic corporations (Didry and Brouté, 2006; Jacoby, 2004; Selznick, 1969). The contractualization of employment relationships was a very gradual process (Deakin, 2009; Le Goff, 2004) but one that in France was nonetheless reaffirmed by the establishment of the French Civil Code in 1804. The Code formalized employment relationships as a relationship of service-renting (*louage*) in which the worker rendered his or her services or work. This conceptualization was perceived by liberals as a step forward: the hiring contract was equal to a contract established by mutual agreement and characterized both by freedom (especially in terminating the contract) and by the security it provided employees with insofar as their compensation was agreed upon in advance and did not depend on the market. Liberals thus believed that salaried employment enabled work its freedom along with a functioning labor market and the security of remuneration agreed upon in advance. Yet others saw salaried employment as being in opposition to the status of a free worker since employees had no right to the products of their work, which were the property of the employer. Charles Gide for instance defined employment as "the situation of the man who, not having the means to produce for himself, is obliged to hire out his services, his arms, his person" (Gide, 1924).

In parallel, during the period of nineteenth-century industrialization, entrepreneurs made greater use of the limited-liability corporation (*société anonyme*) (Djelic, 2013). This was another major break from the past. Up until then, individuals had formed partnerships with unlimited and joint responsibility for the debts of their common activity. In joint-stock corporations, shareholders were no longer liable beyond the value of their investment. As a result, the limited-liability corporation was a preferred tool for raising capital. For a long time the public authorities – fearing that such corporations would be unable to honor their debts – were hostile to them, making the formation of a limited-liability corporation contingent on government authorization. However, during the nineteenth century, the promises made by companies of industrialization as well as scientific and technological progress helped convince the authorities of the benefits that would accrue in any liberalization of the laws regulating incorporation. Thus, a revolution in ownership took place at the end of the nineteenth century: investors were no longer responsible for the use or control of their investments (Berle and Means, 1932).

The limited-liability corporation established a very particular governance structure in which a corporation was a legal entity that owned the assets and outcomes of its operations. While the shareholders no longer managed operations, they retained the right to appoint and dismiss directors. Moreover, from this point onward, the corporation was the contractual party in contracts with employees. This structure is still in use today. Its longevity nevertheless hides a major transformation in the nature of work and work relations.

Early Twentieth Century: Modern Management and the Rise of Labor Law

In Europe, and France in particular, new employment contracts characterized by subordination triggered a radical shift in the economic and legal worlds of work (Deakin, 2009). In France, Cottereau spoke of a "dogmatic coup de force" (Cottereau, 2002). It was indeed in stark contrast to the "contractual" doctrine, which, in nineteenth-century France and America (Deakin, 2009), viewed labor as free and voluntary (Jacoby, 2004; Selznick, 1969).

In the twentieth century, in all these countries, labor law endorsed a view of corporate work as salaried and subordinated work. Labor law, as a specific branch of law separate from corporate law, took shape in the majority of countries between 1900 and 1910 (Commons, 1919). The legal categorization was an extremely long and difficult process and was actually never formalized in hard law (Lefebvre, 2009). But the potential for employers to give orders and directives, of controlling their execution and if necessary sanctioning the employee, introduced the recognition of a discretionary power. Labor law today thus organizes the contestability, responsibility (for instance, in case of occupational accidents) and liability of the employers (the *respondeat* doctrine).

The introduction of the employment contract is mostly seen as the normalization of a relationship of economic domination. In this reading the concept of subordination ratifies an existing legal and economic asymmetry; and by acknowledging submission to the employer, in return, the employment contract is supposed to acknowledge the employer's liability.

Yet recent research has analyzed the recognition of subordination in the law from a new angle. While the terms used in the categories of wage, employment, employer, etc. are stable, they conceal profound transformations in meaning and practice. The nature of work and the relationships within which it takes place underwent a remarkable change in the late nineteenth century in the vanguard or science-based industries that emerged at the time, and these configurations gave rise to an unprecedented figure that would play a decisive role in this transformation: the professional manager or chief executive (*chef d'entreprise*).

Any understanding of why the law accepts and legitimizes subordination will require a better understanding of these figures, their role and the sources of their authority. In what follows, we build upon recent research to argue that managerial authority emerged to organize not only collective production but collective creation. More specifically, subordination can be better explained when we take into account the function of modern innovative management.

Modern management emerged when the traditional know-how and tools of workers had reached their limits. *The role of management was therefore to develop new capabilities that did not yet exist on labor markets.* It appeared with the introduction of science and research and development in business organizations, with the intent not only of producing goods with existing technologies but to develop new products with emerging technologies. New science-based industries arose (e.g., telecommunications, chemistry) (Reich, 1985). With these new organizations, the nature of work changed drastically (Jacoby, 2004). Workers not only sold their ability to work, but also agreed to adopt the methods and tools defined by the organization rather than using their own. They thus agreed to be trained and undergo transformations in their job profiles and occupations. In a way, work could be said to have become "developmental" in the sense that workers invested their potential and expected that the corporation would develop their skills and capabilities in exchange.

While nineteenth-century corporate power was linked to capital ownership, the source of managerial power in modern enterprise is profoundly distinct from capital. Management power is entrusted to managers with clearly defined competencies and legitimacy, rather than to the corporate owners. The legitimacy of management is therefore not based on ownership of the means of production but rather on the ability to create and implement innovative work processes. Management has become a profession in its own right and with a specific skill set. The Taylorist movement clearly showed the utility of replacing the "rule-of-thumb method" with a scientific approach to organization: the management existed so as to "scientifically select and then train, teach, and develop the workman, whereas in the past he chose his own work and trained himself as best he could" (Taylor, 1911). Work became not only the object of bureaucratic rules but, more importantly, a subject of detailed scientific inquiry. In this way, the management profession was progressively institutionalized over the course of the twentieth century through specific training courses such as the MBA (Master of Business Administration) created by Harvard in 1908.

Managerial authority came hand in hand with responsibility. While this new management authority, separated from capital, made many promises as to economic and social progress, it can also be viewed from the perspective of responsibility.

Management authority is legitimate, provided it is competent and exercised with concern for the safety and development of subordinates. This was the intent of labor law when it recognized managerial authority. For instance, managers (*chefs d'entreprises*) were liable for work accidents precisely because they prescribed the work methods without being owners of the machines (Commons, 1919) and because it was their responsibility to develop the skills necessary to safely organize work processes. According to Selznick, the conditions allowing for subordination and managerial power are to be found primarily in administrative methods – that is, the scientific methods of management. Scientific management offered an alternative to conflict through a consensus based on scientifically constructed knowledge and with the intent to create "a new era of productivity and fairness" (Selznick, 1969, p. 86).

The emergence of management profoundly affected the conceptual representation of work. For instance, Commons, who played an important role in the drafting of U.S. labor law in the 1920s, understood modern work as entailing a complete renewal of the theory of work. While "[t]he commodity theory is the merchant's theory of buying and selling," he contended that this old approach needed to be replaced by a new one that was inspired by engineering and managerial views: "The machinery theory is the engineer's theory of economy and output. Man is, after all, the most marvelous and productive of all the forces of nature. He is a mechanism of unknown possibilities" (Commons, 1919, p. 14).

Corporate Work: The Management Lost From View[4]

It is important to emphasize that management has never been formally recognized in law. As Selznick rightly argued, corporate law organizes the relationships between corporate members who decide to put assets in common and share benefits and losses (Selznick, 1969). But corporate law says nothing about labor relations. In the corporation's structure, the executives are mandated by directors who in turn are appointed by the shareholders. The theoretical and legal process of categorizing "corporate work" thus developed in the twentieth century while neglecting the historical sources and conditions pertaining to the legitimacy of management (Segrestin et al., 2019).

Agency Theory: Management Reduced to an Agent of Shareholders

Economic theories of the firm played a decisive role in categorizing corporate work. We will briefly present these theories along two lines.

Transaction-costs theory (Coase, 1937; Williamson, 1985) sees hierarchy as the defining feature of the firm and as an alternative to the market-based coordination of actors. The idea is that hierarchical control allows the reduction of costs, particularly when transactions require specific investments, and is therefore more efficient than the market. This approach, which grants a central role to opportunism, tries to take into consideration the specific nature of the employment contract – a contract based on subordination and not simply a market contract. However, transaction-costs theory hypothesizes that the activities carried out in hierarchical contexts are the same as those in market contexts. It, therefore, overlooks the importance of collective learning inherent to the modern enterprise, which emerged precisely so as to create and develop products that would not have otherwise been invented in market contexts.

The other set of theories is related to the property-rights theory. In this case, the firm is conceptualized on the basis of its contractual structure and the distribution of property rights. For example, Alchian and Demsetz thought the structure of the corporation to have spread because it was optimal in terms of efficiency (Alchian and Demsetz, 1972). They argued that shareholders possessed the ultimate control (appointing and monitoring directors) and had the greatest incentive to manage things well because they were paid only after all the other parties had been compensated. Moreover, if shareholders did not manage the corporation themselves, it was because they preferred to delegate this task to managerial experts; nonetheless, in substance, managers were no more than the "agents" of shareholders.

This summary is of course very brief, but it does explain why the firm is understood as a chain of agency relationships. In the lenses of agency theory, corporate members – the stockholders – appoint directors, and the board of directors can delegate the task of running the business to corporate officers, that is, managers, who in turn mandate workers to do their jobs. Corporate workers have been categorized as the agents of the managers who themselves are the agents of corporate members.

Agency theory thus provided a new theoretical approach to the corporate framework in the 1980s and 1990s to promote new shareholder-oriented principles of corporate governance, starting with the Cadbury Report on Corporate Governance (Cadbury, 1992). The report states that "The shareholders as owners of the company elect the directors to run the business on their behalf and hold them accountable for its progress. The issue for corporate governance is how to strengthen the accountability of boards of directors to shareholders" (Cadbury, 1992, §6.1, p. 47). Managers became more incentivized to work on behalf and in the interests of the shareholders, who had greater control over them.

Legally speaking, this agency view is not completely valid. By law, the stockholders own neither the corporation's assets nor its profits (Robé, 2011; Ciepley, 2013). The corporation is a special legal entity that is the sole owner of its assets and profits (Blair and Stout, 1999). Blair and Stout argue that it is therefore legally inappropriate to consider managers as the shareholders' agents; they are actually trustees of the corporation (Lan and Heracleous, 2010). It is furthermore also inappropriate to consider managers as agents of the shareholders since they are personally liable for business issues, whereas shareholders are not. The recent "team-production theory" of the corporation proposes an alternative approach to the agency theory of the corporation (Blair and Stout, 1999). It holds that the corporation is formed as a third party to allow joint investments by the various team members. As the legal entity is the owner of the joint output, the board is in charge of running the business for the corporation itself and not for shareholders. This view thus proposes a new interpretation of the corporation. But it challenges neither the position of managers as agents nor the right of ultimate control that shareholders have over managers.

Collective Creation Under Threat

It is currently acknowledged that this governance approach has helped create a deep crisis in management, which scholars have called a "great deformation" of the enterprise (Favereau, 2014). The symptoms are well-known and can be evidenced in various ways. As William Lazonick put it, we are now in the era of "Profit without Prosperity" because that which is good for investors is not always good for the collective good (Lazonick, 2014). Moreover, growing profits have been accompanied by a deterioration of work conditions, greater insecurity and a vast increase in wage inequalities. Several studies show that firms' profits have risen substantially in proportion to GDP, as has the share of profits distributed to shareholders in the form of dividends. In contrast, employees' share of GDP is declining (Aubry et al., 2018; Knott, 2017).

Another sign that is less spectacular but just as deleterious is the decline in investment. Everywhere, and Europe in particular, non-financial firms are drawing an increasing proportion of their profits from their financial assets (Auvray et al., 2016). Research and development (R&D) investments are especially threatened. In many firms, including those most commonly associated with renowned traditions of innovation, the change has been significant in recent years. Whereas R&D is the basis of the renewal of a firm's skills and products – and therefore its sustainability – we are witnessing a withdrawal from R&D in exchange for growth strategies based on less risky financial acquisitions (exogenous growth and "Build-Up"[5]) or simply strategies based on purchasing technologies or patents (Knott, 2017). For example, researchers have demonstrated that while the number of patents has continued to increase (including through acquisitions) this increase has not been related to research in firms, which has clearly decreased since 1980 (Arora et al., 2015).

Furthermore, it has been shown that the budget which leading American firms allocate to share buybacks is often larger than that allocated to R&D or even larger than the corporate-net results (Lazonick, 2014)! This phenomenon illustrates the extent to which firms are willing to enhance their financial performance at the risk of sacrificing their long-term sustainability. They are thus failing to address today's large-scale societal and environmental challenges.

Subordination Has Lost Its Foundations and Legitimacy

The category of corporate work views managers as corporate agents. This view neglects the foundations of managerial authority, which are being deeply undermined today. Three sets of evidence are illustrative of this undermining phenomenon.

First, the function of management was to develop new capabilities for action. But how can subordination be accepted and how can managers rally workers if managers run the business in the sole interest of shareholders? Not only does managerial authority become illegitimate, but the economic efficacy of modern business is also jeopardized. If corporations are reduced to pursuing only short-term profits, then the whole point of developing new capabilities through research and development becomes secondary and long-term investment for collective progress is sacrificed.

Second, the legitimacy of management authority was based on specific skills and a creative capacity to invent unprecedented ways of using resources. Under the doctrine of shareholder governance, directors are no longer rated in terms of their skills but with regard to their position as agents responsible for implementing the desires of the board (as opposed to inventing new forms of collective activity).

Lastly, managerial authority was acceptable insofar as it was exercised competently and in the interest of subordinates. This consideration has become secondary in the contemporary governance scheme in which directors' "fiduciary duties" to corporate members prevail over all else.

Avenues for a Recategorization: The New Purpose-Driven Corporations?

Our analysis shows that the category of corporate work obscures the origins and conditions of the possibility of subordination. If it is valid, then our analysis has important implications for further research. It invites us to deepen the theoretical endeavor of "categorization" so that contemporary work may be done in a positive and progressive sense.

In this respect, it is worth noting the introduction of new legal corporate forms. For instance, several countries have introduced "purpose-driven corporations." Particularly in France the "Pacte Law" has introduced the so-called *société à mission* (Segrestin et al., 2021). This law modifies the French Civil Code, requiring that all firms not only be managed while "taking into consideration the social and environmental outcomes of [their] operations" but that they be vigilant with respect to the negative impact their activities could generate. They are furthermore urged to define their *raison d'être* (Article 1835) and commit to social and environmental goals in their bylaws.

A *société à mission* stipulates its purpose in its bylaws, with specific social and environmental objectives. These objectives are included in the corporate contract and are thus corporate commitments for the different stakeholders. In addition, a special board is established for the exclusive purpose of ensuring compliance with these commitments.

By stating the firm's purpose, this law constitutes an unprecedented standard for responsible corporate governance. Contrary to the very numerous reform proposals during the twentieth century, the goal is not to rebalance the powers of the stakeholders at a firm but to specify the orientation of its operations and to involve governance bodies, including shareholders, so as to make corporate work meaningful.

We believe that this new governance scheme combines a principle of efficiency (stating the progress to be achieved, the reason for the action, and the mobilization of stakeholders) with a principle of responsibility (a credible commitment as well as a provision for internal and external oversight) and it is of primary importance to point out that this new legal framework is capable of changing the categorization of corporate work in several ways.

First and foremost, stating the purpose of collective action is a *way to restore the function of the top manager*. As we have seen, the manager is often reduced to being an agent of the shareholders. However, by adopting a mission – that is, a desirable future or a "desirable unknown" – the law reestablishes the creative role of managers, who are now responsible for inventing new models of collective action and for developing the action potential that is precisely lacking today.

Next, writing the firm's *raison d'être* into its bylaws once again grants employees a place in the firm's governance. The mandate given to corporate officers is not reducible to shareholders' interests. And it may designate some desirable future for which the development of workers' capabilities in the long run is crucial (Segrestin et al., 2021). As a result, managers are held accountable in terms of just how the strategy that they implement effectively accords with the mission. It provides the workers with a lever to discuss and control the strategy and the impact of managerial decisions on their own human capital.

Lastly, the new law restores a possible "common purpose" that justifies employee commitment and the acceptance of management authority. In a *société à mission*, a firm's *raison d'être* states what its plans are for making a contribution to a more desirable future (new technologies for non-polluting agriculture, for positive energy buildings, carbon capture, etc.). To be precise, it offers *a principle of responsibility adapted to contemporary innovation issues*. Faced with climate change and the large-scale challenges of the twenty-first century, the law allows firms to make long-term commitments to research and innovation in order to find new solutions. In doing so – through that desirable future to which it commits – the firm thus reconciles freedom of enterprise with the collective good.

Notes

1 See also the chapter "Subordinate Work: How Does the Law Categorize Modern Labor Relationships?" by Linxin He in this volume.
2 See also the chapter "Platform Work: New Workers, New Rights?" by Sophie Bernard and Josépha Dirringer in this volume.
3 This article builds on recent research conducted at Mines ParisTech with Armand Hatchuel and Kevin Levillain and in cooperation with the professorial chair "Theory of the Enterprise: Models of Governance and Collective Creation" and in collaboration with the Collège des Bernardins. See Favereau, 2014; Roger, 2012; Segrestin et al., 2014; Favereau and Roger, 2015; Segrestin and Vernac, 2018.
4 See Johnston and Segrestin (2021).
5 The case of Pfizer is exemplary. Successive acquisitions and a series of streamlining policies, in particular reducing R&D, have allowed it to increase its profits, with less assets allocated to the firm's creative capacities, thus decreasing its contribution to collective progress.

References

Alchian, A.A. and Demsetz, H. (1972) 'Production, Information Costs and Economic Organization', *The American Economic Review*, 62(5), pp. 777–795.

Arora, A., Belenzon, S. and Patacconi, A. (2015) 'Killing the Golden Goose? The Decline of Science in Corporate R&D', NBER working paper 20902.

Aubry, M., Alliot, C. and Ly, S. (2018) *CAC 40: des profits sans partage. Comment les grandes entreprises françaises alimentent la spirale des inégalités*. Paris: Basic & Oxfam France. www.oxfamfrance.org/sites/default/files/file_attachments/vfrapport_oxfam_cac40_des_profits_sans_partage.pdf.

Auvray, T., Dallery, T. and Rigot, S. (2016) *L'entreprise liquidée. La finance contre l'investissement*. Paris: Michalon.

Berle, A. and Means, G. (1932) *The Modern Corporation and Private Property*. New Brunswick, NJ: Transaction Publishers.

Blair, M.M. and Stout, L.A. (1999) 'A Team Production Theory of Corporate Law?', *Journal of Corporation Law*, 24(4), pp. 751–807.

Cadbury, A. (1992) *The Financial Aspects of Corporate Governance*. London: Gee.

Chaigneau, A. and Vernac, S. (2012) 'Repenser la propriété et la responsabilité des personnes morales', in Roger, B. (ed.) *L'entreprise, formes de la propriété et responsabilités sociales: collection 'Cours, Colloques, Conférences du Collège des Bernardins'*. Paris: Parole et Silence/Lethielleux.

Ciepley, D.A. (2013) 'Beyond Public and Private: Toward a Political Theory of the Corporation', *American Political Science Review*, 107(1), pp. 139–158.

Coase, R.H. (1937) 'The Nature of the Firm', *Economica*, 4(16), pp. 386–405.

Commons, J.R. (1919) *Industrial Goodwill*. New York: McGraw-Hill Book.

Cottereau, A. (2002) 'Droit et bon droit. Un droit des ouvriers instauré, puis évincé par le droit du travail (France, XIXe siècle)', *Annales. Histoire, Sciences Sociales*, 57(6), pp. 1521–1557.

Davis, G.F. (2021) 'Corporate Purpose Needs Democracy', *Journal of Management Studies*, 58(3), pp. 902–913.

Deakin, S. (2009) 'Legal Origin, Juridical Form and Industrialization in Historical Perspective: The Case of the Employment Contract and the Joint-Stock Company', *Socio-Economic Review*, 7, pp. 35–65.

Didry, C. and Brouté, R. (2006) 'L'employeur en question, les enjeux de la subordination pour les rapports de travail dans une société capitaliste', in Petit, H. and Thévenot, N. (eds.) *Les nouvelles frontières du travail subordonné, approche pluridisciplinaire*. Paris: La Découverte, pp. 47–70.

Djelic, M.-L. (2013) 'When Limited Liability Was (Still) an Issue: Mobilization and Politics of Signification in 19th-Century England', *Organization Studies*, 34(5–6), pp. 595–621.

Favereau, O. (2014) *Entreprises: la grande déformation*. Paris: Parole et Silence, Collège des Bernardins.

Favereau, O. and Roger, B. (2015) *Penser l'entreprise. Nouvel horizon du politique. Coll. Perspectives & Propositions*. Paris: Parole et silence, Collège des Bernardins.

Freeland, R. (2009) 'The Social and Legal Bases of Managerial Authority', *Entreprises et Histoire*, 57, pp. 194–217.

Gide, C. (1924) *Le programme coopératiste et le salariat: trois leçons du cours sur la coopération au Collège de France*. Paris: Association pour l'enseignement de la coopération.

Jacoby, S.M. (2004) *Employing Bureaucracy: Managers, Unions, and the Transformation of Work in the 20th Century*, Rev ed. Mahwah, NJ: Taylor & Francis Group.

Johnston, A. and Segrestin, B. (2021) 'Lost from View: The Legal Invisibility of Managers in the U.K.', in Colli, A. and Sogner, K. (eds.) *The Emergence of Corporate Governance: People, Power, and Performance*. New York: Routledge, pp. 33–50.

Knott, A.M. (2017) 'The Real Reasons Companies Are So Focused on the Short Term', *Harvard Business Review*. https://hbr.org/2017/12/the-real-reasons-companies-are-so-focused-on-the-short-term.

Lan, L.L. and Heracleous, L. (2010) 'Rethinking Agency Theory: The View From Law', *Academy of Management Review*, 35(2), pp. 294–314.

Lazonick, W. (2014) 'Profits Without Prosperity', *Harvard Business Review*, 92(9), pp. 46–55.

Le Goff, J. (2004) *Du silence à la parole. Une histoire du droit du travail*. Rennes: Presses Universitaires de Rennes, p. 620.

Lefebvre, P. (2009) 'Subordination et "révolutions" du travail et du droit du travail (1776–2010)', *Entreprises et Histoire*, 57, pp. 45–78.

McMahon, C. (2013) *Public Capitalism: The Political Authority of Corporate Executives*. Philadelphia, PA: University of Pennsylvania Press.

Reich, L.S. (1985) *The Making of American Industrial Research: Science and Business at GE and Bell, 1876–1926*. Cambridge: Cambridge University Press.

Robé, J.-P. (2011) 'The Legal Structure of the Firm', *Accounting, Economics, and Law: A Convivium*, 1(1), pp. 1–86.

Roger, B. (ed.) (2012) *L'entreprise, formes de la propriété et responsabilités sociales*. Paris: Parole et Silence/Lethielleux.

Segrestin, B., Roger, B., & Vernac, S. (2014). (Eds.), *L'entreprise, point aveugle du savoir?* Paris: Sciences Humaines.

Segrestin, B. and Hatchuel, A. (2012) *Refonder l'entreprise. La République des Idées*. Paris: Le Seuil.

Segrestin, B., Hatchuel, A. and Levillain, K. (2021) 'When the Law Distinguishes Between the Enterprise and the Corporation: The Case of the New French Law on Corporate Purpose', *Journal of Business Ethics*, 171, pp. 1–13.

Segrestin, B., Johnston, A. and Hatchuel, A. (2019) 'The Separation of Directors and Managers: A Historical Examination of the Status of Managers', *Journal of Management History*, 25(2), pp. 141–164.

Segrestin, B. and Vernac, S. (2018) *Gouvernement, participation et mission de l'entreprise*. Paris: Herman.
Selznick, P. (1969) *Law, Society, and Industrial Justice* (in collaboration with Philippe Nonet and Howard M. Vollmer). London: Russel Sage Foundation.
Supiot, A. (1994) *Critique du droit du travail*. Paris: Presses universitaires de France.
Taylor, F.W. (1911) *Principles of Scientific Management*. New York and London: Harper & Brothers.
Williamson, O. (1985) *The Economic Institutions of Capitalism*. New York: The Free Press.

3

REMOTE WORK

From Employee Telework to Self-Employed Home-Based Work?

Frédérique Letourneux and Gabrielle Schütz

With the COVID-19 pandemic and the lockdown, the term "telework" has become popular. The use of teleworking as a form of health protection means simply working outside the organization using digital tools. In this case the work has merely been physically removed from the organization, with no possible alternatives being considered. In the various OECD countries, the rules governing this exceptional use have varied and more or less left to the employer to impose telework on employees or not. But in most cases we have seen improvised forms of teleworking from the side of both workers and organizations.

Under less exceptional circumstances, telework may cover formal arrangements negotiated as part of the employment contract: part-time (one or two days a week) or full-time work outside the organization. While the majority of telework takes place at home, workspaces are also developing (co-working spaces, shared offices) which offer alternative solutions. Telework can also cover informal arrangements when the activity is partly realized at home, even informally. Metzger and Cleach (2004) speak of "overflowing" telework: the employees, especially executives and especially men (Atkinson and Hall, 2009), continue their work at home in the evening or on the weekend. As we can see, the practical category of "telework" is in itself very porous, with blurred boundaries, even if its definition always contains an implicit reference to a "normal" work-day within an organization.

In this article we reflect on how telework, as a matter of work organization, challenges the concept of "work" itself. As telework introduces a greater degree of autonomy into work carried out by isolated workers, we postulate that telework is not simply a transposition of the work process from the organization to the home; rather, it questions the very foundations of the wage model and the principle of subordination upon which it is based. Work's exit from the

DOI: 10.4324/9781003341321-5

organization also raises questions as to the way in which the use of new technologies can lead to the development of new forms of outsourcing. From this perspective the distance is not only physical but legal. Indeed the use of freelancers at the margins of organizations is growing and encouraged by the possibility of deterritorialized work.[1]

Telework is a particular form of remote work that is salaried. In this article the category "telework" will be used only in this restrictive way, but the challenges posed by the possibility of working remotely go beyond this strict framework of analysis. In order to bring these different dimensions together and analyze the transformations of work and employment triggered by distance – both physical and legal – we use the broader analytical category of "remote work."

After having discussed the different forms of working at distance from the organization, we look at the contemporary evolution of the objectives assigned to telework and the inequalities that it reveals and renews in organizations. Finally we show how remote work is shaking up the wage model by individualizing work relations and blurring the boundaries between wage labor and independent labor.

Definition of the Phenomenon: Homework, Telework, Remote Work?

According to the basic definition of the term itself, telework is a way of working outside the organization through the use of information and communication technologies (ICT) such as the Internet and telephone. But this very simple definition actually covers many situations and issues that go beyond the technical tools. When we look at the modalities of telework today, the definition refers to a particular negotiated form of work at home under salaried status; but the condition of working outside the organization using ICT also applies to self-employed individuals who work from home on behalf of clients.

Remote Working With Communication Devices: The Old Promise of Ubiquity

The belief in the power of ICT to transform the way we work dates back to the early 1980s. Telematics was in the initial stages of its development and associated with futuristic scenarios of deep transformation. The essayist and futurist Alvin Toffler had predicted the massive onset of teleworking in his 1980 book *The Third Wave*. If these scenarios seemed credible at the time, it is only because the tertiary sector was dominating the economies of developed countries, and it seemed that office work could be performed anywhere and anytime by using ICT.

At that time there was an optimistic belief in the future. This promise of ubiquity seemed enormous. The development of telework was seen primarily as a means of developing rural areas on the margins by promising to reduce physical distances through the use of technologies. In France in the 1990s, for example, the Ministry of the Interior and Regional Planning ordered reports on this issue. In its first developmental phase, telework was seen mostly as a way of establishing a kind of *geographical* autonomy rather than any autonomy for *workers*. This planning discourse was associated with a second discourse which perceived telework as a way to better combine work and private life and place a value on the worker's freedom in organizing her time.

Telework: First a Legal Category

At the European level, the social partners signed an agreement on home office on 16 July 2002 so as to frame teleworking. This agreement is non-binding, which leaves each EU member state the choice of whether to implement it in its national legislation and regulations, then agreements are negotiated within the professional branches and within the companies themselves. This stack of agreements results in teleworkers experiencing very different situations.

For example, in France the law of 22 March 2012, known as the Warsmann Law, includes teleworking in the labor code[2] and defines telework as a category of work within a restrictive salaried frame. *This legal definition* emphasizes the voluntary and negotiated character of telework as enshrined in the Europe Agreement. According to this legal frame, work can be performed in the same way inside or outside of organizations and the employer must provide all the equipment.

Telework covers different situations. It is possible to perform all work-related activities at home, but in practice this remains an exception. In the usual implementation, the teleworker alternates working at home (or in a co-working place) and in a workplace. In fact in 2019 only 5.4 percent of the employed persons in the EU-27 *usually* worked from home – a share that has remained roughly constant since 2009. However, over the same period, the share of employed persons working at least *occasionally* from their homes increased from 5.2 percent in 2009 to 9 percent in 2019 (European Commission, 2020).

"Remote Work": Development of Outsourcing and Deterritorialization

Telework in a salaried frame is just one instance of remote work. In recent years we have seen the development of forms of telework that take place on the margins of organizations on a self-employed basis. As European statistics show, in 2019 almost 36 percent of the self-employed were usually or occasionally working from home in the EU-27, which was up from 30 percent in 2009 (European Commission, 2020). With the spread of new technologies there has been the development of what some call "digital labor" (Cardon and Casili, 2019). These workers have no connection with the physical organization. Some work for platforms: they are self-employed and compete for micro-tasks. This is the most deterritorialized form of work, which takes place without any physical constraint or link with the organization (Cingolani, 2021). But remote work covers a variety of other hybrid situations that straddle the line between salaried employment and independence, and it takes place on the margins of organizations (Letourneux, 2017), for instance, self-employed people who depend on a single employer and who occasionally go to the workplace to carry out their tasks, such as freelance graphic designers who work as subcontractors for an agency or freelancers journalists who work from home (or in a shared office) for various newspaper or magazine editorial offices.

The issue of the place where work takes place raises questions as to the employment relationship itself. It questions both the relations with the organizations and the way that teleworkers mobilize to defend their working environment at home, whether they be employees or are self-employed.

Reproduction and Displacement of Inequalities in Telework and Remote Work

Working from home reconfigures not only working times and spaces of work but also the relationship to the organization, whether as an employee or as someone who is self-employed. These reconfigurations tend to reinforce inequalities along lines of gender and qualification that are already present on the labor market.

Telework: From the Margins to the Center of Organizations?

In recent years telework has changed its meaning by becoming a distinguishing feature in organizations that are trying to reinvent themselves as "freedom-form" companies.[3] After being associated with a territorial-development objective and with a societal objective of lifestyle-renewal, in the 2000s and 2010s telework became increasingly associated with a third objective related to the transformation of organizations (Largier, 2001). For example, this is evidenced by the fact that in France the contemporary reports on telework are no longer conducted at the request of the Ministry of Land Management, as in the 1990s, but at the initiative of the Ministry of Labor (Letourneux, 2017). This "third generation of telework" is described by some in terms of nomadism and is associated with the "virtual office," which succeeds the "home office" (Messenger and Gschwind, 2016). Telework is increasingly presented as part of the "digital transformation" of enterprises into "agile" and "resilient" companies. By allowing workers to work anytime and from anywhere, telework should provide greater flexibility. By making workers more "autonomous" and "responsible" and shifting the role of management from control to "support" and "trust," telework is meant to contribute to a horizontalization of relations in the company, a reduction of hierarchies, and a "liberation" of "creativity." Telework is therefore seen as an instrument for optimizing productivity. This way of thinking, particularly within the human-resources departments of companies, is matched by the real-estate departments of these same companies, which see telework as an opportunity to reduce real-estate costs by saving space. The implementation of telework is therefore very often accompanied by a reorganization of the company's premises, with open-plan or even flex-office offices where the number of workstations is lower than the number of employees and where the seats are not allocated in order to allow shifting teams to reconstitute themselves according to the projects they carry out. In short, teleworking is one of those "new ways of work" (NWOW) (Popma, 2013) that are widely reported in the business press and which are giving rise to a flourishing market for consulting firms.

At the same time, the image of the teleworker has changed. Despite the promises associated with telework, it had remained relatively marginal in companies until the 2020 health crisis, and the teleworker was often perceived as a person unsuited to the constraints of the working world and to whom the company generously granted this arrangement to facilitate her adaptation. The teleworker was then the opposite of the "first in, last out" model employee (Blair-Loy, 2003; Munsch, 2016). For example, teleworking was associated with women who wanted to have more flexibility in their schedules so as to take care of their young children. It was also associated with the worker who was nearing retirement and wished to gradually ease the workload by spending a few days of the week at home, or with the worker who had health problems. If these representations of teleworkers are still present in the imaginary of organizations, the rise of the discourse on "new ways of work" has created competing characters who are more desirable and more in line with the managerial discourse. The teleworker is adorned with multiple virtues: flexible, autonomous, hyper-connected, telework allowing her to focus and move forward on highly qualified tasks, without being interrupted, before returning to the organization to carry out "collaborative" work with peers. In contemporary managerial language, the teleworker acts as a mythical figure like Stakhanov in the days of the Soviet mines of the Donbass, pointing the way forward in the world of the "agile" and "digital" company (Rappin, 2018).

But beyond these representations, who are the teleworkers? The practice of telework is unevenly distributed across the workforce. First of all, while the distribution of teleworkers between men and women is nearly balanced in Germany, Hungary and France (where men, however, still predominate), teleworkers in Finland, Sweden and the Netherlands are more likely to be men than women: in the United Kingdom the ratio is even 70/30 (Eurofound and ILO, 2017). Inequalities are also evident in terms of qualifications. According to a European study, the highest share of teleworkers is to be found among so-called knowledge workers – highly qualified employees, often in managerial and professional positions (ibid.). While the health crisis has considerably increased the use of telework, managers and executives still telework much more than workers; on the other hand, the crisis seems to have equalized the use of telework between men and woman (Eurofound, 2020). Finally, the practice of telework also differs across age groups. In France, for example, workers aged 40–49 telework significantly more than those entering the professional world (aged 15–29) or leaving it (over 60) (Hallépée and Mauroux, 2019a). In short, by placing teleworkers on the "right" side of all relationships of domination (gender, class, age) the profile of teleworkers reflects the image of the accomplished worker more than that of the deficient worker.[4] This has not been changed by the health crisis, as it has made telework even more desirable by creating a dividing line between employees who can protect their health by working from home and those who are exposed on the front line, as it were. By becoming increasingly legitimate and desirable, telework has thus brought to the fore new issues of equality and equity within organizations, issues that are all the more important to clarify as telework seems set to expand.

Telework, Remote Work and Inequalities: What Are the Issues?

Indeed, access to telework in organizations is a first source of inequalities. By separating functions, whose activity can be done remotely, from those that require a physical presence, telework reenacts the opposition between intellectual and physical work, between white-collar and blue-collar workers, between skilled and unskilled work, between desirable work and "dirty work." Accordingly, telework also places the majority population in opposition to those racialized minority populations who are overrepresented in unskilled jobs. It further reenacts the opposition between men and women, the latter being more often involved in service relationships and face-to-face interactions (jobs in reception and assistance, commerce and sales, services to individuals, care in the medical or paramedical sector). Beyond the nature of the tasks, which makes them objectively more or less "teleworkable," it is quite obvious that deciding whether a job is teleworkable or not is also the result of a balance of power (Bailey and Kurland, 2002; Beham et al., 2015). Conflicting interpretations of workers' supposed autonomy come into play as well as their resources in negotiating with their employer. Depending on their characteristics, employees are on no equal footing when it comes to making a request for telework. The health crisis suddenly made activities "teleworkable," which prior to the crisis were thought not to be the case, such as working as a personal assistant. While executives preferred to have their secretaries on hand to assist them on a daily basis, the crisis revealed that most secretaries' tasks could be teleworked and that a number of the tasks that could not (such as making coffee) might be dispensed with or reorganized to allow for telework (such as greeting the public, which can be divided among several assistants by rotating them).

Once access to teleworking is established, its unequal features result in effects on the balance between private and work life and they put paid work against unpaid domestic work. This is true for employees who telework as well as for freelancers who work remotely. Remote work puts management of the space-time frame of work on the worker's own shoulders (Greer and Payne, 2014; Tietze and Musson, 2005). It is the worker's responsibility to define her own work space and defend its limits in terms of both space (having a room of one's own) and time (limiting the intrusion of work activities into the private sphere and vice versa) (Allen et al., 2013). However, this ability to define a workplace – be it at home or elsewhere – is unevenly distributed in terms of gender, profession, age and class (Letourneux, 2020). In a context where the indicators of being at work are blurred, the worker's ability to say to his family that "I'm working" calls into question the way in which she defines herself as a worker and, as a mirror effect, the degree to which others respect the professional role thus defined. During the lockdown, gender inequalities were all the more marked as children were also at home. The dual management of children and work reinforced the traditional gendered distribution within teleworking couples. Thus in France the female teleworkers had less opportunity than their male counterparts to have their own office room (Lambert et al., 2020). The gap was particularly striking among executives: only 29 percent of female executives had a specific room dedicated to work as compared to 47 percent of male executives. It is therefore unsurprising that ever since onset of the health crisis the statistical studies have shown that the mental health of female teleworkers has been more negatively affected than that of male teleworkers.

In spite of the fact that telework and, more broadly, remote work is often promoted in the name of a better articulation of the different temporalities of social life, it is uncertain that it allows for a better work-life balance for women in particular. To the contrary, it once more confines them to the domestic sphere but at a renewed cost (Alizadeh, 2012) and undoubtedly entails long-term risks for their careers, whether they be employees or freelancers (Landour, 2019). There has been little research into the effects of telework on promotions and careers in organizations (Glass and Noonan, 2016). However, insofar as the ability to make a career is generally linked to the ability to build a network, to integrate oneself into "clans" or be visible (Guillaume and Pochic, 2007), one must fear that, like part-time work, telework may have deleterious effects on careers by reducing the time spent in the workplace (Cooper and Kurland, 2002). Therefore, even more so than ordinary work, telework requires a person to make her work visible and legible to others so as not to be marginalized (Pralong, 2020). There are different ways of making one's work visible when a teleworker is physically or digitally present (Monneuse, 2013) so telework partly changes the criteria for evaluating work and ways of making a career and can thus create new inequalities among workers.

Making Something New Out of Something Old? The New Clothes of Subordination

Clearly, telework cannot be analyzed as a simple contractual work arrangement, for in many ways it transforms the wage framework and tests its boundaries. On the one hand, telework affects the way salaried work is carried out and brings it closer to that of self-employment. On the other hand, the development of remote work allows for an increase in self-employment situations and thus suggests an extension of the field of independence to the detriment of salaried employment.

The Outsourcing of the Work Environment on Employees

As already seen, the primary impact of telework is on the work environment. In the absence of colleagues and hierarchy, the management of the space-time framework is delegated to the worker herself and her environment (Metzger and Cléach, 2004; Fonner and Stache, 2012). This means that even if the employer theoretically provides equipment for teleworking, in reality the creation of an autonomous office space is the responsibility of the teleworker himself and often he is likewise responsible for providing the office-automation tools. This was particularly crucial during the lockdown period when employees were under great financial pressure, yet many invested in adequate equipment. It is thus possible to identify forms of provision by the teleworker of her own equipment for work done on behalf of others, which contradicts the very definition of salaried employment in which the employer provides the employee with work tools. Concerning the question of time, in practice the teleworker is often responsible for her working hours. A number of studies have pointed out that telework tends to lengthen the working day (as time ordinarily employed for the purpose of traveling to and from work is not necessarily filled by more sleep or leisure time) and make it more dense by reducing distractions and interruptions (Bailey and Kurland, 2002). The issue here is that of the right to disconnect, so difficult to implement in practice (Prost and Zouinar, 2015).

These questions of space and time management raise more general questions of occupational health and the prevention of socio-occupational risks in telework situations. These issues are all the more worrying in view of the teleworker's isolation, cut off from the work group along with its resources and support (Bentley et al., 2016). Until recently, when telework was still very undeveloped and mainly considered as a concession by the employers, risk-prevention was rarely a matter of negotiation in telework agreements. In practice it was up to the teleworker herself to look after her health, which again blurred the boundaries between employee and a self-employed status. While the development of telework may open up new opportunities for negotiation on these subjects, it should be noted that it is unclear how risks at home should be prevented without intruding in inappropriate ways into individuals' private lives. Moreover, the control of working time conflicts with the promise of autonomy in telework – and with the fact that autonomy is usually presented as a prerequisite for being able to telework.

Autonomy or Control?

In general terms it would appear that distance readjusts the very notion of subordination, which in turn structures the wage relationship. How can managers keep control when visual supervision is no longer possible? Some organizations try to solve this issue by implementing digital-control tools that can be much more restrictive than the panopticon surveillance of open-plan offices (Fairweather, 1999). In order to be "teleworked" and remain controllable from a distance, work sometimes becomes more fragmented (Loubaton, 2017, as quoted in Jouan and Mesmin, 2017), which also allows for its intensification (Enel, 2017) in accordance with the principle of the division of labor. This fragmentation increases the disintegration of work collectives and the isolation that telework creates (Bentley et al., 2016). In these cases the employee is alone with her hierarchy, and subordination is also reinforced by telework. Other organizations, to the contrary, bet on the autonomy of the teleworker. In the performance of work, the logic of means is then transformed into a logic of results: what matters is that the work is done, without the company caring about the means used to achieve it or about controlling just how that work is done. However, the company retains the power to sanction the worker's failings and subordination does not disappear but is transformed since only some of its characteristics disappear while others are maintained.

There are thus two main ways of solving the dilemma of controlling telework, which unfold differently depending on the sectors and occupations under consideration. This explains the difficulty of making inferences about the effects of telework on workers' autonomy. It also suggests new inequalities between teleworkers with a multi-speed telework regime where telework can potentially mean less interesting work and less freedom for less qualified workers and more freedom for the more qualified ones (Schütz, 2021).

The Deregulation of Remote Work: The Return of Wages to Piecework?

The emphasis on autonomy, which triggered deep transformations in the sphere of work over many years (Boltanski and Chiapello, 2005), accentuates a feature that has for a long time been associated with self-employment: the increasing number of employees who are entrepreneurs of their own work as well as their own career. Telework deepens this trend by making it even more salient. In a certain way, while remaining salaried, the teleworker revives the figure of the worker at advent of the Industrial Revolution and before the wage-earning system was defined by the relationship of subordination. The worker was then considered a "merchant of his work" who rented out his "services" (when the work was paid by the hour) or his "work" (when it was paid by the piece) (Pillon and Vatin, 2007). The worker entered into a contractual relationship with the owner of capital whereby the parties were supposed to be free and equal, though they were obviously not, since the worker was economically dependent and the capitalist could decide at any time not to use his services anymore. It was a recognition of the inequality of the parties and the worker's dependent status that opened up the fight for rights and protection for the latter, which increased throughout the twentieth century.

Is history repeating itself? We could see an extension of independence becoming a detriment to salaried employees through the development of new technologies, the search for flexibility and the facilitation of self-employment through the use of self-employed status (see Abdelnour, 2017 for the situation in France) along with the despatialization induced by telework. Freelance work could develop in the wake of remote work insofar as teleworking employees are in many respects already quite similar to self-employed workers. As a matter of fact, forms of self-employment are already being deployed on the margins of organizations. Not only does the work leave the spatial framework of the company intact, but all the risks associated with the activity are then borne by the worker.

In this respect the development of contemporary remote work is reminiscent of the role played by home-based work throughout the nineteenth century and the first half of the twentieth century, and this in the textile industry in particular (Kaufman-Scarborough, 2006). While the model of factory work was spreading, home-based work never ceased to exist. The employers had an interest in it because the labor was performed by a docile and low-cost workforce of "isolated workers" who were excluded from the emerging wage framework. It further served as an adjustment variable for the capitalist firm by ensuring flexibility in production. According to Lallement (1990), work at home tends to become more important in times of change in capitalism, for instance at its birth or in phases of technological revolution. It allows for the mobilization of a new workforce and a concerted response to the development of new markets. Along with advent of the new technologies, the deterritorialization of work has thus allowed for the deregulation of labor relations at work ever since the neo-liberal turn of the 1980s, and the development of remote work could be the sign of a new mutation of capitalism.

In the media discourse the health crisis has given rise to the image of a happy teleworker who sees in this new organization of work a gain in autonomy and time. The benefits of telework are opposed to the rigidity of the salary framework: omnipresent hierarchical control, lack of autonomy at work, unnecessary presence. While telework can undeniably result in the alleviation of certain constraints, its extension can be read as part of a process of the deregulation of labor relations. It replicates and reinforces inequalities in organizations and thus participates in an individualization of labor relations and the outsourcing of an increasing number of employer responsibilities onto the employees themselves. Beyond the accelerating role played by the health crisis, its current rise can hence be understood in light of the contemporary changes in capitalism.

Thinking about telework as a category of work as we have done here – that is, thinking about its evolution over time, the power relations it brings into play, its changing boundaries and the way it reenacts other boundaries such as the one between salaried employment and independence – makes it possible to significantly enrich any analysis of the phenomenon by proposing three main shifts. The first shift is to place telework back within the broader framework of an analysis of remote work by not confining the reflection to employees but also including the self-employed. Second, an overview of the academic literature on telework shows that it is dominated by managerial and individual-centered approaches (Schütz, 2021). On the one hand, the issues addressed are primarily about the effects of telework, both positive and negative, its advantages and disadvantages and how to manage it (so that it is productive and the teleworkers are happy). While these approaches are legitimate, they often become prescriptive because of their managerial nature and tend to overshadow a more analytical and critical perspective such as the one we propose. On the other hand, this literature generally favors an individual level of analysis, including interpersonal relationships (with colleagues, hierarchy, family). Although relevant, this level of analysis tends to obscure the meso-level of the organization and what happens when telework is introduced as well as the macro-level involving the relationships of domination and the institutions (such as the wage system) in which individuals are caught. In proposing this triple shift we are thus proposing a truly sociological approach to telework.

Notes

1 Telework allows a "despatialization" of work (Taskin, 2006), that is to say an exit from the physical-spatial framework of the organization. This disjunction allows a competition with workers who can live and work across national borders – what we can define as a "deterritorializon" of work (Cingolani, 2021).

2 "Any form of work organization in which work that could also have been performed on the employer's premises is performed by an employee off the premises on a voluntary basis using information and communication technologies" (Article L.1222–9 Code du travail).

3 A "freedom-form" company refers to an organization that is trying to implement a kind of "liberation" style of management.

4 This finding needs to be qualified somewhat. Although it is unclear whether a causal connection can be made, French executives who telework report poorer health and a greater risk of falling prey to depression than non-teleworkers (Hallépée and Mauroux, 2019b); similarly, in the market sector, telework is more prevalent when employers consider their employees to be exposed to psychosocial risks (Amira, 2016).

References

Abdelnour, S. (2017) *Moi, petite entreprise. Les auto-entrepreneurs, de l'utopie à la réalité*. Paris: Presses universitaires de France.

Alizadeh, T. (2012) 'Teleworkers' Characteristics in Live/Work Communities: Lessons From the United States and Australia', *Journal of Urban Technology*, 19(3), pp. 63–84.

Allen, T.D., Johnson, R.C, Kiburz, K.M. and Shockley, K.M. (2013) 'Work-Family Conflict and Flexible Work Arrangements: Deconstructing Flexibility', *Personnel Psychology*, 66(2), pp. 345–376.

Amira, S. (2016) 'La prévention des risques professionnels. Les mesures mises en œuvre par les employeurs publics et privés', *Dares Analyses*, 13.

Atkinson, C. and Hall, L. (2009) 'The Role of Gender in Varying Forms of Flexible Working', *Gender, Work & Organization*, 16(6), pp. 650–666.

Bailey, D.E. and Kurland, N.B. (2002) 'A Review of Telework Research: Rindings, New Directions, and Lessons for the Study of Modern Work', *Journal of Organizational Behavior*, 23(4), pp. 383–400.

Beham, B., Baierl, A. and Poelmans, S. (2015) 'Managerial Telework Allowance Decisions – A Vignette Study Among German Managers', *International Journal of Human Resource Management*, 26(11), pp. 1385–1406.

Bentley, T.A., Teo, S.T.T., McLeod, L, Tan, F, Bosua, R. and Gloet, M. (2016) 'The Role of Organisational Support in Teleworker Wellbeing: A Socio-Technical Systems Approach', *Applied Ergonomics*, 52, pp. 207–215.

Blair-Loy, M. (2003) *Competing Devotions: Career and Family Among Women Executives*. Cambridge, MA: Harvard University Press.

Boltanski, L. and Chiapello, E. (2005) *The New Spirit of Capitalism*. London: Verso Books.

Cardon, D. and Casili, A. (2019) *En attendant les robots: Enquête sur le travail du clic*. Paris: Seuil.

Cingolani, P. (2021) *La colonisation du quotidien. Dans les laboratoires du capitalisme de plate-forme*. Paris: éditions Amsterdam.

Cooper, C.D. and Kurland, N.B. (2002) 'Telecommuting, Professional Isolation, and Employee Development in Public and Private Organizations', *Journal of Organizational Behavior*, 23(4), pp. 511–532.

Enel, L. (2017) 'Télétravail: entre flexibilité et intensification du travail', *La revue des conditions de travail*, Anact, 6, pp. 161–168.

Eurofound (2020) *Living, Working and COVID-19* (*COVID-19 Series*). Luxembourg: Publications Office of the European Union.

Eurofound and the ILO (2017) *Working Anytime, Anywhere: The Effects on the World of Work*. Luxembourg and Geneva: Publications Office of the European Union, The International Labour Office.

European Commission (2020) 'Telework in the EU Before and After the COVID-19: Where We Were, Where We Head To', *Science for Policy Brief*, https://joint-research-centre.ec.europa.eu/system/files/2021-06/jrc120945_policy_brief_-_covid_and_telework_final.pdf.

Fairweather, N.B. (1999) 'Surveillance in Employment: The Case of Teleworking', *Journal of Business Ethics*, 22(1), pp. 39–49.

Fonner, K.L. and Stache, L.C. (2012) 'All in a Day's Work, at Home: Teleworkers' Management of Micro Role Transitions and the Work-Home Boundary', *New Technology, Work and Employment*, 27(3), pp. 242–257.

Glass, J.L. and Noonan, M.C. (2016) 'Telecommuting and Earnings Trajectories Among American Women and Men 1989–2008', *Social Forces*, 95(1), pp. 217–250.

Greer, T.W. and Payne, S.C. (2014) 'Overcoming Telework Challenges: Outcomes of Successful Telework Strategies', *The Psychologist-Manager Journal*, 17(2), pp. 87–111.

Guillaume, C. and Pochic, S. (2007) 'La fabrication organisationnelle des dirigeants. Un regard sur le plafond de verre', *Travail, genre et sociétés*, 17, pp. 79–103.

Hallépée, S. and Mauroux, A. (2019a) 'Qui sont les salariés concernés par le télétravail ?', *Dares Analyses*, 51.

Hallépée, S. and Mauroux, A. (2019b) 'Le télétravail permet-il d'améliorer les conditions de travail des cadres?', *L'économie et la société à l'ère du numérique édition*, 2019, pp. 43–54.

Jouan, A. and Mesmin, G. (2017) 'Travailler chez soi ou perdre son emploi ? Etude d'un cas de télétravail permanent en France', *La revue des conditions de travail*, Anact, 6, pp. 169–177.

Kaufman-Scarborough, C. (2006) 'Time Use and the Impact of Technology: Examining Workspaces in the Home', *Time & Society*, 15(1), pp. 57–80.

Lallement, M. (1990) *Des PME en chambre: travail et travailleurs à domicile d'hier et d'aujourd'hui.* Paris: L'Harmattan.

Lambert, A. et al. (2020) 'Le travail et ses aménagements: ce que la pandémie de Covid-19 a changé pour les Français', *Population & Sociétés*, 579, pp. 1–4.

Landour, J. (2019) *Sociologie des mompreneurs. Entreprendre pour concilier travail et famille?* Villeneuve d'Ascq: Presses universitaires du Septentrion.

Largier, A. (2001) 'Le télétravail. Trois projets pour un même objet', *Réseaux*, 2(106), pp. 201–229.

Letourneux, F. (2017) 'A distance. Enquête sur les figures contemporaines des travailleurs à domicile' Paris: thèse de sociologie de l'EHESS.

Letourneux, F. (2020) 'Travailler la distance: s'inventer un chez-soi de travail', *Sociologie du travail*, 62(4).

Loubaton, L. (2017) *Le télétravail: une illusion déjà perdue ? La mise en place du télétravail organisationnel dans le cadre d'une restructuration d'une entreprise d'ingénierie informatique,* Master thesis, ENS-EHESS, Paris.

Messenger, J.C. and Gschwind, L. (2016) 'Three Generations of Telework: New ICT and the (R)evolution from Home Office to Virtual Office', *New Technology, Work and Employment*, 31(3), pp. 195–208.

Metzger, J.-L. and Cleach, O. (2004) 'Le télétravail des cadres: entre suractivité et apprentissage de nouvelles temporalités', *Sociologie du travail*, 46(4), pp. 433–450.

Monneuse, D. (2013) 'La stratégie du clair-obscur', *Communication et organisation*, 44, pp. 87–98.

Munsch, C.L. (2016) 'Flexible Work, Flexible Penalties: The Effect of Gender, Childcare, and Type of Request on the Flexibility Bias', *Social Forces*, 94(4), pp. 1567–1591.

Pillon, T. and Vatin, F. (2007) 'La question salariale: actualité d'un vieux problème', in Vatin, F. and Bernard, S. (ed.) *Le salariat: théorie, histoire et formes*. Paris: La Dispute, pp. 29–48.

Popma, J. (2013) 'The Janus Face of the 'New Ways of Work': Rise, Risks and Regulation of Nomadic Work', Working Paper, European Trade Union Institute (ETUI), Brussels.

Pralong, J. (2020) *Full remote skills: quelles compétences pour être un télétravailleur performant ?* Etude de la Chaire Compétences, employabilité et décision RH de l'EM Normandie. https://blog.ecole-management-normandie.fr/wp-content/uploads/2020/04/teletravailsoftskills.pdf.

Prost, M. and Zouinar, M. (2015) 'De l'hyper-connexion à la déconnexion: quand les entreprises tentent de réguler l'usage professionnel des e-mails', *Perspectives interdisciplinaires sur le travail et la santé*, 17(1).

Rappin, B. (2018) 'De quoi la génération Y est-elle le nom ?', *Communication & Organisation*, 53, pp. 133–144.

Schütz, G. (2021) 'Pour une sociologie du télétravail ancrée dans les organisations', *Sociologies pratiques*, 43, pp. 1–12.

Taskin, L. (2006) 'Télétravail: Les enjeux de la déspatialisation pour le management humain', *Revue Interventions économiques*, 34, pp. 73–94.

Tietze, S. and Musson, G. (2005) 'Recasting the Home-Work Relationship: A Case of Mutual Adjustment?', *Organization Studies*, 26(9), pp. 1331–1352.

4

PLATFORM WORK

New Workers, New Rights?

Sophie Bernard and Josépha Dirringer

Western societies have witnessed the emergence of a new economic model in which companies take the form of digital platforms and act as intermediaries between clients and service providers as well as between job seekers and job suppliers. The distinctiveness of this model lies in the fact that the latter are not employees but independent workers (Abdelnour and Bernard, 2018). Yet throughout the world and also in Europe, platform workers have taken legal action to have their labor status upgraded to salaried work. Depending on the jurisdiction, workers have been deemed "employees," "independent workers" or as belonging to the third category of self-employed dependents, a category recognized by certain national legal systems. But in some instances, these actions have failed and workers retain the status of independent workers.

This contentious strategy is interesting in that it shows the extent to which socio-juridical categories of work are not facts but constructs that lie at the heart of conflicts between various interests, not only between economic actors but between institutional actors in the legal realm, for the conflict around the legal classification of platform work has also triggered a reaction on the part of governments as well as international and European authorities. Each party is motivated by a desire to define a new legal framework that can address the issues raised by the growth of this new form of work. Few issues are characterized by such exuberance on the part of actors in the working world, and few matters in the legal realm are so timely, but it is precisely the proliferation of norms that now makes the work of categorization so complicated.

Will we one day find an appropriate legal term for these workers? In this chapter, we are led to ask whether the law structures social life or whether the law constructs itself in society's image. These two alternatives tend to assume the existence of a duality between legal categories on the one hand and social

DOI: 10.4324/9781003341321-6

categories on the other. But shouldn't one instead imagine a continuum in which the social world gradually models itself in reaction to the law, which is itself rooted in the depths of social reality? In other words, shouldn't one abandon the idea of a crude duality and replace it with a dialectical relationship between law and social reality, thus providing a better account of the complexity of the legal and sociological nature of platform work and those tensions – and conflicts – to which categorization gives rise?

The main and most immediately visible factor contributing to this complexity relates to the plurality of actors and the diversity of their interactions. These include national and European legislators; judges (at the local, constitutional and European level as well as lower and higher courts); advisory bodies, professional organizations and think tanks; legal, economic and sociological experts; workers organizations; lawyers, etc. From this plurality of actors, many more or less normative utterances arise. It is of course difficult to predict which of these will succeed in transforming social and economic reality.

We are here focusing on the case of French Uber drivers – the platform emblematic of this controversy – and bringing together a legal and sociological perspective.[1] The legal analysis shows the evolution of the sources of the law and examines the French reforms or plans for reforms with respect to platform work. The sociological perspective reconsiders studies that address the reality of platform work and draws on an ethnographic analysis of Parisian drivers conducted since 2015. The latter includes accounts of collective action and union meetings, the monitoring of social-media exchanges, and interviews with drivers as well as the leaders of collective actions and actors involved in processes seeking to regulate this sector.

In this way, we show what is at stake with regard to the different categories in competition for defining platform work and workers (Section: The Stakes Involved in Categorizing Platform Work) along with the persistent difficulties in transforming them (Section: Difficulties in Changing Categories Applicable to Platform Work).

The Stakes Involved in Categorizing Platform Work

Existing legal categories, which distinguish between the social order governed by labor law on the one hand and the commercial order governed by economic law on the other, will ignore the "gray zone" populated by hybrid workers and of which platform workers are a part. Describing this gray zone and forging new typologies helps make it visible and highlights the gap between the representations that shape the law and realities of work as well as the social conditions of individuals who work or are involved in work-like activities. However, if some sociological categories have a heuristic purpose and serve to reveal the complexity of a work world that is masked by the simplicity of legal categories, others have a more prescriptive intent, serving to sort out just what is work and what is not.

Describing New Forms of Work

The development of digital intermediation platforms has been accompanied by the emergence of a wide range of activities whose characteristics tend to scramble our conventional analytic frameworks. "Indeed, digital platforms render activities on the borderline of work and leisure more visible, easier, and more accessible" (Beauvisage et al., 2018). The conception of "digital work" as "eminently cognitive labor that manifests itself through informal activity, claimed and appropriated in a commercial context by relying on tasks mediated through digital processes" (Cardon and Casilli, 2015, p. 13) throws this borderline into question. The concept encompasses those activities conceived as leisure that nonetheless generate value (Scholz, 2013). Yet apart from the fact that this concept often neglects the genuine work involved in collecting and formatting data through its focus on consumers who work without actually realizing it (Dagiral and Peerbaye, 2012; Denis, 2018) it seems more useful from an empirical standpoint to distinguish between platforms in terms of the commercial or non-commercial character of their exchanges, that is, whether they are for profit or not (Dujarier, 2016).

Sociological studies show a diversity of situations on the platforms and above all a low level of professionalization among platform workers. The activity of platform workers is sometimes temporary, sometimes incidental, sometimes episodic or of a one-time nature. Moreover, there is no real professional identity attached to being a platform worker. The typology of platforms and related forms of employment as proposed by Patrice Flichy (2019, p. 203) thus reveals this diversity and "the fragmentation of platform work." The distinction drawn between amateurs and professionals and between "chosen" work or – for want of a better term – primary work or supplementary work has proven to be a porous one. For sociologists, the category of platform workers encompasses a wide range of variable circumstances that must be accounted for if we are to again lay bare work's porous boundaries.

Yet social protection and workers' rights are the very factors that make the distinction between salaried and independent workers so crucial. Salaried workers benefit from additional protections in exchange for a recognition of their subordinate relationship to employers. The status of independent worker provides access to basic coverage in terms of health insurance and retirement plans but no coverage of work risks or, until very recently, services that protect workplace health.[2] Nor does this status offer unemployment insurance or comparable funding levels for professional development. But despite the risks attached to the status of being self-employed, some workers aspire to become "their own boss." This is the case of French Uber drivers as shown by a sociological survey that one of us conducted (Bernard, 2020). This prioritization of independence can be explained by their professional trajectories. Many come from working-class immigrant backgrounds and have previously held precarious jobs with difficult working conditions and strong hierarchical pressures. Consequently, they tend to associate salaried work with hierarchy and constraint, rather than with social protections and related rights. By comparison, "being one's own boss" gives them a sense of freedom. They rarely mention the vulnerability associated with being an independent worker and see the profession as a "good bad job" (Rosenblat, 2018, p. 59). Yet when drivers learn that the platform can punish them and, without warning, deprive them of their income source, they realize that this autonomy is ultimately very limited.

The conditions under which they can engage in this work are in fact dictated by the platform. Drivers do not set the rates of their rides, and while they theoretically enjoy some autonomy in organizing their work schedules, low rates force them to be available for extensive periods of time. Many respondents said that they work six or seven days a week, between 12 and 14 hours a day, and rarely take days off. This is also why they focus on periods when surcharges apply. To ensure that enough drivers are available to adapt to fluctuations in demand, surcharges are set as a function of supply and demand. As these periods usually occur in the early morning, late in the day, at night and on weekends, they are hardly compatible with family obligations. When a driver signs his partnership contract he also commits to honoring an Uber-imposed charter. Most importantly, the platform has the right to punish drivers, allowing it to disconnect and even permanently deactivate their accounts. This can occur if their ride acceptance rate is below 80 percent, if their cancellation rate is more than 4 percent, if clients complain, and if their client rate is below 4.5 stars. Drivers are rated by clients at the end of each ride. In this way, Uber turns this mechanism for evaluating service quality into a tool for managing and controlling drivers.

However, our study also shows that there exist several types of drivers whose work conditions and compensation as well as their relationship to the platform do indeed greatly differ (Bernard, 2020). Some drivers still manage to establish a private clientele that allows the driver to partially escape from the platform's control and helps to determine his working conditions. Yet faced with competition from Uber, which occupies a quasi-monopolistic position on the French private-drivers market (known as *véhicule de tourisme avec chauffeur* or VTC), they struggle to retain their private clients. The study shows that a majority of drivers work exclusively through platforms and even solely for Uber. Consequently, the Uber driver who is totally dependent on and subordinate to the platform tends to emerge as the prevailing type, and Uber will take full advantage of their independent status. In addition to their labor power, the drivers make some of their production tools (notably cars) available to the company (Abdelnour and Bernard, 2018). They are fully responsible for work-related risks and accept expandable hours to increase their turnover. At the same time, workers must submit to constraints imposed by the platform (Dupuy and Larré, 1998) which attests to their ambiguous situation and dependence on the platform. In particular, their working conditions and remuneration are imposed on them by the platform and they cannot negotiate them collectively. Since they are totally dependent on the hub, it is difficult for them to contest the working conditions imposed on them.

As the discrepancy between representations that shape law and the reality of working conditions grows and becomes more apparent, one must question the law's effectiveness and the appropriateness of the existing legal categories. Particularly in the case of platform workers engaged in work that transports people and goods, the discrepancy is such that the ability of labor law to guarantee the efficacy of fundamental social rights seems weakened. In this still essentially dualist conception in the relationship between law and fact, where law is a reflection of society, there is indeed an alternative for the actors: they have every reason to expect that social reality conforms with the existing legal categories. This is the option embraced by those who request a labor contract. Or they can try to present platform work as a new form of work in the hope of reshaping the law that regulates it. In this case, the relevant legal categories no longer serve to exclusively describe the working world as it exists in a particular legal framework. Instead, they become the instrument of a project for reordering the world of work through law.

Categorizing for Delineating Work From Non-Work

Several reports have attempted to map existing platform work. A report by the European Commission (Kilhoffer et al., 2020) distinguishes between the competencies required for a task (more or less skilled), the task's location (online or in-person) and the selection process (whether decisions are made by the platform, the platform worker or the client). The first category consists of platforms in which the task requires physical proximity and is carried out by low-skilled workers. The second refers to platforms involving physical tasks but with more highly skilled workers. The third comprises platforms in which tasks are carried out online by lower-skilled workers, distinguishing it from a final category in which tasks are performed online by higher-skilled workers. The report's authors note that platform work requiring a person's physical presence is better known and more often debated, due to its greater visibility, than platform work done online. A common denominator of these reports is that they all call attention to the diversity of platform work but ultimately focus solely on platform work requiring a physical presence and performed by lower-skilled workers such as drivers for Uber and Deliveroo.

In their report, Amar and Viossat (Igass, 2016, p. 19) define "job platforms" as "allowing the sale, supply, or exchange of a good or service produced or effectuated by collaborative workers." Within this realm they distinguish between seven different forms, depending on whether the goods and services exchanged are physical or immaterial and whether they operate on a local or international scale. This would include the sharing of platforms through which individuals make mutual use of an asset (AirBnB), organized service operators offering standardized services provided by professionals (Uber), "jobbing" platforms that allow individuals to receive home service (SuperMano), electronic cooperatives that determine collaborative modes for the production, consumption and distribution of the social economy (La Ruche Qui Dit Oui!), marketplaces that are platforms for (re)selling new and used physical goods (Etsy), freelance platforms that pair the supply of high value-added services with their demand (Hopwork) and microwork platforms that do the same for dematerialized microtasks (Amazon Mechanical Turk).

A French Labor Ministry report (Montel, 2017) distinguishes the "sharing economy" from the "economy of platforms of commercial goods and services." The former is based on the sharing and/or production of (material or immaterial) assets through "peer-to-peer" relationships, while the latter encompasses for-profit platforms that play the role of an active third party between the supply and demand of a good or service. While "platforms of commercial goods and services" resemble the "job platforms" identified by Amar and Viossat, the boundaries in this instance are more restrictive, as the goal is "to target platforms that are more likely to raise issues of public regulation" (ibid., p. 8). Hence the emphasis is placed on the platforms' third-party role, and "platforms of commercial goods and services" thus do not confine themselves to connecting supply with demand; they are fully engaged in the production and sale of the product exchanged. They have four characteristics: a triangular relationship between supply, demand and the platform; platform involvement in the quality and price of the product exchanged; a community based on a commercial bond; and membership in a community regulated by the platform. Two indices of the platform's involvement merit consideration: direct remuneration of the platform for exchanges (i.e., commissions) and the platform's regulation of a member's access to rating functions and other criteria relating to exchanges.

While the Frouin report (2020) draws on the categorization proposed by Amar and Viossat to propose a new typology of job platforms, it also tends to narrow the scope of its analysis. It excludes electronic cooperatives and marketplaces that connect those individuals offering commercialized physical goods. It then establishes a new typology based on the degree of workers' dependence on the platform and the distinction made by the French Labor Code in defining platforms to which social responsibility applies. On the one hand, one finds platforms that meet the definition of article L. 7342–1 of the Labor Code because they "determine the characteristics of the service provided or the good sold and set its price" and because their workers are highly dependent on the platform to perform their work. These include platforms based on microwork and those that determine the characteristics of the service provided and set its price, playing the role of organized service operators (essentially in the individualized transportation and delivery sectors). On the other hand, one finds platforms that do not meet the definition of article L. 7342–1 of the Labor Code and whose workers are not dependent on them to perform their activity: those that propose services to individuals and those that bring independent workers and companies into contact (e.g., Brigad). As a result, the latter form does not raise issues of public regulation. The same is true of microwork which, because it generates little revenue, is only an income supplement (Barraud de lagerie and Sigalo-Santos, 2018). Consequently, the report focuses on platforms that function as operators of organized services and almost exclusively on mobility platforms (individualized transportation and delivery sectors). The category of platform workers ultimately refers to a very narrow group: private drivers and deliverers and, within this group, those for whom this is their primary work.

These different typologies have a common denominator. They seek to shed light on the gray area in which platform work finds itself so as to show its specificity and need for regulation. The result is a narrowing of the category of platform workers, reducing them to private chauffeurs and deliverers for whom this is their primary work. The contraction of this category must be connected to the question of public regulation that would appear to apply only to this very limited group. Put differently, the reasons for such a restriction lie not in any effort to better describe social reality but in an attempt to simplify social reality in order to regulate it. Drawing on these restrictive typologies to craft a legal framework, the 2016 law established a body of law unique to digital platforms.

It is for these reasons disturbing when sociologists assert that there is not just one platform (Uber) but multiple platform models, just as there is no single model of platform worker (the Uber driver) but many kinds of platform workers. The same goes for the person – whether a sociologist or a lawyer – who demonstrates that the organization of the work of Uber drivers – who are self-employed – is the same as that of salaried workers; except that the former are paid less, have less social protection and are exposed to the maximum extent to the platform's arbitrary decisions. In 2016, proud to have been able to forge a body of rules specific to platform workers, the legislature preferred to hear such arguments, and claimed to have improved the conditions of these workers. At the same time, the lawmakers have preserved the relevance of the existing legal categories. The employment contract and the relationship of subordination have not been reconceived, any more than the fiction which holds that an independent worker is a company acting on the market. In this way, proposals that seek to complete and bring up-to-date indices of subordination are brushed aside because they are too centered on the power to direct individuals, without consideration of the power inherent in the organization of economic activity. The same is true of proposals that would establish, alongside relationships of subordination, other labor-contract criteria that serve as alternatives to the relationship of subordination, such as the criteria of economic dependence or that of integration in the organization as defined by the dominant economic operator.[3] The study of Uber drivers demonstrates, moreover, that it is their economic dependence on the platform that leads them to submit to the latter's injunctions. In this way, one clings to a simplified and simplistic conception of the law: to respond to the appearance of a new social reality, one has only to create a new body of rules that is specific to this reality. It matters little that this reality could be described differently. Nor does it matter that there might be other ways of conceiving the legal categories applicable to it.

Hence this apparent simplicity can generate tensions and raise difficulties that legislative reform has not always managed to overcome. There is a gaping discrepancy between the legal framework applicable to platform workers and the reality they encounter.

Difficulties in Changing Categories Applicable to Platform Work

To stick with the example of France and the years 2020 and 2021, there have been no less than seven reports relating to independent work and specifically platform work,[4] two of which were government initiatives.[5] This energy testifies to labor law's difficulties in fully acknowledging platform workers. It also attests to the persistent difficulties faced by the commercial economic order in offering platform workers protection equivalent to that provided for subordinate workers.

Workers Inadequately Recognized by Labor Law

Following numerous disputes initiated by platform workers to have their work relationship upgraded to a labor contract, European governments and European authorities took up the problem of the "fake independent workers" and attempted, in various ways, to provide a legal answer (Dirringer, 2018).

Broadly speaking, some legislation attempted to secure the dual legal framework separating independent work from subordinate work, notably by seeking to clarify the criteria characterizing the relationship of subordination. Micro-fiscal measures are often incorporated into the latter with the intention of deterring abusive recourse to independent work. Others have tried – at times before platform work became so pervasive – to establish a third category of workers on the cusp of salaried and independent work. Others still have preferred to build a body of rules specific to platform work. This occurred in France with the establishment of the social responsibility of platform work. Since the approval of the Mobility Guidance Law (LOM, or *Loi d'orientation des mobilités*), rules have been added to it that are solely applicable to platforms involved in individualized transportation and the delivery of goods. Moreover, alongside the question of employment status, several laws in the domain of social protection have recognized that independent workers possess social rights. In this way, they are pursuing the European Union's goal of rendering the labor market more fluid.

Nonetheless, legal actions have continued. Platform workers have continued and still continue to appeal to courts by asking them to recognize the existence of labor contracts. In France, however, court decisions have had a mixed impact. Legal actions are often seen as a risk for platforms, any threat to be avoided. This was the goal of the LOM law, which sought to create immunity against contract upgrades for platforms that had adopted charters. But the Constitutional Council decided that this measure was unconstitutional. Regardless of the number of court decisions issued and despite the position of the Court of Cassation (the highest court of appeals), platforms continue to have recourse to independent workers. Because workers' lawsuits have been of an entirely individual nature (Thomas, 2021), court decisions have remained limited to personal cases and do not require platforms to upgrade contracts in their entirety. A strategy inspired by Italy, which is based not on civil law but on criminal law, may ultimately change matters. For example, in September 2021 a complaint initiated by the CGT for concealed work was filed against Deliveroo. This action is more collective in nature. Above all, it relies on the power of criminal law to both highlight violations of the fundamental values of society and recognize the criminal responsibility of company managers. This complaint has certainly reactivated the investigation begun in 2015, which had strangely been neglected while the government was focused on wanting to secure the economic model of transport platforms. The body responsible for collecting social-security contributions (URSSAF), which had abandoned any prosecution, has finally made a report that has prompted the central office for combating illegal employment to re-launch the investigation.

To find a way out of a conception of the work relationship that has become too individualistic, criminal labor law could help by more clearly posing the question as to the responsibility of platforms. Because they organize other people's work and profit from it, their responsibility should be comparable to that which the law imputes to employers. They should thus be required to insure individuals against professional risks incurred during work-related activity, as was decided in 1898 with the legislation on workplace accidents and the establishment of a system of the mutualization of risk between employers, which facilitated compensation of a worker who experienced a workplace accident or work-related illness.

Abandoning an individualistic conception of the work relationship also implies a recognition of the labor communities that workers form. Collectives exist, some of which resemble unions. Yet the fact that they lie beyond the boundaries of labor law is an obstacle to establishing labor relations. Once again drawing on the Italian model, it would be useful to initiate legal action seeking to recognize the existence of labor communities and related collective rights. These were denied by the constitutional court, which stated that "platforms. . . and workers that have a relationship to them do not constitute, as things stand, a labor community," thus depriving them of the constitutional right to participation (i.e., workers' participation in corporate governance). In these circumstances, drivers' representatives struggle to be recognized as legitimate actors by those they represent as well as those with whom they are supposed to be in dialogue (Abdelnour and Bernard, 2019). Moreover, as independent workers, they are regarded as companies. From the standpoint of European law, this does not deprive them of the right to negotiate collectively and, more generally, of the collective rights granted to (subordinate) workers. The decree of 21 April 2021 does not call this into question. But they are still deprived of the right to information and consultation accorded to workers. No consideration is being given to their right to be represented in the social-protection system. And it is debatable whether the Mouvement des Entreprises de France (MEDEF, the main employers' organization) currently represents independent workers in the bodies of the social-security system.

To these inherent difficulties of the social order must be added the attempts that have been made in economic law to duplicate certain social protections. Yet the protections inscribed in the economic order are only an illusion when their purpose is not to protect individual workers but to ensure the market's proper functioning.

Workers Inadequately Protected by Economic Law

It is perhaps at the European level that the economic order's claim to regulate platform work in conjunction with the social order is most visible.

The question of platform work was first considered in the context of the coordinated employment strategy included in Europe 2020. The European Union lacks normative authority but defines guidelines for member states, who then take them into consideration when writing national legislation. One such guideline calls for "better functioning of the labor markets, with a specific focus on reducing labor market segmentation and improving active labor market measures and labor market mobility." (COUNCIL DECISION (EU) 2018/1215 of 16 July 2018 on guidelines for the employment policies of the Member States) Yet one reason for segmentation resides in the division between salaried and independent workers. It is unnecessary to eliminate this barrier, but these employment categories must be decompartmentalized to ensure that the choice between these employment statuses does not affect the level of social protection. It is notably from this perspective that the preamble to the European Pillar of Social Rights established in 2017 calls for all workers to benefit from "adequate social protection," (principle 12) regardless of their status.

Second, platform work has been the focus of European legislation in both the labor realm and economic realm. The latter sharply distinguishes between what is part of labor law as applicable to subordinate work relationships and what is part of economic law as applicable to commercial relationships between companies acting on the market and subject to competition law. This division is found in the *FNV Künsten* decision handed down in 2014 and relating to the possibility of independent workers entering collective contracts that set minimum rates. According to the Court of Justice of the European Union, collective bargaining is inherent in the salary relationship. By extension, the absence of a salaried relationship should exclude the right to collective bargaining, and the application of the rules of competition law prohibits collective agreements relating to prices. It is for these reasons that the construction of a space for collective bargaining between digital platforms and independent workers has been significantly compromised, at least in the way labor law understands it (Dirringer and Ferkane, 2021). Independent workers are deprived of the right to bargain collectively because it is incompatible with the "internal market."

This general framework allows us to situate two texts relating to the activity of digital platforms that were published on the same day. The first text is directive (EU) 2019/1152 on transparent and predictable working conditions. This text makes it possible to extend the protection of certain social rights to platform workers, taking a first step toward establishing a minimum threshold of social rights for all workers. Upon closer analysis, however, the social rights recognized by the directive are ill-suited to the reality of platform work because most of them are defined in relation to a "normal" employment relationship where the status of the worker and the status of the employer do not give rise to any discussion (Lhernoud and Robin-Oliver, 2020). The second text is regulation (EU) 2019/1150 promoting fairness and transparency for "business users" of "online intermediation services." It defines an array of obligations that platforms – which are dubbed "providers" of online intermediation service – owe to so-called business users (Pellerin, 2022)

Without going into detail about the provisions of these two texts, it is worth heeding the vocabulary they use. Whereas in the first text, European law deals with the situation of workers, in the second it portrays a world comprised of *businesses*, of *providers* of *online intermediation services*, and *business users*. Nowhere is the word "worker" used. Even so, the regulation burdens platforms with a series of obligations designed to inform business users of the platform's evaluation and classification criteria; to motivate decisions seeking to restrict, suspend or cancel the provision of services to a business user; and to allow the latter, through internal procedures, to "defend themselves." In short, in the field of economic law, the regulation recognizes certain guarantees very similar to those found in labor law for limiting employers' power and avoiding the reign of the arbitrary.

Finally, at the European level, no normative order seems privileged, even if economic regulation is clearly more developed than social regulation. This allows differences to persist at the national level, understood as the differences between various states and variations that exist within the framework of a single set of laws. However, this situation may be changing. In the autumn of 2021, the European Commission announced the adoption of a directive introducing a presumption of salaried status for the benefit of platform workers. This would certainly constitute a rejection of the model preferred by France, which has stubbornly chosen to regulate platform work through economic law.

In the case of France, as already emphasized, the social status of independent workers remains fragmented, though improvements have been introduced relating to the universality of the right to social protection. Concerning specific platform workers, the provisions of the LOM law of December 2019 relating to the establishment of platform charters is less an echo of the European directive than the European rule that also encourages platforms to establish codes of good conduct. Similarly, the decree of 21 April 2021, which provides for the creation of collective representation for platform workers, models a form of collective bargaining in the realm of commercial economic law and thus achieves what economic law calls coregulation (Dirringer and Ferkane, 2021).

In terms of social protection, insurance contracts aimed at platform workers have in some instances been introduced not on basis of an obligation but on basis of a legal incentive. The partnership contracts between Axa and certain transportation platforms spring to mind. Upon closer examination, the level of protection they offer remains significantly below what the French social-security system provides for salaried workers (Dirringer and Del Sol, 2021). Moreover, as we have already indicated, equal social services are not enough to end unequal rights. In the economic realm, far from being recognized as entitled to fundamental social rights and as actors in the system of social protection, platform workers appear in the legal realm first as co-contractors of platforms and as co-consumers in relation to insurers. Consequently, the burden of life's social and financial risks falls upon them.

Conclusion

While platform workers constitute a very heterogeneous category, as documented by sociological research, the law focuses on only a very limited number of them, of which Uber drivers are emblematic. This new category of workers, however, is causing difficulties for the legislator, who is struggling to integrate it into existing legal categories. The prevailing legal framework will very largely determine the social reality of the individuals whose interests are at stake, and who in turn will undoubtedly want to modify it. It is precisely in this respect that the role of social groups such as trade unions, workers' collectives, associations and employers' organizations is of particular importance. It is through them that the social group is constituted, giving the category of workers its collective dimension. In Gurvitch's words, let us not forget that "the social rights proclaimed by the Declarations must be rights of collective and individual participation deriving from their integration in communities ensuring their democratic character" (Gurvitch, 2009 [1946], p. 58). It is indeed as a group and collectively that these workers must also be recognized and instituted at the level of the enterprise, of the profession and of all workers. It would seem that under these conditions a return to social law is still possible because – strengthened by their power to act collectively – they would be better able to demand an improvement in their rights and be in a position to influence the decisions that concern them.

Notes

1 Written in September 2020, this chapter does not take into account subsequent legal developments.
2 The law of 2 August 2021 now gives independent workers the option of registering with a prevention and health service for cross-business work, which provides them with a *specific* array of services for mitigating work-related risks, providing individual assistance and preventing professional disqualification.

3 See also the chapter "Subordinate Work: How Does the Law Categorize Modern Labor Relationships?" by Linxin He in this volume.
4 See HCFIPS, Rapport sur la Protection sociale des travailleurs indépendants, September 2020; M. Forissier, C. Fournier and F. Puissat, Travailleurs des plateformes: au-delà de la question du statut, quelles protections?, Rapport d'information de la commission des affaires sociales, May 2020; CNNum, Travail à l'ère des plateformes. Mise à jour requise, 2020; J. Giusti and T. Thévenoud, Pour travailler à l'âge du numérique, défendons la coopérative!, 2020, Fondation Jean Jaurès; and C. Grandjean and D. Obono, La protection sociale des travailleurs des plateformes numériques, Rapport d'information de la Commission des affaires européennes, 20 January 2021.
5 These were the Frouin report, entitled *Réguler les plateformes numériques de travail*, and the Mettling report, submitted in March 2021.

References

Abdelnour, S. and Bernard, S. (2018) 'Mobiliser le travail, contourner les régulations', *La Nouvelle Revue du Travail*, 13. https://journals.openedition.org/nrt/3797

Abdelnour, S. and Bernard, S. (2019) 'Devenir syndicaliste malgré soi. La socialisation militante en tension des chauffeurs de VTC mobilisés', *Politix*, 128(4), pp. 65–90.

Amar, N. and Viossat, L.-C. (2016) Les plateformes collaboratives, l'emploi et la protection sociale. Rapport de l'IGAS.

Barraud de lagerie, P. and Sigalo-Santos, L. (2018) 'Et pour quelques euros de plus. Le *crowdsourcing* de micro-tâches et la marchandisation du temps', *Réseaux*, 212(6), pp. 51–84.

Beauvisage, T., Beuscart, J.-S. and Mellet, K. (2018) 'Numérique et travail à-côté. Enquête exploratoire sur les travailleurs de l'économie collaborative', *Sociologie du travail*, 60(2).

Bernard, S. (2020) 'Des salariés déguisés? L'(in)dépendance des chauffeurs des plateformes numériques', *Sociologie du travail*, 62(4).

Cardon, D. and Casilli, A. (2015) *Qu'est-ce que le digital labor?* Paris: Editions de l'INA.

Dagiral, E. and Peerbaye, A. (2012) 'Les mains dans les bases de données. Connaître et faire reconnaître le travail invisible', *Revue d'anthropologie des connaissances*, 6, pp. 191–216.

Denis, J. (2018) *Le travail invisible des données. Éléments pour une sociologie des infrastructures scripturales*. Paris: Presses des mines.

Dujarier, M.-A. (2016) 'Digital labor, travail du consommateur: quels usages sociaux du numérique?', www.inaglobal.fr/numerique/article/digital-labor-travail-du-consommateur-quels-usages-sociaux-du-numerique-8729

Dirringer, J. (2018) 'Quel droit social en Europe face au capitalisme de plateforme ?', *Nouvelle Revue du travail*, 13, https://doi.org/10.4000/nrt.3965

Dirringer, J. (2021) 'Le travail de plateforme entre ordre social et marché', *Droit Social*, 7, p. 580.

Dirringer, J. and Del Sol, M. (2021) 'Un rapport mutique sur les enjeux de protection sociale', *Droit Social*, 3, pp. 223–231.

Dirringer, J. and Ferkane, Y. (2021) 'Modéliser la négociation collective dans le champ économique', *Droit Social*, 7, pp. 598–610.

Dupuy, Y. and Larré, F. (1998) 'Entre salariat et travail indépendant: les formes hybrides de mobilisation du travail', *Travail et emploi*, 4, pp. 1–14.

Flichy, P. (2019) 'Le travail sur plateforme. Une activité ambivalente', *Réseaux*, 213(1), pp. 173–209.

Frouin, J.-Y. (2020) Réguler les plateformes numériques de travail. Report to the Prime Minister, France. www.gouvernement.fr/partage/11922-remise-du-rapport-reguler-les-plateformes-numeriques-de-travail.

Gurvitch, G. (2009 [1946]) *La déclaration des droits sociaux*. Paris: Dalloz.

Kilhoffer, Z., Pieter de Groen, W, et al. (2020) *Study to Gather Evidence on the Working Conditions of Platform Workers*. VT/2018/032: Research Report.

Lhernoud, J.-P. and Robin-Oliver, S. (2020) 'Travailleurs de plateformes: état des lieux et perspectives du droit social de l'Union européenne', *Revue de Jurisprudence Sociale*, 7, pp. 483–493.

Montel, O. (2017) *L'économie des plateformes: enjeux pour la croissance, le travail, l'emploi et les politiques publiques*. Study paper n° 213, Dares. https://dares.travail-emploi.gouv.fr/publications/l-economie-des-plateformes.

Pellerin, T. (2022) 'Les fonctionnalités du droit économique européen pour de nouvelles régulations du travail de plateforme – l'exemple du règlement P2B 2019/1150', *Revue française des affaires sociales*, 1, pp. 19–39.

Rosenblat, A. (2018) *Uberland: How Algorithms Are Rewriting the Rules of Work*. California: University of California Press.

Scholz, T. (2013) Digital Labor: The Internet as Playground and Factory. New York and London: Routledge.

Thomas, L. (2021) 'Etude du contentieux mené à l'initiative des travailleurs de plateforme', in Dirringer, J. (ed.) *Transformations sociales et économie numérique*. de la recherche TransSEN, research report Rennes 1. https://iode.univ-rennes1.fr/sites/iode.univ-rennes1.fr/files/medias/files/rapport_recherche_TransSEN.pdf.

5

TEAMWORK

From Self-Managed to Lean and Agile Teams

Martin Krzywdzinski and Maximilian Greb

Introduction

Theoretical categories are not timeless. They emerge in specific historical contexts and change with them. No exception is the term teamwork – a central concept in the analysis of forms of work organization in the sociology of work, organizational psychology and management studies. The aim of this chapter is to examine the continuities and changes in the meaning of the category of teamwork and to analyze how these changes are linked to specific economic developments and the history of labor relations.

The chapter, therefore, understands the category of teamwork as a socio-historical construct and examines its development and the driving forces behind it. The origins of the teamwork discussion lie in the early twentieth century in the processes of professionalization of management, which was initiated by the Taylorist revolution and the development of scientific management concepts (Merkle, 1980; Nelson, 1975). As a response, the Human Relations school was formed, which gave birth to the concept of group work (Roethlisberger and Dickson, 1939). In the 1960s and 1970s, the concept's development was carried forward by the institutionalization of organizational psychology and labor sociology as academic disciplines. In addition, research on teamwork was promoted by the Humanization of Work programs, which responded to labor conflicts and a crisis of Fordist-Taylorist work organization.

The 1980s saw a rupture take place. In the context of the deregulation of labor markets and increasing global competition, firms and governments lost interest in group-work concepts. In this context, lean production became the dominant managerial approach (Womack et al., 1990) wherein team self-organization and responsibility for optimization and improvement played an important role, albeit

DOI: 10.4324/9781003341321-7

under more restrictive conditions due to traditional Taylorist thinking. Lean-production concepts also influenced discussions of "agile work organization" which emerged in the 2000s. The influence of discussions on agile concepts reflected a shift in the importance of different economic activities: manufacturing had lost its importance as the core reference for discussions of work organization at the expense of the software industry. While the sectoral focus of the teamwork discussions shifted, nonetheless there were considerable continuities in the category of teamwork.

The structure of our paper follows this historical development. It starts with the Human Relations school and ends with current discussions of agile teamwork. The development of theoretical concepts will be linked with changes in the economic and political framework.

The Origins of Group-Work Research as a Response to Taylorism

From a historical perspective the genesis of the term and concept of teamwork is usually located in the context of Human Relations studies. These studies responded to Taylorist conceptions of work organization (Taylor, 1911) which focused on optimizing individual jobs. The work process was broken down into small steps, each of which was performed by specialized workers. The task of management was to discover the optimal pattern of movement for each work step and to implement it as a standard in the work process. Interaction and cooperation in the group had no place in this concept, especially since elaboration and enforcement of the standards for work execution were seen as the task of management alone.

In contrast to Taylor's approach, the Human Relations school argued that workers and their performance should be studied in a group context. Just as the Taylorist management concepts evolved gradually (Merkle, 1980; Nelson, 1975) the development of Human Relations Studies was the result of an evolution as well. The importance of managerial magazines from the late nineteenth century through to the 1920s was stressed by Kieser (2019, pp. 102–107). In emphasizing the motivational aspects of interpersonal relations between management and workers, these magazine articles paved the way for later research (see also Bruce, 2006; 2013). While the terms "group work" or "teamwork" did not appear in this context, Dennison (1927, p. 12) stated that one of the main tasks of management "will be to study the science and art of so arranging men and women in working groups that the most effective results can be obtained."

Particularly important in the evolution of research on group work were the famous Hawthorne Studies, conducted between 1924 and 1932 by Fritz Roethlisberger, William Dickson and (in part) Elton Mayo. These studies have often been considered the formal starting point of the Human Relations school (Roethlisberger and Dickson, 1939; Mayo, 1949; Wren and Greenwood, 1998; Duncan, 1999).

In the Hawthorne Studies, Roethlisberger (1941, p. 15) argued that in contrast to the Taylorist focus on process standardization, psychological factors played a key role in the productivity of workers (see also Roethlisberger and Dickson, 1939; Mayo, 1949). These psychological factors had to be studied in "a group or configuration" (Roethlisberger and Dickson, 1939, p. 357) as "evidence of social organization" (ibid., p. 357) or as "a social system" (ibid., p. 396). The motivation, behavior and performance of workers were shaped by (1) the formal and informal norms and rules of the work group as well as (2) the working atmosphere. Regarding the influence of the working atmosphere on performance goals, Mayo described "the relation of working groups to management as one of the fundamental problems of large-scale industry" (1945, p. 84). He emphasized management's obligation to develop and sustain cooperation (Mayo, 1945, p. 85) through employee-oriented and cooperative management policies.

Later research pointed out that this early work of the Human Relations school had still not presented an elaborated theory of group work. Added to this, Schein (1965, pp. 62–64) emphasized that the efforts of the Human Relations school were a mere modification of the Taylorist Scientific Management concepts through their emphasis on workers' social needs. Consequently, the central implication for managerial strategies was that managers "should give more attention to the needs of the people who are working for them" (Schein, 1965, p. 63). In this regard, Braverman (1974, p. 100) argued that the Human Relations methods focused mostly on managerial techniques such as "personnel counseling and on ingratiating or nonirritating styles of 'face to face' supervision." Landsberger (1958, pp. 43–47) criticized the Human Relations school for its failure to recognize the role of trade-union organizations.

Nevertheless, the Hawthorne Studies and the Human Relations school became catalysts for the development of organizational psychology as a discipline (Kieser, 2019; Bruce and Nyland, 2011; Gillespie, 1991). In particular, the close association of key actors in the Human Relations movement with the Harvard Business School provided an institutional framework for its consolidation in the social sciences (Gillespie, 1991, pp. 241–250). In the context of the New Deal, the Second World War, postwar industrial reconstruction and the steadily growing transfer of social-science theory to the practice of industrial organizations (Gillespie, 1991, pp. 251–252) the Human Relations school grew in practical influence and importance.

The Rise of Organizational Psychology and Work-Group Research

The Human Relations school was a major driver in psychology's development away from a focus on the individual to a "group-and-systems-oriented organizational psychology" (Schein, 1965, p. 5). Institutes and research facilities were subsequently founded, with the Tavistock Institute of Human Relations in London and its concept of sociotechnical systems (STS) being particularly noteworthy. At the Tavistock Institute, Trist and Bamforth (1951) conducted a highly influential study on productivity and quality of work. Their main question was why technological improvements in the British coal-mining industry did not lead to the expected rise in productivity. Their answer was that technological and social subsystems of organizations had to be coordinated and matched in order to create a successful organizational performance (Cooper and Foster, 1971; Ropohl, 1999). They argued that research must focus on work groups instead of individual workers, and they developed the notion of "responsible autonomy" (Trist and Bamforth, 1951, p. 6), which paved the way for the concept of self-managed and self-directed groups (Batt and Doellgast, 2006; Cohen and Bailey, 1997; Appelbaum and Batt, 1994; Cummings, 1978). The STS approach emphasized several conditions for self-regulation (Barker, 1993; Orsburn et al., 1990) namely task differentiation (including interdependent tasks that pertain to complete products in the group's area of responsibility), boundary control (group members have the skills and right to control interactions with other areas such as quality assurance, maintenance, other teams) and task control (the group chooses work methods and is able to influence performance targets).

It should be noted that the concepts of self-managed teams were largely shaped by research in industrialized Western countries. There was a discussion on group work in socialist countries that was characterized by motives of the humanization of industrial work and the urge to ensure work discipline and create performance incentives. The major concept used in these discussions was brigade work, even if it is worth noting that the Soviet Union, certain Eastern Bloc countries and China had different understandings of this concept (Krzywdzinski, 2018; Krzywdzinski, 2017).

In Western countries from the 1960s onward there was a growing complexity of work-group research in organizational psychology, a development which continues to this day. A multi-level concept of work groups emerged that includes individual, group-level and organizational-level factors (Kozlowski and Ilgen, 2006). The focus of research has been on the necessary conditions for group effectiveness, with highly nuanced discussions on the role of group cognitive processes (group climate, group mental models, group learning), group interpersonal and affective processes (group cohesion, group efficacy, group affects and emotions, conflicts), group behavioral processes (coordination and cooperation, group-member competencies, group self-regulation) and the design of work groups (task design, training and development, leadership). As Schein (2015) described, the research field has also become increasingly differentiated between scholar-practitioners – who rely mostly on qualitative research and work as consultants for companies and other organizations – and highly formalized and specialized academic research driven by an orientation toward the natural sciences.

Group Work and the Humanization of Work Programs

The development of group-work research was spurred by the massive need of companies and politics for consulting services. In the context of the postwar economic boom, full employment and increasing conflicts about the quality of work, calls for change and for the humanization of the working world became ever louder (Silver, 2003).

Scandinavian countries were pioneers in this development. Strongly influenced by the research on socio-technical systems at the Tavistock Institute of Human Relations, in the 1960s Norway became one of the first countries to implement a large-scale research program on the quality of work life in cooperation between researchers, trade unions, employers' organizations and the government. The "Industrial Democracy Program" was the first in a series of programs between 1964 and 1988 (Qvale, 2002) that were intended to combine empirical studies with field experiments in various industrial plants in order to explore more democratic ways of work organization and to provide workers with increased opportunities for direct participation in the workplace (Emery and Thorsrud, 1976). The concept of semi-autonomous work groups played an important role in the search for a new work design (Emery and Thorsrud, 1976, p. 2). Semi-autonomous groups did not reach the level of task differentiation, boundary and task control that was characteristic of self-managed groups. With the introduction of "interlocking tasks, job rotation and physical proximity" in semi-autonomous groups, however, the target was to improve variation and cooperation in already interrelated work processes, to reduce stress caused by isolation and monotony, and to provide workers with a broader perspective on the entire production process (Emery and Thorsrud, 1976, pp. 16–17).

In Sweden, there were similar developments and programs that involved trade unions and management (Emery and Thorsrud 1976, pp. 154–157). These led to the emergence of specific group-work concepts in the automotive industry and were referred to by Berggren as a specific "Swedish version of teamwork" (1992, p. 7). Their particularity was abandonment of the assembly line in favor of stationary assembly with long work cycles in small and autonomous groups. Volvo's Uddevalla plant was a famous and widely discussed example of the Swedish model and was brought forward as an alternative to lean-production systems (Berggren, 1992; Sandberg, 1995).

Labor conflicts and shortages were also the drivers of the "humanization of work" programs in Germany (Fricke, 2003). These governmental reform programs ran from 1974 to 1980 and were supported by trade unions, employers' associations and academics, their purpose being to develop strategies for improving the quality of work. In particular, the group-work approach seemed to promise a win-win situation for trade unions and employers: it was intended to make industrial work more attractive while also improving flexibility in personnel deployment in view of increasing automation. The German metal-worker union, IG Metall, developed a 12-point plan for an emancipatory form of group work that it hoped to propagate in companies (Turner, 1991, pp. 113 f.).

In contrast to the Scandinavian experience, the impact of the German "humanization of work" program was regarded as a limited one by researchers (Fricke, 2003). German industry carried out a large number of group-work projects, ranging from elaborate approaches emphasizing group self-management in work-process planning, training and process optimization, to very restrictive approaches that reduced group work to mere job rotation (Schumann, 1994). After an initial openness to experimentation, however, managerial resistance to these concepts grew over the years as the economic effects of group work failed to really materialize.

In the context of the "humanization of work" programs a comprehensive sociological research program on the topic of group work emerged. While this sociological research was influenced by discussions in organizational psychology, it addressed factors that played no role in psychological studies, for example, emphasizing the embedding of group work in power relations between management and labor as well as the specific product and process-organization strategies of companies (e.g., Kern and Schumann, 1984).

A Rollback? Lean Production and the Turn From Group Work to Teamwork

A number of overlapping developments led to an end of the Scandinavian and German experiments with large-scale programs to implement group work as a way of humanizing work. For one thing, the economic and political climate changed in the 1980s. The era of the postwar boom, full employment, and the resulting strength of trade unions in labor conflicts was over. Now followed a political rollback under the governments of Reagan in the United States, Thatcher in the United Kingdom and Kohl in Germany. The deregulation of labor markets and rising unemployment shifted the balance of power in companies and weakened the position of labor representatives (Emmenegger et al., 2012; Thelen, 2001).

On the other hand, a lively discussion about Japanese production concepts took place in the 1980s, which led to the development of a new management paradigm that was to have a massive influence on work-group research: lean production. The discussion was triggered by the enormous success of Japanese companies in the North American and European markets. While Japan was still a rather poor country in the postwar period, it managed to become a major industrial power within a short period of time. The explanations for this success were sought not only in the country's economic policy (Johnson, 1982) but increasingly in the specific organization of Japanese companies (Krafcik, 1988; Dohse et al., 1985).

A milestone in the discussion was a book by Womack et al. (1990), *The Machine that Changed the World*, which compared the productivity of Japanese, American and European automobile plants and popularized the concept of lean production. The book showed that American and especially European automobile plants were falling behind their Japanese competitors. It jolted the American and European management community, and added to this was the changing global economy. The demise of the Eastern bloc and the liberalization of China and India caused companies to rethink the organization of their manufacturing processes and resulted in a wave of internal restructuring, outsourcing and offshoring.

The original concept of lean production included different dimensions (Womack et al., 1990): factory organization, product-design processes, supplier relations and customer relations. Later writings on lean production had an even more nuanced understanding of its principles, as can be seen in Liker's (2004) 14 points of lean production. In addition to principles of shop-floor organization (pull systems, teamwork, *kaizen*, *heijunka* workload leveling, visual controls and others), his 14 points included general management principles (such as an emphasis on employee development) and elements of corporate culture and governance (compromise orientation, respect and others).

With regard to the shop-floor organization in the context of lean production, teamwork plays an important role. The difference to earlier approaches is also marked by a linguistic shift from "group" to "team." According to the approaches developed in Japan, teamwork combines Taylorist ideas and concepts from group-work debates. Following Taylorist concepts, the idea of standardized work and the flow principle play a central role. Standardized work means that all movements and activities are precisely described and must be performed according to standards. Work processes are broken down into a number of small steps and workers each take on a precisely defined and short cycle with work content whose duration is often about one minute long. The individual work activities are arranged one after the other in a flow. Research has viewed these elements of lean-production teamwork as a clear return to Taylorism (Jürgens, 1997).

However, in a departure from classic Taylorist concepts, teamwork in lean-production concepts emphasizes team tasks and collaboration in problem-solving, the maintenance of equipment and an optimization of work standards. To accomplish these tasks, teams regularly work together in quality circles or so-called *kaizen* workshops. They identify problems in the work process and develop suggestions for improvement. In addition, the teams have a certain degree of autonomy in the distribution (and rotation) of tasks between team members, including issues such as the planning of vacations. It is on this basis that research speaks of the self-organization of teams, but which must be clearly distinguished from the concepts of self-managed or self-directed teams in the group-work debate.

Due to the scope of self-organization, Adler (1995) in particular has referred to the teamwork concepts in lean production as "democratic Taylorism." The participation of teams in continuous improvement activities distinguishes lean production from classic Taylorism (Jürgens and Krzywdzinski, 2016; Liker and Hoseus, 2008). The term continuous improvement describes regular problem-solving and process optimization activities of teams. However, it should be noted that the reality of lean production systems only partially matches the model description. Participation opportunities are often limited (Fucini and Fucini, 1990; Ihara, 2007). Accordingly, authors such as Parker and Slaughter (1988) or Stewart et al. (2009) have criticized teamwork in lean-production systems as a mere facade. Nevertheless, that tension between the standardization of work and the participation of employees in this standardization remains a core point of work design in the context of lean production.

Agile Teamwork: The Reorganization of White-Collar Work

While the 1990s debates about lean production initially focused on teamwork concepts in the context of the automobile and other manufacturing industries, in the 2000s they spilled over into non-manufacturing sectors as well. This development reflects the growing share of white-collar employment in fields like product and process development, engineering, administration and customer relations – and companies increasingly focused on optimizing the processes in these fields. Particularly interesting was the adoption of elements from lean-production concepts of teamwork in the discussion of agile organizational methods.

The original lean-production concepts already went far beyond the field of production alone. Researchers quickly recognized that the competitiveness of Japanese companies was related not only to their production methods but to the way they developed products. The Japanese methods of product development were taken up in the concepts of "New Product Development," which emphasized (among other things) a team-based organization in which, from the outset, there was an intensive exchange between the developers and other corporate functions such as process engineering, manufacturing and logistics as well as external suppliers in order to reduce development time and ensure the manufacturability of the product (Jürgens, 2000; Wheelwright and Clark, 1992; Takeuchi and Nonaka, 1986).

As Rigby et al. (2016) pointed out, New Product Development methods and also the classic problem-solving cycles anchored in lean-production concepts (Plan-Do-Study-Act) were among the important inspirations for the development of agile product-development methods (see also Whiteley et al., 2021). Together with a number of other methodological concepts in software development (Nerur and Balijepally, 2007; Abbas et al., 2008), they influenced the "Manifesto for Agile Software Development" in 2001 (https://agilemanifesto.org/) which became the basis for the development and dissemination of agile methods.

Agile organizational methods go far beyond our focus here, which is the issue of teamwork. The agile teamwork concepts can be illustrated by the example of Scrum, a popular variant of agile organization (see Cohen et al., 2004). At the core of Scrum are small, closely collaborating teams (with a maximum of seven people) that are assigned a project and make self-organized decisions about task-sharing, the organization of work, and problem-solving. The project flow is organized through a formalized series of planning meetings, programming "sprints" lasting several weeks, and then further planning meetings. During the sprints, the teams define and distribute tasks in such a way that each member has a clear assignment. Daily team meetings serve to coordinate the project's status not only within the team but with customers, developers of linked projects and managers in order to ensure the flow of information. A central element of agile leadership is permanent feedback within the team as well as from superiors and customers (Denning, 2018).

Agile teamwork concepts are becoming ever more popular as a framework for team organization in white-collar settings. They are an important driving force to reorganize white-collar work in small teams (Moe et al., 2010) with the aim of enhancing employee motivation and satisfaction (Tessem and Maurer, 2007) while also increasing productivity. With the emphasis on cross-functionality and the authority and responsibility of teams for decision-making in many areas such as scheduling or task assignment to achieve the set targets (Schwaber and Beedle, 2002; Schatz and Abdelshafi, 2005), agile teamwork methods represent a break with traditional hierarchical organization methods in the white-collar sphere (Boes and Kämpf, 2014).

At the same time, we find a similarly polarized discussion with regard to agile teamwork methods, which had already characterized the research on lean production. On the one hand, some studies emphasize the positive aspects of agile teamwork with regard to possibilities of self-organization and stress management (Pfeiffer et al., 2019; Venkatesh et al., 2020; Tuomivaara et al., 2017) while other studies emphasize that stress is a commonplace of agile teams (Meier et al., 2018). The tension between self-organization and the pressure of the organization contained in lean-teamwork concepts is also to be found here.

Conclusion

As shown by our historical analysis of the concept of teamwork – or group work – its development can only be understood if three different processes are connected.

First, overarching economic developments must be taken into account. Development of the category of group work took place in the context of advancing industrialization, which, driven by concepts such as the assembly line, entered the phase of mass production in the twentieth century. In this phase the development of this category was fueled by the search for humane forms of industrial work, culminating in a series of national Humanization of Work programs. The turn to the category of teamwork shaped by lean production took place in a changed economic environment. In the context of intensified global competition, Japanese companies proved particularly successful in combining mass production with a focus on quality and high efficiency. Their success shifted the discussions of teamwork from a pure humanization focus to a search for combining humane and economically efficient forms of organization. Finally, the development of the concepts of agile teamwork reflected the shifts in economic weight from manufacturing to the software industry and from blue-collar to white-collar work in general. The paradigmatic organizational models now increasingly come from the latter.

Second, these overarching economic developments were linked to specific capital-labor relations and their balance of power. The mass-production phase in the twentieth century was marked by the rise of the labor movement and trade unions, which served to focus group-work discussions on the humanization of work. The 1970s and 1980s marked a break in this development and a further weakening of unions, and this is reflected in the increasing focus of teamwork discussions on economic efficiency. Finally, the current discussions on agile teamwork focus on employment areas where unions have hitherto barely been present. It will be a particular challenge for organized labor to impact these discussions.

Third, the development of the categories of group work and then teamwork is closely related to the development of overarching management concepts. The discussion of group emerged as an element of Human Relations thinking in response to classic Taylorist concepts. The shift toward teamwork concepts in the 1980s and 1990s was largely due to the global success of lean production, in which teamwork itself is only a single element. And the discussions about agile team organization are also embedded in a more comprehensive concept of process organization.

The interaction between economic developments, their influence on power relations, and the development of managerial concepts (and managerial fashions too, incidentally) lead to ever new recombinations of the different elements of teamwork – task definition, scope of team autonomy with regard to boundary control and task control, and performance management. In this respect the historical development of teamwork is characterized by continuities – for instance, agile teamwork is nothing completely new – and at the same time by innovations that correspond to the respective economic conditions and power relations. We can expect further new concepts to emerge in the future that continue this recombination.

References

Abbas, N., Gravell, A.M. and Wills, G.B. (2008) 'Historical Roots of Agile Methods: Where Did "Agile Thinking" Come From?', in Abrahamsson, P., Baskerville, R, Conboy, K, Fitzgerald, B, Morgan, L. and Wang, X. (eds.) *Agile Processes in Software Engineering and Extreme Programming: Proceedings of the International Conference on Agile Processes and Extreme Programming in Software Engineering*. Berlin and Heidelberg: Springer, pp. 94–103.

Adler, P. (1995) '"Democratic Taylorism": The Toyota Production System at NUMMI', in Babson, S. (ed.) *Lean Work: Empowerment and Exploitation in the Global Auto Industry*. Detroit: Wayne State University Press, pp. 207–219.

Appelbaum, E. and Batt, R. (1994) *The New American Workplace: Transforming Work Systems in the United States*. Ithaca, NY: ILR Press.

Barker, J.R. (1993) 'Tightening the Iron Cage: Concertive Control in Self-Managing Teams', *Administrative Science Quarterly*, 38(3), pp. 408–437.

Batt, R. and Doellgast, V. (2006) 'Groups, Teams, and the Division of Labor – Interdisciplinary Perspectives on the Organization of Work', in *The Oxford Handbook of Work and Organization*. Oxford: Oxford University Press, pp. 138–161.

Berggren, C. (1992) *Alternatives to Lean Production: Work Organization in the Swedish Auto Industry*. Ithaca, NY: ILR Press.

Boes, A. and Kämpf, T. (2014) 'Agile Methods, Lean Development and the Change of Work in Software Development', in Brunetti, G., Feld, T, Heuser, L, Schnitter, J. and Webel, C. (eds.) *Future Business Software: Progress in IS*. Cham: Springer, pp. 83–92.

Braverman, H. (1974) *Labor and Monopoly Capital: The Degradation of Work in the Twentieth Century*, 2nd ed. New York: Monthly Review Press.

Bruce, K. (2006) 'Henry S. Dennison, Elton Mayo, and Human Relations Historiography', *Management & Organizational History*, 1(2), pp. 177–199. doi: 10.1177/174493590606409.

Bruce, K. (2013) 'George Elton Mayo', in *The Oxford Handbook of Management Theorists*. Oxford: Oxford University Press, pp. 94–112.

Bruce, K. and Nyland, C. (2011) 'Elton Mayo and the Deification of Human Relations', *Organization Studies*, 32(3), pp. 383–405. doi: 10.1177/0170840610397478.

Cohen, D., Lindvall, M. and Costa, P. (2004) 'An Introduction to Agile Methods', *Advances in Computers*, 62, pp. 1–66.

Cohen, S.G. and Bailey, D.E. (1997) 'What Makes Teams Work: Group Effectiveness Research from the Shop Floor to the Executive Suite', *Journal of Management*, 23(3), pp. 239–290.

Cooper, R. and Foster, M. (1971) 'Sociotechnical Systems', *American Psychologist*, 26(5), pp. 467–474. doi: 10.1037/h0031539.

Cummings, T. (1978) 'Self-Regulating Work Groups: A Socio-Technical Synthesis', *The Academy of Management Review*, 3(3), pp. 625–634. doi:10.2307/257551.

Denning, S. (2018) 'The Emergence of Agile People Management', *Strategy & Leadership*, 46(4), pp. 3–10.

Dennison, H.S. (1927) 'Management and Labor's Interest in the Development of an Industrial Psychology', in Metcalf, H.C. (ed.) *The Psychological Foundations of Management* (reprint). Easton, PA: Hive Publishing Co., pp. 11–17.

Dohse, K., Jürgens, U. and Malsch, T. (1985) 'From "Fordism" to "Toyotism"? The Social Organization of the Labor Process in the Japanese Automobile Industry', *Politics & Society*, 14(2), pp. 115–146.

Duncan, W.J. (1999) *Management: Ideas and Actions*. New York: Oxford University Press.

Emery, F. and Thorsrud, E. (1976) *Democracy at Work: The Report of the Norwegian Industrial Democracy Program*. Leiden: Martinus Nijhoff Social Sciences Division.

Emmenegger, P., Hausermann, S, Palier, B. and Seeleib-Kaiser, M. (eds.) (2012) *The Age of Dualization: The Changing Face of Inequality in Deindustrializing Societies*. New York: Oxford University Press.

Fricke, W. (2003) 'Thirty Years of Work Life Programmes in Germany', *Concepts and Transformation*, 8(1), pp. 43–68.

Fucini, J. and Fucini, S. (1990) *Working for the Japanese: Inside Mazda's American Auto Plant*. New York: Free Press; London: Collier Macmillan.

Gillespie, R. (1991) *Manufacturing Knowledge: A History of the Hawthorne Experiments*. Cambridge: Cambridge University Press.

Ihara, R. (2007) *Toyota's Assembly Line: A View From the Factory Floor*. Melbourne: Trans Pacific Press.

Johnson, C. (1982) *MITI and the Japanese Miracle: The Growth of Industrial Policy, 1925–1975*. Stanford: Stanford University Press.

Jürgens, U. (1997) 'Rolling Back Cycle Times: The Renaissance of the Classic Assembly Line in Final Assembly', in Shimokawa, K., Jürgens, U. and Fujimoto, T. (eds.) *Transforming Automobile Assembly: Experience in Automation and Work Organization*. Berlin: Springer, pp. 255–273.

Jürgens, U. (ed.) (2000) *New Product Development and Production Networks*. Berlin: Springer.

Jürgens, U. and Krzywdzinski, M. (2016) *New Worlds of Work: Varieties of Work in Car Factories in the BRIC Countries*. Oxford: Oxford University Press.

Kern H. and Schumann M. (1984) *Das Ende der Arbeitsteilung? Rationalisierung in der industriellen Produktion: Bestandsaufnahme, Trendbestimmung*. Munich: Beck.

Kieser, A. (2019) 'Managementlehren – von Regeln guter Praxis über den Taylorismus zur Human Relations-Bewegung', in Kieser, A. and Ebers, M. (eds.) *Organisationstheorien*. Stuttgart: W. Kohlhammer Verlag, pp. 75–121.

Kozlowski, S. and Ilgen, D. (2006) 'Enhancing the Effectiveness of Work Groups and Teams', *Psychological Science in the Public Interest*, 7(3), pp. 77–124.

Krafcik, J.F. (1988) 'Triumph of the Lean Production System', *Sloan Management Review*, 30(1), pp. 41–52.

Krzywdzinski, M. (2017) 'Accounting for Cross-Country Differences in Employee Involvement Practices: Comparative Case Studies in Germany, Brazil and China', *British Journal of Industrial Relations*, 55(2), pp. 321–346.

Krzywdzinski, M. (2018) *Consent and Control in the Authoritarian Workplace: Russia and China Compared*. Oxford: Oxford University Press.

Landsberger, H.A. (1958) *Hawthorne Revisited*. New York: The New York State School of Industrial and Labor Relations.

Liker, J.K. (2004) *The Toyota Way: 14 Management Principles from the World's Greatest Manufacturer*. New York: McGraw-Hill.

Liker, J.K. and Hoseus, M. (2008) *Toyota Culture: The Heart and Soul of the Toyota Way*. New York: McGraw-Hill.

Mayo, E. (1945) *The Social Problems of Industrial Civilization*. Boston, MA: Harvard University Graduate School of Business Administration.

Mayo, E. (1949) *Hawthorne and the Western Electric Company: The Social Problems of an Industrial Civilisation*. London: Routledge.

Meier, A., Kropp, M, Anslow, C. and Biddle, R. (2018) 'Stress in Agile Software Development: Practices and Outcomes', in Garbajosa, J., Wang, X. and Aguiar, A. (eds.) *Agile Processes in Software Engineering and Extreme Programming: XP 2018 – Lecture Notes in Business Information Processing*, Vol. 314. Cham: Springer, pp. 259–266.

Merkle, J. (1980) *Management and Ideology: The Legacy of the International Scientific Management Movement*. Berkeley, CA: University of California Press.

Moe, N.B., Dingsøyr, T. and Dybå, T. (2010) 'A Teamwork Model for Understanding an Agile Team: A Case Study of a Scrum Project', *Information and Software Technology*, 52(5), pp. 480–491.

Nelson, D. (1975) *Managers and Workers: Origins of the New Factory System in the United States 1880–1920*. Madison, WI: The University of Wisconsin Press.
Nerur, S. and Balijepally, V. (2007) 'Theoretical Reflections on Agile Development Methodologies – The Traditional Goal of Optimization and Control Is Making Way for Learning and Innovation', *Communications of the ACM*, 50(3), pp. 79–83.
Orsburn, J.D., Moran, L, Musselwhite, E. and Zenger, J.H. (1990) *Self-Directed Work Teams: The New American Challenge*. Alexandra: Irwin Professional Publishing.
Parker, M. and Slaughter, J. (1988) 'Managing by Stress: The Dark Side of the Team Concept', *ILR Report*, 25, pp. 19–23.
Pfeiffer, S., Sauer, S. and Ritter, T. (2019) 'Agile Methods as Stress Management Tools? An Empirical Study', *Work Organisation, Labour & Globalization*, 13(2), pp. 20–36.
Qvale, T.U. (2002) 'A Case of Slow Learning? Recent Trends in Social Partnership in Norway with Particular Emphasis on Workplace Democracy', *Concepts and Transformation*, 7(1), pp. 31–55.
Rigby, D.K., Sutherland, J. and Takeuchi, H. (2016) 'The Secret History of Agile Innovation', *Harvard Business Review*. https://hbr.org/2016/04/the-secret-history-of-agile-innovation.
Roethlisberger, F.J. (1941) *Management and Morale*. Cambridge, MA: Harvard University Press.
Roethlisberger, F.J. and Dickson, W.J. (1939) *Management and the Worker* (reprint). New York and London: Routledge.
Ropohl, G. (1999) 'Philosophy of Socio-Technical Systems', *Society for Philosophy and Technology Quarterly Electronic Journal*, 4(3), pp. 186–194.
Sandberg, A. (ed.) (1995) *Enriching Production: Perspectives on Volvo's Uddevalla Plant as an Alternative to Lean Production*. Aldershot: Avebury.
Schatz, B. and Abdelshafi, I. (2005) 'Primavera Gets Agile: A Successful Transition to Agile Development', *IEEE Software*, 22(3), pp. 36–42.
Schein, E. (2015) 'Organizational Psychology Then and Now: Some Observations', *Annual Review of Organizational Psychology and Organizational Behavior*, 2, pp. 1–19.
Schein, E.H. (1965) *Organizational Psychology*. Englewood Cliffs, NJ: Prentice Hall.
Schumann, M. (1994) 'Gruppenarbeit und neue Produktionskonzepte', in Binkelmann, P., Braczyk, H.J. and Seltz, R. (eds.) *Entwicklung der Gruppenarbeit in Deutschland. Stand und Perspektiven*. Frankfurt am Main: Campus, pp. 186–203.
Schwaber, K. and Beedle, M. (2002) *Agile Software Development With Scrum*, Vol. 1. Upper Saddle River, NJ: Prentice Hall.
Silver, B. (2003) *Forces of Labour: Workers' Movements and Globalisation Since 1870*. Cambridge: Cambridge University Press.
Stewart, P., Richardson, M, Danford, A, Murphy, K, Richardson, T. and Wass, V. (2009) *We Sell Our Time No More: Workers' Struggles Against Lean Production in the British Car Industry*. London and New York: Pluto Press.
Takeuchi, H. and Nonaka, I. (1986) 'The New Product Development Game', *Harvard Business Review*, 64(1), pp. 137–146.
Taylor, F.W. (1911) *The Principles of Scientific Management*. New York: Harper & Brothers.
Tessem, B. and Maurer, F. (2007) 'Job Satisfaction and Motivation in a Large Agile Team', in Concas, G., Damiani, E, Scotto, M. and Succi, G. (eds.) *Agile Processes in Software Engineering and Extreme Programming: XP 2007 – Lecture Notes in Computer Science*, Vol. 4536. Berlin and Heidelberg: Springer, pp. 54–61.

Thelen, K. (2001) 'Varieties of Labor Politics in the Developed Democracies', in Hall, P.A. and Soskice, D. (eds.) *Varieties of Capitalism: The Institutional Foundations of Comparative Advantage*. Oxford: Oxford University Press, pp. 71–103.

Trist, E.L. and Bamforth, K.W. (1951) 'Some Social and Psychological Consequences of the Longwall Method of Coal-Getting: An Examination of the Psychological Situation and Defences of a Work Group in Relation to the Social Structure and Technological Content of the Work System', *Human Relations*, 4(1), pp. 3–38. doi: 10.1177/001872675100400101.

Tuomivaara, S., Lindholm, H. and Känsälä, M. (2017) 'Short-Term Physiological Strain and Recovery Among Employees Working with Agile and Lean Methods in Software and Embedded ICT Systems', *International Journal of Human – Computer Interaction*, 33(11), pp. 857–867. doi: 10.1080/10447318.2017.1294336.

Turner, L. (1991) *Democracy at Work: Changing World Markets and the Future of Labor Unions*. Ithaca, NY: Cornell University Press.

Venkatesh, V., Thong, J.Y.L, Chan, F.K.Y, Hoehle, H. and Spohrer, K. (2020) 'How Agile Software Development Methods Reduce Work Exhaustion: Insights on Role Perceptions and Organizational Skills', *Information Systems Journal*, 30, pp. 733–761.

Wheelwright, S.C. and Clark, K.B. (1992) *Revolutionizing Product Development: Quantum Leaps in Speed, Efficiency and Quality*. New York: Simon and Schuster.

Whiteley, A., Pollack, J. and Matous, P. (2021) 'The Origins of Agile and Iterative Methods', *Journal of Modern Project Management*, 8(3), pp. 20–29.

Womack, J., Jones, D. and Roos, D. (1990) *The Machine That Changed the World: The Story of Lean Production*. New York: Rawson.

Wren, D.A. and Greenwood, R.G. (1998) *Management Innovators: The People and Ideas That Have Shaped Modern Business*. New York: Oxford University Press.

6
DEMOCRATIZED WORK
Concepts and Practices

Roberto Frega and Martin Kuhlmann

Introduction

Work is first of all an activity, a task, which means that something "is done," that a goal has been achieved or that something must be done. That "something" of course must not necessarily be anything material or tangible; it can also be immaterial, for example, intellectual or mental, social or emotional. Especially in the service sector, where in more advanced societies an increasing share of work is located, work often means creating specific social or emotional states. But work is more than the accomplishment of a task. When we talk about paid work or even employment, as we do here, work also has an economic dimension. As such, it is embedded in social relations, which often are shaped or at least influenced by economic relations.

Several models have been developed to describe work in its social dimension and explain how its social, economic and technical dimensions should be integrated to achieve effective coordination, namely through the sheer exercise of authority and often by way of managerial hierarchies. But it can also be achieved through bureaucratic procedures: rules and regulations that working people are compelled to follow. Other possibilities include market-based norms, informal values and social norms, or even democratic forms of self-organization and coordination. In most cases, work is shaped by a mixture of different types of coordination.

It is hardly self-evident that work as a social relation might have a democratic dimension and that it can be democratized. Indeed many would consider "democracy" as an appropriate norm only in the public space and for political institutions. Nevertheless, in the search for more democratic forms of work as well as the building of democratic institutions in the world of work, there has

DOI: 10.4324/9781003341321-8

been a long history of thinking about and experimenting with the democratization of work.

This chapter focuses on concepts and practices aimed at improving the democratic quality of work. It first provides an overview of the three mainstream ways of conceptualizing the relation between democracy and work; it then discusses the chief approaches to workplace democracy in contemporary academic debates; and it finally analyzes recent attempts to democratize work. Based on empirical findings from case-study research, some basic elements and conditions for democratizing work will also be discussed.

Three Ways of Understanding the Relation Between Democracy and Work

In the course of the last two centuries, the notion of democratized work and a democratized economy has taken many forms but can be delimited to three main categories.

Economic Democracy

The first category includes approaches that contend that democratizing work requires nothing less than an all-encompassing reform of the economic system aimed at reducing commodification and reining in capitalism. Supporters of this view, which is usually labeled *economic democracy*, hold that capitalism and democracy are uncomfortable bedfellows. The democratization of work is thus predicated on the creation of representative institutions for the management of the economic domain at the regional, sectoral and national levels. Theories of economic democracy usually include the transformation of property relations, notably through a socialization or nationalization of the means of production. The democratic organization of work is seen as closely connected with the democratic organization of politics, and economic and territorial forms of representation are seen as complementary and interdependent. This view has been predominant in the socialist tradition since its beginning and is gaining new momentum in recent literature on property-owning democracy, market socialism, Parecon economy (Muldoon, 2018; Schweickart, 2011), proposals such as a universal basic income (Van Parijs, 2017), extension of the commons (De Angelis, 2017) and the re-municipalization of natural resources (Cumbers, 2020). For supporters of this view, the question as to the internal organization of firms has only secondary meaning since the focus is on the general system within which firms operate.

Industrial Democracy

A second category operates at the meso-level and includes approaches that conceive of democracy in terms of a system of intermediary bodies that coordinate or regulate work, especially by managing conflicting interests and organizing labor issues at sectoral levels. Historically its most distinctive feature is the conception of democracy as a form of collective action organized through voluntary associations. Democracy refers here to the self-organization of workers through elected bodies for achieving an effective voice at a supra-firm level. Usually labeled *industrial democracy*, this view was particularly strong during the high tide of trade unionism, since it gave trade unions a central role in the democratization of work (Budd, 2004). This view is particularly dominant among scholars in the fields of industrial relations and labor history as well as among intellectuals who share a social-democratic, neo-corporatist or consociativist view of continental democracies as based on the mediating role of intermediary organizations (Harcourt and Wood, 2004). Supporters of this view tend to downplay the importance of how workplaces are internally organized, since they consider democratizing work itself as difficult and workers' autonomy at the workplace to be detrimental to the achievement of broader (sectoral or social) forms of labor organization. The most recent instantiation of this approach can be found in the writings of authors such as Colin Crouch, Wolfgang Streeck and Philippe Schmitter (Crouch and Streeck, 2006; Streeck and Schmitter, 1985), who advocate a corporatist model as the unique achievement of social democracy in continental Europe in the second half of the twentieth century.

Workplace Democracy

The third category operates at the micro level of single organizations. It contends that democratizing work first and foremost requires a deep transformation of social relations in the workplace. The focus here is neither on how the broader economy is organized nor on large collective workers' associations, but on how diverse stakeholders (capital owners, managers, employees) interact at the level of a specific workplace. The basic intuition is that in a democratic society any form of authority needs to be legitimated by those who suffer its consequences and that paternalist and authoritarian relationships are inconsistent with the democratic norm. These theories usually go by the term *workplace democracy* since their focus is neither on the economic system at large nor on industrial relations, but on the workplace as a space of power-ridden interactions and different types of hierarchical, market-based or self-organized social relations. Also enjoying a renaissance and having a distinct academic pedigree is the idea that the single workplace, rather than the entire economy, is the appropriate level at which any question as to the democratization of work should be posed (Frega et al., 2019). In addition, recent studies emphasizing the status of corporations as political actors have shifted the focus from markets and economic structures to firms, with regard to both their internal organizational and external actions (Singer, 2018; Ciepley, 2013).

Overview of Theories of Workplace Democracy

Democratization of the workplace has been debated for over a century in a number of academic fields, so there exist a variety of approaches to this theme. Here we identify a set of classical and well-established approaches, mostly from the field of political theory, a series of new approaches that try to enlarge the scope of the idea of workplace democracy as well as filling certain gaps.

Classic Approaches to Workplace Democracy

Many theories of workplace democracy tend to assume political democracy as their model (Frega, 2020a). They thus construe employees as the citizens of the firm and seek institutional solutions to reach a collective form of decision-making. At the level of the workplace, democracy has been conceptualized in many and often contrasting ways, ranging from self-management to institutional systems of representation, voice mechanism and shared ownership. Three approaches have dominated the history of political ideas.

Theories of self-management and workers' control focus on bottom-up participatory decision-making along with power-sharing mechanisms at the level of the plant or workplace. The theory behind this model is participatory democracy: collective self-government achieves its highest form when all the affected parties decide together. Historical examples are the radical anarcho-syndicalist experiments of the early twentieth century (Muldoon, 2018) and work councils (Gumbrell-McCormick and Hyman, 2010). These latter are the paradigmatic representative institutional form of participation at the level of the plant or enterprise. They predominate in Western European countries where they have existed ever since the end of the Second World War (Nienhüser, 2021). Participation can be direct or indirect, depending on the size of the plant. Work councils represent all the workers at a given workplace, irrespective of their status as union members. They are either mandated by state legislation or based on workers' requests, with or without the involvement of trade unions. Their role may be either consultative or constraining, and the scope of their involvement tends to revolve around workplace issues such as work organization, training, health, safety and working hours. Work councils help mitigate a manager's power over his employees in daily workplace life. The 1994 EU directive on European Works Councils (EWC) was the first attempt to establish a mandatory right to workers' representation for multinationals with at least a thousand employees at the European level (Hann et al., 2017).

A second approach emphasizes the constitutional role of board-level employee representation such as company-level employees' chambers (Ferreras, 2017) or mixed supervisory boards which endow workers' elected representatives with direct responsibility in taking strategic decisions (Müller-Jentsch, 2008). These chambers or boards are modeled on political parliaments that steer and oversee executive operations. Co-determination is our best-known historical example of a representational conception of democracy (ibid.). Rather than having one or more work councils for each plant, co-determination consists of workers' representation at the level of either the board of directors or its supervisory board. It was prominent in Germany and Scandinavia in the second half of the twentieth century. In these countries, although the legal framework is a bit different, strong institutions of co-determination are combining works councils with employee representation at the board level. Co-determination gives employees' representatives a supervisory power: while the management board is responsible for running the company, the supervisory board appoints and oversees the management board. The core idea here is that both shareholders and employees are represented on the supervisory board (Müller-Jentsch, 2016, p. 50).

A third tradition of theories and practices has identified democracy with shared ownership. It articulates the basic intuition that economic equality is the necessary condition for political equality (Dahl, 1986) and that to govern themselves collectively, workers should also co-own their workplaces. This view establishes a strong and direct link between property rights and control rights and contends that the former are a necessary condition of the latter. Exemplifying this approach is the cooperative movement as well as mutualism and other forms of bottom-up association for economic purposes (Kaswan, 2014). But there have also been sustained attempts to defend democratization of the workplace through an equal representation of shareholders' rights (Gomez and Korine, 2008). Other types of schemes were later developed to either promote workers' ownership of workplaces or allow other stakeholders – such as consumers, users and local communities – to participate in the governance of firms (Merrett and Walzer, 2004).

Emerging Theories of Workplace Democracy

In the wake of changed economic circumstances as well as the decline and limited achievements of these consolidated views, in the past two decades, there have emerged new approaches to the democratization of work. A common feature of these new approaches is a progressive abandonment of the state/firm analogy and an emphasis on *democratizing* effects rather than democratic forms.

A first set of theories, developed mostly within the field of organization and management studies, has focused on the different types of voice mechanisms developed at the firm level to either handle conflict after the decline of trade unions or give workers institutional protection against organizational abuse (Wilkinson et al., 2020). *Voice* puts emphasis on the protective function of rights embedded in institutional devices that allow employees to articulate their grievances without the risk of incurring retaliation. In its specific and distinctive meaning, voice requires neither representative nor participatory schemes. Indeed its democratic function has greater similarity to that of courts than parliaments. Particularly prominent since the 1980s and in Anglo-Saxon countries, this approach reflects the more liberal orientation of these countries, for example, in their way of replacing collective representation with individualized consultation. It is particularly in the last two decades that scholars, in view of this experience, have begun to theorize more sophisticated forms of employee voice, emphasizing the democratizing potential of employer-initiated practices. Voice mechanisms capture an essential feature of liberal democracy; that is, the existence of institutional protections against the infringement of individual rights.

A second set, particularly prominent in Anglo-Saxon countries, emphasizes the democratizing potential of workers' financial participation through gainsharing programs. This approach extends the idea of shareholders' democracy to workers and contends that financial participation elevates workers to the status of citizens of the firm (Kruse et al., 2010). The democratizing potential of gainsharing schemes is usually predicated on two types of arguments. On the one hand, it is said that by letting employees share in their company's profits, their status is equated with that of shareholders, thus achieving a complete form of shareholder democracy. On the other hand, as discussed more extensively in the next section, employees are fully integrated into a firm's life by participating in profits and their efforts directly connected with the ensuing results. In other words, instead of being merely remunerated for their time, they have a share in the company's success. This fact amounts to a fuller involvement than that allowed by the employment contract. Gainsharing schemes are particularly widespread in Anglo-Saxon countries, in part because pension savings are usually privately managed and thus provide financial resources.

A third set focuses on deliberation as the quintessential democratic method for forming preferences and taking decisions in the workplace (Felicetti, 2018). The central intuition at the core of deliberative approaches is that "binding rules and practices should be determined through open and fair processes of public reason in which parties – be they citizens, political officials or groups – offer arguments and evidence to persuade others" (Fung and Wright, 2003, p. 52). Initially developed in the context of political democracy, deliberative theory has rapidly become a yardstick for assessing the democratic quality of any human association (Parkinson and Mansbridge, 2012). Deliberative approaches do not propose distinctive sets of institutions, per se, but instead provide the justificatory background for diverse institutional solutions such as stakeholder democracy, co-determination and worker councils, thus pointing to deliberative procedures as a basis of legitimation that would guarantee that a given workplace complies with the deliberative norm. Its principal yardsticks are the inclusion of all those who are affected by decisions, and free and uncoerced deliberation as the procedure through which they arrive at collective decisions. Deliberation as a method for democratizing work gained ground in certain Norwegian and Swedish developmental, project-based, action-research approaches (Gustavsen, 1992).

Following in the footsteps of Freeman in the 1980s, a fourth set of theories sees workplace democracy as an inclusive system for representation of the interests of a set of stakeholders outside the firm. Under the banner of stakeholder democracy, the idea is that to be legitimate the governance system of any organization must include all major categories of interested parties. That is, governance structures ought to be organized so as to balance the interests of all concerned parties and not only a limited set such as shareholders and/or employees. Besides shareholders and employees, stakeholder theory emphasizes the rights of local communities, consumers, suppliers and relevant actors from civil society (Matten and Crane, 2005). Stakeholder theory comes in softer forms such as certain variants of Corporate Social Responsibility which consider the inclusion of relevant stakeholders to be a matter of voluntary compliance (Scherer and Palazzo, 2011) and in stronger forms which contend that all relevant stakeholders ought to be represented at the board level (Moriarty, 2014).

Finally, a last set of theories focuses on the lived experience of work, that is, on the conditions through which being a worker can be an emancipatory or alienating experience. These approaches usually emphasize the ethical preconditions of democracy such as individual autonomy and self-esteem but also solidarity at work, contending that meaningful work promotes individual and group-based autonomy, thus enabling a more democratic workplace (Roessler, 2012). The European debate on group work of the 1990s, in particular, focused on workplace practices and the experiences of employees in generating democratizing effects (Kuhlmann, 2002). A sensitivity to the consequences of workplace organization on workers' life emerged parallel to socialist movements and was strongly rooted in trade unionism, but it is mostly in a humanistic manner and, later on, via management and work psychology that a full-blown approach has been developed (Yeoman, 2014).

Open Issues in Democratizing Perspectives on the Workplace

The last set of theories points to a wider dimension of the democratic experience but without clearly specifying its institutional conditions and normative implications. The democratizing potential of the lived experience of work can be recovered through consideration of the social bases of democracy. The theoretical rationale here is a social understanding of democracy as a "form of society" (Lefort) or "way of life" (Dewey). Rather than construing democracy as a formal political institution, it is understood as a distinctive pattern of social interaction, one appropriate to free and equal individuals. As noted by Frega (2020a), starting from this wider view of democracy, one can appreciate the democratizing potential of organizational practices usually neglected by theories of workplace democracy. Employee involvement refers to management practices and organizational patterns through which the concrete activities of workers are transformed so as to promote their individual and team-based autonomy at work as well as the meaningfulness of those activities. By redesigning jobs so as to increase their meaningfulness and variety and by redesigning workplaces to promote competence-based horizontal interactions among peers, employee involvement reduces opportunities for managerial exploitation, enhances inclusion, reduces discrimination and increases autonomy (Frega, 2020b). From this perspective, the social relations at work are made less hierarchical and managerial. Horizontal relations at work and more equal and democratic procedures are also supposed to tame market-driven mechanisms. The basic intuition of employee involvement is that if employees accomplish the complex functions that this new organization of work assigns to them, then they need to know a great deal more about the functioning of the firm, its strategic positioning, productive processes and so forth. They also need to possess a broader array of competencies, be in charge of larger portions of the productive process, be allowed to interact autonomously with individuals in remote parts of the company or outside it, such as customers and suppliers, and be able to control the execution of their work. This entails a form of empowerment that is based neither on higher bargaining power nor on increased recognition and which gains traction by the change in status that follows from the transformation of jobs, since this form of empowerment concretely reduces the gap between managers and employees in terms of knowledge, power and status. Workers are transformed into autonomous human agents by mastering knowledge, achieving autonomy, becoming a source of valuable information and bearers of many skills, being allowed to interact freely with all the social partners of an economic enterprise, and having discussions on an equal footing with their superiors. This kind of empowerment is not reserved for the happy few – who in some accounts of workplace democracy are endowed with political responsibilities (usually trade-union representatives) – since it potentially affects all workers. This is the unique democratizing potential of employee involvement: it taps into the normative resources of workplace practices in which all workers may partake.

Democratizing Work in Action: Elements and Conditions

Employee involvement as a more recent concept of workplace democracy is an important issue in studies on group work or teamwork[1] as well as high-performance work systems (Appelbaum et al., 2000). Thanks to its socio-technical origins (van Eijnatten, 1993), particularly in the northern European debate, the issue of employee involvement has been explicitly connected with the question of democratizing work (Ingvaldsen, 2013). Empirical studies of these forms of workplace innovation reliably show that employee involvement can take many forms at different levels (Turner and Auer, 1994; Benders and Van Hootegem, 1999; Kuhlmann and Schumann, 2001). More democratic forms of work organization elicit higher levels of individual as well as team-based autonomy, so employee involvement tends to promote enhanced working conditions, thus improving employee well-being. All other things being equal, higher levels of employee involvement correlate with a more positive assessment of work (Berggren, 1992; Freeman and Kleiner, 2000; Kuhlmann and Schumann, 2001). On the basis of empirical studies, we can identify a number of elements and conditions of democratizing work through employee involvement.

Developing Horizontal Social Relations at Work

A key element of democratized work based on employee involvement is self-organized team meetings. They have clear democratic implications since they provide a place and dedicated time resources for deliberative practices. Self-organized team meetings are a necessary element in more democratic horizontal social relations at work. In organizations with strong forms of representative industrial democracy based on such things as works councils, the team meetings must be self-organized and protected not only against interventions or domination from supervisors or management but also from employee representatives. Even works councils and union representatives emphasize that the two forms of employee self-organization can and should be complementary, namely the indirect channel via employee representatives and the direct one based on deliberation in team meetings. Different opinions or even disagreements between teams and employee representatives seldom occur, but when this happens they must be resolved by second-order discussions where employee representatives might refer to overarching goals and objectives, the negative side-effects of what teams want, or compliance with legal and/or collective bargaining obligations.

An example from our case-study research of a team meeting in a pharmaceutical plant where employees discussed and planned their vacation time can highlight the horizontal dimension of workplace democracy. The problem the team had to solve is quite common: In the summer almost everybody wants to take a vacation. Migrant workers, in particular, often want to be off from work for three or four weeks, since they want to visit their families in their countries of origin. Normally a supervisor decides who is allowed to take time off, but in our case, an elected spokesperson on each team (*Teamsprecher*) took up this issue in a regular team meeting. Team meetings every second week were backed by a formal binding agreement with the works council. From the employees' perspective, the new regulation was an important achievement because it entrusted them collectively (as a team) with decision-making power. Discussions within the teams about vacation time were sometimes difficult and emotional, but in general, the teams were very satisfied with the approach and were convinced that the vacation issue was often dealt with more quickly and reasonably. The result was also perceived as being fairer. Team meetings provide a place and time to discuss the vacation issue, and this gradually changed the horizontal social relations by promoting more democratic, deliberative and even more solidaristic practices.

Sometimes, when someone asked for a longer period of vacation and somebody else had to replace for this colleague, the team discussed a vacation request at length from different personal and practical perspectives. Pivotal here was the question as to just what reasons can be legitimately claimed and should be applied.

The discussions were learning exercises in taking on the perspective of other people, for example, when a team finally agreed that a colleague should be allowed a longer period of four weeks because of his or her personal situation. Everybody on the team learned more about the situation, the personal backgrounds and their colleagues' preferences. The solidaristic dimension was obvious because the team members assured each other that the decision was embedded in an understanding of "give and take." Self-organized team meetings strengthen a person's ability and willingness to take on the perspective of colleagues, and they fortify workplace solidarity based on a deeper understanding of the personal, social and cultural background of colleagues.

Changing Hierarchical Relations at Work

A second element that improves the democratic quality of work is the transformation of hierarchical managers into facilitators. This organizational solution transforms authority structures in the workplace, thus enhancing their democratic quality. Empirical evidence confirms that the democratic quality of a workplace is strongly related to how first-level supervisors interact with their subordinates: their tasks, their role perception, their style of leadership and what they do. Employee involvement requires that work is not organized by traditional command-and-control forms of leadership but through a managerial approach that emphasizes argumentation, debate, facilitation. Facilitators focus very much on working conditions as well as organizational and technical tools and resources in general. Such a view implies that supervisors must be context-sensitive and engage in constant dialogue with employees. In day-to-day operations, first-level supervisors must take up the role of carrying and promoting ideas and demands from the working level upward. The authority of these supervisors and managers depends not only on formal education, proficiency and the decision-making power they have been delegated from above. Equally important is their technical or professional expertise and knowledge, their communicative skills as well as their willingness and ability to support and develop extended forms of employee involvement.

A second case study on more democratic workplaces – taken from the car industry – makes clear how hierarchical relations at work are likewise changing. Again, it starts from a common problem at most workplaces. From time to time, because of changes in production or natural fluctuation, the transfer of employees between work areas and/or different shift teams becomes necessary. At one point in our case study the three shift teams in a certain working area received information that another employee would be transferred to their unit and would be working on a specific shift team. As a first-level supervisor, the foreman (*Meister*) informed the group speaker (*Gruppensprecher*) of the transfer, who in turn apprised his colleagues, at which juncture the news spread like wildfire – partly because there were rumors that the announced person was less highly qualified, maybe less willing to perform, and even less team-minded. Because of these rumors, the group speaker pressured the foreman to be part of the next team meeting so as to explain and justify the transfer. In the meeting the different points of view, concerns and fears were frankly discussed. Ultimately the team and the foreman agreed that the new colleague would be made welcome and that the team would help integrate him into his new job. Bargaining with the foreman, the team obtained extra time for on-the-job learning so that its flexibility could be increased. The foreman also promised that the next transfer to the unit would be a more highly skilled person. When the new colleague arrived the team set aside time to explain just how they worked and what they expected of him, while simultaneously offering any kind of help that he might need.

In this case, too, the open discussion at the team meeting was a significant part of the story. Even more important was the role and behavior of the foreman and first-level supervisors in general. He was willing and had the authority to enter into a discussion with the team. His responsibility was to explain the situation and justify the decision, while also reacting to what the team was demanding. The foreman could not simply impose his will. He had to make sure that the team would get what it needed in order to cope with the situation of having a new colleague who was less highly skilled and would therefore cause problems in terms of the team's flexibility. This example shows that democratizing work means not only more deliberative and solidaric horizontal social relations but that it also affects hierarchical social relations. First-level supervisors require less of a command-and-control mindset and need to grant more organizational power to the lower ranks.

Questioning Investment Decisions and a Broader Conception of Improvement

A third element of democratized work brought about by employee involvement is the way planning processes are structured and organizational or technical changes are achieved. A democratic perspective on work contends that team-based, employee-driven improvement activities must complement managerial planning activities from above. Similarly, the contribution of external experts to the optimization of production processes should incorporate employees' perspectives. To improve productivity and make processes more efficient and effective is a top priority of any productive unit – and its democratization is a challenging task. Case-study research on different levels of employee involvement in implementing digital technologies has shown that employees perceive non-participatory processes of digitalization as not only detrimental to their working conditions but as entailing a serious disregard for their professional competencies and self-esteem. These days post-Taylorist forms of work organization are quite often based on the assumption that employees should play a role in the ongoing processes of raising productivity and being more cost-efficient and competitive.

Our third case-study example, taken from a mechanical-supplier plant, sheds light on what happens at workplaces where employees are actively involved in improvement initiatives. At this plant, the management and trade-union-led works council agreed to include optimization activities in the objectives of group work. Standard expert-driven improvement activities were therefore supplemented and combined with employee-driven, team-based improvement activities. Notwithstanding the skepticism among managers and planning experts, several teams began discussing solutions to operational problems and strategies to improve production processes. The democratizing potential of these practices stems from two factors: the active involvement of employees in decisions affecting their daily work and the deliberative structure of the decision-making process. Overall, teamwork led to the following results:

(1) In each case study employees quickly agreed on a number of minor improvements that would save money without jeopardizing production or product quality. Employees could achieve these improvements only because of the willingness of management and planning experts to discuss technical and organizational issues with them.
(2) The teams made a distinction between those improvements that had no impact on effort and working conditions and improvements that would require increased efforts – whether immediately, in the long run from the team or from colleagues in other areas. In general, teams were willing to engage in innovations of the first but not the second type. For example, several teams systemized the use of tools on different production batches, so as to produce less waste, along with using the cheapest type of tool for each batch. A side effect of this joint effort was collaborative learning inside the team as well as between team members and planning experts from the tooling department.
(3) Through collective discussion, team members became aware of economic, financial and other strategic issues. Emerging as contested issues were those of where to invest and who had the legitimacy to make decisions about investments. Works council representatives remarked that workplace discussions became comparatively broader and more political, for example, the debate over gainsharing. In our case studies the teams usually committed themselves to improvement activities only when there was an element of mutual gain. From the employees' perspective, improvement activities had to make daily work easier or at least more bearable. In the debates and deliberations related to team-based continuous improvement, a dual perspective on work became visible. Most employees stressed that working life had an economic rationale that had to be taken into account, but that it should also meet social and human needs.

Conclusion

This chapter has presented an overview of theoretical approaches to the democratization of work. Starting from well-established categorizations of workplace democracy and case-study research, we have shown the under-investigated potential for the democratization of work. Deep and radical changes in horizontal and hierarchical social relations at work are necessary. Self-organized team meetings, for example, are important for deliberation and social learning. It is necessary to develop the role and task composition of management so as to facilitate the strengthening of bottom-up processes inside firms. If these related elements of democratic workplaces come together then employee-driven improvement activities can both stimulate and broaden the debate about how work might be organized and developed, about where to invest capital, and especially about the relation between economic and social or human aspects of work.

In a market economy under capitalism, however, work in general is no locus of democracy, and the economic environment places constant pressure on attempts to democratize work. Democratic forms of employee involvement have been rare so far; but as the case studies have shown, democratizing work is possible – both economically and from the employee's perspective.

Finally, two future challenges should be mentioned. First, work-based practices of direct democracy have to be coordinated with representational ones, that is, with the established institutions and practices of industrial democracy. Democratizing work is itself no alternative but needs to be combined with institutions of industrial democracy that grant workers a representative voice in the traditional sense. Second, democratizing work must be embedded in a thriving democratic society, one which is capable of reconciling employees with the interests of consumers and other citizens and begins to address the ecological challenges that mankind faces. There is at least one reason to justify a certain degree of optimism in terms of this bigger picture: employees are also consumers and citizens. Hence there is at least a chance that democratizing work can help to tame the advanced capitalism of our present day.

Note

1 See also the chapter "Teamwork: From Self-Managed to Lean and Agile Teams" by Martin Krzywdzinski and Maximilian Greb in this volume.

References

Appelbaum, E., Bailey, T, Berg, P. and Kalleberg, A.L. (2000) *Manufacturing Advantage: Why High-Performance Work Systems Pay Off.* Ithaca, NY: ILR Press.

Benders, J. and Van Hootegem, G. (1999) 'Teams and Their Context: Moving the Team Discussion Beyond Existing Dichotomies', *Journal of Management Studies*, 36(5), pp. 609–628.

Berggren, C. (1992) *Alternatives to Lean Production: Work Organization in the Swedish Auto Industry*. Ithaca, Ny: ILR Press.

Budd, J. (2004) *Employment With a Human Face: Balancing Efficiency, Equity, and Voice.* Ithaca, NY: Cornell University Press.

Ciepley, D. (2013) 'Beyond Public and Private: Toward a Political Theory of the Corporation', *American Political Science Review*, 107(1), pp. 139–158.

Crouch, C. and Streeck, W. (eds.) (2006) *The Diversity of Democracy: Corporatism, Social Order and Political Conflict*. Cheltenham: Edward Elgar Publishing.

Cumbers, A. (2020) *The Case for Economic Democracy*. New York: John Wiley & Sons.

Dahl, R. (1986) *A Preface to Economic Democracy*. Los Angeles, CA: University of California Press.

De Angelis, M. (2017) *Omnia Sunt Communia: On the Commons and the Transformation to Postcapitalism*. London: Zed Books.

Felicetti, A. (2018) 'A Deliberative Case for Democracy in Firms', *Journal of Business Ethics*, 150(3), pp. 803–814.

Ferreras, I. (2017) *Firms as Political Entities: Saving Democracy Through Economic Bicameralism*. Cambridge: Cambridge University Press.

Freeman, R. and Kleiner, M. (2000) 'Who Benefits Most From Employee Involvement: Firms or Workers?', *American Economic Review*, 90(2), pp. 219–223.

Frega, R. (2020a) 'Democratic Patterns of Interaction as a Norm for the Workplace', *Journal of Social Philosophy*, 5(1), pp. 27–53.

Frega, R. (2020b) 'Employee Involvement and Workplace Democracy', *Business Ethics Quarterly*, 31(3), pp. 360–385.

Frega, R., Herzog, L. and Neuhauser, C. (2019) 'Workplace Democracy – The Recent Debate', *Philosophy Compass*, 14(4).

Fung, A. and Wright, E.O. (eds.) (2003) *Deepening Democracy: Institutional Innovations in Empowered Participatory Governance*. London: Verso Books.

Gomez, P.-Y. and Korine, H. (2008) *Entrepreneurs and Democracy: A Political Theory of Corporate Governance*. Cambridge: Cambridge University Press.

Gumbrell-McCormick, R. and Hyman, R. (2010) 'Works Councils: The European Model of Industrial Relations', in Wilkinson, A., Gollan, P. and Marchington, M. (eds.) *The Oxford Handbook of Participation in Organizations*. Oxford: Oxford University Press, pp. 286–314.

Gustavsen, B. (1992) *Dialogue and Development: Social Science for Social Action*. Stockholm: Arbetslivscentrum.

Hann, D., Hauptmeier, M. and Waddington, J. (2017) 'European Works Councils After Two Decades', *European Journal of Industrial Relations*, 23(3), pp. 209–224.

Ingvaldsen, J. (2013) *Democratic Lean? Work Systems in Norwegian Industry*. Trondheim: NTNU Doctoral Theses.

Kaswan, M. (2014) 'Developing Democracy: Cooperatives and Democratic Theory', *International Journal of Urban Sustainable Development*, 6(2), pp. 190–205.

Kruse, D., Freeman, R. and Blasi, J. (eds.) (2010) *Shared Capitalism at Work*. Chicago, IL: University of Chicago Press.

Kuhlmann, M. (2002) 'Group Work and Democracy', in Docherty, P., Kira, M. and Shani, A.B. (eds.) *Creating Sustainable Work Systems: Emerging Perspectives and Practice*. London: Routledge, pp. 126–138.

Kuhlmann, M. and Schumann, M. (2001) 'What's Left of Workers' Solidarity? Workplace Innovation and Workers' Attitudes Toward the Firm', in Vallas, S. (ed.) *The Transformation of Work*. Oxford: Elsevier Science/JAI Press, pp. 189–215.

Harcourt, M. and Wood, G. (eds.) (2004) *Trade Unions and Democracy: Strategies and Perspectives*. Manchester: Manchester University Press.

Matten, M. and Crane, A. (2005) 'What Is Stakeholder Democracy? Perspectives and Issues', *Business Ethics: A European Review*, 14(1), pp. 6–13.

Merrett, C. and Walzer, N. (eds.) (2004) *Cooperatives and Local Development: Theory and Applications for the 21st Century*. New York: ME Sharpe.

Moriarty, J. (2014) 'The Connection Between Stakeholder Theory and Stakeholder Democracy: An Excavation and Defense', *Business & Society*, 53(6), pp. 820–852.

Muldoon, J. (ed.) (2018) *Council Democracy: Towards a Democratic Socialist Politics*. London: Routledge.

Müller-Jentsch, W. (2008) 'Industrial Democracy: Historical Development and Durrent Challenges', *Management Revue*, 19(4), pp. 260–273.

Müller-Jentsch, W. (2016) 'Formation, Development and Current State of Industrial Democracy in Germany', *Transfer: European Review of Labour and Research*, 22(1), pp. 45–62.

Nienhüser, W. (2021) 'Unternehmen: Diktaturen oder Demokratien? Debatten zur Reform der Unternehmensverfassung', *Industrielle Beziehungen*, 28(3), pp. 283–316.

Parkinson, J. and Mansbridge, J. (2012) *Deliberative Systems: Deliberative Democracy at the Large Scale*. Cambridge: Cambridge University Press.

Roessler, B. (2012) 'Meaningful Work: Arguments From Autonomy', *Journal of Political Philosophy*, 20(1), pp. 71–93.

Scherer, A.G. and Palazzo, G. (2011) 'The New Political Role of Business in a Globalized World: A Review of a New Perspective on CSR and Its Implications for the Firm, Governance, and Democracy', *Journal of Management Studies*, 48(4), pp. 899–931.

Schweickart, D. (2011) *After Capitalism*. Lanham, MD: Rowman & Littlefield Publishers.

Singer, A. (2018) *The Form of the Firm: A Normative Political Theory of the Corporation*. Oxford: Oxford University Press.

Streeck, W. and Schmitter, P.C. (1985) 'Community, Market, State and Associations? The Prospective Contribution of Interest Governance to Social Order', *European Sociological Review*, 1(2), pp. 119–138.

Turner, L. and Auer, P. (1994) 'A Diversity of New Work Organization: Human-Centered, Lean, and In-Between', *Industrielle Beziehungen*, 1(1), pp. 39–61.

van Eijnatten, F.M. (1993) *The Paradigm That Changed the Work Place*. Assen: Van Gorcum.

Van Parijs, P. (2017) *Basic Income*. Cambridge, MA: Harvard University Press.

Wilkinson, A., Donaghey, J, Dundon, T. and Freeman, R. (eds.) (2020) *Handbook of Research on Employee Voice*. Cheltenham: Edward Elgar Publishing.

Yeoman, R. (2014) *Meaningful Work and Workplace Democracy: A Philosophy of Work and a Politics of Meaningfulness*. Basingstoke: Palgrave Macmillan.

PART 2

(In)visible Work

7

FREE VERSUS UNFREE LABOR

Challenging Their Boundaries

Léa Renard and Theresa Wobbe

The COVID-19 pandemic and the accompanying sanitary measures have shed light on "gray zones" of the labor market, on activities that have traditionally either been devalued (e.g., supermarket or cleaning staff) or not been recognized as formal employment, despite their role in very directly supporting the whole economic system such as domestic work (Anderson, 2000). Above all the pandemic is forcing us to rethink the categories with which we segment the world of work and to rethink its boundaries. What counts as work and what is not categorized as work? For these reasons, the pandemic can analytically serve as a "magnifying glass" to enlarge and thereby disclose the representations, cultural restrictions and myths at the basis of today's capitalist system.

The belief in gainful employment as "free labor" is one of these enduring myths in Western societies.[1] Among other things the pandemic challenges a binary conception of coercion and voluntariness (Steinfeld, 2001) and therefore reveals a range of shades between these two poles of the spectrum. Public opinion in Germany was shocked by the revelation of severe labor conditions in German slaughterhouses where (male and female) workers from Eastern Europe are often coerced by suspicious agreements.[2] This case revealed the entanglements between subcontractor systems and the European migration regimes (Wagner, 2015). Coerced or "forced labor" – as formulated by the legal category – thus appears not as an exception to the presumably "free" market system, a holdover from ancient times, but seems to be at the very core of contemporary economic processes in a globalized world.

In the following, we use the notions of *coerced labor* and *violence-based labor* as analytic instruments to address various forms of labor practices based on the threat or use of violence in the past and today. We only employ *forced labor* in referring to the official definition put forward by the International Labour Organization

DOI: 10.4324/9781003341321-10

(ILO) in its convention No. 29 in 1930. "Forced labor" became a legal category in the imperial context of the interwar period, and under it the ILO convention subsumed specific forms of violence-based labor practices, especially targeting those forms in the colonies. Over the course of the twentieth century, this legal classification has undergone changes and was reframed in the ILO Declaration on Fundamental Rights and Principles at Work (1998). Forced labor has shifted from a "colonial problem" to a category of global reach that is the negative counterpart of "decent work" in the human rights terminology of international organizations (Wobbe and Renard, 2019; Wobbe, 2020).

In this article, we argue that forced labor and its opposite "free labor" are historically laden categories reflecting universalist European claims (Engerman, 1999; Petersson, 2005). Our temporal framework is the interwar years during which the ILO was concerned with severe labor conditions in the context of the imperial political system of the first half of the twentieth century. After 1945 we then turn to the late imperial system and the first post-colonial states. In so doing we also suggest looking beyond Europe to include the (former) colonies. Against this background, we will then discuss the renewed ILO interest in the issue of forced labor ever since the late 1990s.

Our article questions the binary opposition between free labor and forced labor – the legal expression of unfree labor in the twentieth and twenty-first centuries – from a historical and sociological perspective. In the second part of the article, we take the international regulation of coerced labor in the ILO as a case in point. We explore under what social and historical conditions forced labor became a category that structured the organization's actions and knowledge production between the wars as well as after 1945 and how the framework shifted around the year 2000. In the last section, we discuss how sociology might unsettle the boundary between free and unfree labor for analytic purposes and the consequences of this analytic shift for our understanding of work today and in the past. We conclude by pointing to the benefits of a reflexive sociology for the study of (coerced) labor practices.

The Critical Relationship Between Free and Coerced Unfree Labor

Forms of coerced labor are very old social and economic phenomena (think of slavery in classical antiquity) but they continue to shape the experiences of today's workers worldwide. Many authors have argued that labor exploitation has been increasing since 1990 (for a critical review on this point, see Patterson and Zhuo, 2018, pp. 426–428). Despite its tremendous relevance – according to the ILO (2017) forced labor can be found in almost every economic sector and in all regions of the world today – coerced labor remains a blind spot for sociology. In particular, the sociology of work takes for granted that work is performed on a voluntary basis while conceptualizing its topic as wage work and contract labor, especially in the industrial sector, though leaving the limitations of this conception implicit. As underscored by Andrew Abbott (2005) sociologists of work have usually focused on paid work and the "wage economy." By doing that mainstream sociology has excluded other kinds of work from its research scope and thus left the study of trafficking, slavery and the like to other disciplines such as history, (international) law and criminology. The consequence of this omission is that coerced labor is thought of as incompatible with "normally" functioning markets rather than a result of the market system and global social inequalities themselves. In this view coerced labor in the sense of forced labor is mainly associated with the worst forms it has taken such as in Nazi Germany and Stalinist Russia, but without connecting them to labor regimes in contemporary liberal democracies (Herbert, 1999; Barenberg, 2017).

Against this background, we suggest exploring the boundary-making of the category of work, rather than starting from a restricted model of wage work that is insufficient in capturing the many facets of labor practices both inside and outside Europe. Historical research shows that the idea of coerced labor is based on a sharp distinction between free and unfree labor, which first emerged in North America and Britain from debates in the late eighteenth century. That idea involved a belief in the economic and moral superiority of free as opposed to unfree labor (Engerman, 1999; Rupprecht, 2014) and introduced the concept of the "civilizing mission" to "educate" so-called backward people in the discipline of "free" work (Petersson, 2005; Osterhammel, 2006). Although the belief in freedom was made up of different streams, they had "enough in common, based on the contrast of free labor with slavery and serfdom" (Engerman, 1999, p. 10).

This critical relationship between freedom and unfree labor is connected to a particular Western meaning of freedom that was first conceptualized in classical antiquity. In his pathbreaking work *Freedom in the Making of Western Culture*, Orlando Patterson (1991) argues that the notion of freedom was generated from the experience of slavery. People constructed it as a "powerful shared vision of life, and response to slavery or its recombinant form, serfdom, in their role as masters, slaves, and nonslaves" (ibid., p. xiii). In Ancient Greece, freedom required slavery insofar as the elite relied on a free space and depended on the work of enslaved people in order to be recognized as an honorable person and to maintain social status.[3] It was within Roman private law, however, that the cultural meaning of freedom was legally systematized in sharp demarcations. A first key aspect was an explicit negative understanding of freedom (*libertas*) as being free from slavery. The second aspect that became decisive refers to the legal meaning of possession as absolute property (*dominium*) that "involved not simply the capacity to derive the full economic value of a thing, to use (*usus*) and enjoy its fruits (*fructus*), as well as 'to use it up' (*ab-usus*), to alienate it" (Patterson, 1982 [2018], p. 31). By placing the idea of freedom and of redemption "at the very center of its theology," the rise of Christianity would provide a specific thrust, which, together with universalism, continues to shape the Western ideal of freedom (Patterson,

1991, p. xvi; see also pp. 203–344). The Roman meaning of freedom that would imprint European continental law was based on the opposition to un-freedom as materialized in the institution of slavery. Freedom in turn became a decisive goal and held the promise of social elevation to "free" persons.

The anti-slavery movements of the eighteenth and nineteenth centuries could connect to that cultural meaning of freedom in a new way. The attack on slavery as the extreme form of coerced labor "was presented as the inevitable and heroic extension of Europe's freedom principle to global dominance" (Drescher, 2017, p. 397). Ever since the 1880s slavery has been presented as the worst evil and as a counterpoint to European civilization, including a new undertone in the strict distinction between free and unfree labor (Cooper, 2000). European colonial powers justified their endeavors by way of this very conception of freedom, while in practice slavery was not only tolerated but new forms of colonial coerced labor were also introduced.

Whereas slavery was being discussed as the ultimate form of unfree labor, the opposite process was taking place in Europe. In the decades preceding the First World War, wage work was promulgated as the achievement of free labor in connection with the new institutions of the welfare state including labor rights. However, in contrast to this narrative of modernization, historical studies have shown that not only were many categories of workers in Europe (agricultural, craft or domestic workers, especially women) excluded from this conception and from the social protection connected to it, but violence and coercion were still perceived as legitimate in the colonies (Stanziani, 2020).

This discourse forms the broader background against which the ILO became concerned with a legal classification of coerced labor practices in the colonies and in particular in Africa.

Forced Labor as a Legal Category: Ruptures and Continuities in the Categorization Process since the Interwar Period

In the field of international organizations, the ILO enjoys a special status. It was created in the aftermath of the First World War by the Treaty of Versailles signed in 1919 under the umbrella of the League of Nations. It survived the Second World War and was later integrated into the system of the United Nations that still exists today. The ILO engages in different forms of knowledge production, standard-setting and categorization in the field of work. One of the main forms is legal classification and international standard-setting at the International Labour Conference, thus forging international legal categories. Beyond that, the International Conference of Labour Statisticians also sets statistical standards of measurement and classifications (for the category "family workers" see Wobbe and Renard, 2017).

Why did the ILO deal with severe labor conditions during the interwar period at all? Spurred on by the strong anti-slavery movement and the Congo Reform movements, the League of Nations was preparing a convention to abolish slavery (for the following, see Miers, 2003; Maul, 2007). Because the final text of the convention (passed in 1926) was only dedicated to the abolition of slavery while leaving labor conditions similar to slavery outside its scope, the League passed the legal codification of forced labor on to the ILO. Although the ILO was the authority for setting labor standards, at the same time its constitution included the "colonial clause" allowing the imperial powers to decide whether to apply these standards in the colonies or not. Therefore the ILO had no procedures in place to make standards for the metropole *and* the colony within the same categorical framework of "labor."[4] The ILO international codifications covered labor standards tailored for European industrial conditions and law. Taken all together this points to the tensions that characterized the ILO in the interwar period – the conflict between the organization's universalist aspirations and its deep roots in the colonial structure of European empires.[5]

That inherent ambivalence was voiced in the legal document adopted by the International Labour Conference during its fourteenth session in 1930 (for the following see Wobbe, 2020). Convention No. 29 prohibited forced labor that was privately carried out, while defining it as "all work or service which is exacted from any person under the menace of any penalty and for which the said person has not offered himself voluntarily" (Article 2 [1]). Accordingly, the threat of punishment and the involuntary nature of the work situation formed the distinctive features of the legal classification. The formulations "all work" and "any person" invoked a universalist understanding; however, it was then stated in the ensuing articles that some obviously coerced work practices were not deemed to be forced labor by the convention, such as compulsory military service, forced labor following conviction, so-called civil obligations, etc. The convention listed a series of labor practices excluded from the general prohibition of forced labor and which were to be found especially or exclusively in the colonies. Furthermore, it depended on the imperial powers as to whether and how they intended to implement the convention.[6] This understanding of forced labor as a problem external to European standards was mirrored in the debate on convention No. 29 during the twelfth International Labour Conference in 1929. Both proponents and opponents of the convention converged in questioning whether the convention would serve the European mission regarding "the educational elevation" of the colonial population.

Altogether the first ILO legal document defining forced labor succeeded in creating an ambivalent category, as it included a general principle of abolition and at the same time highlighted coercive labor conditions that were accepted as legitimate and should not (yet) be banned. The convention attempted to regulate labor in the colonies without delineating clear obligations for the colonial powers. Yet in doing so, the convention also created space for the introduction of a monitoring mechanism as well as for interpretations, controversies and mobilizations.

After the Second World War, the debates over a second convention on forced labor took place within changed historical constellations and societal configurations. The United Nations came into being as an institutional structure of nation-states. While the demise of the colonial overseas empires became apparent, they nevertheless attempted to renew themselves through late colonial reforms until the early 1960s (Steinmetz, 2017). At the same time, the first post-colonial states emerged and often deployed compulsory labor campaigns for the purpose of economic growth (Maul, 2009). As underscored by Samuel Moyn (2010, p. 7) human rights were "peripheral" to postwar reconstruction and, in contrast to conventional assumptions, "there was no widespread Holocaust consciousness." We further add that there was no strong link between human rights and forced labor in the UN, even though the UN Declaration of Human Rights (1948) in Article 4 in reference to the 1926 slavery convention states that "no one shall be held in slavery or servitude; slavery and the slave trade shall be prohibited in all their forms." With regard to human rights and forced labor, the ILO was "the main exception" (ibid., p. 72). Since the Philadelphia Conference of 1944, the ILO placed freedom from forced labor in a human rights frame. During the 1950s, due to the East-West conflict, however, "colonial systems of forced labor very much took a back seat to those of the socialist states of Eastern Europe and Asia" (Maul, 2007, p. 484). It is in this context that the Abolition of Forced Labour Convention (ILO No. 105) (1957) has to be placed (Kott, 2012).

Against the backdrop of the gulag system in the Soviet Union, the ILO began to consider forced labor in a broader sense and explore "new-style forced labor systems" (Maul, 2019, p. 201). Convention No. 105 forbade the use of forced labor "as a means of political coercion or education or as a punishment for holding or expressing political views or views ideologically opposed to the established political, social or economic system" (Article 1 [a]). The convention also reprehended the use of forced labor for "purposes of economic development" (Article 1 [b]), which became a problematic issue in the following years for the new post-colonial states, now being accused of committing a colonial crime par excellence (Maul, 2007, p. 489; Maul, 2009; Tiquet, 2019). Besides the reference to the UN Declaration of Human Rights in its preamble, the convention articles did not evoke or provide any kind of labor rights.

During the late twentieth century, the ILO renewed its interest in the topic and the interpretation of coerced labor underwent a fundamental shift. In the 1990s the increased undercutting of labor standards indicated the severe effects of economic globalization processes that endangered the institutionalized ILO social standards. Given this threat, the ILO decided upon a reorientation, which became manifest in its Declaration of Human Rights and Principles at Work (1998) and was motivated by the desire to create a safeguard against global economic deregulation. The Declaration comprised four core fundamental rights: the abolition of forced labor, freedom of association, the abolition of child labor and the removal of discrimination in employment and occupation.

In contrast to the interwar period, the category of forced labor had now been incorporated into the human-rights set of fundamental labor rights and "decent work" and became thus explicitly part of the universalist agenda of the organization (ILO, 1999). Beyond the legal monitoring of Convention No. 29, the Declaration (1998) set out a follow-up procedure providing new kinds of technical assistance to eradicate forced labor. In founding the Special Action Programme to Combat Forced Labour (SAP-FL) in 2002, the ILO established a dedicated political program on this topic for the very first time. Supplementary to the legal monitoring of conventions, the SAP-FL conducted its own investigations to identify and measure forced labor (ILO, 2001; Plant and O'Reilly, 2003).[7] To this end, the SAP-FL strove to identify forced labor or its absence by analyzing if 1) recruiting procedures, 2) work and life, and 3) the termination of employment were free of threat of punishment, coercion or deception (see Figure 7.1).

The measurement framework presented in Figure 7.1 is related to the ILO international classification system by referring to the international classification of occupations (ISCE-93). But this comes at a price. The central category of the employed worker does not include many practices and kinds of violence-based labor today, in particular those that are "hard to see" or those practiced in a supposedly legal and compliant framework, yet in an opaque and dubious system of sub-contractors (Barrientos, 2013). As during the interwar period, sex work,

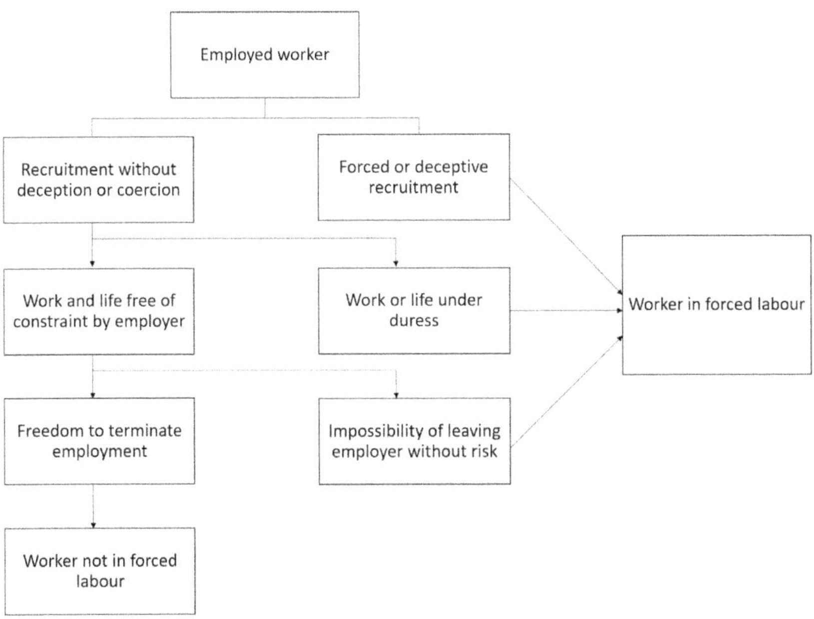

FIGURE 7.1 Schematic presentation of the measurement framework for the labor of adults after ILO, 2012, p. 26

Source: Wobbe, 2020, p. 162

(unpaid) domestic work, care work, etc. are included in neither the definition nor numbers relating to employed work, that is, what is thought of to be respectable work. The notion of the employed worker reinforces the boundary between market-related wage work on the one hand and domestic and sex work on the other.

This can be seen in the distinction made by the ILO in its survey and measurement framework between exploitation for labor purposes and sexual ones. As outlined in the ILO first global report on Stopping Forced Labour (2001), the focus on supposedly new forms of forced labor associated with trafficking, served to heighten awareness of gender issues and child labor. The growing alarm over trafficking provoked a range of responses to address women and children subjected to trafficking for the purpose of sexual exploitation. In particular "for the purpose of estimating the magnitude of forced labour, the ILO has created a simple typology with three broad forms of forced labour," namely 1) imposed by the state or armed forces, 2) forced commercial sexual exploitation, and 3) forced labor for economic exploitation (Belser, 2005, p. 3). By way of this distinction, it was possible for the ILO to highlight the fact that sexual exploitation only constitutes a part of the larger phenomenon of trafficking or forced labor; on the other hand, it connected with the assumption that sexual services cannot be counted as work.

As Frederick Cooper reminds us with regard to free and coerced labor, "the category question was itself part of the history" (2017, p. 144). In particular, it reflects the uneven path of forced labor in emerging as a category of public action. In the interwar period, the ILO was acting in a configuration full of tensions between its imperial location, its universalist ambitions and its technical logics. Thus the ILO had to balance different goals: regulating "colonial" labor (and in the near future ban all forms of forced labor) without rushing the imperial powers and (to a lesser extent) the activist movements. Since the 1990s it has altered its orientation by revising the legal codification regarding coerced labor (ILO, 2014) and by also producing statistics of social situations of forced labor and incorporating them into the internationally comparable framework of labor statistics. Forced labor has already become a category of international law and statistics. At the same time, the category refers to gainful employment and the "employed worker," thus restricting it to a specific legal meaning and socio-cultural conditions which do not match many forms of violence-based and coerced labor inside or outside Europe, for example, in the so-called informal sector (see the chapter by Schalkowski and Braig in this book).

Unsettling the Boundary Between Free and Unfree Labor

As slavery became the prototype of unfree labor and wage work the standard of free labor, the profound interrelation between the two – which have existed for centuries and continue to shape the experience of thousands of male and female workers – were rendered invisible. It was assumed that after abolition then unfree labor would disappear for once and for all, and the analytic tools at the disposal of Western sociology reinforced this assumption.

Building on the understanding of market economy as a standard of civilization, in the interwar period the wage-labor scheme was regarded as the culmination of a specifically European stage of development from which all other forms of work in other regions of the world were to be distinguished (Steinfeld, 1991, 2001; Brass and Van der Linden, 1997; Seibert, 2011).[8] The vocabulary of free labor thus referred to Western Europe and the (northern) United States in Western philosophy and economic thinking.

The liberation from slavery was a common justification for colonization, while at the same time systems of forced labor (such as "indenture") were being set up in the colonial world during the nineteenth century (Hoefte, 2018). Taken all together, "labour as service was at the root not only of serfdom and slavery, but also of the indentured, servants, and wage earners (labour being rented out as a service under a contract)" (Stanziani, 2009, p. 358). Moreover, the imposition of so-called free labor in the colonies was accompanied by financial and corporal violence and coercion during the interwar period (Seibert, 2011, 2016). In fact, economic processes in the colonies and in the metropole were constantly interlinked, the organization of work in the former supporting the organization of work in the latter (Conrad, 2014; Zimmerman, 2010; Stanziani, 2020).

For all these reasons the idea of a clear-cut distinction and linear development from compulsion to freedom is no longer plausible in today's historical research, which urges us to look for alternative concepts able to encompass the parallel existence of free and unfree labor in a spectrum of violence-based conditions, legal regulation, contracts and status (Stanziani, 2009). Arguing from a sociological perspective that is sensitive to gender and other power relations, Orlando Patterson and Xiaolin Zhuo (2018, p. 410) propose to use the concept of "servitude" in order to embrace "all known forms of exploitation or coercion, including forced labor, political imprisonment, forced marriage, sexual exploitation, and other relational or specifically degrading forms of domination not centered around labor exploitation." The authors suggest that today one should reserve the category of slavery for the extreme prototype, namely "that condition in which one or more individuals or organizations exercise complete control and possession of a person's body, labor, capabilities and movement through the overt or threatened use of violence or other forms of coercion" (ibid., p. 411).[9] Consider the use of the term *movement* instead of *freedom of movement*, which exclusively refers to the labor market of the "wage economy" (Abbott, 2005). By contrast the "complete control of movement" also encompasses the room next door. In his sociological conceptualization of slavery as "social death" and "human parasitism," Orlando Patterson (1982 [2018]) has already introduced us to the significant socio-cultural conditions of slavery. One of these conditions is the process of deracination by which enslaved persons are ripped from the context of their cultural origin and denied the social right to belong to any community ("natal alienation"). To locate slavery in current modern societies Patterson suggests employing the broader term of socio-cultural *isolation* instead of natal alienation. Violence and dishonor form further core attributes of being enslaved: "the fact that the slave is a person without honour. . . and that this dishonour parasitically aggrandized the power and honour of the slave-holder" (Patterson, 2012, p. 325). This approach allows comparisons across time and cultures from a sociological-historical perspective (see Greenland, 2019 for women's enslavement).

Concluding Remarks

In this chapter, we have argued that forced labor and its opposite free labor are historically laden categories reflecting the European postulates that soon became part of Western universalist principles. We have suggested exploring that opposition as a problematic interrelationship rather than taking it as a given – as a unique modern standard of Western advancement. As our case study on the ILO's legal definition of forced labor shows, it solidified the ideas of Europe's economic and moral superiority in the field of labor while connecting those same ideas to the European-U.S. postulates of free labor after 1945. Today the imperial and Cold War frameworks have vanished, ceding place to the abolition of forced labor and core labor rights in the globalized economy. But the integration of coerced labor into the general framework of measurement is still a challenge. Neither violence-based labor practices nor unpaid work is covered by the category of the employed worker, let alone the specific social relations of these activities (see Patterson, 2012; Patterson and Zhuo, 2018).

In recent decades a rich body of historical research has explored the variety of violence-based labor conditions and coerced labor, the scopes of dependency and their socio-cultural technologies worldwide. The mainstream of sociology has so far ignored this research, instead adhering to a restricted concept of the wage economy. After 1945 the worldwide spectrum of forms of work was assessed through the lens of modernization theory in light of the specific development of European societies and that of the United States. This view goes back to a longer history of comparison with "other cultures" to which Europe's culture was considered superior. It is this complex nexus, which we have presented here only in its barest outlines, where notions of free labor as a benchmark of Western civilization took shape (historically speaking, see, e.g., Osterhammel, 2006). Sociology has hardly reflected on this connection and therefore often implicitly starts from the premise of free labor. An engagement with this supposedly transmissible universal phenomenon that is appropriate to the developments within and outside Europe has not yet taken place; but as we have shown, there are solid and promising approaches available. So far, however, they have neither taken root in the discipline at an institutional level nor have they become integrated into its understanding or become part of the sociological imagination (see Greenland, 2019; Patterson, 1982 [2018], 1991, 2012, 2017; Steinmetz, 2013, 2017).

Hence we propose to develop a reflexive perspective to unsettle forced labor and its opposite free labor. This involves two epistemological "breaks," namely with everyday assumptions about work and with the dominant sociological presumptions (Steinmetz, 2021). By so doing, we should hope to develop a fresh and more nuanced view of the real practices and meanings of different kinds of labor.

The issue is not only to properly address violence at work in sociological terms. In rethinking its terminology and extending its scope of research, sociology in general and the sociology of work in particular might also question the normative implications of the equation of "work" with "voluntary wage work" for the invisibilization of power relations and inequalities in past and contemporary labor practices.

Notes

"DFG-Project "Forced Labor as a Shifting Global Category: Classification, Comparison and Meanings of Work in the International Labour Organization (ILO), 1919–2017" (FU Berlin and Universität Potsdam)."

1 We use the term *belief* to describe a cultural pattern of behavioral expectation.

2 www.kwa-ekd.de/wp-content/uploads/2020/05/PM-KWA-Moderne-Sklaverei.pdf.

3 In the dual economy of Greece this interrelationship was, on the one hand, based on slave labor in the wine and olive-growing and craft-commercial sectors and, on the other hand, on the non-slave labor of the small free farmer.

4 By metropole we mean the imperial home country, which was thought of as a strictly separated realm from the colonial territories following a "rule of difference" (see Steinmetz, 2014 for a sociology of empire; see also Stoler and Cooper, 1997).

5 On imperialism and the League of Nations, see Pedersen, 2015.

6 See Article 26, ILO Convention, No. 29 (1930) that leaves it up to the member states to decide whether to apply it in the dependent territories or not.

7 During the interwar the ILO fully relied on the reports of the member states.

8 Russia has long served as one of these boundary regions. Stanziani convincingly reverses the "Russian mirror" by highlighting the continuities between labor experiences and institutions in Russia and Western Europe in the eighteenth and early nineteenth centuries. He also points to the many theories and models that circulated between Russian elites and Western European philosophers; see, for example, the impact on Bentham's panopticon (Stanziani, 2020, p. 25ff).

9 Patterson and Zhuo (2018) thereby explicitly distance themselves from the tendency in contemporary campaigns to conflate all forms of exploitation with "modern slavery" in order to attract public and media attention – a tendency that is also observable in the ILO's latest global estimates in which forced labor and forced marriage are lumped together under the umbrella term "modern slavery" (2017).

References

Abbott, A. (2005) 'Sociology of Work and Occupations', *Annual Review Sociology*, 19, pp. 187–209.

Anderson, B. (2000) *Doing the Dirty Work: The Global Politics of Domestic Labour*. London: Zed Books.

Barenberg, A. (2017) 'Forced Labor in Nazi Germany and the Stalinist Soviet Union', in Eltis, D., Engerman, S.L., Drescher, S. and Richardson, D. (eds.) *The Cambridge World History of Slavery*, Vol. 4. Cambridge: Cambridge University Press, pp. 633–654.

Barrientos, S. (2013) '"Labour Chains": Analysing the Role of Labour Contractors in Global Production Networks', *The Journal of Development Studies*, 49(8), pp. 1058–1071.

Belser, P. (2005) 'Forced Labour and Human Trafficking: Estimating the Profits', Declaration Working Paper No. 42. Geneva: International Labour Office.

Brass, T. and van der Linden, M. (eds.) (1997) *Free and Unfree Labour: The Debate Continues*. Bern: Peter Lang Academic Publishers.

Conrad, S. (2014) 'Internal Colonialism in Germany: Cultural Wars, Germanification of the Soil, and the Global Market Imaginary', in Naranch, B. and Eley, G. (eds.) *German Colonialism in a Global Age*. Duke: Duke University Press, pp. 246–264.

Cooper, F. (2000) 'Conditions Analogues to Slavery', in Cooper, F., Holt, T.C. and Scott, R. (eds.) *Beyond Slavery*. Chapel Hill, NC: University of North Carolina Press, pp. 107–149.

Cooper, F. (2017) 'From Enslavement to Precarity? The Labour Question in African History', in Adebanwi, W. (ed.) *The Political Economy of Everyday Life in Africa: Beyond the Margins*. Woodbridge and Suffolk: James Currey, pp. 135–156.

Drescher, S. (2017) 'European Antislavery: From Empires of Slavery to Global Prohibition', in Eltis, D., Engerman, S.L., Drescher, S. and Richardson, D. (eds.) *The Cambridge World History of Slavery*, Vol. 4. Cambridge: Cambridge University Press, pp. 373–398.

Engerman, S. (ed.) (1999) *Terms of Labor: Slavery, Serfdom and Free Labor*. Stanford, CA: Stanford University Press.

Greenland, F. (2019) 'Long-Range Continuities in Comparative and Historical Sociology: The Case of Parasitism and Women's Enslavement', *Theory and Society*, 48, pp. 883–902.

Herbert, U. (1999 [1985]) *Fremdarbeiter. Politik und Praxis des "Ausländer-Einsatzes" in der Kriegswirtschaft des Dritten Reiches*. Bonn: Dietz.

Hoefte, R. (2018) 'Indentured Labor', in Hofmeester, K. and Van der Linden, M. (eds.) *Handbook Global History of Work*. Berlin: De Gruyter Oldenbourg, pp. 363–376.

ILO (1930) *Convention Concerning Forced or Compulsory Labour (No. 29) Adopted at the 14th ILC Session on 28 June 1930 in Geneva*. Geneva: International Labour Office.

ILO (1957) *Convention Concerning the Abolition of Forced Labour (No. 105) Adopted at the 40th ILC Session on 25 June 1957 in Geneva*. Geneva: International Labour Office.

ILO (1998 [2010]) *Declaration on Fundamental Principles and Rights at Work and Its Follow-Up, Adopted at the 86th ILC session on 18 June 1998 in Geneva (Annex revised 15 June 2010)*. Geneva: International Labour Office.

ILO (1999) *Decent Work: Report of the Director-General, International Labour Conference, 87th Session*. Geneva: International Labour Office.

ILO (2001) *Stopping Forced Labour: Global Report Under the Follow-Up to the ILO Declaration on Fundamental Principles and Rights at Work, International Labour Conference Report I(B) 89th Session*. Geneva: International Labour Office.

ILO (2012) *Hard to See, Harder to Count: Survey Guidelines to Estimate Forced Labour of Adults and Children*, 2nd ed. Geneva: International Labour Office (SAP-Forced Labour).

ILO (2014) *Forced Labour (Supplementary Measures) Recommendation (No. 203) Adopted at the 103rd ILC Session on 11 June 2014 in Geneva*. Geneva: International Labour Office.

ILO (2017) *Global Estimates of Modern Slavery: Forced Labour and Forced Marriage*. Geneva: International Labour Office.

Kott, S. (2012) 'The Forced Labor Issue between Human and Social Rights, 1947–1957', *Humanity*, 3(3), pp. 321–335.

Maul, D. (2007) 'The International Labour Organization and the Struggle against Forced Labour from 1919 to the Present', *Labor History*, 48(4), pp. 477–500.

Maul, D. (2009) '"Help Them Move the ILO Way": The International Labor Organization and the Modernization Discourse in the Era of Decolonization and the Cold War', *Diplomatic History*, 33(3), pp. 387–404.

Maul, D. (2019) *The International Labour Organization: 100 Years of Global Social Policy*. Berlin: De Gruyter Oldenbourg.

Miers, S. (2003) *Slavery in the Twentieth Century: The Evolution of a Global Problem*. Walnut Creek, CA: AltaMira.

Moyn, S. (2010) *The Last Utopia: Human Rights in History*. Cambridge, MA and London: The Belknap Press of Harvard University Press.

Osterhammel, J. (2006) *Europe, the "West," and the Civilizing Mission*. London: German Historical Institute London Annual Lectures.

Patterson, O. (1982 [2018]) *Slavery and Social Death: A Comparative Study, With a New Preface*. Cambridge, MA: Harvard University Press.

Patterson, O. (1991) *Freedom. Volume I: Freedom in the Making of Western Culture*. New York: BasicBooks.

Patterson, O. (2012) 'Trafficking, Gender and Slavery: Past and Present', in Allain, J. (ed.) *The Legal Understanding of Slavery: From the Historical to the Contemporary*. Oxford: Oxford University Press, pp. 322–359.

Patterson, O. (2017) 'Revisiting Slavery, Property, and Social Death', in Bodel, J. and Scheidel, W. (eds.) *On Human Bondage: After Slavery and Social Death*. Chichester: Wiley Blackwell, pp. 265–296.

Patterson, O. and Zhuo, X. (2018) 'Modern Trafficking, Slavery and Other Forms of Servitude', *Annual Review of Sociology*, 44, pp. 407–439.

Pedersen, S. (2015) *The Guardians: The League of Nations and the Crisis of Empire*. Oxford: Oxford University Press.

Petersson, N. (2005) 'Markt, Zivilisierungsmission und Imperialismus', in Barth, B. and Osterhammel, J. (eds.) *Zivilisierungsmissionen. Imperiale Weltverbesserung seit dem 18. Jahrhundert*. Constance: UVK Verlag, pp. 33–54.

Plant, R. and O'Reilly, C. (2003) 'Perspectives: The ILO Special Action Programme to Combat Forced Labour', *International Labour Review*, 142(1), pp. 73–85.

Rupprecht, A. (2014) 'From Slavery to Indenture: Scripts for Slavery's Endings', in Hall, C., Draper, N. and McClelland, K. (eds.) *Emancipation and the Remaking of the British Imperial World*. Manchester: Manchester University Press, pp. 77–97.

Seibert, J. (2011) 'More Continuity Than Change? New Forms of Unfree Labor in the Belgian Congo, 1908–1930', in van der Linden, M. (ed.) *Humanitarian Intervention and Changing Labor Relations*. Leiden: Brill, pp. 369–386.

Seibert, J. (2016) *In die globale Wirtschaft gezwungen: Arbeit und Kapitalismus im Kongo (1885–1960)*. Frankfurt am Main: Campus.

Stanziani, A. (2009) 'Labour Institutions in a Global Perspective, From the Seventeenth to the Twentieth Century', *International Review of Social History*, 54(3), pp. 351–358.

Stanziani, A. (2020) *Les métamorphoses du travail contraint. Une histoire globale XVIIIe-XIXe siècles*. Paris: Presses de la FNSP.

Steinfeld, R.J. (1991) *The Invention of Free Labor: The Employment Relation in English and American Law and Culture, 1350–1870*. Chapel Hill, NC: University of North Carolina Press.

Steinfeld, R.J. (2001) *Coercion, Contract and Free Labor in the Nineteenth Century*. Cambridge: Cambridge University Press.

Steinmetz, G. (2013) *Sociology and Empire: The Imperial Entanglements of a Discipline*. Durham, NC: Duke University Press.

Steinmetz, G. (2014) 'The Sociology of Empires, Colonies, and Postcolonialism', *Annual Review of Sociology*, 40, pp. 77–103.

Steinmetz, G. (2017) 'Sociology and Colonialism in the British and French Empires, 1940s – 1960s', *Journal of Modern History*, 89(3), pp. 601–648.

Steinmetz, G. (2021) 'Vergleichende Soziologie, kritischer Realismus und Reflexivität', in Heintz, B. and Wobbe, T. (eds.) *Soziale Praktiken des Beobachtens. Vergleichen, Bewerten, Kategorisiere und Quantifizieren, Kölner Zeitschrift für Soziologie und Sozialpsychologie* (Sonderheft 73). Wiesbaden: Springer, pp. 49–74.

Stoler, A.L. and Cooper, F. (1997) 'Between Metropole and Colony: Rethinking a Research Agenda', in Cooper, F. and Stoler, A.L. (eds.) *Tensions of Empire: Colonial Cultures in a Bourgeois World*. Berkeley, CA: Oxford University Press, pp. 1–56.

Tiquet, R. (2019) *Travail forcé et mobilisation de la main-d'œuvre au Sénégal. Années 1920–1960*. Rennes: Presses Universitaires de Rennes.

United Nations (1948) *Universal Declaration of Human Rights, Adopted by the United Nations General Assembly on 10 December 1948 in Paris*. Paris: United Nations.

Wagner, I. (2015) 'EU Posted Work and Transnational Action in the German Meat Industry', *Transfer, European Review of Labour and Research*, 21(2), pp. 201–213.

Wobbe, T. (2020) '"Hard to See, Harder to Count". Klassifizierung und Vergleichbarkeit der globalen Kategorie "Zwangsarbeit" in der International Labour Organization während der 1920er und 2000er Jahre', in Bennani, H., Bühler, M., Cramer, S. and Glauser, A. (eds.) *Beobachtung und Vergleich. Soziologische Untersuchungen zur Weltgesellschaft*. Frankfurt am Main: Campus, pp. 141–173.

Wobbe, T. and Renard, L. (2017) 'The Category of "Family Workers" in International Labour Organization Statistics (1930s–1980s): A Contribution to the Study of Globalized Gendered Boundaries Between Household and Market', *Journal of Global History*, 12, pp. 340–360.

Wobbe, T. and Renard, L. (2019) 'Der Deutungswandel der Zwangsarbeit in der International Labour Organization (ILO)', in Burzan, N. (ed.) *Komplexe Dynamiken globaler und lokaler Entwicklungen. Verhandlungen des 39. Kongresses der Deutschen Gesellschaft für Soziologie in Göttingen 2018*. https://publikationen.soziologie.de/index.php/kongressband_2018/issue/view/33

Zimmerman, A. (2010) *Alabama in Africa. Booker T. Washington, the German Empire, and the Globalization of the New South*. Princeton, NJ: Princeton University Press.

8

INFORMAL WORK

A Relational Category

Nicola Schalkowski and Marianne Braig

Introduction

The majority of work activities globally do not fit into the construct of a "standard labor relation"; they are described with various terms such as unregulated, casual, marginalized, precarious, invisible, irregular, illegal, unregistered, non-standard, hidden, insecure, or they are assigned to a "petty commerce," "gray labor market" or "shadow economy" (e.g., see Weck-Hannemann, 1984). Legally unprotected, low-paid, temporary-employment relationships increased significantly as a result of neoliberalism implemented by state legislation and progressing de-industrialization and decentralization (Thomas 2002, p. 10). Though in most regions of the world only a small proportion of the population ever pursued formalized wage labor. A category institutionalized globally by the International Labour Organization (ILO) that attempts to capture these activities is *informal work*.

In this chapter, we show how in the 1970s there emerged the problem of labor activities that bear little resemblance to modern urban wage labor (usually understood as urban-industrial wage labor). Modernization theory perceived it as a phenomenon of transition from a traditional to a modern society; for the ILO the problem was a pragmatic one of how to operationally categorize this phenomenon. Both approaches regard informal labor as a residual category rather than a relational one. The only studies that allow us to look at these relations and (inter)dependencies are those sociological and ethnological works on labor relations in Latin America that have emerged in critical engagement with the various modernization theories (including Marxist ones) and in relation to dependency theories. We will reconstruct different debates in relation to informal activities, show their limits and finally seek to demonstrate their persistence and adaptability by focusing on the (inter)dependencies of these activities.

DOI: 10.4324/9781003341321-11

The category of *informal work* is used as a residual category, which means it only describes activities that do not fit the definition of formal work which is embodied in social and labor laws as well as social and economic norms and practices. The legally codified and socially idealized norm of formal work produces the category of informal work as the "other" or the "rest" and serves as a reference point for it. Contextualizing the categorial production of informality situates this dichotomous way of thinking both historically and spatially and aims to dismantle categories of work that are generally taken for granted.

In the second section, we focus on the circumstances surrounding the emergence and conceptualization of the category of *informal work* at the ILO, which institutionalized it on a global scale. The categorization process of *informal work* was bound up with its early conceptualizations in the context of developmental policies, empirical research and employment programs directed at the so-called Third World. The starting point was the attempt to define and measure urban unemployment. We discuss the category's boundaries and blind spots by pointing to the non-coverage of many labor practices (such as paid labor in households or subsistence economy and other labor activities in agriculture and the service sector). In the third section, we reconstruct the parallel but independent sociological debate as it took place in the context of modernization-development theories and the critique by dependency theories, especially in Latin America. This second section therefore historically reconstructs how the ILO category originated and how it has undergone transformations, while the third section examines the theoretical foundations of this concept in (Western) sociology, its colonial premises, and how these foundations and premises have been challenged by Latin American researchers in recent decades. In the fourth and final section, we conclude with a necessary decentration of the sociological gaze and self-reflexivity of the sociology of labor in relation to its Eurocentrism.

Conceptualization of an Operational Category at the ILO

Informality has become an institutional global category, above all through its conceptualization by the ILO. Prior to defining a global statistical category in 1993, there were attempts to conceptualize empirically found income-generating activities which could not be grasped by existing economic categories of work. In order to standardize the reporting practices of government agencies, the ILO's aim was to find an operational category for developmental employment policies in the "Global South." Differing from economists and social scientists, the ILO's interest lay in evaluating and comparing changes in the labor market (Benanav, 2019, p. 108). Reconstructing the process that led to the category of informal work, we can speak of a double narrowing with regard to the ILO's attempt to overcome its self-created dilemma as it sought to distinctly categorize and operationalize a vast variety of relational economic activities. On the one hand, the ILO first constricted the concept of informality to only a small part of the economy: urban micro-enterprises. On the other hand, it disregarded interdependencies by reducing the empirical entanglements and overlapping forms of economic activities.

Conceptualization Based on Diverse Empirical Phenomena in "Developing Countries"

The discourse on informal work in the ILO first developed out of empirical research in the 1970s on employment in cities of so-called developing countries (see Hart, 1973; ILO, 1972). Due to its unsuccessful efforts to operationalize unemployment as a global standard for measuring socio-economic development, the ILO needed to construct another concept (Benanav, 2019, p. 117). Here it is important for our case to discuss the concept of underemployment, which is derived from the term "disguised unemployment."[1] In 1957 the ILO defined underemployment as "the difference between the actual employment and the theoretical full employment of the labor force" (ILO 1957, p. 15) in referring to laborers who wanted to work more hours or referring to low levels of productivity. Wasting human capital for the market economy by not fully exhausting the potential productivity of the labor force was viewed as hindering capitalist development. In order to establish a standardized conceptual and measurement tool, the ILO intended to apply the criteria of underemployment to "underdeveloped countries" (ibid., p. 11). Within the development paradigm, significant parts of the population in these countries were identified as a potential labor force and therefore became the target of employment programs such as the World Employment Programme (WEP).[2] This was the case especially for rural communities and women who were classified as non-working housewives.[3] In these target communities, however, monetized gainful employment was often not the main reference point against which (economic) activities could be measured.[4] As Benanav (2019, p. 108) puts it:

> the recurrent problem that the ILO faced was that real divisions in lived experience – between labour-force participation and non-participation, as well as between the employed and the unemployed – were lacking in economies where only a minority of economic life was organized by means of wage-labour.

Moreover, unemployment was found not to be the most pressing labor-policy issue; instead, the phenomenon of "working poor" with low productivity was detected (ILO, 1972, p. 9; 1991, p. 3). The empirical reality of "the existence of an economic sector that was obscure to labour-force statistics" (Benanav, 2019, p. 108) left ILO economists and statisticians to meet the challenge of developing a conceptual tool that would capture activities outside of a "modern" formalized sector in urban areas, such as persons working as street vendors or producing goods as home workers or small business owners. Sociologists like Keith Hart (1973) coined the term "informal sector," which was readily seized upon by development economists. Hart drew a dualistic distinction in the urban labor force between wage-employed workers ("formal") and small-scale self-employed workers ("informal") (Hart, 1973; see Contreras, 2019, p. 15). Derived from empirically observed phenomena, Hart's descriptive explanation was not backed by any theoretical body of social analysis (see Salas, 2006, p. 194). The concept gained wider international recognition through the ILO's report on employment missions in Kenya, published in 1972 (ILO, 1972).[5] The much-cited ILO report should be understood in the context of an overall development-policy strategy; the urban informal sector is described as "a sector of thriving economic activity and a source of Kenya's future wealth" (ILO, 1972, p. 5). Work practices in rural areas were neglected in debates around the informal sector as the concept was only discussed concerning urban articulations of working people who were not employed in the formal sector but could not be classified as unemployed either. The case of rural (indigenous) communities showed that activities outside the realm of an (urban) capitalist economic logic – for example, community tasks, neighborhood aids, collective cultivation of fields – presented a challenge for economists because these activities could hardly be grasped with Western concepts of wage employment.

Especially the ILO's Regional Employment Program for Latin America and the Caribbean (PREALC) with its structuralist studies on employment of the urban working class, helped to establish and disseminate the term "informal sector." Furthermore, it became apparent that a diversification of definitions had emerged, resulting in a heterogeneous subsumption of activities and production forms under the concept.[6] Contradictions arose concerning the analysis of underlying causes and the evaluation of informal working conditions. In a neoliberal view, small business activity was framed as a positive articulation of emerging entrepreneurship without state intervention (de Soto, 1986). The same activities were described in remedial programs as survival strategies of poor people who are stranded in the informal sector as a last resort (ILO, 1991, p. 13).[7] So the linkages between the formal and the informal within one economic system were insufficiently considered. Also, not taken into account was the relation between work and home and the constructed distinction between production and reproduction. The case of informal activities performed mostly by women as home-based workers producing goods at home for subcontractors or their own use was invisibilized (Prügl, 1996).

Generating employment was an important policy objective, which also influenced the activities of international development organizations. The assumption that informality would remain temporary as well as spatially limited and would decline with increasing "modernization," turned out to be misguided (see Mayer-Ahuja, 2017, p. 265). The active policies of "informalization" (Breman and van der Linden, 2014, p. 927) in the name of flexibilization and global competitiveness reproduced and further established an economic system which profited and depended on the availability of a low-cost, unprotected and flexible workforce. An increasing number of people who used to have secure employment in the formal sector, especially in industry and public services, were compelled to take on informal alternatives in order to generate income.

Since under these conditions employment in the informal sector comprised a growing part of the workforce, it was considered necessary to expand the statistical category system and systematically operationalize and classify these activities in order to formulate labor policies (ILO, 1987).

Conceptualization on the Basis of Economic Units

The conceptualization of informality consistently reproduced the assumption of two separable spheres: "we were still locked into the modern-tradition and urban-rural modes of dualistic thinking, we had just changed the terminology slightly to include formal-informal" (Bangasser, 2000, p. 16).[8] By examining the discussion about the narrowing of the statistical category, it is possible to recognize the demarcations and conceptions of informality as well as the underlying concepts of work.

An international statistical definition of the informal sector in terms of a categorization according to economic models was established in 1993 at the International Conference of Labour Statisticians (ICLS)[9] which "defined the informal sector as a group of production units comprised of unincorporated enterprises owned by households, including informal own-account enterprises and enterprises of informal employers (typically small and non-registered enterprises)" (ILO, 2016).[10] This definition was based on an enterprise approach, not looking at forms of labor but at characteristics of enterprises. Such an economic unit-based ILO definition produces observation and measurement tools that are blind to the complex empirical reality of labor relations and interdependencies between activities and between forms of production. A paradigmatic example is the group of domestic workers. In the debate on the conceptualization and measurement of the informal sector, it has been argued, among other things, that individuals working in the domestic sector (for private households) cannot be classified under the analytic construct of the "productive unit" (see Salas, 2006, p. 201) and that from an empirical standpoint the large proportion of unskilled migrant women in paid domestic work would cause a serious conceptual distortion of the informal sector (Mezzera, 1989, p. 52). As a solution to the question of the statistical treatment of paid domestic workers, the 15th ICLS included the recommendation to optionally include or exclude this group "depending upon national circumstances and the intended uses of the statistics" (Hussmanns and Mehran, 2001, p. 2). This resulted in hardly comparable data for women due to differing national survey practices (ibid., p. 4).[11] Also excluded from the 1993 statistical category were agricultural activities "for practical reasons" (ILO, 1993, Resolution Paragraph 16; see Hussmanns, 2004, p. 9).

As a consequence, blind spots produced by the narrow categorization – seeing informality only as a matter of urban enterprises – resulted in large residuals within censuses as well as calculations on total national income. Criticisms from different scholars along with internal debates and empirical evidence, for example, on informal employment arrangements within the formal sector, led to a shift in the ILO's conceptualization. The 17th ICLS in 2003 broadened the concept of the informal sector, adopting the term of an informal economy including economic activities by workers (ILO, 2003).[12] The definitional boundary separating formal from informal workers was based on legal criteria as follows:

> Employees are considered to have informal jobs if their employment relationship is, in law or in practice, not subject to national labour legislation, income taxation, social protection or entitlement to certain employment benefits.
>
> *(ILO, 2003)*

The shortcomings of definitions based on legal criteria referring to non-compliance with institutional legislations are due to differing sectorial or national configurations. Since the framework of reference – such as labor-law or social-security coverage – underlies recurring reconfigurations, the pool of economic activities subsumable as "informal" increases or decreases.

The conceptual framework as seen in Table 8.1 is an attempt to supplement the enterprise-based concept with a job-based concept. It encompasses three categories: informal employment, employment in the informal sector and informal employment outside the informal sector.

The applicability of this complex framework in diverse national contexts and its practicality for an implementation in national labor statistics continues to be questioned. Sociological as well as economic scholars such as Carlos Salas (2006, p. 214) speak of "conceptual anarchy," pointing to the ambiguous definition and use of the concept. In view of increasing qualitative as well as quantitative data, blurred lines between and entanglements of the static dualistic concepts become apparent (see Meagher, 2013, p. 4). This also concerns the lines drawn between legality and illegality, the latter being used as a synonym for informality by scholars like Hernando de Soto (1989). Critics of this dichotomous assumption (including the ILO)[13] point to the wide range of economic activities which are empirically found on a spectrum between illegal and legal and which are not exclusively found in the informal sector (see Thomas, 2002, p. 5; Parra, 2013, p. 214).

We have now reconstructed the ILO's self-created dilemma arising from the attempt to define unemployment as an internationally standardized category. After unsuccessfully seeking to implement the concept of underemployment, this challenge led to the concept of informal work as a deficient deviation of

TABLE 8.1 Conceptual framework for informal employment[a] (17th ICLS guidelines)

Production units by type	*Jobs by status in employment*								
	Own-account workers		*Employers*		*Contributing family workers*	*Employees*		*Members of producers' cooperatives*	
	Informal	*Formal*	*Informal*	*Formal*	*Informal*	*Informal*	*Formal*	*Informal*	*Formal*
Formal sector enterprises					1	2			
Informal sector enterprises[b]	3		4		5	6	7	8	
Households[c]	9					10			

Notes

(a) Cells shaded in dark grey refer to jobs, which by definition do not exist in the type of production unit in question. Cells shaded in light grey refer to formal jobs. Unshaded cells represent the various types of informal jobs

(b) As defined by the 15th ICLS resolution (excluding households employing paid domestic workers).

(c) Households producing goods exclusively for their own final use and households employing paid domestic workers

Informal employment: Cells 1 to 6 and 8 to 10.

Employment in the informal sector: Cells 3 to 8.

Informal employment outside the informal sector: Cells 1, 2, 9 and 10.

(From International Labour Organization, 2013, p. 37.)

"modern standard employment." As a statistical category, it was defined by ILO statisticians in 1993 and adjusted in 2003 (ILO, 1993, 2003). Blind spots were produced by the attempt to make visible income-generating activities which could not be encompassed by existing economic categories of work. Entanglements and diverse forms of employment relationships and production units are disregarded, as is feminized and rural labor, thus we speak of a double narrowing process.

In the following section, we situate the concept of informal work historically within the modernization paradigm of the mid-twentieth century which influenced dual-economy approaches. We will also elaborate on the disparate developmental debates on centers of urban poverty at the theoretical, sociological and political-economic levels, which have made little reference to each other.

Historical Embedding: Modernization Paradigm and Dualistic Approaches

Sociological and economic concepts of informal work are historically embedded in discourses of modernization as well as dual-economy models drawing from development theories. Within debates on modernization, the emergence of an informal sector is explained as a process of social change within industrialized societies, moving from one stage of development to another. Dual-economy approaches draw on these thoughts by establishing a dualistic concept of two separate economies – formal and informal – while concentrating on relationship constellations between state, household and market (see Teichert, 2000, p. 6). By contrast, other scholars in the field of dependency theories influenced by Marxism have emphasized interdependencies and point to the correlations between economic activities and social exclusion. In order to historically trace the influential theoretical parameters and explanatory approaches, we relate these separate discussions to each other in the context of conceptualizing informal work.

Sociological Debates: From Modernization Theory

Modernization theory approaches construct a dualistic picture of societies that can be classified as "developed" or, in relation to the latter, as in the process of modernization. The approach to the phenomenon called informality is that of a deviation from the norm, meaning that it is constructed in relation to "formality." From the construction of free wage labor, as a formalized labor relation, other labor relations are defined as deficient or illegal. As a default serves the ideal of a "standard labor relation" of the male worker (especially early industrial workers). This idea of a formal "standard employment" should be treated with critical caution, as argued by Jan Breman and Marcel van der Linden (2014, p. 920):

> The real norm or standard in global capitalism is insecurity, informality or precariousness, and the Standard Employment Relationship is an historical phenomenon, which had a deep impact in a limited part of the world for a relatively short period of time.

What is considered as "normal work" is based on notions of productivity and economic behavior as well as on the political interests of social actors and bound to a specific temporal-spatial context.[14] Therefore it is not a universally fixed reference point. Nevertheless, Nicole Mayer-Ahuja (2017, p. 276) argues that after the Second World War there were processes of state-enforced formalization of work relations that took place in different regions of the world through the creation of normative standards. The establishment of formal work and related structures of social security made it possible to observe and distinguish informality from formality (ibid., p. 279). The engagement of a large part of the population in informal work relationships was equated with an economic and social system that was not yet "advanced" but undergoing necessary structural economic and social changes to attain higher stages of development and political stability.

This assumption about development status is largely based on the three-sector theory, which was prominent in the mid-twentieth century (see Clark, 1957; Fourastié, 1954).[15] The emergence of an informal sector outside the formal urban economy was assumed to be a temporary phenomenon. As modernization processes progress, the formal sector would grow and create formal employment opportunities for a larger group of people, thereby absorbing informal labor (ILO, 1988, p. 27). This view of labor-market activities in "developing countries" needs to be deconstructed as a continuity of racialized classification patterns that structured the colonial labor regimes in the name of a "Civilisation Mission" in the twentieth century (Cooper, 2019). Following a Western-European ideal of "free" formalized labor, the imperial powers legitimized the use of forced labor in the colonies by pointing out the need to "educate for work" (see the chapter authored by Renard and Wobbe in this book). This period was understood as a phase of transition leading to the imposition of a "free" labor market (see Rossi, 2017).

. . . To (Inter)Dependencies

In the historical-spatial analysis of the concept of informality, the particular importance of sociological (as well as anthropological) empirical research in urban areas of Latin America should be pointed out (see Castells, 1973; Roy and Alsayyad, 2004). In this context of research in the 1960s and 1970s, scholars reflected on the empirical reality of people who migrated from rural to urban areas and lived in poor housing and working conditions on the periphery of urban societies (see Weinmann and Burchardt, 2013, p. 113). In light of a growing service sector without widely established industrial production, a linear progress – as predicted by modernization theory – could not be observed in Latin American cities. In order to work with suitable concepts and understand the situation of this group of people and their socio-economic position within the urban social order, the concept of "marginalized" persons was generated (Nun, 1971). This scientific debate in Latin America was framed by the thought of the *dependistas* who highlighted historical modes of dependency between the so-called core and the periphery (see Cardoso and Faletto, 1969; Frank, 1970). In contrast to modernization theory, dependency theory points out the persistence of unequal power relations not only in a global context but in a local one. The sociologist José Nun (1971) criticized the Marxist concept of an *industrielle Reservearmee* (industrial reserve army) and a *Lumpenproletariat*, which created the dichotomy of productive and unproductive labor. Nun linked dependency theory to work, developing the concept of "masa marginal" (marginal mass) (1971). This approach focuses on the entanglement of capitalistic processes between peripheries and centers by analyzing the dependencies between different forms of labor. The driving forces of peripheralization are (post)colonialism and long-lasting inequalities (not only socio-economic inequality but also related to gender, race and ethnicity). Looking at the activities of people working beyond the ideal of urban wage labor, Latin American sociologists and anthropologists showed in the 1970s how modern capitalism interrelates different forms of labor in different places throughout the world.

In the 1980s, in the context of debt crisis and economic reforms devised by the Washington Consensus, neoliberal experts saw the interventionist state in Latin America as a causative factor in the growing informal sector. Legislation was seen as responsible for restricting access to the formal labor market, and tax regulation was perceived as limiting entrepreneurship. The Peruvian legalist Hernando de Soto, affiliated with a neoliberal development paradigm, conceptualized the informal sector in terms of legal markers. He characterized informal labor as being unlawful in character by stating that workers chose informal employment based on a rational choice to avoid taxes (De Soto, 1986; see Castells, 1973). In the debates about deregulation, the distinction between formal and informal labor was increasingly overlapped by legal norms that went beyond mere labor laws. The dichotomy of legal and illegal economic activities became ever more relevant to the analysis of informal work relations. The so-called informal sector is not only growing because of a globalizing economy in persistent need of low-cost, unprotected, flexible labor but because of an increasingly rigid normative framework. The illegalizing and penalizing of certain work practices (e.g., the production and sale of pirated goods) and services increases the number of workers laboring outside the regulatory sphere. Moreover, stricter requirements regarding international labor migration minimize the opportunities for migrants to take on formally registered employment. These developments of the increasing number of people entering into complex working relationships are strongly embedded in modern global capitalism (Mathews et al., 2012) without quite fitting into the configuration of free labor relations.

Concepts of informality in spheres of work are still predominantly used to describe worlds of work in the "Global South." This connotation of the concept can be understood by looking at its socio-historical construction within the development paradigm. To conceptualize similar work relations and conditions in the "Global North" social scientists coined the term "precarious work" (Bourdieu, 1998; Dörre, 2006; Mayer Ahuja, 2017). In its guidelines on measuring informality the ILO demonstrates the particularistic application of the category, distinguishing between "developing" and "developed" countries even though the empirically observed forms of labor relations are comparable (ILO, 2013, p. 4):

> In developed countries an increasing share of the labour force works under part-time, temporary work and own-account employment arrangements that offer limited benefits or social protection. Many though not all people working under such arrangements in developing countries would most likely be identified as having informal jobs.

. . . To Focusing on Working People in a Global Context

In the debates we have traced so far the people who secure their living in these activities hardly have a voice. Ethnological studies in Latin America highlighted very early on the importance of different informal activities and their relation to formal ones (Lomnitz, 1975). In recent years the entanglement of different labor relations in global capitalism has been highlighted (Mathews et al., 2012). Above all, the working and living conditions of these people have been given greater attention and they themselves have had a say (Alba and Braig, 2022). Various interdependencies have become apparent: informal activities do not exist for themselves, they are related to domestic work and care activities, hence a large number of women with children can be found among street vendors or helping family members in small enterprises, combining childcare and gainful employment (Mezzadri, 2020). Moreover, informal work within the family is often combined with formal wage labor and, finally, formal work is dependent on macro processes. Globalized and deregulated markets, for many, led to a loss of formal employment. At the same time, cheap imported goods (e.g., from Chinese producers) afforded the opportunity to engage in street vending. Children, young people, mothers, former sex-workers, released prisoners as well as local and international migrants find easier access to street vending (or home-based manufacturing) than to other gainful-employment sectors. Yet they are increasingly confronted with criminalization processes. The goods they sell are considered illegal because no sales tax is paid on them, because they are pirated and property rights are violated, or because they vend their products in public places without permission. More and more working people are fighting not only for the right to work but for the right to have a space to work and thus preserve their dignity against their criminalization.

Conclusion: Decentralizing the Sociology of Work

Informal work is a relational category that is defined by what it is not (Mayer-Ahuja, 2017, p. 270) but it contains more than that. The approach to the phenomenon called "informality" is an abstraction from a norm. In this way, it becomes difficult to see beyond the norm – which itself is socially constructed. An epistemological approach is needed to reconstruct the ambiguity of labor categories and their context of emergence as well as continuities and ruptures in their definition and interpretation. Historical and cultural sociologist Orlando Patterson (2019) warns against the "dangers of presentism" concerning sociological analysis. Presentism is the de-historicization of social phenomena which creates a risk of temporal and regional particularism – that is, losing sight of the broader socio-historical embeddedness of categorization processes. Based on the construction of free wage labor as a legally formalized labor relation, other labor relations are defined as deficient or illegal. Informal work was thus constructed as a deviation from the Western norm of an ideologized formal employment relationship (see Eckert, 2017, p. 303) and has historically been applied primarily to worlds of work in the "Global South" (Mayer-Ahuja, 2017, p. 265). Mostly unaddressed remain the underlying power relations, market dependencies and unequal access to resources not only at the national level but in the context of the capitalist global economy. The case of the category of informal work shows how specific spatial-temporal concepts of employment and economy shape internationally institutionalized interpretive frameworks and measurement tools. Using the benchmark of wage labor in capitalist economies to evaluate development progress perforce excluded a majority of the activities in not only those communities that had different economic structures but in terms of reproductive labor as well.

What shapes informality is not only determined by legislation along with social and economic practices but by categorization and statistical definition, which are connected with normative and legal concepts of labor. The expansion and diversification of work activities that occur outside of contexts defined by (labor) law, tax regulation, the regulation of places to work or by (re)defining (il)legal activities all go to show that the dichotomous notion of two distinct sectors – formal and informal – still exists in the legal framework but is not to be found in empirical reality. Rather, the empirical reality is characterized by relational entanglements and nuances that need to be studied. There is a further need for continued empirical research so as to understand the complexity, diversity and thought structures of work practices outside of these dualistic concepts. And we need to know more about how the working people themselves perceive their activities and how they (re)act to global interdependencies.

Notes

1 For the concept of *disguised unemployment*, see Joan Robinson (1936).
2 The WEP was the ILO's flagship initiative, launched in 1969, "to make productive employment for large numbers of people a major goal of national and international policies for development" (ILO, 1969, p. 7).

3 For the invisibilization in development plans of women's economic contribution (such as social reproductive labor or home-based manufacturing), see Lourdes Benería (1982).
4 For example, when all members of a household contribute to subsistence without any distinction being drawn between productive and reproductive activities and between economic and non-economic activities (e.g., ILO, 1988, p. 28).
5 Only in a footnote it is mentioned that researchers at the Institute of Development Studies at the University of Nairobi actually did the conceptual work on the idea of informal work (ILO, 1972, p. 6; see Bangasser, 2000, p. 10).
6 In his report for the ILO, 1991, ILO Director Michel Hansenne called the conceptualization of the informal sector a "hazardous undertaking" (ILO, 1991, p. 2).
7 In light of its persistence, the ILO itself attests to a "Dilemma of the Informal Sector" based on the question of promoting the associated entrepreneurial potential or regulating it in the name of labor standards (ILO, 1991, p. 54).
8 Yet the ILO's Kenya report claimed that it was a universal concept: "to describe a duality that avoids the bias against the low-incomes sector inherent in the traditional-modern dichotomy. Both sectors are modern" (ILO, 1972, 503f.).
9 The request was put forward at the ICLS 1987 which problematized the "elusiveness of the concept" and the "formidable measurement problems" (ILO, 1987, p. 9).
10 Acknowledging the ILO's lead, the United Nations System of National Accounts (SNA) included the ICLS' resolution and henceforth distinguished informal from formal sectors (SNA 1993; see also Bangasser, 2000, p. 22).
11 Another reason why mostly the labor of women was left unseen in statistics on informality is the non-coverage of homeworkers (see Prügl, 1996; Thomas, 2002, p. 4f.).
12 The updated guidelines at least address the agricultural sector by requesting that its member states find adequate definitions for informal jobs in agriculture (Hussmanns, 2004, p. 9).
13 ILO statistician Ralf Hussmanns points out how "it is widely known that in developing and transition countries most informal sector activities are neither underground nor illegal, as they represent simply a survival strategy" (Hussmanns, 2004, p. 10). Though in the Kenia report (ILO, 1972, p. 504) the distinction between legal and illegal had already served as an analytic parameter.
14 Mayer-Ahuja rightly states that "Normality is obviously not an ontological quality, but a profoundly historical concept, when the stable yardstick against which undercutting of standards is measured is stretchable" (Mayer-Ahuja, 2017, p. 276).
15 This approach divides an economy into a primary (agriculture), secondary (industrial production) and tertiary sector (service) and presupposes that with increasing economic growth employment in the primary sector decreases in favor of the secondary sector. This is followed by decreasing employment in the secondary sector in favor of the tertiary sector.

References

Alba Vega, C. and Braig, M. (2022) *Las Voces del Centro Histórico. La lucha por el espacio en la Ciudad de México*. Mexico City: El Colegio de México.

Bangasser, P. (2000) *The ILO and the Informal Sector: An Institutional History*. Geneva: ILO.

Benanav, A. (2019) 'The Origins of Informality: The ILO at the Limit of the Concept of Unemployment', *Journal of Global History*, 14(1), pp. 107–125.

Benería, L. (1982) 'Accounting for Women's Work', in Lourdes, B. (ed.) *Women and Development: The Sexual Division of Labor in Rural Societies*. New York: Praeger, pp. 119–147.

Bourdieu, P. (1998) *Gegenfeuer. Wortmeldungen im Dienste des Widerstands gegen die neoliberale Invasion*. Konstanz: UVK Universitätsverlag Konstanz.

Breman, J. and van der Linden, M. (2014) 'Informalizing the Economy: The Return of the Social Question at a Global Level', *Development and Change*, 45, pp. 920–940.

Cardoso, F.H. and Faletto, E. (1969) *Dependencia y desarrollo en América Latina. Ensayo de interpretación sociológica*. Mexico City: Siglo XXI Editores.

Castells, M. (1973) *Imperialismo y urbanización en América Latina*. Barcelona: G. Gili.

Clark, C. (1957) *The Conditions of Economic Progress*. London: Macmillan.

Contreras, T. (2019) 'Empleo informal. Evolución teórica y criterios para su estimación derivados de la Organización Internacional del Trabajo (OIT)', *Revista Lebret*, 11, pp. 11–35.

Cooper, F. (2019) *Von der Sklaverei in die Prekarität? Afrikanische Arbeitsgeschichte im globalen Kontext*. Oldenburg: De Gruyter Oldenbourg.

De Soto, H. (1986) *El Otro Sendero. La Revolución informal*. Lima: Editorial El Barranco.

De Soto, H. (1989) *The Other Path: The Invisible Revolution in the Third World*. New York: HarperCollins.

Dörre, K. (2006) 'Prekäre Arbeit. Unsichere Beschäftigungsverhältnisse und ihre sozialen Folgen', *Arbeit*, 15(3), pp. 181–193.

Eckert, A. (2017) 'Von der "freien Lohnarbeit" zum "informellen Sektor"? Alte und neue Fragen', *Geschichte und Gesellschaft*, 43(2), pp. 297–307.

Fourastié, J. (1954) *Die grosse Hoffnung des 20. Jahrhunderts*, 3rd ed. Cologne: Deutz.

Frank, A. (1970) *Latin America: Underdevelopment or Revolution. Essays on the Development of Underdevelopment and the Immediate Enemy*. New York: Monthly Review Press.

Hart, K. (1973) 'Informal Income Opportunities and Urban Employment in Ghana', *The Journal of Modern African Studies*, 11(1), pp. 61–89.

Hussmanns, R. (2004) *Statistical Definition of Informal Employment: Guidelines Endorsed by the Seventeenth International Conference of Labour Statisticians (2003)*. Geneva: ILO.

Hussmanns, R. and Mehran, F. (2001) *Statistical Definition of the Informal Sector – International Standards and National Practices*. Geneva: ILO.

ILO (1957) *Measurement of Underemployment*. Geneva: ILO.

ILO (1969) *World Employment Programme: Report of the Director-General, Part 1, International Labour Conference Fifty-Third Session, Geneva 1969*. Geneva: ILO.

ILO (1972) *Employment, Incomes and Equality: A Strategy for Increasing Productive Employment in Kenya*. Geneva: ILO.

ILO (1987) *Report I, General Report: Fourteenth International Conference of Labour Statisticians, Geneva, 28 October – 6 November 1987*. Geneva: ILO.

ILO (1988) *Rural Employment Promotion, Report VII, International Labour Conference, 75th Session, Geneva, 1988*. Geneva: ILO.

ILO (1991) *The Dilemma of the Informal Sector: Report of the Director General, International Labour Conference, 78th Session (1991)*. Geneva: ILO.

ILO (1993) *Resolution Concerning Statistics of Employment in the Informal Sector*, Geneva: ILO.

ILO (2003) *Guidelines Concerning a Statistical Definition of Informal Employment: Seventeenth International Conference of Labour Statisticians (ICLS)*. Geneva: ILO.

ILO (2013) *Measuring Informality: A Statistical Manual on the Informal Sector and Informal Employment: International Labour Office*. Geneva: ILO.

ILO (2016) *Minimum Wage Policy Guide: 4.5. Informal Economy Workers: Distinguishing the Concepts: The Informal Sector, Informal Employment and the Informal Economy*. www.ilo.org/global/topics/wages/minimum-wages/beneficiaries/WCMS_436492/lang--en/index.htm.

Lomnitz Adler, L. (1975) *Como sobreviven los marginados*. Mexico City: Siglo XXI Editores.

Mathews, G., Lins Ribeiro, G. and Alba Vega, C. (eds.) (2012) *Globalization From Below: The World's Other Economy*. London and New York: Routledge.

Mayer-Ahuja, N. (2017) 'Die Globalität unsicherer Arbeit als konzeptionelle Provokation: Zum Zusammenhangzwischen Informalität im "Globalen Süden" und Prekarität im "Globalen Norden'," *Geschichte und Gesellschaft*, 43, pp. 264–296.

Meagher, K. (2013) 'Unlocking the Informal Economy: A Literature Review on Linkages Between Formal and Informal Economies in Developing Countries', WIEGO Working Paper 27.

Mezzadri, A. (2020) 'The Informal Labours of Social Reproduction', *Global Labour Journal*, 11(1), pp. 156–163.

Mezzera, J. (1989) 'Excess Labour Supply and the Urban Informal Sector: An Analytical Framework', in Berger, M. and Buvinic, M. (eds.) *Women's Ventures: Assistance to the Informal Sector in Latin America*. West Hartford: Kumarian Press, pp. 45–64.

Nun, J. (1971) *Superpoblacion relativa, ejercito industrial de reserva y masa marginal, Series Históricas 66*. Santiago de Chile: Naciones Unidas Comisión Económica para América Latina y el Caribe (CEPAL).

Parra, J. (2013) 'Complicaciones de lo ilegal y de lo informal – el business – una propuesta conceptual', *Antipoda. Revista de Antropología y Arqueología*, 17, pp. 205–228.

Patterson, O. (2019) 'The Denial of Slavery in Contemporary American Sociology', *Theory and Society*, 48(6), pp. 903–914.

Prügl, E. (1996) Home-Based Producers in Development Discourse, in Boris, E. and Prügl, E. (eds.) *Homeworkers in Global Perspective: Invisible No More*. New York and London: Routledge, pp. 39–59.

Robinson, J. (1936) Disguised Unemployment, *Economics Journal*, 46(182), pp. 225–237.

Rossi, B. (2017) 'What "Development" Does to Work', *International Labor and Working-Class History*, 92, pp. 7–23.

Roy, A. and AlSayyad, N. (2004) *Urban Informality: Transnational Perspectives From the Middle East, Latin America, and South Asia*. Oxford: Lexington Books.

Salas, C. (2006) El sector informal: auxilio u obstáculo para el conocimiento de la realidad social en América Latina, in de la Garza Toledo, E. (ed.) *Teorías sociales y estudios del trabajo: nuevos enfoques*. Mexico City: UAM, pp. 130–148.

System of National Accounts (1993) *Commission of the European Communities – Eurostat, International Monetary Fund, Organisation for Economic Co-operation and Development, United Nations, World Bank*. Brussels, Luxembourg, New York, Paris and Washington, DC: System of National Accounts.

Teichert, V. (2000) *Die informelle Ökonomie als notwendiger Bestandteil der formellen Erwerbswirtschaft: Zu den ökonomischen, sozialen und ökologischen Wirkungen informellen Arbeitens*, WZB Discussion Paper P00–524. Berlin.

Thomas, J. (2002) *Decent Work in the Informal Sector: Latin America*. Geneva: ILO.

Weck-Hannemann, H. (1984) *Schattenwirtschaft*. Munich: Vahlen.

Weinmann, N. and Burchardt, H.J. (2013) Politikzyklen der In-Formalität? Dynamiken informeller Arbeit in Lateinamerika, in Burchardt, H.J., Peters, S. and Weinmann, N. (eds.) *Arbeit in globaler Perspektive. Facetten informeller Beschäftigung*. Frankfurt and New York: Campus, pp. 97–122.

9

MIGRANTS' WORK

An Anthropological Perspective From West Africa

Isaie Dougnon

Introduction

The categorization of foreign workers in ways that facilitate their exploitation, turning them into human machines for capitalist profit, can be seen throughout history from the period of slavery through colonization to contemporary forms of capitalism (Greene, 2004). In West Africa, we need to reexamine our colonial history to understand the process of categorizing different groups of migrant workers, such categories designed to exploit the labor of these workers. Central to the exploitation of colonial labor were ideas about the virtues entailed in work and physical, professional and moral superiority or inferiority according to race or ethnic origin. The regulation of labor and recruitment, along with the status of foreign labor, has undergone many alterations since the nineteenth century. Whether we call them new slaves, clandestine captives, "new freemen," legal migrants, seasonal migrants, illegal or clandestine migrants, border workers, artists, sportsmen, sailors, trainees – they are all workers placed outside the "common law" in their host countries.

Migrants are "categorized" on the basis of national laws governing the employment of foreign labor. Migrants are "named" according to their nationalities, geographies, length of stay, cause of migration, distance of migration, level of qualification and by generation (first or second generation, as if migration and work were hereditary). In fact, states often use strategies of (mis)categorization to grant, refuse or limit migrants' work rights. Many researchers as well as actors in civil society denounce this denial of justice, this systematic segregation and exploitation of migrant workers. They also denounce the fact that these categories serve to devalue the important role of migrant labor in the economic systems of host countries.

DOI: 10.4324/9781003341321-12

But why does migration intensify despite such discriminatory categorizations? Do legal or sociological categories really reflect the migrant's own views of his or her work in the host country? To answer these questions we need to consider the cultural, social and economic factors that enable migrants to formulate their own definitions of work in the migratory context. Yet for more than 50 years those researching African migration have focused on migrants in search of wage labor and the process of their proletarianization (Cooper, 1987; Ferguson, 1999; Macmillan, 1993). What has been largely ignored is the question of how migrants themselves define their work in their destination countries. What social, economic and symbolic values do they attach to their work, and how do different African migrants categorize themselves as either self-employed or as employees?

Based on my field research in West Africa – in Accra from 2000 to 2003, Timbuktu in 2005, Niono in 2011 and Bamako in 2014 – this chapter analyzes how African migrants define work in material, social and symbolic terms. The material dimension is determined by the financial impact of migrants' work on their community of origin or family. The social dimension is related to the expectations which migrants encounter during visits to their village or city of origin. Finally, the symbolic dimension refers to the perception of migrants as "heroes"[1] who have overcome various risks. After describing the embeddedness of migrants' work in networks of communities, I will contrast two different self-categorizations by two different communities of migrant workers. Then I will discuss the three dimensions of migrants' own conceptualization of their work in relation to their home countries.

The Sense of Belonging to a Community and Its Networks

In previous publications (Dougnon, 2012, 2013, 2016) I have shown that West African migrants see their having migrated for work as a heroic act. To examine work from the perspective of migrant workers serves to demonstrate that the latter enter into it with their own social, cultural and economic backgrounds and that these, in turn, influence their perception of work.

The idea that migrants can realize themselves through their work is formed in their communities of origin. They are culturally, socially and economically influenced by the ideas, identities and social capital that their immigrant elders have transferred and continue to transfer to their communities. Their primary motivation is the possibility of obtaining work and then importing the earnings from their host country to their community of origin. Prospective migrants seek employment in the same jobs as their predecessors as well as having a keen interest in just how much income they can save per year and how much they can send back to their country to be redistributed in their community, where it will serve to establish symbols of success such as building a house or opening a family business.

From the vast migratory flows organized by the public authorities according to the needs of national economies, and through to the era of spontaneous migration, the professional paths of migrants are based on the types of work that each immigrant community has had the opportunity to perform or control over a more or less extended period. If the first migrants were employed in a given activity, those who come after will be engaged in the same activity (through intermediation of the first). Thus a sort of "monopolization" or "professionalization" of certain activities by certain migrant communities takes place. Some communities organize themselves to keep to themselves, for as long as possible, in the activity that they consider to be rightly theirs or for which they feel most qualified. In these situations, a migrant who retires will be replaced by another migrant who may be a son, younger brother, cousin or any other individual from the same community. The new worker is informed in advance by the one he or she replaces as to the forms and terms of employment. As regular salaried work with social protection becomes rarer for migrant workers, this form of mutual aid is the key to survival for many migrants. At the same time, it is a transfer of the moral order of the community of origin to the context of migrant work. This order reinforces the migrant's sense of belonging to his or her community and gives their work a community-specific value.

In the mid-1970s, in order to better analyze the strategies of immigrant communities in protecting their work sectors, the social sciences abandoned the approach of examining push-and-pull factors, instead using concepts such as "networks" or "chains" to describe the biographies, experiences and trials of migrants who organize themselves into communities to help each other in the search for work and the development of careers. In the migration process, the network constitutes social capital in Bourdieu's sense of the term. For potential migrants, the network is vital not only for the journey but especially for finding work in the host country. It is a social infrastructure that comprises individuals, families and immigrant communities, and which constitutes a web of relationships that fulfill specific functions, one of the most important of which is to find work for newcomers (Pompo and Dolores, 2019; Guilmoto and Sandron, 2000). The feeling of not being able to achieve fulfillment through work outside this social chain is very strong within many migrant communities, especially in host societies where migrants encounter xenophobic reactions. In some countries, the new migrants create or develop their own activity and workspaces. They engage in self-employment in which priority is given to workers from the same family or community. This is the case of a community of West Africans, commonly called "Senegalese," in Central African cities (Whitehouse, 2009a), the Lebanese in several francophone African countries (Charnay, 2014) and more recently the Chinese in certain African capitals.

Through analysis of the functions that the "network" plays in the work of migrants, we can see that the three dimensions of migrant work – material, social and symbolic – are inseparable. We can even say that the social dimension takes precedence over the material and instrumental aspects. Work is first of all a matter of being part of a social network and only secondarily a means of creating an income. The arriving immigrant is welcomed and accommodated by someone who comes from the same community, for example, the same village. The latter then finds work for the immigrant in the same department or in one where he or she has worked before. If the migrant finds himself in a situation of failure (e.g., prolonged unemployment, legal problems, incurable illness or death) then the costs of the repatriation are carried by the community.

This solidarity between elders and young people in facing the adversities of migration is recognized and valued in the community of origin. In the host countries, by contrast, it is rare to see migrants gain recognition and dignity through their work. In recent years, in Europe and elsewhere, institutional and socio-economic violence has marginalized migrants who are often despised while also being economically exploited. For migrants, however, the question is not whether they work in precarious, informal, clandestine or formal jobs – these are not the categories that matter. The central question for them is the impact of the material benefits of their work and the social and symbolic recognition that accompanies it back in their home country. This recognition counterbalances the suffering that they undergo in the host country where most of them work under indecent conditions, sometimes even endangering their health. The true fulfillment of migrants' work, during their long or short stay abroad, happens in their native country where this work is primarily conceived as a means of intra-family and community solidarity. Sometimes immigrants from the same community compete for social recognition by bringing more financial and material goods to the village of origin. This rivalry shows a process entailing the individualization of professional trajectories among the youngest immigrant strata.

Different Migrant Communities, Different Types of Work

In pre-colonial Africa, custom and tradition determined the type of work that a man of a given status was permitted to do (Neff, 1977).[2] In societies where the system of castes exists and where cultural forces determine the forms of institutions and social organization, certain occupations are hereditary (healers, priests, traders, tanners and so on). With colonization and waves of migration, the local divisions of labor changed abruptly. The upheavals associated with the displacement of peoples as well as the introduction of new methods of production and the extension of frontiers of trade and employment all served to disrupt the ancestral prerogatives of work. My research on the migration patterns of the Dogon and Songhay to Ghana illustrates these upheavals. (Dougnon, 2015)

When Jean Rouch published his work "Migration to Ghana" (1957) he suggested that researchers working on migration in Africa could raise the question of how different groups of migrants specialize in particular activities, specifically those where they have a comparative advantage. In the early 2000s when I carried out most of my research in Ghana's migrant districts, known as *zongo*,[3] the Dogon and Sonhay immigrant communities developed two completely different patterns of work. Thanks to migration, the migrant Songhay found themselves earning their living by trading at Kumasi's central market which their parents, who remained in the village, had never heard of. The Songhai community became liberal and entrepreneurial to a degree that would be hard to find in their villages of origin. The Dogon community, by contrast, basically relied on the security of colonial work.

The history and culture of these two ethnic groups' countries of departure have had a fundamental effect on their choice of work and adaptation strategies. The Songhai, founders of an empire which had developed thanks to trans-Saharan trade and the inheritors of an Islamic culture, soon responded by engaging in commerce and quickly prospered through it. By contrast, the Dogon transferred their ancestral notion of work to Ghana. According to this concept, the value of work is a function of the total effort needed and the sweat expended to perform it. Agriculture, their main activity, basically consists of working the fields. It conjures up images of pain, effort and tenacity. In light of this notion of work, it is easy to understand how Dogon migrants state that the forms of hard work of the "White Man" – which referred to public works and mining – were by definition a Dogon activity that suited their abilities.

Let us return to the Songhai. In Ghana, from the 1920s through to the 1940s, they were known by the curious name of *kayakaya*, literally "carry on the head." The notion of *kayakaya* or Gao people was used in reference not only to a particular type of work – as head porters – but also to the community which engaged in this activity. In fact, *kayakaya* expressed their new identity as migrant workers in Ghana, whereas the name "Gao" referred to their geographical origin. The word *kayakaya* had a pejorative connotation because the work to which it referred was reserved for migrants. Stigmatization of the "*kayakaya* community" and their work was linked to the fact that these communities continued to be perceived as foreigners despite the length of their stay in Ghana. In addition, no Ghanaian native would have agreed to work as head porter, which was seen as degrading.

However, over time the *kayakaya* community became one of the respectable business people. They went from being head porters for others to traders in their own right (Dougnon, 2016). This new status has enabled them to occupy a large part of Kumasi's central market and thus dominate the trade in basic commodities. The natives did not accept this control of commerce by communities who had become masters after having been mere servants. In April 1948 a ruling by the municipal authorities in Kumasi gave the *kayakaya* one month to vacate the market. After this deadline, their goods were to be seized and they would be expelled by force. According to a rumor which gained wide currency, the Songhai were responsible for the price inflation of basic goods. Allegedly this inflation had been orchestrated by the Songhai who knew that they had established a monopoly on the trade in foodstuffs at the Kumasi market. The ruling was implemented despite appeals to the colonial and traditional authorities of the Ashanti region and mediation by the district's religious and political leaders. The proactive economic approach of the Songhai is in contrast to the conservatism of the Dogon community, who tended to stick to jobs in the service sector of the colonies and preferred the regular rhythms of the White Man's work, which in Ghana means public works or mining, to which security work and caretaking were later added. The account of a former mining worker from the manganese sites in Nsuta included the following remarks:

> I left my village for Kumasi, but there was no work in that city apart from kayakaya [carrying loads on one's head]. This wasn't the sort of work for Dogon. They can't do that. The Dogon work in mines and in P.W. (Public Works). Kayakaya is for the Songhai, the Bella, the Hausa and the people from round here. The Dogon, no.

In Kumasi, there were two occupations: land and wood. The Dogon rejected both as unsuitable for them, which is why they traveled to Accra where they were convinced they would find "White Man's work," said one old Dogon woman who has lived in this city since 1942.

The migrants chose this "White Man's work" for different reasons. First, it provided money (the material dimension of work) so that they could take luxury items back to their villages. The young migrants were between 15 and 30 years of age. None of them came to Ghana to stay. The young people would become engaged in their own village before leaving. If no news was received from a departing young man within three years, his fiancée would leave him for another. A number of young men would come back to prepare for their marriage and take part in traditional festivals. At these local festivals and in the markets, the former migrants would dress in their finest clothes so as to celebrate in fitting style (the social dimension of work).

A number of migrants also say that they sought "White Man's work" because of its clearly determined nature. This was an everyday activity where hard workers could keep their jobs right up until retirement. In contrast, when a migrant worked for Black or Levantine traders, the latter would recompense the employee once the work was finished and there were no claims to any further income, for example, a pension. A number of pensioners say that the reason they receive a pension is because they did White Man's work. Second, choosing White Man's work facilitated a professional qualification. Many migrant workers chose White Man's work because they were fascinated by the resources, the methods and the nature of the work (fueling the heroic dimension of work). According to the migrants, they had been attracted by White Man's work because this work was characterized by (1) modern technologies such as caterpillars, long trucks and other heavy construction machines, (2) a hierarchical organization of work, and (3) the nature of that work (construction of roads, buildings, dams, plants and other modern infrastructure).[4]

The Three Dimensions of Migrants' Work

How would migrants themselves categorize their work, and what dimensions matter to them? I adopted certain anthropological and historical perspectives that allowed me to show the formation of "cultural heroes" through the transfer to and consumption of foreign items in villages. I examined both migration for colonial wage work and the modern lifestyle of returnee migrants, while scrutinizing the symbolic relationship between the two (Dougnon, 2016). To be cultural heroes, migrants must have a taste for adventure, a taste originating particularly from exposure to the accounts of those who come back from remote foreign countries. In familial conversations, they tell other young ones about the sensations they experienced while exploring these lands. They influence the young ones in the village and make them believe that migrants participate in the creation of the country they visit and work in, as can be seen in Malians and Burkinabe migrants recounting their role in birth of the Ivory Coast or of the Gold Coast, now the country of Ghana (Gary-Tounkara, 2008).

But it is not enough for the migrant to simply have memories and stories of success. He – most migrants being men – must expose other men to what he has brought back. In order to be complete, the stories demand many objects of prestige as well as proficiency in foreign languages. Material opulence thus nurtures social prestige and symbolic capital. Before the 1960s, migration was considered a dangerous adventure, and one's return from abroad was perceived as a victory. The one who came back was considered a hero. During his time spent abroad, he stoically conquered all difficulties. This foreign endeavor bespoke a form of courage that honored not only the migrant but his parents. He became a role model for all the young people his age. The foreign objects brought back – umbrellas, shoes, clothing, fabrics and bracelets – were seen as proof of his success, a success coveted by others who themselves were now tempted to undertake such an adventure.

But the adaptation of a migrant community to a foreign country depends on its fit with the economic conditions. Here the differences between different communities, which I discussed previously, become relevant once more. The Dogon, who favored colonial work rather than self-employment, have in the post-colonial period now found themselves in a lamentable financial situation (chronic unemployment, children lacking education, etc.). On the other hand, the Songhay, who excel in trade, have asserted themselves over the course of several years as essential economic actors.

The material success of the Songhay was based on their decision to become self-employed, seeing their sojourns abroad as an investment. According to certain seasonal workers, the Songhay do not engage in migration for wage labor but for trading purposes. For many of the migrants interviewed, working away from home meant to count their money at the end of the day or month. It is this notion of return on investment that underlay the entrepreneurial spirit of Songhay migrants in the 1930s and 1940s. It explains why they all involved themselves in petty trade, ranging from the sale of yams to rags. They opted for self-employment, considering it more rewarding and more profitable than wage labor for others.

As I have described in previous work (Dougnon, 2012) the seasonal migrants are also imbued with this entrepreneurial spirit. The seasonal worker is insofar defined as someone who returns home when he believes he has earned sufficient funds to provide for his needs and those of his family. One of the reasons these seasonal workers engage in petty trade is that their store of goods is to be found at the market. As they are wont to say, "When a man eats thanks to the market, he can work only at the market." Furthermore, the length of their stay is an important factor for this category of migrants. Someone who migrates for six months will not take the risk of engaging in a job that requires a year or more to accumulate sufficient income. Freedom of movement is also an important factor. Trade allows seasonal workers to go from one place to another, depending on which location might prove more profitable to them. They can abandon a country, a region, a town or a market for alternative ones if they learn that the commercial conditions there are better. Speed of movement and profitability are the two essential aspects of the capitalist spirit among Songhay migrants in Ghana and in the south of Mali.

The idea of luxury, comfort and social prestige are factored into my analysis of the Songhays' conception of return on investment, which unites material and symbolic conditions as embedded in a social community. Often underscored here is their need for money to buy clothes for their women and themselves. According to these seasonal workers, in returning to their homeland they must appear beautiful; their bodies must be glowing. In this regard one of my interlocutors raised his large *boubou*, showing off his arms and expressing himself with humor: "I have just arrived from Sikasso. You see how I shine. But in three months you will no longer recognize me, so pale will I be under the weight of bad conditions." If the needs of the body are satisfied, the seasonal worker can buy himself a goat or sheep or even a cow. However, the migrant does not easily embark upon commercial activity without entering into competition with the host country's traders and their customers. And this competition increases with the growing economic power of the migrant.

The cultural and economic influence exercised by migrants who return to their villages reflects the relations between the different generations of migrants in the host countries. In both cases, it is the immigrant's economic success that determines his status in his family as well as with his loved ones and the community as a whole. The successful migrant returning with plenty of resources will adapt better to conditions in the village, which are often precarious, and he also finds it easier to escape the shackles of tradition. In his host location, he had more opportunities to adapt to the host culture whilst retaining his own culture and maintaining regular links with his family in the village (frequent visits and sending gifts). These are still the reasons put forward by young people to justify leaving their village for African cities and Europe.

Conclusion

Current discussions of mobility, mass migrations, working-class categorizations and transnational cultural flows reflect much older concerns. In Europe, the book *The Polish Peasant in Europe and America* (Thomas and Znaniecki, 1927) and more recent publications such as *Culture, Power, Place* (Gupta and Ferguson, 1997) and *Modernity at Large* (Appadurai, 1996) describe the global historical character of urbanization and the movement of rural peoples to centers of work. These studies show how the general circulation of population across the globe continually places individuals in countries whose language they do not understand and in social systems where they have no place; and even if they do find a place, it is permanently called into question. Durkheim was the first to thematize the relationship between the division of labor and the mobility of people as Everret Hughes (1958) reminds us when he affirms the thesis that the secularized division of work is the most important factor in the mobility of people. In the course of his argument, he refers to this passage from Durkheim:

> For to live by a métier one must have clients, and he must sally forth from his house to find them; he must sally forth also to enter into relations with his competitors, to struggle against them, and to converse with them. Moreover, métier suppose more or less directly, cities, and cities are always formed and recruited principally by means of immigrants who have quitted their *milieu natal*.[5]

In the colonial era, West Africans migrated within and outside Africa not to obtain a *métier* but simply to work for money in whatever job that might have been available. They were willing workers, in the etymological sense of the term, and all of this still pertains today.

These migrant workers and their work have been classified in many discriminatory ways. An analysis of migrants' work in a dual historical and anthropological perspective shows them in opposition to native workers. Historians and anthropologists have tried to understand the difference between the native's work and a migrant's work (Atkins, 1993). The term *kayakaya*, which I have described earlier, was in the beginning a professional category but has been gradually transformed into a social category: *kayakaya* ended up meaning both the migrant and the migrant's work. One of the social effects of this categorization was the overt conflict between the *kayakaya* and the natives in Kumasi's central market. As soon as their work garnered a certain prestige and recognition, the *kayakaya* workers were excluded from the market and relocated to a remote area of the city. If a migrant's work became prestigious, steps were taken to reserve it for native workers.

In the course of my fieldwork in Ghana and Mali, I noticed that when people spoke of these migrants' work they meant degrading work. "Expat" workers (mostly Europeans and Chinese) received varying treatment and different definitions. In rich capitalist countries, the notion of unskilled work is associated with migrants' work (Anderson et al., 2021; Chalof, 2008; Varreau and Perrieaux, 1991). In our digital era, these latter seem to be less in demand, as Donald Trump openly declared. In the competition between developed countries to attract "desired migrant workers," he said that the United States would welcome Norwegian and other Scandinavian workers over people from Africa.

In this chapter, however, my focus has been on internal African migration. In the last four decades, such migration has substantially increased. The African economic Eldorado – countries such as Gabon, Angola, Congo and South Africa – continue to attract migrant workers from all over the continent. In these countries, the migrant workers are assigned humiliating labels. In South Africa the Nigerian and Somali migrants are called "clandestine workers" (Demeestère, 2016); in the Congo, West Africans are known as "Senegalese," meaning merchants/businessmen, or "Zaïrois" which refers to workers involved in illegal activities (Whitehouse, 2009b). Such degrading classifications help to explain why many natives are unwilling to work in those sectors dominated by migrant workers. While these are core features of categorization, looking at a migrant's self-categorization from the viewpoint of their native community, as this chapter does, shifts the focus to narratives of material opulence, social prestige and heroism.

These findings are confirmed by discussions I recently led within the framework of a community-engaged-learning class with West African community leaders about their migration trajectories to New York City. They traveled to New York with the expectation of receiving dignified, well-paid ed jobs and then later returning home to become bosses back in their own communities. But the reality turned out to be different. Many got jobs that they would never have done in their country of origin. For the men it was carwashing, dishwashing or as cabdrivers; for the women, it was hair-braiding and babysitting. As they acknowledge, such work is considered low-class, but once they are paid and they invest their money in their respective cities and villages in Africa (into the building of houses, helping family members obtain their social needs, building a small business in the agricultural or service sector) they have a feeling of pride. In the eyes of their community, they became someone, were regarded as successful migrants and a valuable asset to their relatives. This can take decades or more, but the myth of returning home as a "hero" helps to strengthen a migrant's will to work against all odds.

Notes

1 It is worth mentioning that the category of migrants analyzed in this chapter are essentially men. In the historical period under consideration (1910–1950) the women did not migrate for reasons of wage labor but so as to join their husbands. They remained in charge of domestic work and sometimes participated in street commerce.

2 Jean Rouch (1957, p. 195) recalls "the shame of work" in speaking of the migrants from Niger, the *zabrama* (Gao). According to him, these populations

> consider all work, apart from that of their culture, to be shameful for people who are not members of a servile caste; a free man must not work in front of the women of his country. The migrant, in emigrating, can therefore work without shame on the condition that he not migrate with his wife. He chooses the Gold Coast in preference to the Côte d'Ivoire because he knows that no one in his village will know what he is doing there.

3 *Zongo* is a Hausa word meaning "foreigners' district." During the colonial era it was the mining companies who, on the colonial government's instructions, established the *zongo* so that they could settle the migrant workers there.

4 More details on this notion of work are to be found in my book *Travail de Blanc, travail de Noir* (Dougnon, 2007).

5 Emile Durkheim, *De la Division du travail social* (Paris, 1902), preface to the second edition; "Quelques remarques sur les groupements professionnels," as cited by Hughes (1958, p. 330).

References

Anderson, B., Poeschel, F. and Ruhs, M. (2021) 'Rethinking Labour Migration: Covid-19, Essential Work, and Systemic Resilience', *CMS*, 9(45).

Appadurai, A. (1996) *Modernity at Large*. Minneapolis, MN: Minnesota University Press.

Atkins, K. (1993) *The Moon Is Dead! Give Us Our Money: The Cultural Origins of an African Work Ethic – Natal, South-Africa 1843–1900*. London: Pearson Education.

Chalof, J. (2008) 'Gérer les migrations de travailleurs peu qualifiés', in *Perspectives des migrations internationales*. Paris: SOPEM, Edition OCDE.

Charnay, J. (2014) *Le cèdre et le baobab: L'immigration syro-libanaise dans les colonies française d'Afrique de l'Ouest (1890–1939)*. Paris: Mémoire de Master, Université Paris Ouest La défence, département d'Histoire.

Cooper, F. (1987) *On the African Waterfront: Urban Disorder and the Transformation of Work in Colonial Mombasa*. New Haven, CT: Yale University Press.

Demeestère, R. (2016) 'Même si tu as des papiers, ils t-embarguent: gestion policière de l'immigration africaine ou institutionnalisation de la xénophobie dans l'Afrique du Sud post-apartheid', *Politique Africaine*, 142, pp. 145–167.

Dougnon, I. (2007) *"Travail de Blanc," "Travail de Noir": la migration des paysans dogons vers l'Office du Niger et au Ghana 1910–1980*. Paris: Karthala.

Dougnon, I. (2012) 'Comparing Dogon and Songhai Migrations Towards Ghana', in Berriane, M. and de Haas, H. (eds.) *African Migrations Research: Innovative Methods and Methodologies*. Trenton, NJ: Africa World Press, pp. 211–236.

Dougnon, I. (2013) 'Migration as Coping With Risk and State Barriers: Malian Migrants Conception of Being Far From Home', in Leedy, T. and Kane, A. (eds.) *African Migrations Today: Patterns and Perspectives*. Bloomington, IN: Indiana University Press, pp. 35–58.

Dougnon, I. (2015) 'Migration and Competition Over Commercial Spaces: The Case of Songhay Migrants in the Kumasi Central Market, Ghana 1930–1948', in Akinyoade, A. and Gewald, J.-B. (eds.) *African Roads to Prosperity: People en Route to Socio-Cultural and Economic Transformations*. Leiden: Brill, pp. 74–93.

Dougnon, I. (2016) 'Reinterpreting Labor Migration as Initiation Rite: "Ghana Boys" and European Clothing in Dogon Country (Mali) 1920–1960', *African Economic History*, 44, pp. 73–79.

Ferguson, J. (1999) *Expectations of Modernity: Myths and Meanings of Urban Life on the Zambian Copperbelt*. Berkeley, CA: University of California Press.

Gary-Tounkara, D. (2008) *Migrants soudanais/maliens et conscience ivoirienne (1903–1980)*. Paris: L'Harmattan.

Greene, J. (2004) 'Spaniards on the Silver Roll: Labor Troubles and Liminality in the Panama Canal Zone, 1904–1914', *International Labor and Working-Class History* (New Approaches to Global Labor History), 66, pp. 78–98.

Guilmoto, C. and Sandron, F. (2000) 'La dynamique interne des réseaux migratoires dans les pays en développement', *Population*, pp. 105–135.

Gupta, A. and Ferguson, J. (1997) *Culture, Power, Place, Exploration in Critical Anthropology*. London: Routledge.

Hughes, C.E. (1958) *Men and Their Work*. Glencoe, IL: The Free Press of Glencoe.

Macmillan, H. (1993) 'The Historiography of Transition on the Zambian Copperbelt: Another View', *Journal of Southern African Studies*, 19(4), pp. 681–712.

Neff, W.S. (1977) *Work and Human Behaviour*. Chicago, IL: Chicago University Press.

Pompo, P. and Dolores, M. (2019) 'Réseaux migratoires et réseaux de pouvoir: les triquis en Californie', in du Moulin Kervran, D. and Pépin-Lehalleur, M. (eds.) *Agir-en-Réseau, modèle d'action ou catégorie d'analyse*, Presses Universitaires de Rennes, Rennes. pp. 205–219.

Rouch, J. (1957) 'Migration au Ghana (Gold Coast) (Enquête 1953–1955)', *Journal de la société des africanistes*, XXVI, p. 33–196.

Thomas, W.I. and Znaniecki, F. (1927) *The Polish Peasant in Europe and America*. New York: Knopf.

Varreau, G. and Perrieaux, A.-S. (1991) 'Les sens d'une catégorisation: Les O.S. immigrés', *Language et société*, 58, pp. 5–36.

Whitehouse, B. (2009a) 'Discrimination, Despoliation and Irreconcilable Difference: Host-Immigrant Tensions in Brazzaville, Congo', *Africa Spectrum*, 44(1), pp. 39–59.

Whitehouse, B. (2009b) 'Migrants et insécurité existentielle', *Hommes & Migrations*, 1279, pp. 80–87.

10

DOMESTIC WORK

The Invention of a Gendered Relationship

Michel Lallement

Introduction

In ordinary language as well as in academic semantics, domestic work usually refers to all the unpaid activities of the production of goods and services carried out within the family (e.g., preparation of meals, housework, education of children). The use of the notion of work to describe such social practices is both obvious and paradoxical. It is obvious insofar as it refers to the production-of-use values whose social utility is hardly in doubt, resulting from the mobilization of a predominantly female labor force. It is paradoxical because this analytical category results from a historical construction which, since the Industrial Revolution, denies domestic work the very status of work. This denial is obvious when one considers the first formulations of neo-classical economic theory (Faugère, 1980). Because work can be a source of pain, this theory equates it with a disutility. From this perspective, rational individuals will only agree to perform work that is remunerative, thus domestic work is regarded as non-labor or even a leisure-time activity.

The paradox, however, can be resolved by distinguishing between two different definitions of work (Joyce, 1987). In the first, all activities that require the expenditure of energy in order to produce goods and services are understood as work. In the second, the determining criterion is that of status, raising the issue of how a society creates different social "worlds" within it, or, if one prefers, universes composed of entities, cultures and practices that are specific to them (Goodman, 1978). In this respect the sphere of domestic work is opposed to that of paid work, the partition having taken shape thanks to the industrial development in modern societies. This chapter highlights some of the salient manifestations of the ambivalent relations between domestic and paid work. It aims to

DOI: 10.4324/9781003341321-13

illuminate the category of domestic work by not only contrasting it to paid and unpaid work but to productive and reproductive work.

However, in this chapter, the focus will be less on analyzing domestic work as a social sphere than as a category. Like any such abstract entity, domestic work includes some social activities and excludes others. It is the modalities but also the fragilities of this partition that I would like to emphasize. To do this, I will look at the historical conditions which produced the category of domestic work, then I will discuss the limits of the opposition between household production and professional activities. To complete the picture, I will draw on the feminist literature which, since the 1970s, has helped to denaturalize domestic work in favor of perspectives that invite us to think of the different components of work in a relational way.

A category is not only a theoretical instrument that enables us to see the social universe by dividing it into different parts (Bourdieu, 1980) but more generally a means of knowing and acting. One particularly meaningful activity, from this point of view, is measuring. By asking what the measurement of domestic work means, we are in fact led to question the criteria that make up the category, the conventions that govern its definition and, in return, the impact that measuring processes have on our categories and practices. Domestic work is no exception with respect to these characteristics. I will show this by addressing the methodologies of the economic evaluation of domestic work as used by national accountants since the Second World War. The last point that I discuss is the reconfiguration of the category of domestic work in a period when its boundaries are being recomposed, and I shall give priority to care work. Contemporary research would seem to agree that we are currently witnessing the production of new ways of thinking, classifying and evaluating what has long been referred to as domestic work.

The Historical Construction of Domestic Work

Contrary to certain representations which, even today, mainly define professional activity in masculine terms, there is nothing incongruous about associating work with the female gender. On the contrary,

> in many languages the same word can be used to identify both work and pain of childbirth, as if the two activities – named production and reproduction in modern socioeconomic language – belonged to the same domain and were two different but equally painful gendered ways to reach the same goal, i.e. making sure that both human life and mankind would live on.
>
> *(Sarti, Bellavitis and Martini, 2018, p. 10)*

If there is any general conviction shared by an increasing number of historians, it would be that women have always worked (Kessler-Harris, 1981; Schweitzer, 2002). This holds true for whatever period one considers – whether it be that of the "first societies" or today. It is true, however, that the forms of productive activity have evolved over time. The *oikos* economy that has long prevailed in Western societies brought together, in elementary domestic units, men, women and children who worked collectively to provide for their own needs as well as others outside their immediate circles.

Governed by the capitalist law of value highlighted by Karl Marx, today's dominant mode of production organizes the use and exchange of labor differently. The formal split between the domestic sphere and the professional sphere is one of its characteristic features. In summarizing a very long history in this way, one must beware of overly simplistic schemes. The pre-industrial world had a variety of social conditions. Robert Castel (1995) reminds us that in pre-industrial society there coexisted two regimes of work – that of regulated work (the professions) and that of forced work (which compelled the poor to become laborers in order to benefit from social assistance schemes). In this period, women did not work less than men (Marinella, 1999). The situation changed with the invention of a market in which labor power is bought and sold according to the needs of the productive system. In the dynamics of the industrial revolutions of the eighteenth and nineteenth centuries, labor was reduced to a commodity, the use of which determined the production of wealth. The theorists of classical political economy, from Adam Smith to Karl Marx, made productive work the cornerstone of their theories of value.

At a time when industrialization and urbanization were disrupting the old order, labor was also ejected from its home base. Against the backdrop of the workforce's resistance to this great mobilization, practices and representations gradually established the segmentation between two spheres of social action: public versus private, the market versus the family, the technology versus the natural, the masculine versus the feminine, paid work versus non-paying domestic work. This opposition was not only an expression of material changes. Between the late eighteenth century and the mid-nineteenth century, one also finds multiple European enterprises that tried to forge what Claudia Honegger (1991) names an "ontology of the differences of sex." Largely driven by the medical profession, the process came to an end in the mid-nineteenth century with the construction of a universal figure of Man and, at the same time, the institution of Woman as a specific object of study. In France, Ernest Legouvé, author of a famous *Histoire morale de la femme* (1848), was directly indebted to this episteme of gender. For Legouvé the man's body was on the side of power and woman on the side of grace, beauty and delicacy. With regard to the mind, the woman showed a higher practical sense than the man, which gave her the "natural" privilege of daily domestic work. In the nineteenth century, medical rhetoric reinforced the idea that men were responsible for the material and moral well-being of their families, while women were responsible for the upkeep and education of their children. The many treatises on household economy published during this century set the tone for this division of labor.

By way of illustration, here is a short excerpt from a work significantly entitled *La future ménagère* (*The Future Housewife*):

> The authority of the mother is exercised above all within the family; the domestic home is her domain. The woman was created to be the queen of the domestic home; there she is above all competition; there man finds in her his providence and the most powerful artisan of his happiness.
>
> *(Wirth, 1892, pp. 1–2)*

However, depending on social class, the relegation of women to domestic work took on different forms. Bourgeois families, under the leadership of the wife, delegated to other women the tasks of carrying out domestic and educational activities. At bottom of the social hierarchy, by contrast, subcontracting was unthinkable. Despite pressure from hygienists, doctors and philanthropists who iterated that a woman's place was with her children, to whom she had a maternal duty, the fact is that paid labor occupied a large portion of the time of women from the working class (Tilly and Scott, 1987). Intermediate situations were also possible. In France, for instance, in the middle of the 19th century

> the wife of a "modest employee," of a junior doctor could be satisfied with a housekeeper, she could do the cooking, go to market, do the sewing, she could be forced to abandon drawing and music in order to devote herself to occupations necessary to the good running of the household, yet this "Parisian housewife" nevertheless remained a "lady."
>
> *(Daumard, 1987, p. 83)*

Limits of the Rationalization of Domestic Work

The preceding considerations show that the category of domestic work is a historical construction whose constitutive modalities can only be understood if the representations associated with it are placed in a long-term perspective. Sociology provides a fairly simple key to explaining this phenomenon when, in observing the evolution of Western European societies, it makes the differentiation of social-action spaces one of the major characteristics of "modernization." The thesis appears very clearly in the work of Max Weber, for example, when he gives an account of the rationalization movements that preside over the institution of modern capitalism (Weber, 1992 [1904–1905]). Domestic work here appears as the product of a process of differentiation which, in the name of efficiency, sets the household against the firm.

However, these two spheres were equally permeable to the spirit of Taylorism that developed during the twentieth century. The rationalization of work by matching means to ends has never been the sole prerogative of professional worlds. Following the example of the American high priestess of efficiency, Christine

Frederick (Rutherford, 2003), zealots of the scientific organization of work tried to convince housewives that they too could improve the way they washed their clothes, moved around in the kitchen, spent their money – in short, that they could keep their homes tidy by using the methods *en vogue* in the industrial world. Ernestine Gilbreth Carey and Frank Bunker Gilbreth's famous book *Cheaper by the Dozen* (1948) did much to spread this idea to the general public.

Even if this double movement of rationalization strongly established the legitimacy of the category of domestic work, its importance should not be overestimated. The line that divided the domestic sphere from other spheres was never clear-cut; often the boundaries were blurred. Women did not suddenly stop working because, as early as the eighteenth century and throughout Europe, manuals of conduct had encouraged women to prepare themselves to dedicate their lives to the management of a domestic kingdom once they married (Chatenet, 2009). Apart from women at the top of the social hierarchy, who were disinclined to engage in remunerative activities (for material reasons in particular), most others

> worked with men in a familial situation, operated their own business or trade, worked on their own to support themselves or a family of children to save a dowry. Some women were employers, other were employees. Some work was waged, and some not. Some was paid annually, like servants, and some was paid by piece or day rates.
>
> *(Simonton, 2006, p. 139)*

And it was not much different thereafter. Davidoff and Hall (1987) have shown that bourgeois women, whose lives are sometimes presented as alternating between private languor and assiduous socializing, indeed deviated more often from the rule of domestic work than is generally believed. At the end of the eighteenth century and during the first half of the nineteenth century, the English bourgeoisie promoted the precepts of a dissident Protestantism that advocated the association between an active and pious man (in the image of a pastor) and a wife entirely devoted to his cause and well-being. In fact, married women have never been entirely restricted to the domestic sphere. Not only were they far from inactive but they also contributed capital to the family business. To maintain the appearance of asymmetry between domestic and paid work, however, the law was a particularly effective instrument. The generalization of the principle of *fideiscommis* allowed men to benefit from the resources of their wives while keeping the latter in a condition of dependence and domination.

There is one final point worth considering so as to make clear that the opposition between paid work and domestic work was probably less clear-cut than the rhetoric of the dominant classes would have us believe: the distortion of statistics from this time. In Victorian England, women were looked upon (as in other countries) as veritable "angels" of the home. Those who did not conform to the norm were subject to public condemnation (Abrams, 2006). And interestingly, surveys and censuses bear the trace of this moral opprobrium. The collection and processing of data was primarily done by males who were tempted to underestimate the importance of women's work by imputing the hours worked by their wives to their husbands, or by tinkering with the categories used so as to better portray women as inactive (Higgs and Wilkinson, 2016). In France, an artifact of a slightly different nature had a similar effect. In the 1896 census, it was decided to classify homeworkers (mostly women) as "isolated" workers on the grounds that they did not work under the direct physical control of their employers. Separated from other employees, they were thus unable to benefit from certain rights (such as the right to be declared unemployed in the event of the cessation of orders) and, although they had an employment contract, they have long been considered as belonging exclusively to the world of domestic work (Lallement, 1990).

The "Male Breadwinner" Moment and the Renewal of Feminist Approaches to Domestic Work

The gap between the discourse on the "natural" place of women in the domestic sphere and actual social practices narrowed in the twentieth century, due in particular to the increase in levels of remuneration. In England, the beginnings of this rapprochement can be observed in the middle classes from the second half of the nineteenth century onward (Blunden, 1982). In France, this movement took place a little later. It was not until after the Second World War and the establishment of social security systems that the separation of male and female roles was fully effective.

> Even if the housewives of this period, often in charge of large families, faced time- and energy-consuming activities (for example the washing machine was not widespread before the late 1960s), their tasks, performed in a non-market and non-wage fashion within the confines of the domestic space, were perceived by those around them and experienced by themselves as the "natural" expression of their role as wife and mother and not as "work."
>
> *(Dussuet, 2017, p. 104)*

In the main Western countries (North America, Europe) a new era of domestic work thus began at the dawn of the *Trente Glorieuses*. The 1950s and 1960s, more precisely, corresponded to the golden age of the "male breadwinner" model, a period during which the media celebrated the figure of the "housewife" who gave up any professional ambition to devote herself to the well-being of her family. Domestic work became a full-time female activity that benefited from new household technologies and for which young girls were trained early on. Two observations on this phenomenon deserve particular attention. First, this model took hold in different countries in different ways. It was for example strongly established in Germany, France, Italy and the United Kingdom but left a much weaker imprint on Scandinavia, which promoted greater formal equality between women and men (Lewis, 1992) and was reflected in the construction of a two-breadwinner model which broke with the asymmetry in the allocation of domestic tasks. Secondly, ever since the 1970s, women's participation in the labor force has been on the rise again in Western Europe. In spite of economic crises, and in ways that varied from country to country, it then rose steadily to the point where the strict division of labor that prevailed for two short decades appears in retrospect as a parenthesis in the history of women's work. The moment was nevertheless sufficiently influential to give rise to renewed feminist reflection.

The status of domestic work had already been questioned long before the male-breadwinner period. To name but one critic, in a short and incisive text published in 1912 the German sociologist and feminist Marianne Weber (1919) questioned the evaluation of the singular social practice of *Hausfrauenarbeit* ("housewife work") and concluded that it was necessary to reform matrimonial relations in order to take into account the contribution of women through their domestic work and to break the financial dependence of wives on their husbands. It was several decades later that Marxism irrigated feminist thinking in a slightly different way. The dichotomy of productive and reproductive work took center stage in quite a surprising way – surprising because, as Allesandra Pescarolo (2018) reminds us, reproductive work for Karl Marx corresponded to the expenditure of energy that a worker must make in order to garner a salary in the factory that would ensure a simple reproduction of his labor power. Productive labor, on the other hand, was equivalent to surplus labor, the product of which feeds the accumulation of capital and the expanded reproduction of the economic system. By appropriating the Marxist semantics, a part of the feminist literature changed its meaning. It defined as reproductive labor the female activities that consist in producing (through childbirth) and reproducing (through the provision of domestic goods and services) the labor power that capitalism needs to function.

This position was notably defended by Mariarosa Dalla Costa and Sema James in *The Power of Women and the Subversion of the Community* (1972), a manifesto that quickly gained international recognition. They argued that women

> have been isolated in the home, forced to carry out work that is considered unskilled, the work of giving birth to raising, disciplining, and servicing the worker for production. Her role in the cycle of social production remained invisible because only the product of her labor, the laborer, was visible there. She herself was thereby trapped within pre-capitalist working conditions and never paid a wage.
>
> *(Dalla Costa and James, 1972, p. 28)*

The diagnosis gave life to the *International Wages for Housework Campaign*, a social movement in England, Italy, the United States and Canada which was in favor of recognizing and remunerating the labor carried out by all those who worked in the home without the benefit of any financial compensation.

As early as 1970, Christine Delphy also developed a critical view of domestic work, while arguing from a different standpoint. In a seminal article that she published under the pseudonym Christine Dupont, she asserted that if female domestic work was not paid, it was not because of the nature of its production. It also served to keep agriculture, crafts and commerce going. Its specificity lay in the patriarchal relationship of production in which it was inserted. In such a system, "the appropriation of women's labor power tends to be limited to the exploitation (the free provision by them) of domestic work and the raising of children" (Dupont, 1970, p. 165). In the decades that followed, feminist sociologists insisted even more strongly that domestic work not be considered a separate category. They proposed to insert it into analytical schemes that made it possible to link the professional and the familial, paid and unpaid work or, if one prefers, production and reproduction, in one and the same way.

This type of displacement has a double advantage. It forces us to think about domestic work in relation to other activities that make up daily life. This research thus highlights the importance of family concerns, which women never broke with, even in situations of paid work. In the case of the United States, Arlie Hochschild (Hochschild with Machung, 1989) referrers to a "second shift" to designate the unpaid work of childcare and housework taken on by working women. Not only is this additional work exhausting, but the women can hardly count on companies to help them assume this double burden. They can count no more on the public authorities, which are too ungenerous in terms of schemes (such as paid parental leaves) that would encourage a better articulation between domestic and professional work. In France, Danielle Chabaud-Rychter et al. (1985) describe in the same spirit the burden of the "double day," domestic and professional, which is imposed on working women. They describe in detail what characterizes domestic commitment – in contrast to industrial or office work – namely the fragmentation of tasks, the invisibility of the work done and permanent availability. A few years later the permanent overload imposed by domestic work was added to the various other elements used to explain women's specific difficulties in making a career in the professional world.

Categorizing and Measuring Domestic Work

The categorization of domestic work through censuses and surveys, and then by means of sociological and feminist analyses, is a first form of rationalization albeit an imperfect one. But there is a second and equally important form which consists of measuring domestic activities. When economists invented national accounting at the time of the Second World War, they were aware of the importance of domestic production. But each time they addressed the question, they refused to integrate it into the national accounts, except at best through satellite accounts.

The reasons given are statistical in nature: difficulties in collecting relevant information, the risks of producing erroneous data because of incompleteness, etc. (Lützel, 1989). Those who examine the status of domestic work nevertheless admit that it is possible to define its contours theoretically. One can thus define domestic production as "non-market activities which produce goods or services for the members of the household not desired in and of themselves, but rather for the utility which they yield" (Hawrylyshyn, 1977, p. 89). Even if we exclude practices corresponding to the satisfaction of biological needs (sleep, personal care) from the scope of actions concerned, this definition remains unsatisfactory, for it makes it impossible to clearly differentiate domestic work from leisure. In order to overcome this difficulty, national accountants have adopted the third-person principle defined early on by Margaret Reid (1934). On this principle, activities that one enjoys but that can be done by someone else (cooking, gardening, etc.) have the status of housework, not leisure.

With such a grid, it is possible to quantify domestic work. In the case of the United States, for example, Valerie Ramey (2009) has shown that the number of hours spent each week by people aged 18–64 on domestic production remained more or less constant throughout the twentieth century (around 25 hours per week). However, this apparent continuity in fact conceals two opposing trends: a decline in female domestic work and a steady rise in male participation (3.9 hours on average per week in 1900 vs. 16.8 in 2005). To be more precise, the trajectory of women's domestic work first signaled an erosion of the male-breadwinner model before finally stabilizing. The figures are as follows: 46.8 hours spent on average each week by American women on domestic production in 1900, 40.9 hours in 1965, 32.1 hours in 1975, and 29.3 hours in 2005.

Thanks to the household time-use surveys implemented around the world, this type of investigation has been extended to many other national areas. A comparative study by the OECD shows that the average duration of unpaid domestic work in 2011 varied from about 2.3 hours in Turkey to 4.3 hours in Mexico, passing through a whole series of intermediate situations (with a group of countries whose duration was around 3.5 hours, such as France, Hungary, Finland, Germany, the United States and the United Kingdom) (Ahmad and Koh, 2011). This way of running the surveys is illuminating in that it allows us to reevaluate the usual hierarchies between "poor" and "rich" countries. Most of the time, in fact, international comparisons stick to classifications based on indicators such as market labor expenditures or economic performance. By including domestic work, we get a more accurate view of the wealth produced by each country. However, because of the coding and measurement of activities (especially those relating to personal care), the method is still far from perfect (Folbre, 2009).

Another way of objectifying domestic work is to evaluate its contribution to the wealth of a country. There are two methods employed in doing this. The first is based on market costs (either globally or by activity category). In this method, the value attributed to domestic work corresponds to what it would cost if the tasks were assigned to a person who would be paid to perform them. The second method uses an opportunity-cost approach. Here it is stipulated that housework is worth what the person doing it would earn in his or her paid occupation. The economic value of domestic work thus depends on the social status of the person performing it. In France, Ann Chadeau and Annie Fouquet (1981) carried out a pioneering study that used these measurement strategies. They arrived at estimates of the value attributable to domestic work that vary between 15 and 70 percent of the GDP. Using a similar methodology, other researchers have been able to show that in Canada, the Netherlands, Norway, the United Kingdom and the United States the share of home production in GDP had been steadily decreasing between 1971 and 2008 (Ahmad and Koh, 2011). In the Netherlands, where the most comprehensive data are available, the share fell from 42 percent in 1975 to 19 percent in 2018 when using market-cost estimates, and from 96 to 45 percent when using the opportunity-cost method. The level of economic development, the share of retirees in the total population, and public-policy choices (whether or not they encourage women to work in paid jobs) (Gornick and Meyers, 2003) are three factors that explain these medium-term changes.

From Domestic Work to Care Work

Since the 1990s, research on care has shaken up the ways in which domestic work is represented and categorized even more so than the developments just mentioned. The interest in care is directly related to the growing role played by personal services in Western economies, whether it be medical care, domestic help for the elderly or the disabled, etc. It is also linked, in some countries, to the promotion of "small jobs" of a neo-domestic nature, which public authorities believed could help fight unemployment (Devetter and Rousseau, 2011). The term "care" was first used in 1982 by Carollyn Gillian (1982). She argued that, for social reasons, the capacity to care was unequally shared by the sexes. A few years later, Berenice Fisher and Joan Tronto provided a definition of care that is now authoritative:

> On the most general level, we suggest that caring be viewed as a species activity that includes everything that we do to maintain, continue, and repair our 'world' so that we can live in it as well as possible. That world includes our bodies, ourselves, and our environment, all of which we seek to interweave in a complex, life-sustaining web.
>
> *(Tronto, 1993, p. 103)*

As can be seen, the definition encompasses a wide range of activities, including those typically associated with the unpaid production of goods and services in a family setting.

The success of care as a new concept, first in the United States and then a little later in Europe, cannot therefore leave anyone indifferent. Since the 1980s, feminist sociologists have insisted on the need to develop a relational analysis of professional and domestic work. With care, the way of seeing things is no longer the same: by emphasizing the importance of subjective involvement, another type of connection is made, this time in favor of personal-service jobs. In all cases, whether domestic work, professional home help, hospital care and the like, an ideal type of the "good" care service is formed through solicitude, free gesture and the place given to social ties (if not to emotional relationships). To these components we can add the desire to adjust one's service to personalized needs and the anticipation of future demands. Finally, care work often goes hand in hand with an unclear definition of the tasks to be accomplished, the temptation not to count one's time, and the invisibility of the services provided (Hirata, 2021).

More generally, social practices lie at quite some distance from the idyllic picture that has been painted. Nurses testify to this: it is sometimes necessary to do violence to oneself in order not to react too abruptly to patients whose requests may seem abusive (Molinier, 2005). This is also confirmed by employees specializing in domestic help: care forces one to walk a narrow path between empathy and total support (at the risk of being accused of taking the place of loved ones) and aloof professionalism (at the risk of appearing devoid of compassion). The experience of family caregivers confirms this in another way. Because such work involves physical fatigue and psychological exhaustion, it is difficult to maintain the role of care provider on a day-to-day basis for the benefit of dependent relatives. But the most difficult thing is sometimes the impossibility of admitting and recognizing the hassle and distress that the practice of care imposes.

All these elements make it possible to understand the effective scope of the small revolution of which care is the epicenter. Its introduction fundamentally shakes up the category of domestic work since, while encompassing the latter, it emphasizes structuring dimensions, in this case the capacity to take care of others, which until now had been little valued by specialists in domestic production. But such a shift is no guarantee that care can claim a categorical homogeneity as strong as that of domestic work. The difficulty in drawing a dividing line between what is care and what is not is proof of this. As a result,

> the vague and all-encompassing nature of this term is a real difficulty in working in a somewhat constructed and pragmatic way on the subject. The (general, generous, programmatic) definition of care does not constitute a practical category for those who want to study it.
>
> *(Cresson, 2011, p. 197)*

Depending on the perspective, moreover, the status assigned to care can vary greatly. In some cases the emphasis is placed on the disposition that care requires; in others, attention is focused on the actual practice of providing care; in still others, it is the political stakes of the use of care that are the focus of reflections (Giraud, 2017).

Conclusion

As a historical construction that owes its fundamental origins to the process of social differentiation that accompanied Western societies in the era of industrial modernity, domestic work has acquired a categorical thickness under the combined weight of various rationalizations, of which statistics, law and social theory have been powerful vectors. It is no coincidence that one of the main sociologists of the twentieth century, Talcott Parsons, tried to justify the almost exclusive attribution of domestic tasks to the female gender. In the nuclear family of his time, explained the Harvard professor, men and women jointly assume the function of socializing their children. But they did so in a rational and complementary way: while the man took on the role of breadwinner and guaranteed the family's main income, the woman took care of the household and educational tasks (Parsons and Bales, 1955).

Feminist movements have taken on the task of proposing less functionalist and more critical readings of domestic work. Recent historical developments have also shown the provisional nature of the conventions that have structured our understanding and use of the category of domestic work. Since the 1980s, policies to make work more flexible and the increasing use of new information and communication technologies have had the massive effect of blurring boundaries between the spaces and times dedicated to the family and those traditionally reserved for professional activities. The long hiatus caused by the health crisis of 2020 and 2021 has only made the situation worse. In the 28 countries of the European Union, the proportion of teleworkers (regular or occasional) has suddenly risen from 16.1 percent in 2019 to 44.6 percent in 2020, this mainly benefiting the most educated populations (Dayan, 2021). As a result, it seems possible that in the near future the already fragile resistance to the categories of non-salaried domestic work and professional work may suddenly give way to new forms of categorizing work activities.

References

Abrams, L. (2006) 'At Home in the Family', in Simonton, D. (ed.) *The Routledge History of Women in Europe Since 1700*. London and New York: Routledge, pp. 14–53.

Ahmad, N. and Koh, S.-H. (2011) Incorporating Estimates of Household Production of Non-Market Services Into International Comparisons of Material Well-Being. OECD Statistics Working Papers, 07.

Blunden, K. (1982) *Le travail et la vertu. Femmes au foyer: une mystification de la révolution industrielle*. Paris: Payot.

Bourdieu, P. (1980) 'L'identité et la représentation. Éléments pour une réflexion critique sur l'idée de région', *Actes de la recherche en sciences sociales*, 35, pp. 63–72.

Castel, R. (1995) *Les métamorphoses de la question sociale. Une chronique du salariat*. Paris: Fayard.

Chabaud-Rychter, D., Fougeyrollas-Schwebel, D. and Sonthonnax, F. (1985) *Espace et temps du travail domestique*. Paris: Méridiens.

Chadeau, A. and Fouquet, A. (1981) 'Peut-on mesurer le travail domestique?', *Économie et statistiques*, 136, pp. 29–42.

Chatenet, A. (2009) 'La femme, maîtresse de maison? Rôle et place des femmes dans les ouvrages d'économie domestique au XVIIIe siècle', *Histoire, économie et société*, 28(4), pp. 21–34.

Cresson, G. (2011) 'Le care: soin à autrui et objet de controverses', *Travail, Genre et Sociétés*, 26, pp. 195–198.

Dalla Costa, M. and James, S. (1972) *The Power of Women and the Subversion of Community*. Bristol: Falling Wall Press.

Daumard, A. (1987) *Les bourgeois et la bourgeoise en France*. Paris: Aubier.

Davidoff, L. and Hall, C. (1987) *Family Fortunes: Men and Women of the English Middle Class 1780–1850*. London: Hutchinson Education.

Dayan, J.-L. (2021) 'Le télétravail est-il l'avenir du travail en Europe ?', *Document de travail Malakoff Humanis, Metis*. https://lecomptoirdelanouvelleentreprise.com/wp-content/uploads/2021/05/2021-125-cne-mh-teletravail-avenir-travail-en-europe.pdf.

Devetter, F.-X. and Rousseau, S. (2011) *Du Balai. Essai sur le ménage à domicile et le retour de la domesticité*. Paris: Raisons d'agir.

Dupont, C. [pseudonym of C. Delphy] (1970) 'L'ennemi principal', *Partisans*, 54–55, pp. 157–172.

Dussuet, A. (2017) 'Le 'travail domestique': une construction théorique féministe interrompue', *Recherches féministes*, 30(2), pp. 101–117.

Faugère, J.-P. (1980) 'L'allocation du temps entre travail domestique et travail marchand. Discussion autour d'un modèle', *Revue économique*, 31(2), pp. 313–346.

Folbre, N. (2009) 'Inequality and Time Use in the Household', in Nolan, B., Salverda, W. and Smeeding, T.M. (eds.) *The Oxford Handbook of Economic Inequality*. Oxford: Oxford University Press, pp. 342–363.

Gilbreth Carey, E. and Bunker Gilbreth, F. (2002 [1948]) *Cheaper by the Dozen*. New York: HarperCollins.

Gillian, C. (1982) *In a different Voice: Psychological Theory and Women's Development*, Cambridge, MA: Harvard University Press.

Giraud, O. (2017) 'L'introuvable démocratie du *care* ? La gouvernance multiscalaire des systèmes d'aide et de soins à domicile des personnes âgées entre néo-familialisme et privatisation: les cas de Hambourg et Édimbourg', *Revue européenne des sciences sociales*, 55(1), pp. 127–147.

Goodman, N. (1978) *Ways of Worldmaking*. Indianapolis, IN: Hackett Publishing Company.

Gornick, J. and Meyers, M. (2003) *Families that Work: Policies for Reconciling Parenthood and Employment*. New York: Russell Sage.

Hawrylyshyn, O. (1977) 'Towards a Definition of Non-Market Activities', *The Review of Income and Wealth*, 23(1), pp. 79–96.

Higgs, E. and Wilkinson, A. (2016) 'Women, Occupations and Work in the Victorian Censuses Revisited', *History Workshop Journal*, 81, pp. 17–38.

Hirata, H. (2021) *Le* care*, théories et pratiques*. Paris: La Dispute.

Hochschild, A., with Machung, A. (1989) *The Second Shift: Working Parents and the Revolution at Home*. New York: Viking.

Honegger, C. (1991) *Die Ordnung der Geschlechter. Die Wissenschaften vom Menschen und das Weib 1750–1850*. Frankfurt am Main: Campus.

Joyce, P. (ed.) (1987) *The Historical Meanings of Work*. Cambridge: Cambridge University Press.

Kessler-Harris, A. (1981) *Women Have Always Worked: A Historical Overview*. New York: The Feminist Press, The McGraw-Hill Book Company.

Lallement, M. (1990) *Des PME en chambre. Travail et travailleurs à domicile d'hier et d'aujourd'hui*. Paris: L'Harmattan.

Legouvé, E. (1897 [1848]) *Histoire morale des femmes*, Paris: J. Hetzel et Cie.

Lewis, J. (1992) 'Gender and the Development of Welfare Regimes', *Journal of European Social Policy*, 2(3), pp. 159–173.

Lützel, H. (1989) 'Household Production and National Accounts', *Statistic Journal of the United Nations*, 6, pp. 337–348.

Marinella, L. (1999) *The Nobility and Excellence of Women, and the Defects and Vices of Men*. Chicago, IL: University of Chicago Press.

Molinier, P. (2005) 'Le Care à l'épreuve du travail – Vulnérabilités croisées et savoir-être discrets', in Paperman, P. and Laugier, S. (eds.) *Le Souci des autres. Éthique et politique du care*. Paris: EHESS, pp. 299–316.

Parsons, T. and Bales, R. (eds.) (1955) *Family, Socialization, and Interaction Process*. Glencoe: Free press.

Pescarolo, A. (2018) 'Productive and Reproductive Work: Uses and Abuses of an Old Dichotomy', in Sarti, R., Bellavitis, A. and Martini, M. (eds.) *What Is Work? Gender at the Crossroad of Home, Family, and Business From the Early Modern Era to the Present*. New York and Oxford: Berghahn, pp. 114–138.

Ramey, V. (2009) 'Time Spent in Home Production in the Twentieth-Century United States: New Estimates from Old Data', *The Journal of Economic History*, 69(1), pp. 1–47.

Reid, M. (1934) *Economics of Household Production*. New York: John Wiley & Sons.

Rutherford, J.W. (2003) *Selling Mrs. Consumer: Christine Frederick and the Rise of Household Efficiency*. Athens, GA and London: The University of Georgia Press.

Sarti, R., Bellavitis, A. and Martini, M. (2018) 'Introduction: What Is Work? Gender at the Crossroad of Home, Family, and Business From the Early Modern Era to the Present', in Sarti, R., Bellavitis, A. and Martini, M. (eds.) *What Is Work? Gender at the Crossroad of Home, Family, and Business From the Early Modern Era to the Present*. New York and Oxford: Berghahn, pp. 1–87.

Schweitzer, S. (2002) *Les femmes ont toujours travaillé. Une histoire du travail des femmes aux XIXe et au XXe siècles*. Paris: Odile Jacob.

Simonton, D. (2006) 'Women Workers: Working Women', in Simonton, D. (ed.) *The Routledge History of Women in Europe Since 1700* London & New York: Routledge, pp. 134–176.

Tilly, L. and Scott, J. (1987) *Women, Work and Family*. London: Routledge & CRC Press.

Tronto, J. (1993) *Moral Boundaries: A Political Argument for an Ethic of Care*. New York: Routledge.

Weber, Marianne (1919) 'Zur Frage der Bewertung der Hausfrauenarbeit (1912)', in Weber, M. (ed.) *Frauenfragen und Frauengedanken*. Tübingen: J.C.B. Mohr, pp. 80–94.

Weber, Max (1992 [1904–1905]) *The Protestant Ethic and the Spirit of Capitalism*. London and New York: Routledge.

Wirth, E. (1892) *La future ménagère. Lectures et leçons sur l'économie domestique, la science du ménage, l'hygiène, les qualités et les connaissances nécessaires à une maîtresse de maison*. Paris: Hachette.

11

UNPAID WORK

Expansion and Mobilization of a Feminist Category

Maud Simonet

The COVID crisis has shone a bright light on a fact that feminist theories uncovered more than 40 years ago, namely that a huge amount of work is undertaken by women in the home, unpaid and invisible, and often framed in terms of love and natural duties toward other family members. As many scholars and journalists observed during the first lockdown, women were not only over-represented among "essential workers"[1] at the frontlines in healthcare services, education and supermarkets. They were also on the frontlines at home during the pandemic, cooking, providing home-schooling and many other forms of unpaid care. Calls for unpaid service also emerged outside the home, to volunteer in hospitals or deliver food to the elderly, to sew desperately needed masks, and women again were overrepresented in answering these calls.

This chapter will follow the category of "unpaid work" inside and outside the home in the last 50 years, studying its use both in the literature and in social movements. I will first recapitulate the political and scholarly discovery of "unpaid work" through an analysis of domestic work and the feminist controversies that swirled around it in the 1970s and 1980s. What is the value of unpaid domestic work? Who benefits from it? Does it mean the same for every woman assigned to it? How do other social relations such as race and class play a role in it? Secondly, I will explore the contemporary expansion of the category of "unpaid labor" outside the "home," namely the more or less institutionalized forms – from volunteering to workfare, from unpaid internships to digital labor, which have been categorized by scholars (Kaplan Daniels, 1988; Terranova, 2000; Krinsky, 2007; Taylor, 2015; Mensitieri, 2020) but also by social movements as "unpaid/invisible work" or "free labor." Drawing lessons from the feminist approach to "unpaid work," I will finally attempt to shed light on the institutionalization of unpaid work in the labor market today, analyzing both its politics and its conflicts.

DOI: 10.4324/9781003341321-14

I will then conclude by questioning the consequences of unpaid work as well as its meaning in terms of work transformation and work frontiers.

In the Name of Love: The Feminist Discovery of Domestic Work as Unpaid Work

> *They say it is love, we say it is unwaged work.*
>
> Silvia Federici (1975)

To start with domestic work[2] is to start at the beginning, and the concept of unpaid work is undoubtedly anchored in the feminist political and scientific revolution of the 1970s. Then, as French feminist Daniele Kergoat (Kergoat, 2000, p. 37) put it,

> it became collectively "obvious" that a huge amount of work is realized for free by women, that this work is invisible, that it is not done for oneself but for others, and always in the name of nature, love or maternal duty.

While fighting to make domestic activities visible as "work," both in the streets and through their statistics and analysis, feminist scholars and activists raised all those questions about "domestic work" that could possibly be broached regarding "unpaid work" and its value (Simonet, 2018). They did not necessarily agree on the answers, but there is a great deal which can be learned from the questions themselves and the controversies that engendered them.

In order to make domestic work visible, to reveal its importance to the economic system and its burden on women, feminist scholars and activists decided to measure it. Measuring domestic work, though, raised a series of questions and opened an "enduring debate" (Benaria, 1999) as to what the definition of "domestic work" precisely is. What is the unit that one should use to measure it? How should it be done? As technical as they might sound, such questions do indeed raise issues of a highly political nature. For instance, the "third-person criterion" (Hawrylyshyn, 1977; Hill, 1979), which was mainly chosen to elaborate an objective definition that would allow for comparisons across time and space, has largely been questioned. To what extent can we use it for activities such as playing with your child, walking your dog or washing yourself? Could one really delegate these activities? Conversely, other home-based activities that can be delegated to third parties – such as sexual intercourse in the form of prostitution – are "chastely eluded in the literature" (Roy and Poissonnier, 2017, p. 9).

Another set of questions concerned the "value issue" as framed by the statistician Annie Fouquet, that is, for domestic work "to become a social issue," and socially visible then "its estimation had to borrow the terms of the dominant economy: money" (Fouquet, 2001, p100).[3] But because the valuation operation implies relying on women's wages,[4] putting a price on domestic work perpetuates the gender inequalities already present in the labor market, such as wage discrimination and the occupational segregation of women (Benaria, 1999; Chadeau, 1992; Jany-Catrice and Meda, 2011). According to French economist Jean Gadrey (2012), existing monetary valuations of domestic work not only reproduce but even "amplify the inequality of which (women) are victims in the sphere of wage labor." As these inequalities partly rely on the fact that women's work is often assimilated to domestic work, and not properly valued on the labor market for that reason, the attempt to impose a monetary value on domestic work traps it in a vicious circle of devaluation.

If that first debate was about the "how" – how do we place a value on domestic work? – then a second controversy among Marxist feminists raised the question of "who." Who benefits from that unpaid domestic work which is mostly assigned to women? In other words, who is "the main enemy" (Delphy, 1977): capitalism or patriarchy?

Anchored in a feminist reading of Marx, second-wave feminist scholars opened up the debate "with and against Marx" (Bidet-Mordrel et al., 2016, p. 7) and among themselves. Feminist materialists all agreed on one point: Marx did not sufficiently theorize domestic work, and due to this "void" he evaded any analysis of the specific kind of oppression and exploitation that women endure. Marxist feminists intended to complete Marx's work, using his own legacy to amend it, but they did it in different ways. A famous international attempt was that of the "Wages for Housework" movement (Toupin, 2018) which laid the foundations for social-reproduction theory (Battacharya, 2017). Members of the international "Wages for Housework" movement such as Mariarosa Dalla Costa, Silvia Federici, Leopoldina Fortunati and Selma James developed an analysis of domestic work as reproduction work: the work that capitalism needs in order to reproduce the labor power. In order to function and develop itself, the capitalist system needs the workers to be fed, wear clean clothes, be loved, and be produced and reproduced. Women were assigned that task: "servicing the wage earner physically, emotionally, sexually, getting him ready to work day after day for the wage" (Cox and Federici, 1975, p. 4). "Behind every factory, behind every school, behind every office or mine is the hidden work of millions of women" (ibid, p. 5) and home is the place for that hidden factory, based on women's invisible and unpaid work. This international feminist movement asked for "wages for housework" (Federici, 1975) in order to denaturalize women's assignment to domestic work, to repoliticize this work and challenge the relation between houseworkers, mostly housewives, and capital by integrating housewives into the labor class.

It is not the capitalist class that benefits from the unpaid domestic work that women are doing, so stated radical-materialist feminists, it is the class of men! Like Christine Delphy (1978) in France, radical feminists also used the Marxist apparatus but in a way that was different from the social-reproduction perspective. According to Delphy, women are subject to capitalist exploitation but they are also subject to another type of exploitation, a domestic exploitation, which is the basis for a domestic – or patriarchal – mode of production. Domestic work then is not defined by a range of tasks but instead by its social conditions of production. It includes any type of work that the householder will extort and appropriate – the wife's cleaning or cooking for her family but also the clerical or accounting work for her husband's office. But when you bake your own cake or clean your own socks, this cannot account for unpaid work according to Delphy, as she believes "only services furnished *for others* should be so designated" (Delphy, 1978, p. 88). Delphy insists that patriarchal exploitation is not a relic of the past, nor are serfdom or slavery. Different types of exploitation coexist; they are not doomed to be subsumed by the capitalist variety. If Federici and Dalla Costa view capitalism as being in itself patriarchal, the radical-materialist position sees patriarchal and capitalist exploitation as coexisting and even combining with each other, while yet still referring to different processes.

Another important debate on domestic work emerged around the 1980s in the United States and opposed black feminism to "mainstream" feminism – that is, of the white middle-class variety. As described by bell hooks,

> middle-class women shaping feminist thought assumed that the most pressing problem for women was the need to get outside the home and work – to cease being 'just' housewives. . . . Work outside the home, feminist activists declared, was the key to liberation.
>
> *(hooks, 1984, p. 95)*

But bell hooks emphasized that

> when these women talked about work they were equating it with high-paying careers; they were not referring to low-paying jobs or so called "menial" labor. They were so blinded by their own experiences that they ignored the fact that a vast majority of women were . . . already working outside the home, working in jobs that neither liberated them from dependence on men nor made them economically self-sufficient.
>
> *(ibid., p. 95)*

So while "many white women's liberationists were saying 'we are tired of the isolation of the home, tired of relating only to children and husband, tired of being emotionally and economically dependent; we want to be liberated to enter the world of work," not only a great many black women but also working-class white women were saying "we want to have more time to share with family, we want to leave the world of alienated work" (ibid., p. 146).

The critical eye that bell hooks cast on 1970s feminist social movements and their analysis of unpaid domestic work merits our attention at two levels. The first one is the necessity of thinking beyond gender and bringing class and race relations into any analysis of the experience and meaning of domestic work. Laying the foundation for an intersectional analysis of work, she underscores how the feminist approach to domestic work (as a symbol of women's alienation) and to the labor market (as the source of their emancipation) is a class approach rooted in a white middle-class or upper-class experience of the world. In so doing she dishomogenizes the category of "woman." In contrast to an understanding of domestic work as dirty work or as a mental or physical burden, bell hooks calls our attention to the intimate and political meaning it can have. In her famous article "Homeplace (A Site of Resistance)" (hooks, 1990) she emphasizes the value of domestic work for black families in a society controlled and dominated by white people. Taking the example of her mother and grandmother she depicts how their involvement at home, creating and transmitting political subjectivity through housework, was an expression of subversion rather than of alienation. Domestic work can be considered a devaluated activity for some women, the most dominant ones, and a valuating one for others. Thus there is no one single social value for unpaid work but instead several that are socially constructed according to just how class and race relations intersect with gender.

In the end, all three of these debates raise the question of the value of unpaid work – albeit from different angles and in different registers – while also highlighting both the breadth and complexity of the issue. The debate about the monetary valuation of domestic work, for instance, simultaneously underscores the political need for this monetary equivalence as well as its limits and even perverse effects. The debate over the "main enemy" seeks to understand who ultimately appropriates this economic value produced by unpaid work and, as such, addresses the complex relations between capitalism and patriarchy. As for the debate whipped up by black feminism, it reminds us that our valuation of a certain activity depends on our position in the social space, which in turn is contingent on our class and race.

Lessons to be Learned: Domestic Work as the Matrix for Unpaid Work Outside the Home

Whether they defined unpaid domestic work relationally – through its domestic appropriation like Delphy, or as the process of reproduction like Federici – no materialist-feminist approach to domestic work strictly limited it to invisible unpaid work performed *in the house*. The house, and more precisely the home, was understood as the center of exploitation for the former and a center of production for the latter, but never as the one and only workplace for unpaid work. Baking your own cake in your own kitchen was not defined as unpaid work by Delphy, while doing your husband's accounting in his professional office was. And reproductive work takes place not only at home but in the schools, daycare, hospitals and retirement homes where the workers are mostly women, and their work partly invisible, naturalized and severely un(der)paid. Therefore it is important to keep in mind that the various feminist definitions of unpaid work that were mobilized in the aforementioned debates laid the foundation for an analysis of women's unpaid work beyond the home. Feminists not only questioned the dichotomy between work and family life but they provided us with a strong theoretical understanding of unpaid work and with crucial lessons so as to analyze the exploitation that characterizes it.

The first lesson, undoubtedly, concerns the definition of unpaid work. Analyses of domestic work teach us that it cannot simply be defined in a negative fashion – as work that is *not* paid. Feminists stress that unpaid work is not a simple matter of subtraction (work minus pay) but a denial process. It is a non-recognition of the worker as a worker in the name of her recognition as something else: as "woman," "mother" or "wife." Domestic work is at the same time unpaid and invisible as "work," per se, because it is visible as "love." Its monetary devaluation is justified by this other form of valuation: this is not work, this is love! Therefore the notion of unpaid work, as it emerges from this feminist perspective, is an appropriation as work of an activity that is neither subjectively experienced nor socially defined as such but as something else. It is through this denial and in the name of this value that this appropriation operates.

Therefore this specific definition of unpaid work lays the groundwork for an understanding of exploitation that is significantly different from the traditional Marxist one. In order to function, reproduction-theory feminists state, capitalist exploitation reaches far beyond the factory, the firm and the market, into "our kitchens and our bedrooms" (Cox and Federici, 1975, p4). The radical-materialist feminist perspective, for its part, invites us to consider exploitation beyond its capitalist form. Delphy insists that not all forms of exploitation are rooted in the market. Despite their different understanding of the "nature" of domestic-work exploitation, both of these Marxist-feminist approaches converge in forcing us to step out of the traditional equation: exploitation = wage labor = market. They open up another understanding of where and how exploitation happens – in our intimate and supposedly "non-work" spheres – and invite us to bring values back in our theory of value.

Last but not least, feminist debates on domestic work have shed light on the extent to which unpaid work is caught up in social relations, gender relations of course, but also relations of class and race. This is the case both in its process of assignment (unpaid work is mainly assigned to women) and in its social uses (it has different meanings for different women, depending on their class and race).

Paying attention to various more or less institutionalized forms of unpaid work in the last 20 years, scholars from assorted disciplines have taken the analysis of unpaid work far beyond the four walls of the "home."

From Arlene Kaplan Daniel's pioneering analysis of volunteering as "invisible work" (1988) to the contemporary studies of "hope labor" (Kuehn and Corrigan, 2013) or "sacrificial labor" (Ross, 2009) in the cultural industries; from media scholar Kylie Jarrett's "digital housewife" (2017) to information technology theorist Titziana Terranova's (2000) or workfare specialist John Krinsky's "free labor" (2007), the issue of unpaid work has emanated in many strands of work and labor studies. Studying internship, volunteering, and user collaboration, scholars have analyzed the role of unpaid work in the development of various industries: the media (Hesmondhalgh and Percival, 2014), fashion (Mears, 2011, 2020; Mensitieri, 2020) or the online economy (Kuehn and Corrigan, 2013; Duffy, 2017). They made unpaid labor – such as volunteering, civic service and workfare – visible in the running of public services (Chambré, 1989; Muehlebach, 2012; Krinsky and Simonet, 2017). They also disclosed its importance in the functioning of the labor market (Krinsky, 2007; Hustinx and De Waele, 2018) and in the construction of individual lives and careers (Kaplan Daniels, 1988; Taylor, 2015; Simonet, 2010; Ihaddadene, 2018; Aubry, 2018; Jourdain and Naulin, 2019).

The reference to feminist studies and their analysis of domestic work as unpaid work broadly varies among these different research approaches, ranging from an uninformed silence to a strong tribute. Many of the questions raised by digital-labor scholars over the definition and frontiers of work, for instance, echo those debated by feminist statisticians 40 years earlier. Should writing a blog, configuring one's Facebook page or posting an online comment be considered work? Can one speak of exploitation if value is derived from my online activities but no one forces me to engage in them and I actually take pleasure in doing so? Only a few scholars have acknowledged that echo, though, and even fewer have built theories upon it. While Kyllie Jarrett's *Digital Housewife* (2017) fully embraces and applies Federici's perspective to her analysis of digital labor, Trebor Scholz (2012, p. 6) mainly underscores how "shifts of labor markets to the Internet are described as an intensification of traditional economies of unpaid work" and how "casual digital labor is much akin to those less visible, unsung forms of traditional women's labor such as child care, housework and surrogacy."

Nevertheless, taken together, these contemporary studies of unpaid work in the labor market undoubtedly pursue the feminist perspectives initiated with the domestic-work debates. They analyze how unpaid work is not necessarily obtained through coercion but voluntarily – in the name of love, art, passion, citizenship, training, a job to come or a "jackpot to win" (Ross, 2009). As Evelyn Nakano Glenn asserted in *Forced to Care* (2010, p. 11) these studies invite us to trace the "different strands of coercion" and acknowledge the fact that "exploitation has been made possible by multifarious forms of coercion, ranging from personal moral persuasion to the force of impersonal legal doctrines, from internalized feelings of obligation to external constraints of the labor market." Krinsky in his studies of workfare – the shift in welfare programs whereby they have beneficiaries work off their benefits – and Terranova in her analysis of digital labor both stressed that multifarious character by using the notion of "free labor" and playing with the double meaning of "free." Referring to activities such as "building Web sites, modifying software packages, reading and participating in mailing lists, and building virtual spaces," Titiziana Terranova's pioneering article on digital labor emphasized that they are "simultaneously voluntarily given and unwaged, enjoyed and exploited" (Terranova, 2000, p. 33). The question mark in Krinsky's title – *Free Labor? Workfare and the Contested Language of Neoliberalism* – challenges the "freedom" of the workfare-unpaid worker when considered as a worker and not just as a welfare recipient.

These contemporary studies also challenge the traditional work/non-work dichotomy by illustrating how unpaid work is not only performed outside the labor market (in the "non-work" spheres) but clearly in its center, as emphasized by the frequent use of (unpaid) *labor* instead of (unpaid) *work*. People do for free (as an intern, volunteer, passionate blogger) what other people right adjacent to them (in a nonprofit, a public service or online) are being paid for and sometimes perform as their main professional activity.

But if unpaid work is both fully developed and inscribed in the labor market today, it neither takes on the same meaning nor comes at the same cost for everyone. While women are still predominantly assigned to unpaid work – whether in volunteering, civic service, workfare or unpaid internships – studies such as Mensitieri's (2020) on unpaid work in the fashion industry or Ross Perlin's *Intern Nation* both raise a class issue, pointing to those privileged individuals who can afford to work for free, whereas other parts of the workforce cannot afford to "earn nothing" (Perlin, 2012).

Last but not least, it is not only academics who have mobilized the category of unpaid work. Concomitant to this prolific but fragmented literature, various forms of unpaid work, ranging from workfare to internship, have been the stage for social mobilization and the fight against both their social invisibility and economic appropriation . . . just as domestic work was in the 1970s, and sometimes with an explicit reference to it.

The Institutionalization of Unpaid Work: Politics and Conflicts on the Frontier of Work

Whether they explicitly refer to the feminist approach or not, scholars studying the development and institutionalization of unpaid work on the labor market have analyzed it as a capitalist neoliberal policy aiming to provide goods or services at the lowest possible cost and put people to work at any price, namely through a new regime of proof and promise.

Studying unpaid work as the result of a public policy hardly goes without saying. If workfare is usually understood as such, volunteering is commonly perceived as the opposite: as a grassroots activity in an autonomous civil society, mostly described in the Anglo-Saxon context as "the community," that is, distinct from the state and government. American sociologist Susan Chambré's article "Kindling Points of Light: Volunteering as Public Policy" (1989) and political scientist Theda Skocpol's 1996 article "What Tocqueville Missed: Government Made All That 'Volunteerism' Possible" both seriously question this common perception. By bringing the state back into the analysis of volunteering (Skocpol, 1985) they pave the way for an analysis of public policy that makes political use of volunteering and volunteers that goes beyond the American example.

Studying David Cameron's "Big Society" narratives and achievements, Britain sociologist Stephen Bach wrote that this program supporting the development of civil society against "big government" was "integrally connected to deficit reduction with the voluntary sector and an increased emphasis on volunteering promoted as a more user–centered and cost–effective way of delivering public services in tough times" (2012, p. 399). In *The Moral Neoliberal*, anthropologist Andrea Muehlebach also analyzed, in the Italian context, the growing reliance on volunteers for the delivery of public services, its rhetoric, and the shift in citizenship that it illustrates. Visiting several sites across the region of Lombardy, from Milanese high schools to the offices of state social workers to the homes of the needy, Muehlebach showed the rise of an ethical citizenship where volunteer work was proof of good citizenship in the wake of the state's withdrawal of social-service programs: "The Italian State has in the last three decades, intent to mobilize a part of the population in a volunteer-work regime, a regime that allows the State to amalgamate volunteer work and good citizenship, unpaid work and gift" (Muehlebach, 2012, p. 6).

This analysis of a neoliberal citizenship becoming "conditional on conduct" (Rose, 2000, p. 1407) connects the politics of volunteering to the politics of workfare where this notion of active and responsible citizenship is enforced and prominently so through compulsory unpaid labor in exchange for benefits.[5] In New York City's parks, after the 1975 fiscal crisis, both workfare recipients and volunteers were enrolled in order to take on part of the public employees' maintenance work (Krinsky and Simonet, 2017). Beyond workfare, scholars have recently studied the development of "volunteer programs for migrants" in Switzerland (Aubry, 2018) and in Italy (Di Cecco, 2021) where migrants are encouraged to spend time cleaning the city streets or serving food in soup kitchens in order to show proof of good citizenship. It is through this unpaid work in the public sphere that a new "figure of deserving migrants" (ibid, p. 185) has emerged, that of the "volunteer migrant, grateful and active, willing to perform free activities of general interest" and reflecting a broader "moral economy of civic worth" in migration policies (Chauvin and Garces-Mascareñas, 2012).

In the meantime different work and labor-research studies – mostly on the art, media and the technology sector, – have pointed out how "unpaid internships, 'runner' positions or 'working for free' are an embedded part of careers in these industries" (Taylor, 2015, p. 493). In a study conducted in 2005 on the English film and television industries, Percival and Hesmondhalgh showed that 75 percent of 1,071 independent workers had been subject to unpaid work, which the authors estimate as having benefited their employers to the tune of 28 million pounds. In wondering whether "working for nothing" has become "the latest high-growth sector," the American sociologist Andrew Ross analyzed developments in the creative industries and of " 'working for exposure' as a normative career mentality" (Ross, 2017, p 189).

Whether they focus on the public sector or the media and fashion industries or platform capitalism, these studies disclose and question the growing political use and economic reliance on unpaid labor. But they also converge in pointing out the progressive institutionalization of a regime of proofs on the labor market and where unpaid labor stands as the ultimate proof of value. In the same way that domestic work proved your quality as a mother and a spouse and attested to your "full femininity," working for free attests that you are "a real artist," a "passionate writer," "a good citizen" or a "deserving migrant."

That regime of proof is inscribed in a regime of promise, or as Bascetta (2015) phrased it "a political economy of promise." The notion of "hope labor" introduced by Kuehn and Corrigan (2013, p. 21) encapsulated this phenomenon. They defined it as "un- or under-compensated work carried out in the present, often for experience or exposure, in the hope that future employment opportunities may follow." In her book *(Not) Getting Paid to Do What You Love* (2017), social-media scholar Brooke Erin Duffy developed the concept of "aspirational labor" to describe the "highly gendered, forward-looking and entrepreneurial enactment of creativity" that pushes many women to work for free on social media platforms. Duffy argues that "aspirational labourers pursue productive activities that hold the promise of social and economic capital; yet the reward system for these aspirants is highly uneven" (2017, p. 12) and she empirically and theoretically connects the activities of these women on media platforms to larger shifts in unpaid and gendered labor.

From the class-action lawsuit of unpaid bloggers against Huffington Post (Simonet, 2018) to the organizing of workfare beneficiaries (Krinsky, 2007) or the recent strike of interns in Quebec (Schirmer, 2019), in the last two decades the political and economic use of unpaid work has been contested by various social movements and through different repertoires. Interestingly, the link between these contests and the feminist contest against domestic work was made explicit in many of these movements' slogan. While the interns on strike in Montreal in 2017–2018 were walking the street claiming that "the intern strike is a women's strike" and asking for a "wage for students" to end students' invisible and unpaid work, artists in Geneva launched a "Wages for/against Artwork" campaign to contest the exploitation of artists through unpaid labor. A few years before, in 2014, the manifesto "Wages for Facebook"[6] was put online to denounce the appropriation of Internet users' work on and by social networks. It opened with a rewrite of Federici's famous sentence – from "They say it is love. We say it is unwaged work," – to "They say it's friendship. We say it's unwaged work." The first "Wages for/against Artwork" manifesto also ended with that same poetry, replacing "women" with "artists" and "housewife" with "worker."

With regard to contemporary references to the "Wages for Housework" movement, Silvia Federici (2018, p. 28) commented that at "a time when unpaid labor is expanding like an oil stain into every corner of the capitalist organization of work. . . . more workers are today recognizing the essential similarity of their work condition with that of a housewife." Her comment echoes previous feminist analyses of the transformation of work under current capitalism, which pictured the housewife not as a relic of the past but as the new model worker of capitalism's future. While Claudia von Werlhof predicted a housewife-ization of work in "The proletarian is dead. Long live the housewife!" (1984), Donna Haraway (1991, p. 166) observed the development of a "homework economy outside the home" in which "work is being redefined as both literally female and feminized, whether performed by men or women." Depicted as an unpaid worker who is always at an employer's behest, with no right to strike, no working hours, no conditions of work, no contractually stipulated holidays or leisure time, who is individualized and atomized and "works out of love and (whose) love becomes work" (von Werlhof, 1984, p. 140), the housewife may very well be the ideal worker for today's "capitalist's dream" (Ross, 2011).

Thus, decades after the feminist scientific and political revolution of domestic work, a growing but fragmented number of studies, along with various social movements, are shedding light on the institutionalization of unpaid work at the heart of the labor market – in the running of public services, nonprofit organizations and private industries. Scholars are pointing out how volunteering, internship, digital labor, workfare and more generally "working for nothing" are all embedded within a regime of proof and promise, unveiling the rhetoric and practices of capitalism's work on the frontiers of work (Simonet, 2020). Yet when sociologists observe, analyze and talk about "work" the majority of them still do not include domestic work, volunteer work and more broadly unpaid work in their operational and theoretical concept and their empirical settings.

In the four decades since the "domestic labor debate," women as workers have been integrated or "added" – as suggested by Wajcman (2003) – to labor and work studies. Then again, women's work and the sexual division of labor – and more broadly gender at work – have become increasingly legitimate as perspectives for studying work and labor today. But the feminist definition of work in its questioning of our "folk understanding of work" as "paid work" (Kaplan Daniels, 1988) has not yet fully broken into the mainstream sociology on work and labor. If women count as workers then "the concept of worker" itself, as Nancy Fraser put it, still "has an implicit gender subtext" (2013, p. 38). And by being epistemologically gender-blind with our categories, by equating work with paid work, we may "fail to grasp the full character of the spirit of neoliberal capitalism" (Fraser, 2013, p. 220). For instance, we might merely focus on its "masculinist romance" of the "free, unencumbered, self-fashioning individual" (ibid., p. 220) and miss those other driving forces which are putting people to work and sometimes (increasingly so) for nothing. Nothing but love, care, passion, citizenship or hope . . .

By neglecting this feminine face of neoliberalism, its work denial process and its value rhetoric, we may fail to grasp, in a more materialistic way, the big picture of capitalism's current modus operandi, that is, exploitation and value production, and how it actually transforms work experience, conditions and careers. It does so for women, as feminists' approaches to unpaid work have long emphasized, but not *only* for them and not necessarily for all of them in the exact same way. Maybe it is time to return the analysis of unpaid work "from margin to center" (hook, 1984) so as to realize the feminist project of fully grasping how social relations intersect with work in all its forms.

Notes

1 See also the chapter "Essential Work: A Category in the Making?" by Lisa Herzog, Katrin Sold and Bénédicte Zimmermann in this volume.
2 See also the chapter "Domestic Work: The Invention of a Gendered Relationship" by Michel Lallement in this volume.
3 Twenty years later, recalling her pioneer article on the measurement of domestic work in France (Chadeau and Fouquet, 1981), Fouquet noted that another article based on the same data and published in the same journal the exact same year but measuring domestic work in terms of time spent (Rousse and Roy, 1981) was received with "irony and mockery" by the press while hers, which converted domestic work into monetary units, was regarded as a "revelation."
4 Whether it uses the market-replacement approach, which imputes wages that reflect the market price of the domestic tasks, or the opportunity-cost approach which assumes that time spent on unpaid work is at the expense of earning a market wage.
5 As Sylvie Morel wrote, "unpaid work" is "the activity that best represents the notion of reciprocity associated with workfare" and coincides with "a pattern of conduct ruled by the ethic of work" (Morel, 2000, p. 20, 188).
6 http://wagesforfacebook.com/

References

Aubry, A. (2018) 'Immigrant Men and Voluntary Work in a Swiss City', *Metropolitics*, 15 May.

Bach, S. (2012) 'Shrinking the State or the Big Society? Public Service Employment Relations in an Era of Austerity', *Industrial Relations Journal*, 43(5), pp. 399–415.

Bascetta, M. (ed.) (2015) *Economia Politica della promessa*, Rome: Manifesto libri.

Battacharya, T. (ed.) (2017) *Social Reproduction Theory: Remapping Class, Recentering Oppression*. London: Pluto Press.

Benaria, L. (1999) 'The Enduring Debate Over Unpaid Labor', *International Labor Review*, 138(3), pp. 298–309.

Bidet-Mordrel, A., Galerand, E. and Kergoat, D. (2016) 'Analyse critique et féminismes matérialistes. Travail, sexualité, culture', *Cahiers du Genre*, 3, pp. 5–27.

Chadeau, A. (1992) 'Que vaut la production non marchande des ménages?', *Revue Économique de l'OCDE*, 18, pp. 95–114.

Chadeau, A. and Fouquet, A. (1981) 'Peut-on mesurer le travail domestique?', *Economie et statistique*, 136, pp. 29–42.

Chambré, S.M. (1989) 'Kindling Points of Light: Volunteering as Public Policy', *Nonprofit and Voluntary Sector Quarterly*, 19, pp. 249–268.

Chauvin, S. and Garces-Mascareñas, B. (2012) 'Beyond Informal Citizenship: The New Moral Economy of Migrant Illegality', *International Political Sociology*, 6(3), pp. 241–259.

Cox, N. and Federici, S. (1975) *Counter-Planning From the Kitchen*. Bristol: Falling Wall Press.
Delphy, C. (1977) *The Main Enemy: A Materialist Analysis of Women's Oppression*. London: Women's Research and Resources Centre Publications.
Delphy, C. (1978) *Close to Home: A Materialist Analysis of Women's Oppression*. London: Verso.
Di Cecco, S. (2021) 'Le demandeur d'asile bénévole, nouvelle figure du "migrant méritant"?', *Revue européenne des migrations internationales*, 37–1(1–2), pp. 185–206.
Duffy, B. E. (2017) *(Not) Getting Paid to Do What You Love: Gender, Social Media, and Aspirational Work*. New Haven, CT; London: Yale University Press, 320 p.
Federici, S. (1975) *Wages Against Housework*. Bristol: Fallling Wall Press and the Power of Women Collective.
Federici, S. and Austin, A. (2018) *The New York Wages for Housework Committee, 1972–1977: History, Theory and Documents*. New York: Autnomedia.
Fouquet, A. (2001) 'Le travail domestique: du travail invisible au "gisement" d'emplois', in Laufer, J., Marry, C. and Maruani, M. (eds.) *Masculin-Féminin- Questions pour les sciences de l'homme*, Paris: Presses Universitaires de France, pp. 99–127.
Fraser, N. (2013) *Fortunes of Feminism: From State-Managed Capitalism to Neoliberal Crisis*. London: Verso.
Gadrey, J. (2012) 'Le travail domestique: 33% du PIB pour 160% du travail rémunéré?', https://blogs.alternatives-economiques.fr/gadrey/2012/11/28/le-travail-domestique-33-du-pib-pour-160-du-travail-remunere.
Haraway, D. (1991) *Simians, Cyborg, and Women – The Reinvention of Nature*. London: Routledge.
Hawrylyshyn, O. (1977) 'Towards a Definition of Non-Market Activities', *Review of Income and Wealth*, pp. 79–96.
Hesmondhalgh, D. and Percival, N. (2014) 'Unpaid Work in the UK Television and Film Industries: Resistance and Changing Attitudes', *European Journal of Communication*, 29(2), pp. 188–203.
Hill, T. (1979) 'Do-It-Yourself and GDP', *Review of Income and Wealth*, 25(1), pp. 31–39.
hooks, b. (1984) *Feminist Theory: From Margin to Center*. Boston, MA: South End Press.
hooks, b. (1990) 'Homeplace (A Site of Resistance)', *Yearning: Race, Gender and Cultural Politics*. Boston, MA: South End Press, pp. 41–49.
Hustinx, L. and De Waele, E. (2018) 'Governing Through Volunteering: The Discursive Field of Government-Initiated Volunteering in the Form of Workfare Volunteering', *Nonprofit and Voluntary Sector Quarterly*, 48(2 suppl), pp. 72–102.
Ihaddadene, F. (2018) 'Politiques d'engagement ou d'employabilité? Concurrences au sein des programmes de volontariat à Madagascar', *Critique internationale*, 81(4), pp. 63–82.
Jany-Catrice, F. and Méda, D. (2011) 'Femmes et richesse: au-delà du PIB', *Travail, genre et sociétés*, 2(26), pp. 147–171.
Jarrett, K., (2017) *Feminism, Labour and Digital Media: The Digital Housewife*. New York: Routledge.
Jourdain, A. and Naulin, S. (eds.) (2019) *The Social Meaning of Extra Money: Capitalism and the Commodification of Domestic and Leisure Activities*. London: Palgrave Macmillan.
Kaplan Daniels, A. (1988) *Invisible Careers: Women Civic Leaders from the Volunteer World*. Chicago, IL: The University of Chicago Press.
Kergoat, D. (2000) 'Division sexuelle du travail et rapports sociaux de sexe', *Dictionnaire critique du féminisme*. Paris: Presses Universitaires de France, p. 37.

Krinsky, J. (2007) *Free Labor? Workfare and the Contested Language of Neoliberalism*. Chicago, IL: The University of Chicago Press.

Krinsky, J. and Simonet, M. (2017) *Who Cleans the Park? Public Work and Urban Governance in New York City*. Chicago: The University of Chicago Press.

Kuehn, K. and Corrigan, T. (2013) 'Hope Labor: The Role of Employment Prospects in Online Social Production', *The Political Economy of Communication*, 1(1), pp. 9–25.

Mears, A. (2011) *Pricing Beauty: The Making of a Fashion Model*. University of California Press.

Mears, A. (2020) *Very Important People: Status and Beauty in the Global Party Circuit*. Princeton, Princeton University Press.

Mensitieri, G. (2020) *The Most Beautiful Job in the World: Lifting the Veil of the Fashion Industry*. London: Bloomsbury.

Morel, S. (2000) *Les logiques de la réciprocité, les transformations de la relation d'assistance aux États-Unis et en France*. Paris: Presses Universitaires de France.

Muehlebach, A. (2012) *The Moral Neoliberal: Welfare and Citizenship in Italy*. Chicago, IL: The University of Chicago Press.

Nakano, G.E. (2010) *Forced to Care: Coercion and Caregiving in America*. Cambridge, MA: Harvard University Press.

Perlin, R. (2012) *Intern Nation: How to Earn Nothing and Learn Little in the Brave New Economy*. London: Verso Books.

Rose, N. (2000) 'Community, Citizenship, and the Third Way', *American Behavioral Scientist*, 43(9), pp. 1395–1411.

Ross, A. (2009) *Nice Work If You Can Get It: Life and Labour in Precarious Times*. New York: NYU Press.

Ross, A. (2011) 'A Capitalist's Dream', *London Review of Books*, 33(10).

Ross, A. (2017) 'Working for Nothing: The Latest High-Growth Sector?', in Armano, E., Bove, A. and Murgia, A. (eds.) *Mapping Precariousness: Labour Insecurity and Uncertain Livelihoods*. London: Routledge, pp. 189–198.

Rousse, H. and Roy, C. (1981) 'Activités ménagères et cycle de vie', *Economie et statistique*, 131, pp. 56–67.

Roy, D. and Poissonnier, A. (2017) 'Household Satellite Account for France: Methodological Issues on the Assessment of Domestic Production', *Review of Income and Wealth*, 63(2), pp. 353–377.

Schirmer, E. (2019) 'Pay Your Interns Now: An Interview With Isabelle Cheng and Paolo Miriello-Lapointe', *Jacobin*. https://jacobinmag.com/2019/03/quebec-unpaid-internships-strike-university.

Scholz, T. (ed.) (2012) *Digital Labor: The Internet as Playground and Factory*. London: Routledge.

Simonet, M. (2010) *Le travail bénévole: Engagement citoyen ou travail gratuit?* Paris: La dispute.

Simonet, M. (2018) *Travail gratuit, la nouvelle exploitation?* Paris: Textuel.

Simonet, M. (2020) 'Having or Blurring It All? Capitalism's Work on the Frontier', in Naulin, S. and Jourdain, A. (eds.) *The Social Meaning of Extra Money: Capitalism and the Commodification of Domestic and Leisure Activities*. London: Palgrave Macmillan, pp. 269-273.

Skocpol, T. (1985) *Bringing the State Back In: Strategies of Analysis in Current Research*. Cambridge: Cambridge University Press.

Skocpol, T. (1997) 'The Tocqueville Problem: Civic Engagement in American Democracy', *Social Science History*, 21(4), pp. 455–479.

Taylor, R. (2015) 'Volunteering and Unpaid Work', in Edgell, S., Heidi, G. and Granter, E. (eds.) *The Sage Handbook of the Sociology of Work and Employment*. London: SAGE Publications, pp. 485–501.

Terranova, T. (2000) 'Free Labor: Producing Culture for the Digital Economy', *Social Text*, 63(18–2), pp. 33–58.

Toupin, L. (2018) *Wages for Housework: A History of an International Feminist Movement*. London: Pluto Press.

Von Werlhof, C. (1984) 'The Proletarian Is Dead: Long Live the Housewife?', in Smith, J., Wallerstein, I. and Evers, H.-D. (eds.) *Households and the World-Economy*. Beverly Hills, CA: SAGE Publications, pp. 131–147.

Wajcman, J. (2003) 'Le genre au travail', in Laufer, J., Marry, C. and Maruani, M. (eds.) *Le travail du genre, les sciences sociales à l'épreuve des différences de sexe*. Paris: La Découverte.

12

EMOTIONAL LABOR

Concept and Practical Categorizations in Light of COVID Critical Care Nursing

Robert McMurray, Nicki Credland, Martyn Griffin, Peter Hamilton, Oonagh Harness and Kimberly Jamie

Introduction

Within masculine traditions of management and organization studies, emotion has long been placed in ontological opposition to reason (Ward and McMurray, 2016). Whether considered in terms of positivistic accounts of management research and practice (Shuler and Sypher, 2000) Weberian bureaucratic archetypes (Weber, 1946) or rationalizing processes (Taylor, 1911; Ritzer, 1993) reason was separated from and raised above emotion, downplaying the importance of the later in organized work. Preoccupations with abstraction, taxonomy, rules, efficiency and structure positioned emotion as inferior, invalid and unwanted when it comes to the workplace (Hancock and Tyler, 2001; Ward, 2019; Lawley and Caven, 2019). It encouraged us to forget that organizing and managing are primarily about seeing and working with people (McMurray and Pullen, 2019) and that emotions are central to such work.

By the turn of the twentieth century, scholars had established that which every laborer knew: emotion is ever-present in work and organizing (Hochschild, 1983; Fineman, 2001; Korczynski, 2009). As humor emotion is at the heart of the entertainment industries; as aggression it is writ large in military campaigns; and as compassion it is central to health provision. Emotion may be formally recognized in the constitution of job roles and work tasks, or informally present in gallows humor and office intimacy. Depending on context and audience, any given emotion can be framed as good or bad: to be encouraged or sanctioned. In this sense, emotion is central to organizing. Indeed, rather than eschewing emotions; managers now seek to control and commodify the feelings of workers in exchange for a wage. In short, our organizations, managers and customers require most of us to labor emotionally (Hochschild, 1983; Korczynski, 2001).

DOI: 10.4324/9781003341321-15

This chapter considers the conceptualization and categorization of emotional labor over the past 40 years. We begin by outlining emotional labor as a concept: as a class of that which is being represented and analyzed during categorization. Hochschild's (1983) foundational work in this area gives rise to a singular concept that usefully distinguishes between the performance of emotions for use and exchange value. From here it is possible to identify the enactment of different categories of emotional labor according to style and depth. We consider those categories by drawing on research with Critical Care Nurses working amidst the COVID-19 global pandemic.[1] Laboring at the extreme edge of medical and nursing care, Critical Care Nurses specialize in attending to those who are critically ill or suffering from life-threatening conditions, while at the same time managing sorrow, anger, hope, despair, joy, death and recovery at the bedside of the patient. Nurses such as these are instructive in terms of their long association with emotions and emotional labor (see, e.g., Katz, 1969; Abbott and Meerabeau, 1998; Bolton, 2001; Nelson and Gordon, 2004; Bolton, 2005; Kirkpatrick et al., 2005; Currie et al., 2008; Morgan and Ogbonna, 2008; Maben et al., 2009; McMurray, 2012) and our analysis extends understanding of the ways in which emotional labor not only describes a facet of occupational work, but also as a site of power, politics and contestation that informs personal positions and professional identities.

We proceed by defining emotional labor as a concept, before exploring the ways in which such work is categorized according to "depth" of performance and the mediating effects of temporality and context. The third section considers how we might categorize different "styles" of emotional labor and the interplay between them. As the chapter draws to a close, we consider the personal-professional effects of such labor and our collective duty of care.

Conceptualizing Emotional Labor

Writing about the work of flight attendants and debt collectors, Hochschild (1983) was among the first to consider the trend for employers to commodify not just our physical and mental capabilities but also our emotional capacities (Ward and McMurray, 2016). Her work shed light on the ways in which managers were increasingly concerned with controlling that which had been regarded as the private domain of individuals, namely, feelings. Identifying the root of emotional labor in her reading of Marx, Hochschild defined the phenomenon as:

> the management of feeling to create a publicly observable facial and bodily display; emotional labour is sold for a wage and therefore has *exchange value* . . . This labour requires one to induce or suppress feeling in order to sustain the outward countenance that produces the proper state of mind in others.
>
> *(Hochschild, 1983, p. 7)*

The aforementioned definition draws attention to the distinction between "use" and "exchange" value when it comes to feelings. Something can be said to have *use* value when it has utility to the individuals involved, is not compensated and the individual has sole discretion over the performances offered. Often grouped under the term emotion work, examples might include a joke between friends or pretending to like an unwanted gift from a much-loved aunt. In these contexts, the management of feelings is unpaid and intended to maintain a relationship in our private life and social spheres, including the workplace.

Emotional labor refers to feelings that are performed and traded for payment. It describes the requirement placed on employees to express organizationally desired emotions in order to complete tasks or deliver services in exchange for a wage (Morris and Feldman, 1996). Emotional labor takes place within organized relations informed by wider sets of feeling and display rules. Preferred emotional displays are encouraged by "feeling rules" that circulate through an organization and are intended to encourage workers to offer performances that contribute to the collective good (e.g., the smile of the airline steward, the enthusiasm of the Disney performer or the empathy of the pallbearer). Feeling rules determine "what is 'due' in each relation, each role" (Hochschild, 1983, p. 18) and may be reinforced by training, mentoring, professional codes, guides to best practice, the implicit rules for "getting on" in an organization, the expectations generated in advertising, relations between workers and, the traditions of interaction within a given context. Because these rules seek to prescribe what counts as an appropriate performance in terms of timing content and form, workers are often required to express emotions they do not feel: to suppress or fake that which is felt in return for a wage. This gives rise to different categories of emotional labor. Our first categorization pertains to the depth of emotional offering.

Categories: Surface and Deep Acting

The requirement to act or present that which one does not feel is labeled "surface acting" by Hochschild (1983). Surface acting describes the practice of deceiving others about how we really feel while not deceiving ourselves. When surface acting, a worker complies with the service or relational requirement for which they are being paid by faking happiness, empathy or aggression as part of their attempt to manipulate an encounter. Examples might include the fast-food operative who wishes a rude customer "a nice day," the bored lecturer faking excitement for a subject, or the bartender who feigns interest in drunken stories and wears a "wooden smile" (Seymour and Sandiford, 2005, p. 556) in hope of a better tip. Within the context of the COVID pandemic and the work of Critical Care Nurses, surface acting manifests somewhat differently. For many, it took the form of masking feelings of stress, depression and burnout with a positive demeanor:

> During Covid times, I really didn't want to be there at all. The morale was just so low. It was just awful. . . . And then feeling it yourself as well, but trying to be upbeat.
>
> *(CCN001)*[2]

At other times workers may engage in what is known as deep acting. Going beyond the "smile that's just painted on" (Hochschild, 1983, p. 33) deep acting requires the worker to self-induce a real feeling (based on a past event or imagined scenario) that is then offered up in the new context of the service encounter. In essence, the worker learns to feel that which they perform, such that the customer is less aware of the socially engineered nature of the encounter. Years of enculturation within a given organization or field mixed with a daily carrot-and-stick discipline, conspire to push corporate feeling rules further and further away from self-awareness. Eventually, these rules about how to see things and how to feel about them come to seem "natural", a part of one's personality. (Hochschild, 1983, p. 155)

Returning to the example of the Critical Care Nurse earlier, we can see how on a "normal basis" she had learned to self-induce the identity of the upbeat person, this despite unwanted early starts:

> Normally, I'm a really upbeat person, a positive person at work. Don't get me wrong (laughs), nobody wants to get up at six o'clock in the morning and go to work, but as much as that was hard – that is hard on a normal basis – as soon as I got to work, I'd be fine. . . . I know if you ask my colleagues what kind of nurse/person I am, they'd say the jolly one with a smile on her face all the time.
>
> *(CCN001)*

In the aforementioned case, the routine of work initiated the performance of "a positive person at work": a performance that the nurse had come to see as part of her natural personality. It was also a performance and identity which colleagues accepted and expected.

Temporality, Intensity and Depth

The ability to engineer deeper performances often takes time (Harness et al., 2020). Examining the work of hairdressers, Harness et al. (2020) note that temporality has the potential to impact performance depth. Where interactions recur over an extended period and affective relations flourish, deep acting may emerge as "faking" becomes unnecessary (Price and Arnould, 1999). In the case of worker–client relations "commercial" or "quasi" friendships can develop that allow greater interpersonal sharing and even favors (Harness et al., 2020). Moreover, rather than being premised upon conformity with prevailing social norms and occupational display rules, the development of shared narratives may lead to the transgression of normal display rules (Bolton and Boyd, 2003) as worker and client share confidences, display unregulated emotion and reciprocate in the exchange of information over life events, confidences and personal details not usually shared as part of working interactions (Harness et al., 2020).

There is, however, no simple linear relationship between the recurrence of interactions over time and the depth of emotional performance. Our work with Critical Care Nurses suggests that relatively brief relations (days or weeks) which are characterized by high-intensity or extreme context can lead to the rapid development of deep acting which some nurses frame as an attachment to clients and their families:

> the emotional attachment . . . if you have the same patient that's very sick four nights in a row and then taking that home is very emotionally distressing . . . it's almost like you have this emotional attachment to them and to the family because you're constantly in contact with them.
>
> *(CCN030)*

Alternatively, a shift from surface to deep acting may not occur at all. Client or worker may resist the development of commercial or quasi friendships. Where interactions are fleeting, infrequent or one-off (as in the case of cabin crew, fast food counter staff, call center interactions) there is also less likelihood of developing shared narratives that impact on the depth of emotional labor. Within Intensive Care Units interaction may be limited by the condition of the patient (e.g., lack of consciousness). Alternatively, the avoidance of deep acting and attachment may form part of defense mechanisms designed to prevent nurses from becoming too emotionally invested in a patient:

> you detach yourself. You've got to be able to detach yourself from the situation. You cannot think – like when I was a student, you cannot think, "that could be my dad, that could be my daughter". You can't do that. You just physically can't do it because it will drag you down. . . . It's a strange thing. You've got to be able to sit there, wipe someone's poo up and then still go and have a butty [hot sandwich].
>
> *(CNN050)*

In this last case, deep acting is resisted by the worker to reduce the possibility of burnout (see later). They resist the requirement to self-induce a real feeling (. . . you cannot think, "that could be my dad, that could be my daughter" . . .) – as required by deep acting – because this level of emotional performance will "drag you down." As the last line of the quote suggests, you have to be able to deal with the issue and move on. For some nurses in some contexts, this is best achieved through surface acting.

Thus far we have conceptualized emotional labor in terms of its relations to emotion work, wage and feeling rules. We have considered how performances might be categorized as surface or deep and the ways in which temporality, intensity and coping mechanisms might alter performance depth. We turn now to how we might categorize different "styles" of offering.

Categories: Styles of Emotional Labor

This section considers how different types of emotions are suppressed or performed according to the particularities of a given context. We focus on three distinct styles of performance: empathy, neutrality and antipathy.

Empathy

Workers employed in front-line service roles or caring professions are often expected to offer up positive *empathetic* displays (Rafaeli and Sutton, 1987; Korczynski, 2003) that leave others feeling safe, valued and comfortable. Empathy describes an ability to understand and experience the position of another and respond appropriately (Moudatsou et al., 2020). We see this in the work of cabin crew (Hochschild, 1983; Taylor and Tyler, 2000) resort workers (Van Maanen, 1991; Tracy, 2000) and nurses (Bolton, 2000; Chiappetta-Swanson, 2005).

Nursing is an interesting case in point because, in addition to their technical competencies, empathy (and its counterpart compassion) are often identified as central components of their professional identity and values (Chowdhry, 2010; RCN, 2021; Wu, 2021) with the performance of empathy being linked to more efficient role fulfillment and the ability to deliver quality patient-centered care (Moudatsou et al., 2020). Broadly, such performances are about understanding the plight, fears, pain and condition of the patient. It manifests in a caring demeanor and, often, the attempt to evoke a positive or stable frame of mind in those they treat. There is also empathetic care of patient's friends and family who may be "distressed" in "turmoil" or "screaming" as they fear for the well-being of loved ones:

> We just talk to them and try to comfort them (family), try and get whoever I need to get to speak to that person, if it's a doctor, if they want to speak to the doctor a bit more. Just obviously assess how they are and what they're saying. Just be there for them, really, and comfort.
>
> *(CCN002)*

While empathic performances are associated with positive work they can be problematic in terms of occupational identity. Within nursing, associations with empathy have contributed to a narrative that positions nursing as something less than the "science" of medicine (Katz, 1969; Raelin, 1985; Kirkpatrick et al.,

2005; Currie et al., 2008; Maben et al., 2009; McMurray, 2012). The empathy offered by nursing was said to be based in "knowledge which everyone ought to have" whereas the doctor was privy to "medical knowledge, which only a profession can have" (Nightingale, 1860 preface). Humanism and emotion were thus placed in subservient opposition to science and rationalism: nurses as the "servants of medicine, surgery and hygiene" (Holliday and Parker, 1997, p. 487). The result is that nurses have repeatedly found themselves in a position of material, social and political disadvantage as compared to members of the medical profession (Abbott and Wallace, 1998; Nelson and Gordon, 2004). Worse still, nursing itself appears trapped by apparently irreconcilable binaries which recursively question whether its members believe in extending competencies or caring compassion. The reality is that they, like other professions, combine both. They also practice other categories of emotional labor, including emotional neutrality.

Neutrality

As a form of emotional labor, *neutrality* describes a position in which the absence of facial or bodily emotion is itself a performance (Smith and Kleinman, 1989; Ward and McMurray, 2011). The worker dons a mask of impartial disinterest to conceal their true feelings such that swan like serenity on the surface belies emotional tumult below. The archetypal example would be the Weberian bureaucrat whose performance of rule-bound impartiality and rational objectivity in the face of anger, sadness, suffering or joy describes a matter-of-fact approach to work encounters. Other examples might include the receptionist, bartender or ticket inspector who is sworn at or abused by an irate customer. In their private life, the worker might retaliate with equal vigor, giving free reign to their own anger at being so sorely abused. Within the context of a service encounter in which feeling rules are shaped by a presumption of consumer sovereignty (Korczynski, 2001) such a response is denied to the laborer. Where empathy is inappropriate and aggression denied, the only course left is the performance of emotional neutrality. In such cases, the absence of emotion masks the laborer's own feelings of hurt, rage, fear, sadness or disappointment. As considered below, maintaining a neutral professional mask in the face of abuse is far from easy:

> The level of abuse that, you know, you would receive from either the patient or their family, and that was obviously exceptional because there were some difficult times (pandemic) and I accept that, you know, aggression and anger would be an emotion that anybody would show in those difficult times, but that was a very difficult part of my job.
>
> *(CCN007)*

Within neutrality the response is to understand rather than condone outbursts, anger and violence. In a context of care and death, professionals labor to understand the root of the unwanted emotion before then speaking to, explaining and ideally defusing the situation:

> Again, they [families] were experiencing so much anger and frustration and because all they'd wanted to do is just come and be with their relatives and they can't do that [due to covid hospital restrictions] . . . so we just tried to explain that to them: this is just unfortunately what the situation is.
>
> *(CCN030)*

In the aforementioned cases, aggression flows from the consumer or client toward the worker. There are however cases where the flow is deliberately reversed.

Antipathetic

The final category to be considered here is *antipathetic* emotional labor (Korczynski, 2003). This may be observed in the work of the soldier, bouncer or debt collector (Hochschild, 1983; Sutton, 1991; Ward and McMurray, 2016) who, through facial, verbal and bodily display work to discomfort or subjugate the would-be combatant, argumentative drunk or debtor. At a surface level, such workers may be required to summon-on-command aggression that they do not feel, while suppressing their own fears, pain, anxiety or excitement (Ward et al., 2020). This is the least researched style of emotional offering: most attention being given over to empathetic performances. This relative neglect reflects the unacceptability of open aggression in most workplaces coupled with the presumption that antipathetic displays are antithetical to the notion of consumer sovereignty. Finally, the stereotypical association of emotion and emotional labor with women's work has served to shift focus away from antipathetical labor; this despite efforts to disrupt and deconstruct dualistic normative assumptions that erroneously associate occupations, tasks and performances with a particular sex. That said, it is difficult to locate examples of antipathetic labor within caring professions such as nursing. Where anger is evident, as in verbal or written outbursts at managers or colleagues ("I wrote an email in anger to some of the seniors . . . and it was putting my true thoughts down and thinking I'll get this off my chest because actually you've really annoyed me" (CCN 046)) the emotion in question is felt and raw. There is no masking or performing.

It is worth noting that most occupational members are called upon to offer more than one style of emotional performance. Accordingly, while the soldier may exhibit aggression in the face of the enemy this is replaced by empathy in the face of the refugee, and neutrality in the face of a commanding officer. The critical care nurse may switch between empathy and neutrality depending on a patient's condition, the behavior of families or the norms for interaction with other occupations such as medical doctors. This emotional switching depends on the specifics of the task, changes in context or client, the skills of the laborer, and an ongoing assessment of what is "due" in a given set of relations (Ward and McMurray, 2011).

By now it should be clear that, as a concept, emotional labor can inform our understanding of the nature of occupational roles and tasks. Its performance can be categorized in terms of the depth and style of emotional offering, the exact nature of which being determined by the particularities of the given context. We draw the chapter to a close with a consideration of the effects of such work on those who undertake it.

Emotional Labor and Its Effects

There has been a long concern over the negative effects of emotional labor. Personal effects tend to be described in terms of the dissonance, burnout and alienation that are said to arise from the attempt – under capitalism – to commodify emotions. Dissonance occurs where workers are coerced into performing organizationally desired emotions that they do not feel in return for a wage (Morris and Feldman, 1996). The inauthenticity this evokes is said to estrange the worker from self and, where workers are required to maintain the pretense for an extended period of time, it may engender the sort of exhaustion associated with burnout.

Burnout describes a condition under which "workers in jobs with high levels of emotional demands eventually lose the ability or energy to meet the demands of the job" (Briner et al., 2008, p. 2). Burnout is comprised of three dimensions: emotional exhaustion, lack of personal accomplishment and depersonalization (Maslach and Jackson 1986). The first of these dimensions is generally seen as the most important (Byrne et al., 2013) and is linked to experiences of tiredness and overload. Individuals perceive their job to be excessively burdensome such that they may feel "at the end of their tether" (Friedman, 2000. p. 597). Lack of personal accomplishment (second dimension) is indicative of feeling incompetent or ineffective when dealing with others, while depersonalization (third dimension) suggests negative or cynical feelings toward clients that is closely linked to alienation and a sense of estrangement from self and others. Nurses working at a time of crisis exhibit many of these negative effects. One nurse offered a heart-wrenching account of her own struggles:

> I just felt like really, I had no energy at all, I couldn't get out of bed, I just felt really depressed, I just felt, like I was just living in these moments, of these patients, and then it got to such a point that. . .. The second week was more nightmares and flashbacks about my patients . . . I felt I kind of failed my patients and I wanted to be with my patients, and I couldn't find any way out of these thoughts all the time. I basically threatened to kill myself and my daughter by driving into a wall. I was sectioned twice over the summer.
>
> *(CNN 036)*

The above is an extreme case that demonstrates the emotional impact of working in extreme environments. The sense of being at the end of one's tether, of somehow failing personally and of estrangement was common to many working during the pandemic (and many in other times and occupations). It reminds us that work and life cannot be separated and that our categories have the power to explain and assess the impact of work on real people. It reminds us that work and how it is managed has consequences.

Hochschild herself denies that there was any necessary emphasis on the damaging and alienating consequences of emotional labor in her original conceptualization, going as far as stating that "one can enjoy emotional labour immensely . . . providing one has an affinity for it and a workplace supports that affinity" (Hochschild, 2013, p. 25). Indeed, there is a growing body of research that points to the ways in which workers might take pride, pleasure and satisfaction in difficult emotional labor as part of positive identity work (Tyler, 2012; McMurray and Ward, 2014). Even so, for many workers, emotional labor is all too often part of a "tragic cycle" (Hochschild, 2013) in which "one might take great pride in caring for others through emotional labour performances but the organizations in which this work is carried out demonstrates very little by way of care for those employed" (Ward, 2019, p. 26). As in the case above, our organizations can ask too much.

Finally, our work with critical care nurses also highlighted the ways in which the denial of emotional labor, or its distortion due to a change in context, can have negative effects on workers. Being unable to physically personally comfort the relatives of those who were ill or dying was particularly hard on nurses. This was brought about by the exclusion – on health and contagion grounds – of relatives and friends from hospital wards. The lack of access had the effect of removing the possibility that nurses could labor to deal with and manage the emotions of family and friends in person. What had at one time been an important, and occasionally annoying, part of the role – speaking with and comforting relatives at the bedside of the patient and learning about the life of the patient – was now denied to workers as an embodied practice. The impact for many was a sense of personal professional failure and regret:

> Families, saying goodbye via FaceTime, that was just horrific, I mean how do you ever give them back that? How do you . . . ?
>
> *(CCN039)*

For critical care nurses, this was a very specific effect of the isolation and exclusion brought about by the COVID-19 pandemic. It led to difficult conversations for nurses:

> we had to tell the relatives of the people that they couldn't see their relatives again because we couldn't allow them in the hospital. That was bad. That will never leave me. I'm in counselling now for little things like that.
>
> *(CC029)*

As was the case for so many during the pandemic, virtual contact was substituted for physical interaction. In terms of emotional labor, the substitute was generally perceived to be an inadequate one:

> We pride ourselves on looking after relatives and communicating with relatives and we weren't able to do that. Things like patients dying over FaceTime is just not something [pause] . . . I am all for technology but having to hold an iPad to someone's face while they are dying to their relative is just awful – absolutely awful. You'd hear cries from one end of the unit to the other from wives who knew their husband was dying effectively, and, I can still hear one particular relative's screams, she was inconsolable, hysterical as you would be, and the whole unit just went deathly quiet. All we could hear is this lady. I can still hear her now. We just felt so frustrated that we could not do what we like to do, what we should be doing. . . . There is just a much dignity in saving someone's life as helping them die with dignity and it just didn't feel like we were able to do that. We were overwhelmed with emotions.
>
> *(CNN0023)*

In circumstances such as these the performance or denial of emotional labor can have profound and lasting impacts on workers. At its most positive it defines a category of complex work that is a source of pride. It stands alongside technical competencies, discrete tasks and role responsibilities as a defining feature of personal and professional identity. Where such labor is taken to the extreme – to points at which workers can no longer cope with all that is heard, seen, felt, performed and masked – it threatens the immediate and long-term well-being of those involved.

Conclusion

Emotional labor and the performance of specific categories of labor, such as empathy, describe not only a facet of occupational work, but also the relation of a profession to its clients, other professions and wider systems (Chowdhry, 2010). It emerges as a site of power, politics and contestation at work. It informs personal and professional identity. Moreover, its value shifts depending on the context of its application.

We have seen the ways in which emotional labor is to be differentiated from emotional work, and can vary in both depth and type of performance. Emotional labor is altered by contextual factors such as the site of enactment, temporality and embodied versus virtual encounters. In terms of its effects, emotional labor can act as a source of professional pride and occupational virtue. It can also result in harm through dissonance, burnout and alienation. These effects draw attention to the obligations that might attend such categories of work. Responsibilities are likely diffused, touching upon the individual, educators, occupational bodies and, perhaps most importantly, the managers, leaders and systems that constitute employers. If emotional labor is an increasingly important category of work, then is it equally important that employers support and care for those who are paid to undertake that work, as in the case of the nurse who, in the midst of a pandemic, dares to care.

Notes

1 Critical Care Nursing data in this chapter is part of a longitudinal study of their experience of working during the COVID-19 pandemic. Data is drawn qualitative interviews with 54 nurses in Ireland and the United Kingdom. Interviews were fully transcribed and thematically analyzed by the authors.
2 Notation at the end of quotes (i.e., CCN004) stands for anonymized participants in the research study. So, CNN004 stands for Critical Care Nurse number 4 in the study.

References

Abbott, P. and Meerabeau, L. (1998) 'Professionals, professionalization and the caring professions', in Abbott, P. and Meerabeau, L. (eds.) *The Sociology of the Caring Professions*. London: UCL Press, pp. 1–19.

Abbott, P. and Wallace, C. (1998) 'Health Visiting, Social Work, Nursing and Midwifery: A History', in Abbott, P. and Wallace, C. (eds.) *The Sociology of the Caring Professions*. London: UCL Press, pp. 20–53.

Bolton, S.C. (2000) 'Who Cares? Offering Emotion Work as a 'Gift' in the Nursing Labor Process', *Journal of Advanced Nursing*, 32(3), pp. 580–586.

Bolton, S.C. (2001) 'Changing Faces: Nurses as Emotional Jugglers', *Sociology of Health and Illness*, 23(1), pp. 85–100.

Bolton, S.C. (2005) 'Women's Work, Dirty Work: The Gynaecology Nurse as 'Other', *Gender Work and Organisation*, 12(2), pp. 169–186.

Bolton, S.C and Boyd, C. (2003) 'Trolley Dolly or Skilled Emotion Manager? Moving on From Hochschild's Managed Heart', *Work Employment and Society*, 17(2), pp. 289–308.

Briner, R., Poppleton, S., Owens, S. and Kiefer, T. (2008) *The Nature, Causes and Consequences of Harm in Emotionally-Demanding Occupations*. Norwich: HSE Books.

Byrne, M., Chughtai, A., Flood, B., Murphy, E. and Willis, P. (2013) 'Burnout among Accounting and Finance Academics in Ireland', *International Journal of Educational Management*, 27(2), pp. 127–142.

Chiappetta-Swanson, C. (2005) 'Dignity and Dirty Work: Nurses' Experiences in Managing Genetic Termination for Fetal Anomaly', *Qualitative Sociology*, 28(1), pp. 93–116.

Chowdhry, S. (2010) 'Exploring the Concept of Empathy in Nursing: Can it Lead to Abuse of Patient Trust?', *Nursing Times*, 106, p. 42.

Currie, G., Finn, R. and Martin, G. (2008) 'Accounting for the 'Dark Side' of New Organizational Forms: The Case of Health Care Professions', *Human Relations*, 61, pp. 539–564.

Fineman, S. (2001) *Emotions in Organizations*. London: Sage.

Friedman, I. (2000) 'Burnout in Teachers: Shattered Dreams of Impeccable Professional Performance', *In Session: Psychotherapy in Practice*, 56(5), pp. 595–606.

Hancock, P. and Tyler, M. (2001) *Work, Post Modernism and Organization: A Critical Introduction*. London: Sage.

Harness, O., Jamie, K. and McMurray, R. (2020) 'They've Been With Me the Whole Journey': Temporality, Emotional Labor and Hairdressing Work', *Work Employment and Society*, 35(6), pp. 1073–1090.

Hochschild, A. (1983) *The Managed Heart: Commercialization of Human Feeling*. London: University of California.

Hochschild, A. (2013) *So How's the Family and Other Essays*. Berkeley, CA: University of California.

Holliday, M. and Parker, E. (1997) 'Florence Nightingale, Feminism and Nursing', *Journal of Advanced Nursing*, 26, pp. 483–488.

Katz, F. (1969) 'Nurses', in Etzioni, A. (ed.) *The Semi-professions and their Organization*. London: The Free Press, pp. 54–81.

Kirkpatrick, I., Ackroyd, S. and Walker, R. (2005) *The New Managerialism and Public Service Professions*. London: Palgrave.

Korczynski, M. (2001) 'The Contradictions in Service Work: Call Center as Customer-oriented Bureaucracy', in Sturdy, A., Grugulis, I. and Willmott, H. (eds.) *Customer Service: Empowerment and Entrapment* (Critical Perspectives on Work and Organisations). London: Palgrave.

Korczynski, M. (2003) 'Communities of Coping: Collective Emotional Labor in Service Work', *Organization*, 10(1), pp. 55–79.

Korczynski, M. (2009) 'The Mystery Customer: Continuing Absences in the Sociology of Service Work', *Sociology*, 43, pp. 952–967.

Lawley, S. and Caven, V. (2019) 'Lillian Moller Gilbreth', in McMurray, R. and Pullen, A. (eds.) *Routledge Focus on Women Writers in Organization Studies: Beyond Rationality in Organization and Management*. London: Routledge.

Maben, J., Cornwell, J. and Sweeney, K. (2009) 'In Praise of Compassion', *Journal of Nursing Research*, 15(1), pp. 9–13.

Maslach, C. and Jackson, S. (1986) *Maslach Burnout Inventory Manual*. Palo Alto, CA: Consulting Psychologists Press.

McMurray, R. (2012) 'Embracing Dirt in Nursing Matters', in Simpson, R., Slutskaya, N, Lewis, P. and Hopfl, H. (eds.) *Dirty Work Concepts and Identities*. Basingstoke: Palgrave Macmillan, pp. 126–142.

McMurray, R. and Pullen, A. (2019) 'Introduction: Beyond Rationality in Organization and Management', in McMurray, R. and Pullen, A. (eds.) *Routledge Focus on Women Writers in Organization Studies: Beyond Rationality in Organization and Management*. London: Routledge, pp. 1–5.

McMurray, R. and Ward, J. (2014) ''Why Would You Do That?': Defining Emotional Dirty Work', *Human Relations*, 67(9), pp. 1123–1143.

Morgan, P.I. and Ogbonna, E. (2008) 'Subcultural Dynamics in Transformation: A Multi-Perspective Study of Health Care Professionals', *Human Relations*, 61, pp. 39–65.

Morris, J. and Feldman, D. (1996) 'The Dimensions, Antecedents, and Consequences of Emotional Labor', *The Academy of Management Review*, 21(4), pp. 986–1010.

Moudatsou, M., Stavropoulou, A., Philalithis, A. and Koukouli, S. (2020) 'The Role of Empathy in Health and Social Care Professionals', *Healthcare*, 89(1), p. 26.

Nelson, S. and Gordon, S. (2004) 'The Rhetoric of Rupture: Nursing as a Practice With a History', *Nursing Outlook*, 52(5), pp. 255–261.

Nightingale, F. (1860) *Notes on Nursing: What It Is and What It Is Not*, Kindle ed. London: Harrison.

Price, L. and Arnould, E. (1999) 'Commercial Friendships: Service Provider – Client Relationships in Context', *Journal of Marketing*, 63(4), pp. 38–56.

Raelin, J. (1985) *The Clash of Cultures: Managers and Professionals*. Boston, MA: Harvard Business School Press.

Rafaeli, A. and Sutton, R.I. (1987) 'Expression of Emotion as Part of the Work Role', *Academy of Management Review*, 12(1), pp. 23–37.

RCN (2021) 'Principles of Nursing Practice', www.rcn.org.uk/professional-development/principles-of-nursing-practice.

Ritzer, G. (1993) *The McDonaldization of Society: An Investigation Into the Changing Character of Contemporary Social Life*. Newbury Park, CA: Pine Forge Press.

Seymour, D. and Sandiford, P. (2005) 'Learning Emotion Rules in Service Organizations: Socialization and Training in the UK Public-house Sector', *Work, Employment and Society*, 19(3), pp. 547–564.

Shuler, S. and Sypher, B.D. (2000) 'Seeking Emotional Labor: When Managing the Heart Enhances the Work Experience', *Management Communication Quarterly*, 14(1), pp. 50–89.

Smith, A.C. and Kleinman, S. (1989) 'Managing Emotions in Medical School: Student's Contact With the Living and the Dead', *Social Psychology Quarterly*, 52, pp. 56–69.

Sutton, R. (1991) 'Maintaining Norms About Expressed Emotions: The Case of Bill Collectors', *Administrative Science Quarterly*, 36, pp. 245–268.

Taylor, F.W. (1911) *The Principles of Scientific Management*. New York and London: Harper and Brothers.

Taylor, S. and Tyler, M. (2000) 'Emotional Labor and Sexual Difference in the Airline Industry', *Work Employment and Society*, 14(1), pp. 77–95.

Tracy, S.J. (2000) 'Becoming a Character for Commerce: Emotional Labor, Self-subordination, and Discursive Construction of Identity in a Total Institution', *Management Communication Quarterly*, 14(1), pp. 90–128.

Tyler, M. (2012) 'Glamour Girls, Macho Men and Everything in Between: Un/Doing Gender and Dirty Work in Soho's Sex shops', in Simpson, R., Slutskaya, N, Lewis, P. and Hopfl, H. (eds.) *Dirty Work Concepts and Identities*, Basingstoke: Palgrave Macmillan, pp. 65–90.

Van Maanen, J. (1991) 'The Smile Factory: Work at Disneyland', in Frost, P.J. (ed.) *Reframing Organisational Culture*. London: Sage, pp. 58–76.

Ward, J. (2019) 'Arlie Russell Hochschild', in McMurray, R. and Pullen, A. (eds.) *Routledge Focus on Women Writers in Organization Studies: Beyond Rationality in Organization and Management*. London: Routledge.

Ward, J. and McMurray, R. (2011) 'The Unspoken Work of General Practitioner Receptionists: A Re-examination of Emotion Management in Primary Care', *Social Science and Medicine*, 72(10), pp. 1583–1587.

Ward, J. and McMurray, R. (2016) *The Dark Side of Emotional Labor*. London: Routledge.

Ward, J., McMurray, R. and Sutcliffe, S. (2020) 'Working at the Edge: Emotional Labor in the Spectre of Violence', *Gender, Work and Organization*, 27(1), pp. 82–97.

Weber, M. (1946) *Essays in Sociology*. New York: Oxford University Press.

Wu, Y. (2021) 'Empathy in Nurse-patient Interaction: A Conversation Analysis', *BMC Nursing*, 20(18). https://doi.org/10.1186/s12912-021-00535-0.

PART 3
(In)valuable Work

13

DIRTY WORK

Physical, Social and Moral Taint

Natalia Slutskaya and Annilee M. Game

Introduction

Ashforth and Kreiner (1999) demarcate three kinds of taint that workers might face as a result of their proximity to dirt (both the material and the symbolic): physical taint produced by direct involvement with material dirt or danger (e.g., refuse collectors, miners); social taint formed by regular contact with people from stigmatized groups or where the job is seen as servile to others (for instance, prison officers, domestic workers); and moral taint implicated in sinful or less virtuous occupations (examples include debt collectors, sex workers).

There is a significant overlap between tainted categories of dirty work and stigmatized categories of socio-economic status, racio-ethnicity and gender (see, e.g., Anderson, 2000; Mendonca and D'Cruz, 2021). In this sense, the category of dirt gestures toward power differentials, and correspondingly to how exclusion and oppression are produced. Marginalized groups are often held to be "filthy and hardly human"(Elias, 1994, p. xxxvii) and dirtiness is often internalized by these groups in a way that undermines their sense of self-worth, producing "paralyzing" empathy and curbing these groups' resilience (Elias, 1994). The proximity to dirt, therefore, constitutes a divide between those who have little choice in life and those who can withdraw from whatever bears traces of contamination (Simpson et al., 2016).

Thus, understanding the category of dirty work is as much about *shifts in our understanding* of *class, caste, race, and money* as it is about individual or group experiences at work. In chasing "dirt," not only do we reorder the environment, separating the pure from the contaminated, but we also distance ourselves from those who come to be associated with impurity. For example, in her discussion of social mobility, Todd (2021) considers how being upwardly mobile meant differentiating

DOI: 10.4324/9781003341321-17

oneself from those involved in manual and servile labor by showing eagerness to learn and by being "impeccably clean." To illustrate how the class divide could be rooted in a demarcation between the dirty and the clean, Todd draws on the account of a railway clerk, who described how clerks were encouraged to consider themselves of higher status than manual workers, commenting that "there was a rule that you had to present yourself at the office 'in a clean and tidy manner'" (Todd, 2021, p. 50). Similarly, as noted by McClintock, the bodily relation to dirt expresses a social relation to labor. Historically, unlike the working class, the middle class and in particular its female members, could not bear on their bodies the visible evidence of manual labor – "dirt was . . . a scandal because it was the surplus evidence of manual work" (McClintock, 1995, p. 153). Thus, proximity to or distance from dirt defined the threshold of "normal work," "normal money," "normal sexuality" and came to "be figured increasingly in the iconography of 'pollution', 'disorder' . . . 'moral contagion' and racial 'degeneration'" (ibid., p. 154). From this perspective, proximity to dirt produces a series of sub-oppositions by the symbolic divide between mind/body, clean/dirty, governing/governed, and what role they play in attributing value (Thiel, 2007).

Taint is not independent but instead constitutes part of an interactive, complex, and iterative process of social construction. In other words, the sociopolitical and cultural context shapes workers' self-understanding and the strategies they adopt to battle stigmatization (Ashforth and Kreiner, 2014). In addition, different types of taint or stigma might determine the level of sensitivity to historical and cultural circumstances. For example, there is likely to be greater divergence and more context-specific differences "between societies about what is socially or morally stigmatized than what is physically stigmatized because social and moral stigma tend to be symbolically (as opposed to physically) threatening" (ibid., p. 85). Symbolic codes reflect systems of values and implicitly, therefore, the cultural, geographic and historical context (Lai and Lam, 2012; Tyler, 2011).

Dirty work is a category that hinges on ever-changing and historically determined societal classifications of what is clean or dirty, what groups are normal or stigmatized, and/or what is moral or immoral (Makkawy and Scott, 2017). In this sense, the concept is not only central to a better understanding of a specific type of labor, but it unlocks grounds for exploring interdependencies and relations between *shifts in the structure of society and changes in the structure of behavior* (Elias, 1994, p. xv). What is designated as "dirty" has emerged and changed over time, varying according to "the historical processes through which current labor configurations have arisen" (Duffy, 2007, p. 333). In other words, dirty work cannot be understood in terms of *ahistorical abstraction* as it is simultaneously historically conditioned and variable. In sum, the "dirty work" category captures how historical circumstances emerged and changed, what progress, agency and power might mean and what the implications are for those involved in this work. This chapter explores how changes in historical, economic and social conditions might affect the material and symbolic status of tainted jobs and what consequences these changes might have for conceptualizing "dirty work."

Origins of the "Dirty Work" Concept

The concept of dirty work was first adopted from the original studies of Hughes (1951, 1958), which unlocked the connections between status and occupations. For Hughes, status is conditioned not just by major differentiating categories of the society in which one lives, but by acquiring a place in a series of sub-groups. "The division of labor provides many such sub-groups in which a man may live and have his being" (Hughes, 1958, p. 23). In other words, occupational selection becomes a major process of establishing hierarchies, classifying people, and producing forms of inclusion and marginalization. As Hughes notes, "the delegation of dirty work to someone else is common among humans. Many cleanliness taboos, and perhaps even many moral scruples, depend for their practice upon success in delegating the tabooed activity to someone else" (ibid., p. 51). Governing through delegation becomes a practice of power, it is central to the reproduction of the social order. In his writings, Hughes is attentive to the need to study occupations "from the points of view of all the kinds of people involved in it, whether their position be high or low, whether they are at the center or near the periphery of the system" (ibid., p. 77) but also how shifts and changes in the system of work might disadvantage some and benefit others. Hughes's invitation to investigate the peripheries resonates with Culler's insistence that "since systems of classification depend upon exclusions, one looks at what is apparently marginal to understand the system (. . .). What is marginal turns out to be essential to the study of the system that excludes it" (Culler, 1985, p. 2).

Initial research in this area tended to assume that dirty work was associated with "pathological" and "defective" individual attributes, thereby furthering the stigmatization of such work (see Saunders, 1981, for a review). In later research, the association with personality traits became less important as organizational psychologists focused on the way that workers' perception of their work might be shaped and sustained by their interactions with others. Yet early researchers still interpreted social identity theory in dispositional terms (Kreiner et al., 2006), arguing that stigmatization would result in adverse consequences, such as low self-esteem (Dovidio et al., 2000). A number of scholars in the field stressed that occupational stigma negatively affected individuals by relegating workers to "out-groups" associated with devalued and demeaning work (Tajfel and Turner, 1979; Mejia et al., 2021). The same researchers observed how stigmatization might fashion the dynamic between in-groups and out-groups (Crocker et al., 1998; Mejia et al., 2021). In addition, these studies drew attention to varied processes of stigmatization and the variety of predicaments it could create for the individual; how stigma may stick to individuals (Bergman and Chalkley, 2007); how easily it could be discovered in social interactions (Ashforth and Humphrey, 1997;

Crocker et al., 1998); how effectively it can be removed (Crocker et al., 1998), and the extent to which the individual could be seen as responsible for their own stigmatization.

Yet dirty work research was not simply a venture of studying the peripheral and the pathological. It was, as importantly, an exploration of how those who found themselves marginalized and stigmatized could maintain a positive sense of self. As noted by Hughes (1971), even in low-status occupations, people develop collective pretensions or "dignifying rationalizations" in order to give their work, and consequently themselves, value in the eyes of each other and outsiders. A growing number of studies of dirty work highlight the interrelated processes of "attribution" (i.e., ascriptions/perceptions of others) and "reattribution" (e.g., the reworking of meanings) through which dirty workers endeavor to gain a positive identity, in spite of cultural tendencies toward stigmatization and negative framing. In so doing, research has moved away from its original focus on personal attributes in order to explore the cognitive, affective and behavioral strategies used to cope with the "taint" of dirty work (see examples Ashforth et al., 2007; Kreiner et al., 2006; Deery et al., 2019; Torelli and Puddephatt, 2020).

More attention has been paid recently to gaining a better understanding of cultural differences in the psychological arrangements and devices by which employees may make their work meaningful or tolerable. For example, scholars have investigated how the "dirtiness" of such occupations as the gambling industry, mining and nursing is managed in China (Lai and Lam, 2012). These studies of Chinese workers considered the role of Confucian work ethics and Buddhist beliefs in dealing with occupational stigma (ibid.). In Africa, dirty work careers offered opportunities for a significant number of African immigrants to find employment (Hart and Acs, 2011; Vinogradov and Jorgensen, 2017); however, it came at the price of stigmatization (Peberdy and Rogerson, 2000). In South Africa, for example, those involved in dirty work are often perceived as semi-literate, and physically dirty (Van Rooyen et al., 2010). A growing number of studies have looked into the underlying motives influencing migrants' decisions to revert to dirty work careers and different rewards and dangers of being involved in dirty work in African countries (e.g., Fatoki and Patswawaire, 2012; Fredericks, 2018). More recent studies have also encouraged consideration of workers' experiences in such places as India highlighting the intractability of dirty work for ragpickers in Mumbai (Shepherd et al., 2021), and the role of forgetting in the dignity claims of Dalit janitors, Chennai (Mahalingam et al., 2019).

In sum, studies of "dirty work" concur that the value of what is dirty is mutable and conferred rather than fixed and inherent, and there is also a significant variability across time and space in what persists and what changes as "dirt." Questions about what prevents values from changing, what social conventions disallow certain value transformations, and under which circumstances these transformations might occur remain pertinent.

Physically Tainted Jobs

Many studies have specifically looked at how physical taint can be managed. This category of occupations tends to remain fairly stable (i.e., less affected by historical and cultural context), since physical dirt is more likely to stimulate the often innate and universal responses of disgust and fear (Rozin et al., 2008). In addition, culturally, disgust is never ambivalent about its object, it strengthens and polices the boundaries (Ngai, 2005). The literature on physically tainted jobs captures the experiences of those who found themselves in direct proximity to material dirt. Examples of physically tainted jobs might include garbage handlers (Perry, 1998), morticians (Thompson, 1991; Batista and Wanderley, 2018) and butchers (Meara, 1974; Simpson et al., 2014), slaughterhouse workers, (Ackroyd and Crowdy, 1990; McCabe and Hamilton, 2015), firefighters (Tracy and Scott, 2006; Perrott, 2019), and miners (Fitzpatrick, 1980; Kesküla, 2015). This classification of people's work has been updated but not much changed over the past decades.

Gold (1952) offered the first account of stigma attached to cleaning up the dirt of others. He drew attention to the acute awareness of those involved in dealing with garbage that not only did the public consider their job to be lowly, but that many held them, as people, in low esteem because of their apparent willingness to do other people's dirty work (Gold, 1952, p. 488). Similarly, Hughes (1958) reinforced the idea that the physical disgust present in jobs such as janitoring was not merely a "thing" between the worker and the garbage, but moreover a reflection of the public's attitudes and of the antagonistic nature of the relationship between janitors and the people whose dirt they clean. Hughes remarks on the consensus among janitors, prison guards, and mental-hospital attendants that while society at large puts dirty work upon them, and acknowledges the necessity of such work, its value to society is nonetheless refuted.

Most studies on the experiences of dirty workers in a *Western context* focus on the ability of workers to resist devaluation by imbuing their work with value. As Ashforth et al. (2007) argue, perceived negative attributions can be "neutralized" by drawing discursively on occupational ideologies that include "reframing," whereby the work is infused with positive value (e.g., presented as a badge of honor or mission) and "re-focusing" which involves an emphasis on the non-stigmatized aspects of the job. Thiel (2007) stresses that such traditional norms and values as relying on the job's usefulness and on workers' ability to undertake unpleasant and strenuous tasks have historically provided a potent source of leverage over participants' more powerfully positioned, higher-status counterparts. Workers in physically tainted jobs continue to feel capable of digesting the impurities as they continue collecting garbage or cutting animals as these jobs are necessary. They feel that the necessity of the job shields them from the stigma attached to the dirtiness of their work. In Ackroyd and Crowdy's (1990) study of slaughterhouses, the greatest esteem was found through adherence to traditional norms of masculinity – norms that rely on dominance, strength and differentiation from women.

Although the classification of physically tainted jobs has remained fairly stable, scholars have noted the emergence of new approaches to de-stigmatization adopted by workers, such as professionalism and service orientation. Both butchers in the Simpson et al. (2014) study and home carers in Stacey's (2005) research emphasized the importance of their interactions with customers and clients, to redirect attention from the physical taint associated with their proximity to flesh or bodies. Chiappetta-Swanson (2005) highlighted how routinization could function as a coping strategy in nurses' attempts to battle the taint associated with managing genetic termination for fetal anomaly. Lemmergaard and Muhr (2012) discussed the tactic of reframing the dirty aspects of work as "good," professional, useful and necessary. Lemmergaard and Muhr (2012) reflect upon different types of professional indifference as a form of creating a neutral-from-taint space.

Studies of physically tainted jobs *in a non-Western* context could be divided into two broad categories – research that engages with how dirty workers in such countries as India, China, Ghana, Philippines, etc., may contest and reframe the socially accepted meanings of their work through communication strategies and projects that focus on how dirty work is often a survival opportunity for those who find themselves in desperate circumstances. As Furedy (1990) notes in her examination of Asian cities, in nations without social welfare systems, those who are laboring in low-paid "dirty" jobs often draw on their occupations as an informal survival strategy. For instance, garbage pickers might resort to eating food waste or those who gather bones would boil them to make a soup, before delivering them for recycling as fertilizer and animal feed. The same pickers might then build their shelters with scavenged materials, often on the edge of dumps (Furedy, 1990).

More recent studies invited attention to the complexities of resisting devaluation in the non-Western context. For example, Shepherd et al. (2021) explored how intersectionality shapes the experiences of ragpickers in Mumbai, India. The study shows how ragpickers are tainted by the nature of the work they do (handling and disposing of garbage) as well as belonging to the lowest caste in Indian society and living in slums. Similarly, the role of caste and class were examined in a study of Dalit janitorial labor in the aftermath of floods in Chennai, India, in 2015 (Mahalingam et al., 2019). The study attests to various ways through which caste, dirty work, and dignity intersect in the narrative accounts of Dalit janitors and how processes of remembering and forgetting play an active role in their claims for dignity.

In sum, the list of physically tainted occupations tends to remain fairly stable (i.e., less affected by historical and cultural context) and there is also significant overlap in what is defined as physically tainted across geographical locations, different cultures and economic orders. It seems that some physical contaminants, such as spittle, are so unpleasant that they are unanimously perceived as repulsive

(Sandvoll et al., 2015). Workers in this category tend to belong to already marginalized groups and show very little social mobility. Although some new de-stigmatization strategies have evolved, overall, those involved in physically tainted occupations incline to similar discursive (class-relevant) strategies in their struggles against devaluation. In addition, non-Western accounts highlight the intractability of dirty work for those who need it to survive.

Socially and Morally Tainted Occupations

Stigmatization is experienced not only by those involved in low-paid, low-prestige occupations but also by those in high-status professions (for instance, physicians who treat alcoholics, psychiatric nurses, prison wardens and public defenders) as a result of their association with disease, infection, or criminal activities (Lemmergaard and Muhr, 2012). Some of these occupations are often described as socially tainted. Hughes (1962) foregrounds the fact that those involved in such occupations as prison wardens, police officers, public defenders, and mental health professionals have to deal with people or environments from which others want to distance themselves. For example, though policing may be known for some prestigious and glamorous dimensions, police officers also often deal with gruesome crimes and crime scenes (De Camargo, 2019).

In the context of socially tainted jobs, as Tracy and Scott (2006, p. 32) argue, "employees feel 'clean', when the work's 'filth' can be pinned on another," and contamination is most successfully redirected when "blaming one that is perceived as low-class, criminally inclined, and socially marginal." For example, condemning the actions of prisoners justifies the use of coercive authority in the study of the police officers; it also enables the construction of a moral and valued occupational identity (Dick, 2005; Hughes, 1958). The common taint-management techniques used by security guards and prison wardens are to develop contempt against those policed, who come to be depicted by officers as "deserving" targets (Lofstrand et al., 2016). Other strategies might include attempts to restore their devalued identities by focusing on the cognitive ability that the work might require (Löfstrand et al., 2016), redirecting attention away from the stigmatized aspects of their jobs, or by emphasizing the usefulness to wider society. As an illustration, security guards infuse their work with a sense of importance and responsibility by viewing their patrons and clients as "akin to children over whom security officers need to exercise paternal oversight" (Löfstrand et al., 2016, p. 311).

It is reasonable to assume that status shields and prestige do not just reflect the nature of work performed but are simultaneously wrapped up in notions of class, race and gender (De Camargo, 2019). Todd (2021) offers us an account of how class mattered in the occupational prestige of nurses at the beginning of the twentieth century. At this time, the higher status of professional nursing resulted from the fact that it was only open to recruits from middle-class families (Todd, 2021). Edith Hall, born into a working-class home, admitted pretending to be more middle-class by giving "no information as to any previous employment except to say that my parents didn't believe in young women going out to work with the exception of nursing . . . With this white lie I obtained the first post" (Todd, 2021, p. 84).

Belonging to the middle class and the ideas around women's emancipation were resources to draw on to supersede the dirtiness of the job, the long hours and the poor pay for those involved in nursing at the time. Later, it became more realistic for both working - and middle-class women to enter the nursing profession. Yet, nursing remained a profession in which "women so divided by class that their common oppression based on gender could not unite them" (Reverby, 1987, p. 6). The aforementioned example illustrates the vitals of history to understand how the status of occupations changes over time and how such categories as class, gender and race might contribute to or lessen stigmatization. This is also particularly relevant to socially tainted (and, maybe, morally tainted) occupations, as they were more likely to be gendered, classed and undertaken by ethnic minorities.

In addition, such shifts in political, social and economic contexts as globalization and new technologies have not only produced new forms of labor but also shaped how taint is formed and understood. For instance, commercial surrogacy in a developing country setting is rendered "dirty" for poor rural women. This new reproductive technology freed some and stigmatized and disadvantaged others (Pande, 2009). In addition, legal protections are often not available to protect women who may engage in commercial surrogacy (Rotabi and Bromfield, 2012). Surrogates find themselves under constant domination by the medical system and had no decision-making power in the surrogacy process (Rozée et al 2020).

The other area related to new forms of social taint has emerged at the intersection of sex crimes and the digital world. Sex crimes investigators and digital forensics examiners spend a significant proportion of their time handling transgressive material, watching and listening to video evidence of sex crimes (Spencer et al., 2019). Such exposure results in a potential taint, the view that there is something psychologically "wrong" with individuals that can engage in such work (Powell et al., 2014). In the discussion of mitigating strategies adopted by those involved in these occupations, scholars show that cynicism plays an important role in how they cope with stigmatization. Similarly, the growth of social medial platforms triggered demand for commercial content moderators. This professional activity gets described as "digital laborer's dirty work" due to workers' exposure to racist, homophobic, misogynist images and language (Roberts, 2016). Research in this area is concerned with the invisibility of this type of work and the expectations from workers to stomach the most disturbing content. As Roberts (2016) stresses, for as long as these workers stay hidden, the ramifications of being involved in this profession will remain unknown.

Liberal and neoliberal economics, as well as emerging cultural agendas, generate diverse experiences of marginalization and stigmatization. For example, areas such as banking or advertising have been deemed morally tainted since they are seen as contributing to either the ascendancy of the idea that the "good life" is derived from consumption, or to prosperity that is gained at the expense of others. As Stanley and Mackenzie-Davey (2012) argue, moral taint is more personal and value-based taint. For example, taint derives from bankers' values (greedy and reckless) and their remuneration (excessive and unwarranted), rather than banking itself. The same writers note that there are more dramatic (though not always long-lasting) shifts in perceptions of morally tainted occupations including such examples as corrupt corporate CEOs, or military commanders who turn a blind eye to the abuse of detainees by soldiers (Oshana, 2006).

Conclusion

This chapter sets out to provide neither an exhaustive list of emerging dirty work occupations, nor the strategies that those involved in these occupations might employ to mitigate taint. Instead, it aims at inviting more reflections on historical processes that might interfere in the production of stigma. These processes are not only reflective of shifts in the nature of tasks performed by those involved in those jobs, but more importantly, by the norms of accessibility, ever-changing economic circumstances, political agendas and cultural assertions.

We recognize that most "dirty work" occupations have multiple forms of taint attached to them, and even jobs that are not seen by the general public as tainted might have some "dirty" elements that need to be negotiated by employees (Sanders-McDonagh, 2014). Yet even if most of us find ourselves dealing with emerging dirty aspects of our jobs,

> "some people get good wages, and some do not; some have a relatively high degree of control over their working conditions and some have little control; some have many employment options and some have very few. And some are socially stigmatized, and some are not."
>
> (Nussbaum, 1998, p. 693)

References

Ackroyd, S. and Crowdy, P. (1990) 'Can Culture Be Managed? Working With Raw Material: The Case of the English Slaughterhouse Workers', *Personnel Review*, 19(5), pp. 3–14.

Anderson, B. (2000) *Doing the Dirty Work?: The Global Politics of Domestic Labour*. London: Zed Books.

Ashforth, B.E. and Humphrey, R.H. (1997) 'The Ubiquity and Potency of Labeling in Organizations', *Organization Science*, 8(1), pp. 43–58.

Ashforth, B.E. and Kreiner, G. (1999) '"How Can You Do It?" Dirty Work and the Challenge of Constructing a Positive Identity', *Academy of Management Review*, 24(3), pp. 413–434.

Ashforth, B.E. and Kreiner, G. (2014) 'Dirty Work and Dirtier Work: Differences in Countering Physical, Social and Moral Taint', *Management and Organization Review*, 10(1), pp. 81–108.

Ashforth, B.E., Kreiner, G, Clark, M. and Fugate, M. (2007) 'Normalising Dirty Work: Managerial Tactics for Countering Occupational Taint', *Academy of Management Journal*, 50(1), pp. 149–174.

Batista, A. and Wanderley, C. (2018) 'Dirty Work and Stigma: Caretakers of Death in Cemeteries', *Revista de Estudios Sociales*, 63, pp. 72–83.

Bergman, M. and Chalkley, C. (2007) '"Ex" Marks the Spot: The Stickiness of Dirty Work and Other Removed Stigmas', *Journal of Occupational Health Psychology*, 12(3), pp. 251–265.

Chiappetta-Swanson, C. (2005) 'Dignity and Dirty Work: Nurses' Experiences in Managing Genetic Termination for Fetal Anomaly', *Qualitative Sociology*, 28(1), pp. 93–116.

Crocker, J., Major, B. and Steele, C. (1998) 'Social Stigma', in Gilbert, D.T., Fiske, S.T. and Lindzey, G. (eds.) *The Handbook of Social Psychology*. Boston, MA: McGraw-Hill. pp. 504–553.

Culler, J. (1985) 'Junk and Rubbish: A Semiotic Approach', *Diacritics*, 15(3), pp. 2–12.

De Camargo, C. (2019) "You Feel Dirty a Lot of the Time': Policing 'Dirty Work', Contamination and Purification Rituals', *International Journal of Police Science & Management*, 21(3), pp. 133–145.

Deery, S., Kolar, D. and Walsh, J. (2019) 'Can Dirty Work Be Satisfying? A Mixed Method Study of Workers Doing Dirty Jobs', *Work, Employment and Society*, 33(4), pp. 631–647.

Dick, P. (2005) 'Dirty Work Designations: How Police Officers Account for Their Use of Coercive Force', *Human Relations*, 58(11), pp. 1363–1390.

Dovidio, J. F., Major, B. and Crocker, J. (2000) 'Stigma: Introduction and Overview', in Heatherton, T., Kleck, E., Hebl, M. and Hull, J.G. (eds.) *The Social Psychology of Stigma*. New York: Guilford Press, pp. 1–30.

Duffy, M. (2007) 'Doing the Dirty Work: Gender, Race and Reproductive Labour in Historical Perspective', *Gender and Society*, 21(3), pp. 313–336.

Elias, N. (1994) *The Civilizing Process*, Vols 1 and 2. Oxford: Blackwell.

Fatoki, O. and Patswawairei, T. (2012) 'The Motivations and Obstacles to Immigrant Entrepreneurship in South Africa', *Journal of Social Sciences*, 32(2), pp. 133–142.

Fitzpatrick, J.S. (1980) 'Adapting to Danger: A Participant Observation Study of an Underground Mine', *Sociology of Work and Occupations*, 7(2), pp. 131–158.

Fredericks, R. (2018) *Garbage Citizenship*. Durham, NC: Duke University Press.

Furedy, C. (1990) 'Social Aspects of Solid Waste Recovery in Asian cities', *Environmental Sanitation Reviews*, 30, pp. 2–52.

Gold. R. (1952) 'Janitors Versus Tenants: A Status-Income Dilemma', *American Journal of Sociology*, 57(5), pp. 486–493.

Hart, D.M. and Acs, Z.J. (2011) 'High-Tech Immigrant Entrepreneurship in the United States', *Economic Development Quarterly*, 25(2), pp. 116–129.

Hughes, E. (1951) 'Work and the Self', in Rohrer, J. and Sherif, M. (eds.) *Social Psychology at the Crossroads*. New York: Harper and Brothers, pp. 317–371.

Hughes, E. (1958) *Men and their Work*. Glencoe, IL: Free Press.

Hughes, E. (1962) 'Good People and Dirty Work', *Social Problems*, 10(1), pp. 3–11

Hughes, E. (1971) *The Sociological Eye: Selected Papers*. Chicago, IL: Aldine-Atherton.

Kesküla, E. (2015) 'Reverse, Restore, Repeat!: Class, Ethnicity, and the Russian-speaking Miners of Estonia', *Focaal*, 2015(72), pp. 95–108.

Kreiner, G.E., Ashforth, B.E. and Sluss, D.M. (2006) 'Identity Dynamics in Occupational Dirty Work: Integrating Social Identity and System Justification Perspectives', *Organization Science*, 17(5), pp. 619–636.

Lai, J.Y.M. and Lam, L.W. (2012) 'Dirty Work in Chinese Societies', in Huang, X. and Bond, M. (eds.) *Handbook of Chinese Organizational Behavior: Integrating Theory, Research and Practice*. Cheltenham: Edward Elgar Publishing, pp. 103–117.

Lemmergaard, J. and Muhr SL. (2012) 'Golfing with a Murderer – Professional Indifference and Identity Work in a Danish Prison', *Scandinavian Journal of Management*, 28(2), pp. 185–195.

Lofstrand, H.C., Loftus, B. and Loader, I. (2016) 'Doing 'Dirty Work': Stigma and Esteem in the Private Security Industry', *European Journal of Criminology*, 3(3), pp. 297–314.

Mahalingam, R., Jagannathan, S. and Selvaraj, P. (2019) 'Decasticization, Dignity, and 'Dirty Work' at the Intersections of Caste, Memory, and Disaster', *Business Ethics Quarterly*, 29(2), pp. 213–239.

Makkawy, A. and Scott, C. (2017) 'Dirty Work', in *The International Encyclopedia of Organizational Communication*. Hoboken, NJ: Wiley, pp. 1–8.

McCabe, D. and Hamilton, L. (2015) 'The Kill Programme: An Ethnographic Study of 'Dirty Work' in a Slaughterhouse', *New Technology, Work and Employment*, 30(2), pp. 95–108.

McClintock, A. (1995) *Imperial Leather*. London: Routledge.

Meara, H. (1974) 'Honor in Dirty Work: The Case of American Meat Cutters and Turkish Butchers', *Work and Occupations*, 1(3), pp. 259–283.

Mejia, C., Pittman, R., Beltramo, J.M.D., Horan, K., Grinley, A. and Shoss, M.K. (2021) 'Stigma and Dirty Work: In-group and Out-group Perceptions of Essential Service Workers during COVID-19', *International Journal of Hospitality Management*, 93, 102772.

Mendonca, A. and D'Cruz, P. (2021) 'Workplace Bullying, Emotional Abuse and Harassment in the Context of Dirty Work', in D'Cruz, P., Noronha, E, Keashly, L. and Tye-Williams, S. (eds.) *Special Topics and Particular Occupations, Professions and Sectors. Handbooks of Workplace Bullying, Emotional Abuse and Harassment*. New York: Springer, pp. 551–585.

Ngai, S. (2005) *Ugly feelings*. Cambridge, MA: Harvard University Press.

Nussbaum, M. (1998) 'Whether from Reason or Prejudice: Taking Money for Bodily Services', *Journal of Legal Studies*, 27(2), pp. 693–724.

Oshana, M. (2006) 'Moral Taint', *Metaphilosophy*, 37(3–4), pp. 353–375.

Pande, A. (2009) 'Not an 'Angel', Not a 'Whore': Surrogates as 'Dirty' Workers in India', *Indian Journal of Gender Studies*, 16(2), pp. 141–173.

Peberdy, S. and Rogerson, C. (2000) 'Transnationalism and Non-South African Entrepreneurs in South Africa's Small, Medium, and Micro-enterprise (SMME) Economy', *Canadian Journal of African Studies*, 34(1), pp. 20–40.

Perrott, T.A. (2019) 'Doing Hot and 'Dirty' Work: Masculinities and Occupational Identity in Firefighting', *Gender, Work & Organization*, 26(10), pp. 1398–1412.

Perry, S.E. (1998) *Collecting Garbage*. New Brunswick, NJ: Transaction Books.

Powell, P.A., Overton, P.G. and Simpson, J. (2014) 'The Revolting Self: An Interpretative Phenomenological Analysis of the Experience of Self-disgust in Females with Depressive Symptoms', *Journal of Clinical Psychology*, 70(6), pp. 562–578.

Reverby, S.M. (1987) *Ordered to Care: The Dilemma of American Nursing, 1850–1945*. Cambridge: Cambridge University Press.

Roberts, S.T. (2016) 'Commercial Content Moderation: Digital Laborers' Dirty Work', in Noble, S. and Tynes, B.M. (eds.) *The Intersectional Internet: Race, Sex, Class and Culture Online*, New York, NY: Peter Lang, pp. 147–160.

Rotabi, K.S. and Bromfield, N.F. (2012) 'Intercountry Adoption Declines Lead to New Practices of Global Surrogacy in Guatemala: Global Human Rights Concerns in the Context of Violence and the Era of Advanced Fertility Technology', *Affilia*, 27(2), pp. 129–141.

Rozée, V., Unisa, S. and de La Rochebrochard, E. (2020) 'The Social Paradoxes of Commercial Surrogacy in Developing Countries: India Before the New Law of 2018', *BMC Women's Health*, 20(1), pp. 1–14.

Rozin, P., Haidt, J. and McCauley, C.R. (2008) 'Disgust', in Lewis, M., Haviland-Jones, J.M. and Barrett, L.F. (eds.) *Handbook of Emotions*. New York: The Guilford Press, pp. 757–776.

Sanders-McDonagh, E. (2014) 'Conducting "Dirty Research" With Extreme Groups: Understanding Academia as a Dirty Work Site', *Qualitative Research in Organizations and Management: An International Journal*, 9(3), pp. 241–253.

Sandvoll, A., Grov, E, Kristoffersen, K. and Hauge, S. (2015) 'When Care Situations Evoke Difficult Emotions in Nursing Staff Members: An Ethnographic Study in Two Norwegian Nursing Homes', *BMC Nursing*, 14(40), pp. 1–6.

Saunders, C. (1981) *Social Stigma of Occupations: The Lower Grade Worker in Service Organisations*. Farnborough: Gower.

Shepherd, D.A., Maitlis, S, Parida, V, Wincent, J. and Lawrence, T.B. (2021) 'Intersectionality in Intractable Dirty Work: How Mumbai Ragpickers Make Meaning of Their Work and Lives', *Academy of Management Journal*, published online 2 August 2021.

Simpson, R., Hughes, J. and Slutskaya, N. (2016) 'Resistance in Dirty Work: Street Cleaners and Refuse Collectors', in Simpson, R., Hughes, J. and Slutskaya, N. (eds.) *Gender, Class and Occupation*. Basingstoke: Palgrave Macmillan, pp. 147–167.

Simpson, R., Slutskaya, N, Hughes, J. and Balta, M. (2014) 'Sacrifice and Distinction in Dirty Work: Men's Construction of Meanings in the Butcher Trade', *Work Employment and Society*, 28(5), pp. 754–770.

Spencer, D.C., Ricciardelli, R, Ballucci, D. and Walby, K. (2019) 'Cynicism, Dirty Work, and Policing Sex Crimes', *Policing: An International Journal*, 43(1), pp. 151–165.

Stacey, C. (2005) 'Finding Dignity in Dirty Work: The Constraints and Rewards of Low-wage Home Care Labour', *Sociology of Health and Illness*, 27(6), pp. 831–854.

Stanley, L. and Mackenzie-Davey, K. (2012) 'From Highflyer to Crook – How Can We Understand the Stigmatization of Investment Bankers During the Financial Crisis?' in Simpson, R., Slutskaya, N., Lewis, P. and Höpfl, H. (eds.) *Dirty Work. Identity Studies in the Social Sciences*. Basingstoke: Palgrave Macmillan, pp. 49–64.

Tajfel, H. and Turner, J.C. (1979) 'An Integrative Theory of Inter-group Conflict', in Austin, W.G. and Worchel, S. (eds.) *The Social Psychology of Inter-group Relations*. Monterey, CA: Brooks/Cole, pp. 33–47.

Thiel, D. (2007) 'Class in Construction: London Building Workers, Dirty Work and Physical Cultures', *The British Journal of Sociology*, 58(2), pp. 227–251.

Thompson, W.E. (1991) 'Handling the Stigma of Handling the Dead: Morticians and Funeral Directors', *Deviant Behavior*, 12(4), pp. 403–429.

Todd, S. (2021) *Snakes and Ladders: The Great British Social Mobility Myth*. London: Chatto & Windus.

Torelli, J. and Puddephatt, A. (2020) 'Reframing "Dirty Work": The Case of Homeless Shelter Workers', *Symbolic Interaction*, pp. 1–29.

Tracy, S. and Scott, C. (2006) 'Sexuality, Masculinity and Taint Management Among Firefighters and Correctional Officers: Getting Down and Dirty With 'America's Heroes' and the 'Scum of Law Enforcement', *Management Communication Quarterly*, 2(1), pp. 6–38.

Tyler, M. (2011) 'Tainted Love: From Dirty Work to Abject Labour in Soho's Sex Shops', *Human Relations*, 64(11), pp. 1477–1500.

Van Rooyen, L., Du Toit, D.H, Botha, E. and Rothmann, S. (2010) 'Artisan Retention in an Organisation in South Africa', *SA Journal of Human Resource Management*, 8(1), pp. 1–8.

Vinogradov, E. and Jorgensen, E.J.B. (2017) 'Differences in International Opportunity Identification Between Native and Immigrant Entrepreneurs', *Journal of International Entrepreneurship*, 15(2), pp. 207–228.

14

EFFICIENT WORK

Exploring Algorithmic Approaches to Categorization

Sasha Disko, Bruce Kogut, Hanyu Li and Jennifer Zhang

Forward

> When we come to say "we just don't speak the same language," we mean something more general: that we have different immediate values or different kinds of valuation, or that we are aware, often intangibly, of different formations and distributions of energy and interest.
>
> Raymond Williams (1976, p. 9)

Introduction

How can analyzing definitions of efficiency and inefficiency help us to understand how the category of work has shifted over time and what the future of work could look like? And by whom and to what ends were competing definitions invoked? What are the semantic interconnections between categories and how do they manifest themselves in material and experiential ways? In what relationship does efficiency and innovation stand to labor, as both practice and social category, or to the corporations who employ technology in seeking higher productivity? How do these categories, as Williams writes, "embody different experiences and readings of experience" and how do they exist in "active relationships and conflicts"? (ibid., p. 21).

In this chapter, we take a novel approach to analyzing the complex category of efficiency and its relationship to the equally slippery term, innovation. We first briefly trace its historical semantic definitions using historiographical methods and then compare two very different textual sources, the *International Labor Review* (*ILR*) and the *Harvard Business Review* (*HBR*) published, respectively, published by the International Labor Organization (ILO) and by the Harvard Business School (HBS), the world's oldest Masters of Business Administration (MBA)

DOI: 10.4324/9781003341321-18

program. The *ILR* and the *HBR* clearly represent different perspectives on efficiency and work. Some might say they hold antagonistic views: the *ILR* formally representing "labor" and the *HBR* siding with "capital." Thus, built into our research design is the recognition that the act of categorizing efficiency embodies different forms and experiences of power. By using natural language processing tools, we trace the usage of "efficiency" from the founding of these publications in the early 1920s to 2019.

Efficiency: Saving Labor? Distributing Wealth?

Like so many categories of work, efficiency is often invoked unreflectively. Although all categories are normative, efficiency is notably positivistic. As a historian of technology, Jennifer Karns Alexander argues, "Efficiency has . . . become a central value in the world's advanced industrial cultures, an apparently self-evident value associated with individual discipline, superior management, and increased profits" (Alexander, 2008, p. 1). Despite its actual semiotic openness, efficiency often carries the weight of a scientific measure and appears to have an authoritative quality that puts it beyond questioning.[1] In order to unpack efficiency as a category, we first turn to the *Oxford English Dictionary* (OED-Online, 2020).

The first definition in the OED of efficiency is philosophical. It refers to the "fact of being an operative agent or efficient cause," giving efficiency a Faustian quality. The second two definitions, both of which are more common today, relate to economics on the one hand, and mechanics and physics on the other hand. The second one is "Fitness or power to accomplish, or success in accomplishing, the purpose intended; adequate power, effectiveness, efficacy." This definition first appears, according to the OED in 1633, and becomes commonplace in the course of the nineteenth century. It increasingly becomes an expression related to power, for example, of the navy, or of labor. The OED cites British economist Henry Fawcett, who used this concept of efficiency in his 1863 *Manual of Political Economy*: "Nothing more powerfully promotes the efficiency of labor than an abundance of fertile land."

According to the OED, efficiency in an explicitly business sense is first cited in the British context in a 1906 title of a book by A. Shadwell: *Industrial efficiency. A comparative study of industrial life in England, Germany and America*. Efficiency becomes closely tied to the concept of "scientific management" and "industrial organization" in the first decade of the twentieth century. By the 1920s, this use of "efficiency" as a category was much *en vogue*, as we can see in these quotes from an article that appeared in the *Harvard Business Review*:

> These facts are sufficient to show the striking tendency toward making the workman the director of energy, rather than the supplier of energy. It is the accelerated movement in industry to substitute the use of brains for the use of muscle . . . The question, therefore, of measuring increased efficiency

> in American industrial enterprise becomes a complex one, as well as one possessing social significance.
>
> *(Duncan, 1927, pp. 275, 279)*

Thus, the category of economic efficiency could already operate on multiple levels: on an individual level regarding the efficiency of an individual worker, as we see in Fredrick Winslow Taylor's *Principles of Scientific Management*, (1911) or on the enterprise level, as we see in Harrington Emerson's *The Twelve Principles of Efficiency* (1913). In these works, efficiency is posited as beneficial not only for management, but for workers as well, as the gains are purportedly fairly shared through piece-rate compensation (Taylor, 1895; Nelson, 1974; Nolan, 1994).

Economic efficiency, however, was not limited only to shop floors and public debates. Within the growing discipline of economics, the late nineteenth-century marginalists such as Jevons, Menger and Walras were exploring efficiency from the perspectives of markets. They defined optimality as the equation of marginal costs of outputs and prices consumers paid. At the turn of the twentieth century, the Italian economist and sociologist Wilfredo Pareto formulated a welfare measure to evaluate the efficient distribution of resources, using Walras' derivation of general equilibrium. Marginalist ideas revolutionized economics and economic policy. Their influence was reflected in the OED, which cites Keynes' theory on the "marginal efficiency of capital" in his 1936 *General Theory of Employment.* Moreover, in the late 1930s, Kaldor and Hicks developed the new Keynesian model as a policy tool that relied upon the concept of economic efficiency that applied Pareto efficiency to compare the desirability of alternative policy choices. Any distributional consequences were waved away by the argument that individuals who lose under the policy can be compensated by larger gains to society. Thus, growing inequality did not challenge the dominance of market marginalist efficiency but transformed it into a political economy dilemma: will those who are hurt by the policy be compensated?

Still, in the following decades, economic efficiency became a dominant measure in policymaking, often in the form of cost-benefit analysis, making it a category that demands closer inspection for its fairness. As Yale Law School Professor Zachary Liscow argues, efficiency as a policy guide is often applied to increase the economic pie, but it has all the same a tendency toward distributional consequences that favor the wealthier (Liscow, 2018). Similarly, many economists spoke about the dangers of large corporations not only because of their economic power, but also due to their negative incentive effects on economic efficiency.

The second definition of efficiency in the OED is technical and continues to develop and diversify over the twentieth century. According to the OED, in the 1960s, a differentiation is established between "economic efficiency" and "technical efficiency," with economic efficiency being evaluated at market prices, measuring the "output per unit cost of the resources employed," while technical efficiency is evaluated by engineering measures, indicating "output of energy per unit of energy applied." The technical approach precipitated the growth in operations research and cybernetics in the decades in the post-World War II era. Not only was it applied in the public and the private sector in the West, but it also found wide reception in the microeconomic textbooks in the Soviet bloc countries.[2]

The third definition in the OED defines efficiency in relation to mechanics and physics. The first obsolete definition, in use especially in the first decades of the nineteenth century, pertains to "the work done by a force in operating a machine or engine; the total energy expended by a machine." It is replaced in the mid-nineteenth century by the physical/mechanical definition of efficiency that is still in use today, namely "the ratio of useful work performed to the total energy expended or heat taken in." In the OED, this definition appears to apply solely to machines, however, as Anson Rabinbach has shown in his magisterial study *The Human Motor: Energy, Fatigue, and the Origins of Modernity* this concept of efficiency was applied to human energy as well; for the scientists of work of the late nineteenth and early twentieth century, efficiency meant conserving human energy (Rabinbach, 1992, also Nolan, 1994 and Alexander, 2008). In today's debates, efficiency is often a marker for the possibility of substituting human work, both physical and mental, by machines equipped with artificial intelligence.[3]

Economics, Technology and the Intercourse Between Productivity and Organizational Arrangements

In the first decades of the twentieth century, the world of work was thus continuing to undergo a massive transformation. This led to both the development of the MBA as an academic discipline, first established at Harvard in 1908, and the ILO, based in Geneva, as a formalization, in 1919, of efforts to create a body responsible for international social legislation.[4] Returning to the question of categorization, the establishment of both the ILO and business schools, such as the HBS, were tied to the semantic shift over the eighteenth and nineteenth centuries of the keyword of industry, with the development of the related terms industrial revolution and industrialism. The category of labor, as Williams has traced, likewise underwent a profound shift to become an abstract category, one that was quantifiable and objectifiable. He cites Fabian socialist, economist and social commentator Beatrice Webb, incidentally the first woman to publish in the *ILR* in its first year of circulation, to explain how "labor was an abstraction, which seemed to denote an arithmetically calculable mass of human beings, each a repetition of the other" (Webb, 1921, cited in Williams, p. 147). Speaking historically and currently, an important underlying assumption often contained within the category of efficiency is that purportedly, by definition, its presence is the result of productivity gains in which work is accomplished due to changes in technological and organizational arrangements. What is especially important to note here is that the hegemonic use, aside from notable critiques such as those offered by Harry Braverman and Stephen Meyer, frames both changes in technological and organizational arrangements and boosts in productivity as normatively beneficial to all (Braverman, 1974; Meyer, 1981).

The long shift to defining labor as a commodity is key to any study that seeks to understand the history of the category of efficiency. Intrinsic to the transformation of labor from a "human activity which goes with life itself, which in turn is not produced for sale" to a "fictitious commodity" (Polanyi, 1944, p. 75) was a shift in the real and abstract treatment of time, whereby time was increasingly understood as a monetized unit (Biernacki, 1995). Technologies, such as the mechanical clock and later the stopwatch, played a central role in this process (Thompson, 1967). Within the concept of efficiency, it is possible to read struggles over the objectification of social relations, above all of time and labor. Needless to say, these struggles played out and play out differently in different temporal and geographical settings and among different actors in different political contexts (Biernacki, 2001).

As the pace of technical and social change in the twentieth century accelerated, the notion of efficiency was challenged as an inadequate, if not misguided, concept. Innovation is a term that gradually superseded the earlier focus on cost efficiency. For example, even though Taylorism represented the implementation of cumulative technical advances in the management of workers and materials, the term innovation was not applied to these cost-savings practices.[5] However, over the course of the twentieth century, innovation is often not only semantically tied to new ways of achieving efficiency, but it also becomes associated with technological and product breakthroughs.

Arguably, the most important text from which the differentiation of innovation from efficiency is Schumpeter's classic study *The Theory of Economic Development* that lays the groundwork for a new definition of innovation adopted by the OED. In this book, he identifies five types of innovations, three of which can be considered more technologically oriented and two of which are work process and skill oriented (Schumpeter and Redvers, 1934). Thus, an important aspect, not often highlighted in the subsequent literature, is that skill adaptations are often at the center of changes in work routines. Schumpeter himself was clear that "innovation is possible without anything we should identify as invention and invention does not necessarily induce innovation" (Schumpeter, 1939, p. 84, OED-Online, 2021). Still, the late Schumpeter emphasized the growing role of commercial scientific research housed in the labs of large bureaucratic corporations. He proposed that, as government bureaucrats could manage these labs, late industrial society would slide to socialism.

This late Schumpeterian thesis reflects a critique of cost efficiency as the driver of productivity, especially concerning the emergence of multi-divisional corporations that came to dominate many of the most successful economies in the last century through what Alfred Chandler labeled "scale and scope" economies.

Others accepted the historical evolution of the multidivisional firm, but rejected its inherent efficiency, instead pointing to changes in markets toward preferring innovation that led also to a decay in market competition and the rise of regulation (Chandler, 1994).[6] With the evolution of firms and markets, other dimensions central to the evaluation of productivity fitted better to the growing appreciation of top management and the formulation of strategy. Two industrial psychologists proposed a particularly insightful distinction: with efficiency as minimizing waste in pursuit of a goal, and effectiveness as the choice of what goals to pursue (Katz and Kahn, 1966). After all, improvements in the technology of horse-pulled wagons did not cease even long after the casual evidence of motor-driven vehicles, such as autos and motorcycles, suggested a change in eras.[7]

Perspectives and Geometries Through Comparative Topic Analysis

In order to better understand the social construction of the category of efficiency, we have chosen to review the perspectives of two major publications that were found almost conterminously: The *International Labor Review*, first published in 1921, and the *Harvard Business Review*, first published in 1922.[8] By assembling a collection of documents from two journals related in their ambitions and founded at about the same time, we create a research design that permits two comparisons along two dimensions. The first is a comparison of the topics that most strongly describes the social and political issues emphasized in the respective corpus. There is no question that *HBR* favored a perspective from business. The *Harvard Business Review* was initiated by the second dean of Harvard Business School, Wallace B. Donham. In his opening essay, "Essential Groundwork for a Broad Executive Theory," Donham argues that the purpose of the *HBR* will be to provide cases, such as were used in the development of legal theory, to develop a theory of business (Donham, 1922, p. 9). On the other hand, the *International Labor Review* saw its mission to provide a factual basis for institutions throughout the world to address challenges of employment labor, and government policy post-World War I. More specifically, the *ILR* was established within Article 396 of the Treaty of Peace, and was to be "a periodical paper dealing with the problems of industry and employment of international interest," and to publish monthly, "information and statistics presented in a uniform manner upon all the more important phases of industrial life" (*ILR*, 1921, pp. 3–4; Bollé, 2013).

The second dimension of our research design parses the collection of documents over the duration of almost one hundred years to observe and compare changes within the total corpus. Each of these journals was and is important for defining boundaries, and their fields of interest intersect and overlap. Clearly, over the hundred years of their existence, the *ILR* and *HBR* were shaped by historically major external events ranging from technological change, wars, mobilization of the war economy and formal decolonization, the growing presence of women in the formal economy and accelerated migration, and the rise of the multidivisional corporation, and, with few notable exceptions, such as Chile and Iceland, the waning power of collective bargaining. The editors and contributors of these two journals were themselves often actors, whether through their academic expertise or through their engagement in these events.

While the communities around these journals were working through the same world historical events, their experiences, responses and actions embodied, we propose, different perspectives that led, in turn, to differences in the ways these journals tended to categorize these experiences as well. Quite simply, the journals provided different interpretations on world events, and yet these perspectives were hardly static over time and one-dimensional in their focus. Borrowing a term from Kozlowski, Taddy and Evans, the textual documents expressed a geometry defined by many dimensions that reveal a richer and more polysemous interpretation than available by a single perspective (Kozlowski et al., 2019). For the purpose of classification, these dimensions represent topics. For a single topic – for example, politics – a document is placed along a line with extreme politicism and the absence of politics at polar opposites. By adding a second topical dimension of religion, a document now is assigned to an interior position on a plane; a third topic creates a three-dimensional space; and this geometric expansion continues to increase to as many topics as the amount of data can support. Once this space is defined by choosing the number of dimensions (expressed as topics), documents as groups (here *HBR* and *ILR* as two distinct groups), the distance between these groups can be observed and the evolution in the changes in the intensity of their interest for each topic can also be observed.

At some point, some argue, the sheer quantity of texts and topics surpasses the ability of humans to thoroughly process the information without recourse to artificial intelligence assistance. An alternative is to use a generative model that learns from the text data to assign words to latent topics. Topic analysis belongs to a history of efforts to categorize bibliographic documents in such a way as to facilitate information retrieval.[9] One of the most common NLP models is called latent Dirichlet allocation (LDA). Each document (for example, article, book, etc.) in a collection (here, *HBR* and *ILR*) is characterized by all topics. The job of the LDA program is to discover the assignment of words to topics and topics to documents for documents in a corpus that might be a few thousand to millions of words.[10] The generative model assigns words to the topics by their association with other words in that topic. Using these associations, LDA learns that some words will have a high probability to be in a topic, and others will have a low probability. The words with the highest probability are the keywords. Similarly, for each document, the relevance of a topic to describing the text is probabilistically scored. LDA makes these calculations for all topics per document in a corpus. Finally, a topic proportion that gives the relevance of a topic for the entire corpus can be calculated by taking the average of a topic score across all the documents. This average gives a topic proportion score to each topic. These scores are normalized so that they all add up to one. Topic proportions can also be calculated for partitions of text. We partition the corpus by source – *HBR* or *ILR*, as discussed later.

As noted earlier, LDA requires that the researcher chooses the number of topics. But how does one decide this number? A popular statistic is coherence which measures the degree of semantic similarity between each topic's keywords. A simple rule is to fix the number of topics that are most coherent with each other. We rely also on expertise concerning how sensible are the words assigned to a given topic. Ultimately, these two methods, of coherence and human judgment, led us to the decision to fix the number of topics at 30.

Human expertise is needed to increase the interpretability of LDA-generated topics by expert labeling of topics. Unlike systems where labels are determined beforehand, LDA does not know the labels, meaning the data are "unsupervised." Instead, LDA lets topics be generated from the data, for example, through the association among words. As these generated topics are not labeled by the program, common practice is for researchers to assign labels. We labeled the ten most important topics using our judgment.

Comparing the Geometry of Text Over Space and Time

A point of entry into a distant reading of text extracted from over a hundred years of two very different journals is to get a sense of changes in the salience of the word efficiency over time by looking at its frequency. To provide a calibration of this salience, we plot also the frequency of the word innovation in the entire merged corpus. This comparison corresponds to microeconomics where efficiency is clearly related with minimizing costs to the supply of goods and innovation is associated with increasing the demand for products through novelty.

The first plot (Fig. 14.1a) shows that the frequency of the word efficiency is volatile, as it reflected the urgency of production, above all in the context of World War II.[11] Nevertheless, the mean trend is stable. On the other hand, the plot of the word innovation (Fig. 14.1b) shows a striking pattern, moving from relatively lower frequencies to considerably higher in the last decades. Compared to efficiency, innovation is over 4 times more frequent after 2000. When the text is split into *HBR* and *ILR* (not reported visually here), it is evident that *HBR* is primarily responsible for the sudden rise of innovation. This trend should not be surprising, as one of the notable and most cited contributors to the *HBR* was Peter F. Drucker, author of *Innovation and Entrepreneurship* and a "management guru" who viewed Schumpeter as a "modern prophet" (Drucker, 1983).

Besides its uncomfortable relationship with innovation, there is another way in which efficiency failed to retain dominance. As discussed earlier, the pursuit of efficiency left open the question of efficiency in pursuit of what? Over the course of the twentieth century, globally, incomes grew due to increases in "efficiency," favoring the adoption of high-resource intensity products at higher costs and prices. The exploitative side effects of increases in efficiency, were, however, not

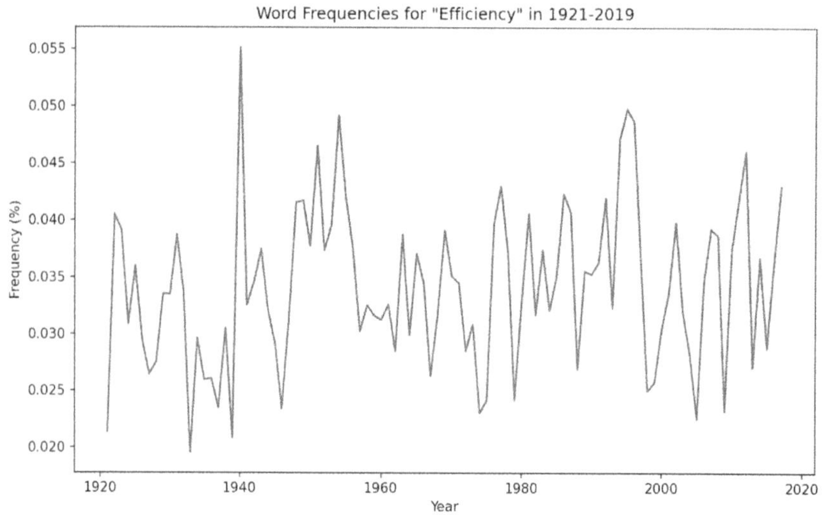

FIGURE 14.1A Word Frequencies for "Efficiency" (1921–2019)

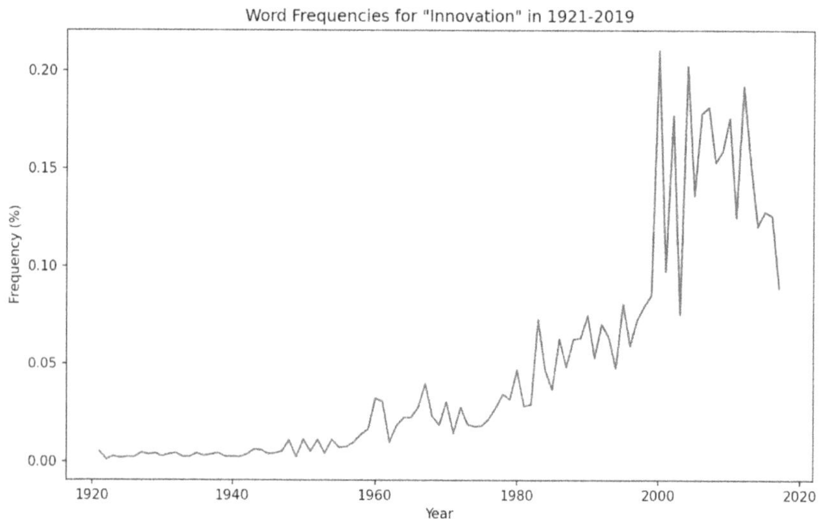

FIGURE 14.1B Word Frequencies for "Innovation" (1921–2019)

only accompanied by exploitative working conditions. By the turn of the twenty-first century, environmental issues were undeniable, requiring a more sophisticated and longer-term tradeoff between efficiency, innovation and effectiveness. If we take the climate crisis as an indicator of the "effectiveness" of efficiency, we can identify a shift in the twenty-first century toward reassessing dominant models, as indicated in recent articles in both the *ILR* and the *HBR*.[12]

Frequencies provide a broad context; however, they do not provide insight into the geometry of semantic perspectives. For this, topic analysis is useful insofar as it places words into a high-dimensional space that reveals what authors, and journals, are writing about. Sometimes, a close reading of a central writer charts the changes in the Zeitgeist over time. For example, Schumpeter's ideas evolved over his lifetime regarding innovations. The word efficiency was less implicated in this evolution, remaining static in its frequency of appearance and also in its semantic connection to the organization of work and to the regulatory arrangements of the state and of trade unions.

This stability in the frequency of efficiency is consistent with the topic analysis we conducted that split the merged *HBR* and *ILR* into two periods: 1921–1972 and 1973–2019. The first period covers the period of the collapse of 1920s economic gains in efficiency due to the diffusion of Taylorism and similar methods to the great boom in productivity after World War II and the era of the *trente glorieuses*. The first period ends with the publication of "Limits to Growth," the signing of the Paris Peace Accords and the collapse of the world economic order built on the pivotal role of the United States, challenged by oil cartels, a rebuilt Europe and a rising Asia. The second period covers the turn to neoliberal economic arrangements, including the brief revival of the United States as the economic hegemonic world power and the disintegration of the Soviet empire before morphing into a wider predicament of dispersed economic and political competitors, especially China. Our periodization is associated with the events already presaged in the frequency plots, namely the growing dependence of the United States and the West on innovations as a response to the diffusion of technological and managerial knowledge to the rest of the world. The so-called American century captured in our collection of *HBR* and *ILR* documents ends with the collapse of US hegemony and the establishment of dispersed and competing power constellations.

In the first period, from 1921 to 1972, the topic proportions of the total corpus of both the *ILR* and the *HBR* reflect the dominance of Taylorist methods of scientific management, as well as its adaptation in the European discourse on "rationalization." This discourse is closely tied to debates on state intervention and planning, including laws and regulations, topics that were hotly debated on both sides of the Atlantic and that gradually emerged as two different perspectives on the ideal relationship between the economy and the state. Viewed from the perspective of the heyday of the power of labor movement in the global North as well as the United States-dominated formalization of both management studies and the growth of the large-scale corporation, the topics generated from the corpora over this period demonstrate how marginalist discussions of efficiency were closely aligned with arguments about welfare provisions and the institutional relationship between labor and capital. The topic analysis also shows how both World

Wars, but particularly World War II, were important fields of experimentation in terms of possibilities for active political intervention into economic relations, including industrial relations, in order to increase productivity. The second half of this period also witnessed a large wave of decolonization and the consolidation of developmentalist discourses, as is reflected in the concern with employment and workforce improvement.[13]

In the second period, from 1973 to 2019, we see the influence of the unraveling of ideological foundations that structured the world economic order into two competing camps and the decline of state-centered approaches to organizing the economy.[14] Reflective of the increasing hegemony of neoliberal ideologies, this second period has a far stronger focus on the individual, as customer, employee, manager or executive. The dominant discourse in the overall corpus is shaped by firm-level interventions regarding job process and performance, managerial analysis and reporting, and management strategies more generally. Macroeconomic considerations are, however, still of concern, and the organization of the economy on a global scale, including the labor market, comes increasingly into focus. This includes the broadening of the geographic scope; both China and Japan are clear vectors of interest. Also, while neither "workers" nor organizational factors drop out entirely, the data allows us to observe a transformation in the efficiency discourse to highlight the role of technology and innovation. Information processing technologies, including computers and the internet, join developmentalist discourses and the global expansion of formal labor rights as important fields of inquiry.[15]

Earlier, we sought to understand the changing reception and usage of the term efficiency in contrast to innovation. We now expand this idea of understanding efficiency from the perspective of related and competing term of innovation to consider its semantic categorization in relation to a *topical* analysis of the entire corpus of text extracted from the *ILR* and *HBR*. For this purpose, we rely upon natural language processing (NLP) tools to categorize documents, and words, by the topics to which they belong to. This effort moves beyond the single comparison with one word (for example, innovation) to placing efficiency in the context of many ways by which a document can be described by topics and their vocabularies.

The *HBR* and *ILR* sources differ in their orientations by design in order to contrast the perspectives (what we call "geometries") from capital and from labor.[16] Looking at the period 1921–1972 (Figure 14.2a), the four topics more favored by the *ILR* always include the word "worker," no matter the other keywords assigned to that topic. Compared to *ILR*, the *HBR* documents favor slightly topics concerning rationalization and Taylorism. These are of course classic coded words for efficiency. The keywords all include the word "time." Both *HBR* and *ILR* favor topics that include the word "war." *HBR* mentions war along with price and union, and *ILR* groups war with worker and employment. Clearly, *HBR* and *ILR* are not speaking the same language even when discussing similar topics.

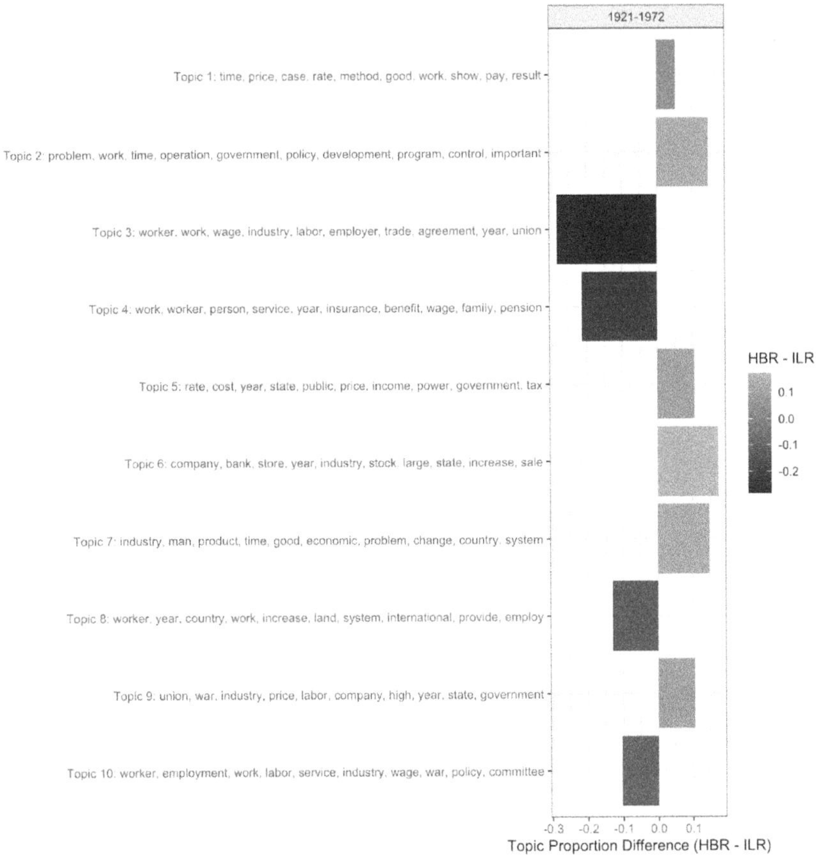

FIGURE 14.2A Difference in Topic Proportion by Topic and by Journal (1921–1972)

In the second period of 1973–2019 (Figure 14.2b), the *ILR* topics mention worker only twice, instead discussing employment, economic and growth. Still, traditional concerns of labor are present, with topics reflecting the theme of child (work) adjacent to social, law and contract. Indeed, the word "social" is present in 4 of the 5 topics characterizing the *ILR* text. While time is included in the keywords for two of the topics favored by the *HBR*, its most preferred topic is about marketing, products, customer, people and sales. The growth of articles devoted to the word "strategy," cited in one topic, is accompanied by a glut of modern business terminology: cost, product, customer, team, manager and organization. Here we note a strong trend that sees efficiency as increasingly less salient in relation to other considerations for both the ILO, which increasingly focused on social aspects of work, and for the HBS, mirroring new business vocabularies, standardized in MBA programs.

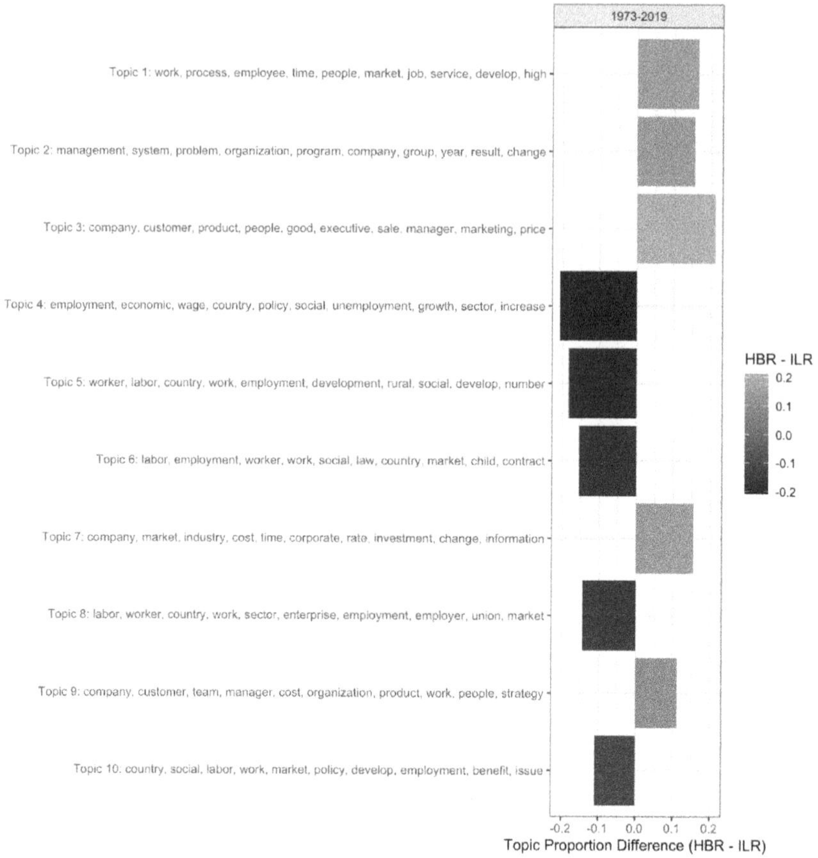

FIGURE 14.2B Difference in Topic Proportion by Topic and by Journal (1973–2019)

In all, even when constraining the analysis to the same topics, the topical differences between the *HBR* and *ILR* appear more differentiated post-1972. *HBR* is less concerned with the state and more fixated on the corporation that undertakes product development, marketing, and sales, giving relatively less attention to time and cost efficiencies so closely associated with the Taylorist currents in the first half of the twentieth century. There is a general shift in language. The *ILR* still writes of the social and of employment, but less of unemployment and more of the market. Here, we may see a correspondence of broad macroeconomic trends that have come to dominate the early twenty-first century – stagnant wages, weakening of unions and historic levels of income and wealth disparity.

Conclusion: Babbling Words, Finding a Common Vocabulary?

So how do these journals contribute to the construction of the category of efficiency over time? A simple test is whether their writings echo the historical record. While the period of 1921–1973 was filled with battle and reconciliation between labor and capital, with both parties focused on the dynamics of wages and costs and of markets and the state, the second period is marked by new categorizations reflecting the dominance of larger and more global corporate entities who compete in the richer markets through innovation, marketing and strategy.[17]

Thus, through identifying clusters of words collected in expansive datasets, machine learning tools prove useful for validating how definitions of categories and keywords shifted over time. As Jo Guldi and Benjamin Williams (Guldi and Williams, 2018) have argued, the use of topic modeling in tracing the development of categories holds significant potential in particular for helping social scientists and historians chart longer durée trends and for potentially identifying the impetus for a shift in a category. There is, however, an active debate on whether the outcome of introducing AI will favor the substitution of skilled by lower-skilled workers. This suggests a trade-off between new gains in efficiency brought by innovation at the cost of human motivation, for which there is evidence (Dell'Acqua et al., 2020). If such methods are "objectively more efficient" for historians who seek to gain insights into change over time than tried and true methods are, is a question that also remains open to debate (Evalyn 2021; Guldi, 2018).

Critical inquiries into categories and processes of categorization can help us understand what is at stake in the

> shaping and reshaping, in real circumstances and from profoundly different and important points of view: a vocabulary to use, to find our own ways in, to change as we find it necessary to change it, as we go on making our own language and history.
>
> *(Williams, 1976, p. 22)*

Oligarichism, digitalization, climate change and tectonic shifts in geopolitical arrangements are breaking down the long-standing consensus around productivity and efficiency. On the one hand, traditional understandings of efficiency have given way to other categories, such as innovation and flexibility. On the other hand, categories previously understood as "inefficient," such as "the commons" and the "common good," express an entirely different way of measuring costs and benefits (Bollier and Helfrich, 2019; Felber, 2018). Currently, these historic relics are being revisited and revised. In any case, the multifaceted crises we currently face, regardless of our politics, will inform how these categories evolve. After all, technological shifts, wars and economic crises precipitated past shifts in understanding and experiencing the category of efficiency.

Appendix: Topic Proportions, Keywords and Labels

Topic Labels, First 50 years

Top 10 topics explained 64.1% of documents.

LL/token: −9.03182 (also call as "bound")
Perplexity = 2^(-LL/token) =523.42 (lower is better)
Coherence score = 0.3681 (higher is better)

TABLE 14.1A 10 Top Topics per Topic Proportion (1921–1972)

Topic	*Size (%)*	*Top 10 Words in Topic*	*Label*
1	11.5%	time, price, case, rate, method, good, work, show, pay, result	*Taylorization & Rationalization*
2	9.1%	problem, work, time, operation, government, policy, development, program, control, important	*State Intervention & Planning*
3	9.0%	worker, work, wage, industry, labor, employer, trade, agreement, year, union	*Industrial Relations*
4	6.9%	work, worker, person, service, year, insurance, benefit, wage, family, pension	*Welfare Provisions*
5	5.9%	rate, cost, year, state, public, price, income, power, government, tax	*Laws & Regulations*
6	5.6%	company, bank, store, year, industry, stock, large, state, increase, sale	*Commerce & Banking*
7	5.0%	industry, man, product, time, good, economic, problem, change, country, system	*Industry & Economic Change*
8	4.4%	worker, year, country, work, increase, land, system, international, provide, employ	*Employment & Workforce*
9	3.4%	union, war, industry, price, labor, company, high, year, state, government	*Wartime Industrial Relations*
10	3.3%	worker, employment, work, labor, service, industry, wage, war, policy, committee	*Wartime Employment Policy*

* Model Coherence Score is 0.3681

Topic Labels, Second 50 years

Top 10 topics explained 70.3% of documents.

LL/token: −8.97887 (also call as "bound")
Perplexity = 2^(-LL/token) =504.56

TABLE 14.1B 10 Top Topics per Topic Proportion (1973–2019)

Topic	*Size (%)*	*Top 10 Words in Topic*	*Label*
1	13.3%	work, process, employee, time, people, market, job, service, develop, high	*Job Process & Performance*
2	11.6%	management, system, problem, organization, program, company, group, year, result, change	*Managerial Analysis & Reporting*
3	7.6%	company, customer, product, people, good, executive, sale, manager, marketing, price	*Retailing & Commerce*
4	7.5%	employment, economic, wage, country, policy, social, unemployment, growth, sector, increase	*Macroeconomics, Growth & Unemployment*
5	6.5%	worker, labor, country, work, employment, development, rural, social, develop, number	*Employment & Labor Policy*
6	5.5%	labor, employment, worker, work, social, law, country, market, child, contract	*Protective Labor Provisions*
7	5.4%	company, market, industry, cost, time, corporate, rate, investment, change, information	*Investment & Technological Change*
8	5.1%	labor, worker, country, work, sector, enterprise, employment, employer, union, market	*Union & Industrial Policy*
9	3.9%	company, customer, team, manager, cost, organization, product, work, people, strategy	*Management Strategy*
10	3.9%	country, social, labor, work, market, policy, develop, employment, benefit, issue	*Global Labor Market*

* Model Coherence Score is 0.3977

Notes

1 For a fascinating and thought-provoking exploration of efficiency as a facet of the attempt to construct "mass utopia," see Buck-Morss (2002). Link (2020) also recently explored this question from a different perspective.
2 For example, the prominent textbook used in the DDR in the 1970s and 1980s, Arnold et al. (1973). On cybernetics, see Mirowski (2001).
3 Keynes made a famous argument for economic progress hurting labor (Keynes, 1930 [2010]). For a current up-beat assessment of the perennial debate over the substitution of labor by capital, see Brynholfson and McAfee (2011). For a relatively pessimistic critique, see Ford (2015).
4 The historiography of the world of work, even for the twentieth century, is of course too broad to attempt even a cursory bibliography. However, a recent anthology provides a good overview, touching on topics such as "The Economy of Work" and "Work, Skill and Technology," see Walkowitz (2019), as well as Kocka (1969 and 1999).
5 The oldest definitions of innovation in the OED date back to the sixteenth century. The first definition regards "the action of innovating; the introduction of novelties; the alteration of what is established by the introduction of new elements or forms" and is closely related to a second definition: "A change made in the nature or fashion of anything; something newly introduced; a novel practice, method, etc." The definition related to "commerce," meaning, "the action of introducing a new product into the market; a product newly brought on to the market" only appears in the 1930s. Interestingly, two obsolete definitions of innovation are aligned with revolution (OED-Online, 2021).
6 For the argument that changes in the market environment forced firms to change their orientations from manufacturing, to marketing and to finance, see Fligstein (1990).
7 The fossil-fuel-driven automobile era could, however, lead to the ultimate ineffective inefficacy: mass-extinctions, including of humankind. Bicycles, however, which have endured from the horse-drawn era of mobility until today, are an example of a mobility technology that is both efficient *and* effective.
8 For *ILR*, we retrieved all the text from Heinonline in digital form. For *HBR*, we downloaded the HTML articles from EBSCOhost website in pdf format after failing to receive the consent of Harvard Business School to the well-curated *HBR* corpus.
9 NLP has been used in humanities research since the early 2000s and has become more well-developed in the last decade. A few examples that we found particularly useful in thinking about the pros and cons of using this approach are Guldi (2019); Guldi and Williams (2018); Schmidt (2012); Heuser and Le-Khac (2012). A prominent publication dedicated to exploring the use of digital tools in the humanities is the *Journal of Cultural Analytics*.
10 We used a combination of Gensim (Python) and Mallet Package for LDA which is coded in Java and hence runs slower than in Python, especially for very large corpus of text.
11 As discussed earlier, efficiency is a polysemous word and its lower frequency compared to innovation might reflect the omission of highly similar words, including "efficient."
12 For example, Ghosh (2010) and Winston (2020).
13 See Table A 1a. 10 Top Topics per Topic Proportion (1921–1972) in the Appendix.
14 See Table A 1b. 10 Top Topics per Topic Proportion (1973–2019) in the Appendix.
15 Some transformations only become more apparent when looking at the full dataset of 30 topics.
16 We recalculated the topic proportions separately for the *HBR* and *ILR* texts, preserving the topics and keywords from the pooled sources. Figures 2a and 2b plot the differences between the *HBR* and *ILR* topic proportions, highlighting the topics over which they most *disagree*.
17 In the Appendix, we include two tables that give the keywords for the top 10 topics that the topic analysis algorithm generated as well as author-assigned keywords characterizing the algorithm-generated words.

References

Alexander, J.K. (2008) *The Mantra of Efficiency: From Waterwheel to Social Control*. Baltimore, MD: John Hopkins University Press.

Arnold, H., Borchert, H. and Schmidt, J. (1973) *Sozialistische Betriebswirtschaftslehre*. Berlin: Verl. Technik.

Biernacki, R. (1995) *The Fabrication of Labor: Germany and Britain, 1640–1914*. Berkeley, CA: University of California Press.

Biernacki, R. (2001) 'Labor as an Imagined Commodity', *Politics & Society*, 29(2), pp. 173–206.

Bollé, P. (2013) 'The International Labour Review and the ILO: Milestones in a Shared History', *International Labour Review*, 152, pp. 1–12.

Bollier, D. and Helfrich, S. (2019) *Frei, fair und lebendig: die Macht der Commons*. Bielefeld: Transcript Verlag.

Braverman, H. (1974/1998) *Labor and Monopoly Capital*. New York: Monthly Press Review.

Brynholfson, E. and McAfee, A. (2011) *Race Against the Machine: How the Digital Revolution Is Accelerating Innovation, Driving Productivity, and Irreversibly Transforming Employment and the Economy*. Lexington, MA: Digital Frontier Press.

Buck-Morss, S. (2002) *Dreamworld and Catastrophe: The Passing of Mass Utopia in East and West*. Cambridge, MA: MIT Press.

Chandler, A. (1994) *Scale and Scope: The Dynamics of Industrial Capitalism*. Cambridge, MA: Harvard University Press.

Dell'Acqua, F., Kogut, B. and Perkowski, P. (2020) 'When Mario Meets AI: Automation, Knowledge, and Skill Effects on Team Performance and Coordination in Video Game Play'. https://www.fabriziodellacqua.com/s/Mario_meets_AI_paper.pdf.

Donham, W.B. (1922) 'Essential Groundwork for a Broad Executive Theory', *Harvard Business Review*, 1(1).

Drucker, P.F. (1983) 'Schumpeter and Keynes', in *Forbes,* May 23, https://www.forbes.com/2007/10/10/schumpeter-keynes-economics-biz-cz_pd_1011schumpeter.html?sh=6c68cd25d4f7.

Duncan, C.S. (1927) 'New Elements in American Business Efficiency', *Harvard Business Review*, 5(3), pp. 269–280.

Emerson, H. (1912) *The Twelve Principles of Efficiency*, New York: The Engineering Magazine.

Evalyn, L. (2021) 'Have an Expert Do It by Hand', Blog Entry, *Journal of Cultural Analytics,* October 27, https://culturalanalytics.org/post/1213-have-an-expert-do-it-by-hand.

Felber, C. (2018) *Die Gemeinwohl-Ökonomie: ein Wirtschaftsmodell mit Zukunft*. Wien: Paul Zsolnay Verlag.

Fligstein, N. (1990) *The Transformation of Corporate Control*. Cambridge, MA: Harvard University Press.

Ford, M. (2015) *Rise of the Robots: Technology and the Threat of a Jobless Future*. New York: Basic Books.

Ghosh, J. (2010) 'Global Crisis and Beyond: Sustainable Growth Trajectories for the Developing World', *International Labour Review*, 149(2).

Guldi, J. (2018) 'Critical Search: A Procedure for Guided Reading in Large-Scale Textual Corpora', *Journal of Cultural Analytics* (Online).

Guldi, J. (2019) 'Parliament's Debates About Infrastructure: An Exercise Using Dynamic Topic Models to Synthesize Historical Change', *Technology and Culture*, 60(1), pp. 1–33.

Guldi, J. and Williams, B. (2018) 'Synthesis and Large-Scale Textual Copora: A Nested Topic Model of Britain's Debates Over Landed Property in the Nineteenth Century', *Current Research in Digital History*, online first, https://scholar.smu.edu/

hum_sci_history_research/11/?utm_source=scholar.smu.edu%2Fhum_sci_history_research%2F11&utm_medium=PDF&utm_campaign=PDFCoverPages.

Harvard Business Review (abbreviated HBR).

Heuser, R. and Le-Khac, L. (2012) *A Quantitative Literary History of 2,958 Nineteenth-Century British Novels: The Semantic Cohort Method*. 4th Pamphlet of the Stanford Literary Lab, https://litlab.stanford.edu/LiteraryLabPamphlet4.pdf.

International Labor Review (abbreviated ILR).

Katz, D. and Kahn, R. (1966) *The Social Psychology of Organizations*. New York: Wiley.

Keynes, J.M. (1930 [2010]) 'Economic Possibilities for Our Grandchildren', in Keynes, J.M. (ed.) *Essays in Persuasion*. London: Palgrave Macmillan, pp. 321–332.

Kocka, J. (1969) 'Industrielles Management: Konzeptionen und Modelle in Deutschland vor 1914', *Vierteljahrschrift für Sozial-und Wirtschaftsgeschichte*, 56(3), pp. 332–372.

Kocka, J. (1999) *Industrial Culture and Bourgeois Society: Business, Labor, and Bureaucracy in Modern Germany*. New York: Berghahn Books.

Kozlowski, A., Taddy, M. and Evans, J. (2019) 'The Geometry of Culture: Analyzing the Meanings of Class Through Word Embeddings', *American Sociological Review*, 84(5), pp. 905–949.

Link, S.J. (2020) *Forging Global Fordism*. Princeton, NJ: Princeton University Press.

Liscow, Z. (2018) 'Is Efficiency Biased?', *University of Chicago Law Review*, 85.

Meyer III, S. (1981) *The Five Dollar Day: Labor Management and Social Control in the Ford Automobile Company, 1908–1921*. Albany, NY: State University of New York Press.

Mirowski, P. (2001) *Machine Dreams: Economics Becomes a Cyborg Science*. Cambridge: Cambridge University Press.

Nelson, D. (1974) 'Scientific Management, Systematic Management, and Labor, 1880–1915', *Business History Review*, 48(4), pp. 479–500.

Nolan, M. (1994) *Visions of Modernity: American Business and the Modernization of Germany*. Oxford: Oxford University Press.

OED-Online (2020) 'Efficiency, n', in *OED Online*. Oxford: Oxford University Press.

OED-Online (2021) 'Innovation, n', in *OED Online*. Oxford: Oxford University Press.

Polanyi, K. (1944 [2001]) *The Great Transformation: The Political and Economic Origins of Our Time*. Boston, MA: Beacon Paperback.

Rabinbach, A. (1992) *The Human Motor: Energie, Fatigue and the Origins of Modernity*. Berkeley, CA: University of California Press.

Schmidt, B.M. (2012) 'Words Alone: Dismantling Topic Models in the Humanities', *Journal of Digital Humanities*, 2(1), pp. 49–65.

Schumpeter, J.A. (1939) *Business Cycles*, Vol. 1. New York: McGraw-Hill.

Schumpeter, J.A. and Redvers, O. (trans.) (1934) *The Theory of Economic Development; An Inquiry Into Profits, Capital, Credit, Interest, and the Business Cycle*. Cambridge, MA: Harvard University Press.

Taylor, F.W. (1895) 'A Piece Rate System Being a Step Toward Partial Solution of the Labor Problem', *Transactions of the American Society of Mechanical Engineers*, pp. 856–903.

Taylor, F.W. (1911) *The Principles of Scientific Management*. New York: Harper & Brothers.

Thompson, E.P. (1967) 'Time, Work-Discipline and Industrial Capitalism', *Past and Present*, 38, pp. 56–97.

Walkowitz, D.J. (ed.) (2019) *A Cultural History of Work in the Modern Age*. London: Bloomsbury.

Webb, S. Mrs. (sic), (1921) 'The Co-operative Movement of Great Britain and its Recent Developments', *ILR*, 4(2), pp. 15–44.

Williams, R. (1976) *Keywords: A Vocabulary of Culture and Society*. Oxford: Oxford University Press.

Winston, A. (2020) 'Leading a New Era of Climate Action', *HBR*, January 23, https://hbr.org/2020/01/leading-a-new-era-of-climate-action.

15

SKILLED AND UNSKILLED WORK

From Theoretical Concepts to Social Practices

Philipp Grollmann and Michael Tiemann

Introduction

The distinction between "skilled" and "unskilled" work is omnipresent, for example, in invoices for artisanal work with different hourly rates or in worries over an insufficient supply of skilled work. This categorial dichotomy describes *how* work is performed – "skillfully" or not – and thus also refers to the quality of the *outcome*. Beyond this layman's meaning, however, there are further implications related to this concept's use in policy or theory. Although the term is used quasi-universally, there are significant differences not only across disciplines (Green, 2013) but in different linguistic and cultural contexts. Table 15.1 shows a variety of possible translations in English, French and German.

The last row in particular shows that when applying the term to the noun "work" or "labor" a change of meaning takes place that goes beyond a mere individual attribution. While in English this change remains unnoticed on the linguistic level – the wording stays the same – in German and French the notion of "skilled" changes into "qualified."

The term "qualified" points to social practices of formalizing what is considered "skilled." On the other hand, labeling work "unqualified" or "unskilled" cannot actually mean that no skills or qualifications are required at all. These practices are intrinsically connected to different national and cultural concepts of work, education and the labor market (Brockmann et al., 2011). An important sociological distinction is the differentiation of work into the multidimensional categories of "job," "occupation" and "profession," all three of which involve the skill dimension (Carr-Saunders and Wilson, 1964). Hence the categorization of work as "skilled" or "unskilled" is embedded in broader social practices. In the following, we discuss these practices by looking at the *acquisition* of skills, their role in *social and organizational processes*, and their *socio-economic valuation*.

DOI: 10.4324/9781003341321-19

TABLE 15.1 Possible translations and meanings of skill, skillful and skilled work(er)/labor(er)

English	*German*	*French*
skill	Fertigkeit, Fähigkeit, Kompetenz . . .	competence, habilité, savoir, talent . . .
skillful	geschickt, gekonnt, kunstfertig, kompetent . . .	compétent, habile . . .
skilled labor/work	qualifizierte Arbeit, "Facharbeit"	travail qualifié

Skills in Context: The Acquisition of Knowledge and Skills

In the sociology of skills, there is the understanding that they can be made *productive* at work, that they are *expandable* through training and learning, and that they are *socially* determined (Green, 2013, p. 10). In this section, we focus on the training and learning aspect. When looking at the "outcomes" of learning, policymakers and academics use measurements of learning that have been developed over the last 30 years and provide a basis for comparing different educational systems, for example, in the large-scale measurements of the International Association for the Evaluation of Educational Achievement (est. 1958). According to the OECD, "PISA measures 15-year-olds' ability to use their reading, mathematics and science knowledge and skills to meet real-life challenges."[1] Of course, "basic" skills such as numeracy, literacy and problem-solving are very important in skilled work. There is a huge body of literature examining the effect that personal cognitive dispositions – similarly measured through the OECD-PIAAC study for adults – have on opportunities for participation in economic practices. They are predictors of success on the labor market. However, the monetary "value" attached to such cognitive skills in work (in earnings) varies considerably in different countries (Hanushek et al., 2015).

So, what then are "skills"? While having such "skills" is an important prerequisite for participating in modern economic and social processes, it is hardly sufficient. Excellent numeracy skills are an advantage for professions in technical fields or business, but a technician will need to conjoin her numeracy skills with technical-mechanical expertise, while an insurance salesman will have to assess specific risks or perhaps the perceived need for security on the part of his customer. In the tradition of cognitive psychology, such dispositions are labeled "domain specific." The notion of "competence" is more integrative than that of "skills" because it by definition includes different types of learned and inherited capacities such as abilities and intelligence; interestingly, it always relates to a designated field of application (Sternberg and Grigorenko, 2003; Hartig and Klieme 2006). Even when trying to isolate the significance of individual learning and development for what we call "skilled" work, we cannot avoid looking at the context, be it just a body of written knowledge (as in very few occupations) or, as is more often the case, a certain practice that is observable and distinctive from other social and occupational practices (Mieg, 2001). Hence we are back to the "work" component of our theme. Exploring further what psychologically driven research has found on the nature of skills, we enter the territory of *expertise* research. A fundamental finding here is that a high amount of training *and* practical learning is necessary in order to perform well in most domains. Even though there is a discussion, as in educational psychology, about the role of nature and nurture, it has clearly been shown that being involved in practice and constantly improving one's own performance under structured supervision is a fundamental component of expertise (Ericsson and Harwell, 2019).

Skills and abilities are also used as defining characteristics of jobs and occupations. The multidimensionality of "skills" can be traced back to how professions and craftsmanship evolved historically. Richard Sennett (2008) explains how, within crafts and occupations, tasks are being performed by individuals in the best way possible, namely from an intrinsic motivation. While this is what he calls "craftsmanship," it is at the same time what one would call "skillful" work. Skills are part of the knowledge we acquire in occupational practice (Tiemann, 2014).

The contexts for occupational practices are defined by workplaces. It is necessary to look at specific combinations of occupational and firm-specific divisions of labor (Tiemann, 2014) in which production processes are organized. But even without assuming identical organizations within branches, there are similarities in the way workplaces for incumbents of the same occupation are organized in firms. Illustrating this are data from the BIBB/BAuA Employment Survey 2018, which we examined in greater detail. We focused on four groups of work tasks: production, information-handling, direct services (e.g., teaching or caring) and indirect ones such as organizing.[2] Figure 15.1 shows the differences in the mix of skills for the occupational groups situated at the first level of the German classification of occupations. Even with such a broad overview, one sees that the mix of skills in the varying occupations can be quite distinct.

Taking a view where skills equate with qualifications, we might assume that there would be a fairly clear difference between the skills mix where formal qualifications are required – and the skills mix where none are. We will come back to this point in a later section. But we will not find any (occupational) activities requiring *no* skills.

How does the idea of completely "unskilled" activities relate to the possibility of substituting work with digital machines? Can such tasks be automated? One commonality of different theoretical views of the development of technology, society and their relations is an implicit reference to a continuum of man–machine relations from anthropocentric to anthropomorphic.[3] These are reflected in the extremes of machines working for and under the control of humans, centered around humans (anthropocentric) or combined with them (as in prostheses).

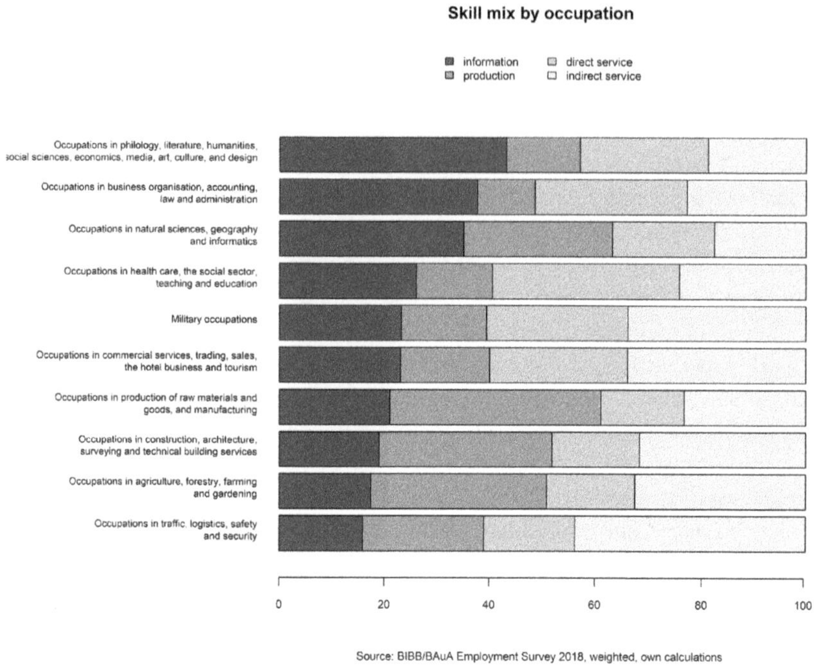

FIGURE 15.1 Skill mix by occupation (BIBB/BAuA Employment Survey 2018, weighted, own calculations)

Among these, we find numerous positions where human workers feed machines with input (Maier, 2021) and such tasks require some sort of skills and training. On the extremes of the continuum, where machines do all the work or are direct parts of human–machine entities, this will not be the case. For example, one can simply put on a pair of "smart glasses" and read their input. Technical advances might therefore bring about situations where no skills are needed.

In contrast to accounts of skills and their development that focus on individualistic or organizational levels, there is also a sociocultural view (Stasz, 2001; Billett et al., 2018). It puts a much stronger emphasis on the social prerequisites of learning and skilled work. According to this view, skills are being developed in social networks of practitioners where the learner constantly develops the knowledge and skills required and also incrementally changes his or her role from that of a learner to being an accepted member of the professional community. This perspective provides a series of indications as to how practices can be shaped in order to provide an environment for the development of skills. It also emphasizes the role of those who already perform skilled work for those who are learning to become skilled. The interaction of experienced professionals and those in the process of acquiring skills is necessary because these jobs involve continuous evaluations, subjective experience-building and behavioral changes that will ultimately make the difference between skilled and unskilled work. Some of the learned skills and abilities may not be adequately represented by cognitive psychology models, for the processes involved in both the transfer of knowledge and the knowledge itself are often referred to in the literature as "implicit" (Nonaka and Takeuchi, 1995; Neuweg, 2000).[4] We have already explained that even immediate practices and interactions take place within a socially framed environment, as can be seen in cross-national differences in work practices. Analogous to our rough distinction between manufacturing, information-processing and services, we will now restrict ourselves here to "blue collar occupations" – in other words, to manufacturing.

The evidence base is not particularly favorable. Nevertheless, a few data sets are available that allow for an international comparison of occupational work tasks. Tasks are the requirement of jobs corresponding to necessary *skills and knowledge*. The focus of available studies is often not on specialized professional knowledge or skills but rather on general job characteristics. Figure 15.2a shows the extent to which employees in blue-collar occupations can decide for themselves just how they will perform their work (discretion) for a number of selected countries (Grollmann et al., 2020).

It is noticeable that blue-collar workers in Germany and Austria have the greatest scope for discretion in comparison to the other countries examined in our study. Discretionary powers are also high in Japan; the United Kingdom and the United States have lower ratings in this regard, as do Spain and Italy.

On the other hand, the United States and the United Kingdom show a high incidence of "complex problem-solving" at work (Figure 15.2b). By including

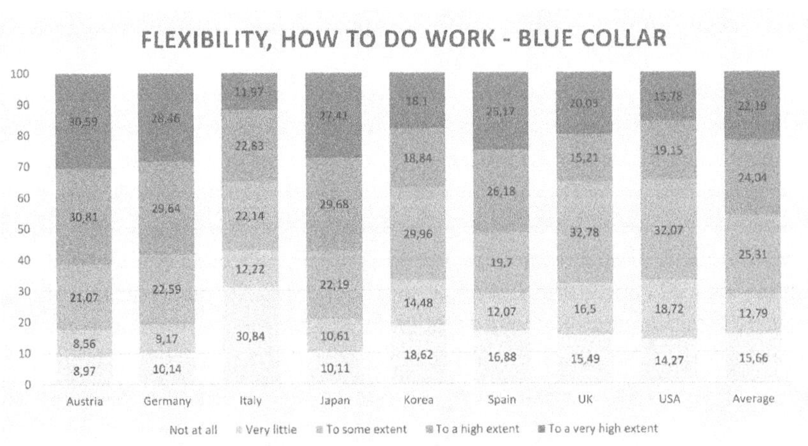

FIGURE 15.2A Flexibility, How to Do Work – Blue Collar based on data from OECD PIACC 2012

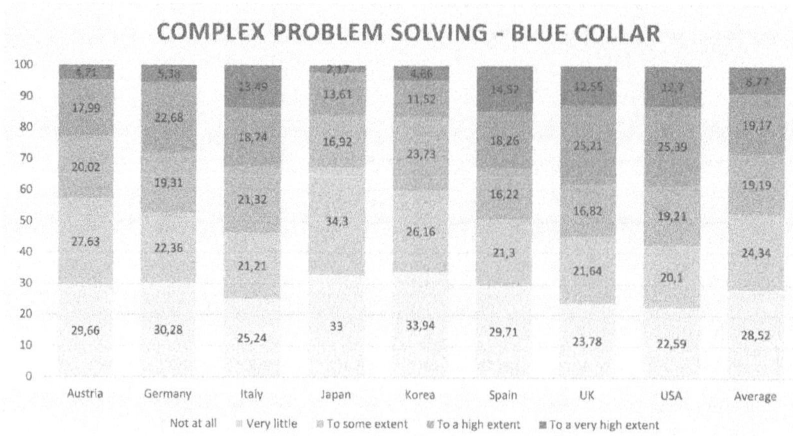

FIGURE 15.2B Complex problem-solving – Blue Collar based on data from OECD (2012) PIACC

further items in our analysis, it becomes quite clear that there are considerable differences in how work within occupations is organized across countries. Accordingly, there will be different types or conceptions of skilled work and skills required for performing these jobs. Of course, this can be attributed to genuine economic factors such as the distribution of company size or sectoral features, but it is also likely that there is an interaction between the structures of general education and that of the vocational-education system as well as the demand for skilled labor through employers, especially on a long-term basis. We have only been able to show this here with a single instance, but there are many other findings that point to these differences in the weighting of knowledge and skills in the context of different national labor markets and firms.

This leads us to the relation between skills and educational systems. While becoming skilled is a learning process that is highly dependent on the respective occupational context, in turn the latter is integrated into various other contexts. A decisive factor in the way in which this integration takes place is the system of general and vocational qualification. The supply of labor is significantly shaped by educational and qualification traditions. While considerable differences in the governance and coordination of labor supply and demand and the importance of educational systems have been highlighted by comparative political economy, we know very little about the implications that this has for skills along with their content and their emergence in the occupational and educational contexts. In the European Union, with its diverse education and training systems, differences in the national concepts of skill have led to great challenges with regard to the establishment of a European labor market. The European Qualifications Framework (EQF) was instituted so as to translate various qualifications from

TABLE 15.2 Concepts, principles and structures of qualifications across three countries (Brockmann et al., 2011)

France	*Germany*	*England*
Knowledge	Competence	Skills
Education	Dual apprenticeship	Training

different national and subnational systems of education and training. Based on extensive research into terminology and concepts, this framework has been a matter of complex political negotiations between the EU Commission and the member states. It attempts to overcome considerable differences in the design of educational structures, training practices, and the organization and distribution of responsibilities by referring only to the "learning outcomes" that are (supposed to be) expressed by qualifications (European Commission, 2008).

A comparative research project examining the content of selected occupations in Germany, the Netherlands, France and England as well as the development of the EQF have been able to successfully demonstrate just how different training traditions are linked to different guiding principles and ideas. According to the authors, the guiding principle of France's school-dominated qualification system is "knowledge," that of the German dual vocational-training system is "action competence," and that of the English system – which is characterized by a pragmatic and fit-for-purpose orientation – is "skills" (Brockmann et al., 2011). Interestingly, Table 15.2 can be read as a continuation of Table 15.1, further specifying the various understandings of the skilled/unskilled dichotomy.

Skills in Social and Organizational Processes

Whereas the EQF formally defines skills more from an educational perspective, the project of a European Taxonomy of Qualifications, Skills and Occupations (ESCO) aims to establish core skills defining occupations across Europe from an organizational perspective. Skills here are detailed aspects of occupations as categorized in the International Standard Classification of Occupations (ISCO)[5]. They are seen as building blocks enabling individual and organizational flexibility and easier labor migration within the EU.

Social practices are embedded in the definition of what is counted as an occupation or a job as well as in the categories themselves. Jobs in ISCO are seen as "a set of tasks and duties performed . . . by one person" with occupations referring "to the kind of work performed in a job . . . as a set of jobs whose main tasks and duties are characterized by a high degree of similarity" (ISCO-08, 11). This reflects a socio-cultural perspective on occupations, which is open to a definition of occupations as "institutions" (Tiemann, 2014) or "forms" (Kurtz, 2005). Within this framework, skills are seen "as the ability to carry out the tasks and duties of a given job" (ISCO-08, 11). Thus skills have levels, which also means they can have the lowest level, but unskilled work is per definition impossible. The basic skill levels "involve the performance of simple and routine . . . tasks," "basic skills in literacy and numeracy" and might also require some "on-the-job training," for instance, "handling equipment," "operating non-motorized vehicles" or "assembling goods by hand" (ISCO-08, 12). Skills also have domain specificity ("skill specialization"). Occupations are conceived as bundles of tasks or the combination of skills and experiences needed to perform those tasks, even if these skills might not be formalized in a vocational qualification.

In Germany the national classification of occupations defines occupations as skill-oriented, combining a bundle of tasks and having two dimensions: *Berufsfachlichkeit* (field of occupation) and *Anforderungsniveau* (required level of skills). Here the lowest level of required qualifications (1 of 4) would indicate low-skilled occupations. This applies to 60 of the 1,286 occupations on the most detailed level. From a classificatory perspective, it seems nearly impossible to think of a bundle of tasks as not requiring some kind of skill.

Another approach to understanding skill levels as related to jobs is subjective accounts. Respondents in the Employment Survey were asked to state "[w]hat type of training is usually required for performing your activity" as a worker in their respective occupation. One of the four possible answers was: "No vocational training degree required." Given our considerations so far, this could be another way of gaining an idea of unskilled work, since respondents choosing this answer might work in specific occupations or with a specific mix of skills. Overall, 17.2 percent of employed individuals in Germany (or 6.4 million persons) state that there would be no vocational qualification required to perform their current occupation. But do these persons also work in occupations that are classified as not requiring vocational training degrees (i.e., skill-level 1)? Roughly a third of them do (30.2 percent) but 55 percent work in an occupation for which, according to the classification, vocational training degrees are required. This illustrates how complicated it is to empirically grasp a concept like "unskilled" work and also shows why one can safely argue that there might not be such a thing as "unskilled work."

If we look at the required skill levels (*Anforderungsniveaus*) of occupations as given by the German national classification of occupations (KldB2010), which can be roughly translated to the ISCO-08 skill levels, we return to the question of whether these levels are associated with different skill mixes. Figure 15.3 shows that in 2018 employees on the German labor market had a fairly distinct mix of skills according to the classificatory skill levels of their occupations. When no vocational training is required, they most often carry out tasks in the realm of indirect services and least often in information handling. The rates for direct services are also quite comparable, with the exception of occupations where no vocational training is required, where we see a lower share of these skills. In occupations where incumbents need some kind of academic degree (typically one

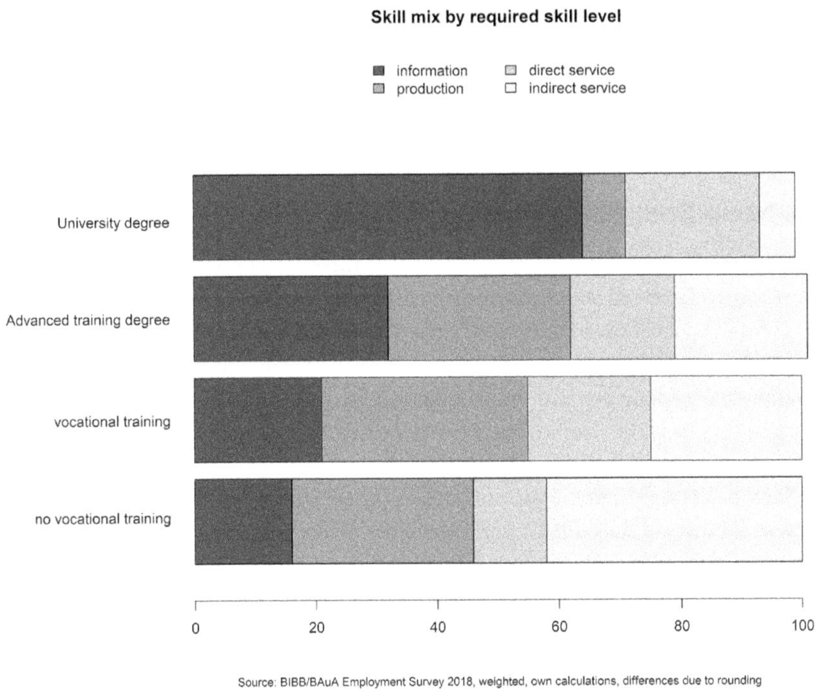

FIGURE 15.3 Skill mix by required skill level (BIBB/BAuA Employment Survey 2018, weighted, own calculations, differences due to rounding)

from the university) the information-handling skills are most prominent and we find the lowest rates of indirect services and production skills.

One could then reasonably only speak of "low-skilled" rather than "unskilled" work. Low-skilled would mean less complex tasks being performed and for which only skills that can be easily learned or adapted are needed. But since all four skill groups are represented in these occupations, there will also be some complexity due to alternating and different tasks.

This is also an indication that "unskilled" work will probably be socially or culturally defined. The current debate on job automation or "task based technological change" (Autor et al., 2003) reflects this in its core idea of programmability. It is predicted that these programs will replace those tasks which are defined in such a way that they can be translated into computer programs. Referring again to data from the Employment Surveys, we can evaluate the percentage of persons in workplaces where "the execution of the work is prescribed to you in every detail" and "one and the same operation is repeated in every detail" (Hall et al., 2020). We find that there can still be a considerable number of programmable tasks even for high skill levels. The normative reflection of "unskilled" work comes into play here with the term "routine" tasks for programmable tasks, which might easily lead one to assume that such tasks require less skills. Yet a highly trained technician overseeing the operation of a nuclear-power plant or a journalist undertaking the same steps in every investigation would be able to state that even though their work is programmable and routine it is hardly "unskilled."

The Socio-Economic Valuation of Skills

In the preceding sections, we have shown that there are considerable differences in the organizational and social anchoring of the category of "skills," which relates to the cultural and national contexts of their acquisition and development. There are also differences between societies in how they value different skill sets. A more or less universally applicable pattern for distinguishing the amount and quality of skills required in jobs is the distinction between "jobs," "occupations" and "professions," differing in terms of scope, specificity and quality of knowledge and education required to exercise certain tasks or perform them competently. While "jobs" can be associated with "unskilled" work, there are plenty of workplaces that fulfill the criteria of "occupations" and few that would be referred to as "professions." With regard to professions, there are typically additional characteristics used to describe their particular role within the societal division of labor. Self-governance of the members of a professional group is just as much a characteristic as is the assumption that professionalized work is required when there is a special capacity for ethical reflection and the ability to empathize with the needs of "clients." Typical examples of such professions, across all contexts, are medical doctors or lawyers.

Finally, the combination of these characteristics with the societal valuation of the services that professions provide and the exclusivity of their entry requirements leads to relatively high status and good incomes. This classical understanding of the professions has increasingly given way to analyses that are particularly concerned with the specificity of the knowledge base and its subjective and objective conditions of emergence, the ethical relevance of the work and approaches that see the particular characteristics of professional work, especially in the interaction with their clients and the corresponding counseling work. However, this view also involves a high degree of contingency.

Let us first consider the special nature of the consulting activity which characterizes the work of professionals. Their special expertise should be brought into any interaction with their clients for benefit of the latter. Typical examples of these kinds of activities are health services or teaching jobs. The findings on the importance of advisory activities (Figure 15.3) underscore their omnipresence across all positions on the labor market. Hence the question arises as to why we don't use the term "professional" in referring to the building technician who implements building regulations as well as integrating certain other requirements that both he and the client deem necessary, while also anticipating any future ecological and economic developments.

In Figure 15.3, the work of this person would be located on level 2 or 3. Interestingly, these are precisely the characteristics of work and expertise that the American psychologists Howard Gardner, Mihaly Czikszentmihaly and William Damon address in their long-term research project "Good Work" (2001) in which they scrutinize the development of expertise in different "domains" and "fields" of professional work, which might include the requirement to make difficult ethical judgments and adhere to ethical standards. There is no principal theoretical or empirical argument why this research approach could not be applied to the level of "skilled work" that is commonly associated with intermediate qualifications and mid-level jobs on the labor market.

In a seminal article on the importance but also the limitations of the human-capital approach in explaining differences between the United States and German labor markets, Wolfgang Streeck (2011) elaborated on those considerable historical institutional differences which lead to quite different meanings in terms of the categories assigned to general and specific education or skills. American company unions and closed-shop recruitment practice have historically led to a relatively visible segmentation of intra-company labor markets and thus also to the possibility of demarcating company-specific knowledge. In Germany, by contrast, the category of "specific skills" can be understood as the special ability of vocationally qualified persons to competently take on inter-company technical-task profiles.[6] This significantly changes the possibility of earning an income on the labor market with a corresponding certificate. The example illustrates that the hierarchical and content-related classification of skills in production and workplaces is not merely the result of company decisions but a subject of negotiation between companies and employee representatives. This is also the basis on which the differences with regard to discretion at the workplace shown in Figure 15.2 are classified in the literature. Craft organizations can also play a role in the social and economic definition of skilled/unskilled work, but this depends on their position and strength in different societies. In England, for example, the influence of craft organizations was gradually diminished in the context of freedom of trade; in Germany, craft forms and organizational characteristics were transferred to industry and integrated into the development of its system of skill formation.

While we could not unambiguously show how occupations might be (empirically) classified as unskilled, we did find increasing information on the handling of skills with higher levels of required qualifications. A culturally sensitive understanding of skills would have to take this into consideration. Maybe "unskilled" work refers less to the performance of tasks requiring no skills and more to the performance of tasks that are less highly regarded. This should be reflected in measures of social status or just simply wages.

The category with the highest share of skills for those occupations with no vocational qualification is indirect services. If these skills are seen as less valuable than something like information-handling skills, we should find that measures of status and income are lower for these skills. The Employment Survey 2018 (Hall et al., 2020) contains information on just such status measures, and here we will be considering the International Socio-Economic Index of Occupational Status (Ganzeboom, 2010). We report the mean ISEI values of different occupational groups[7] in the classification (KldB2010) as well as their mean wages. Although there is a strong relation between ISEI values and hourly wages, we look at both measures since it might well be the case that some skills are associated with a lower occupational status but are still more highly paid than other occupations having the same status, which would thus provide incentives to people to take up these occupations. For the grouping into skills groups, we use the group with the highest share within the occupational group. Thus, an occupation given here as a "production" occupation still has a skills mix, but the highest share of skills is in production skills.

Figure 15.4 plots the information we have on occupational status, hourly wages and dominant skill groups within the occupational groups considered here. As expected, we find that most of the occupations where information skills are dominant will show the highest values for ISEI and the highest hourly wages. Occupations dominated by production skills show roughly average wages, but some of them already have low ISEI values and seem to be regarded as less

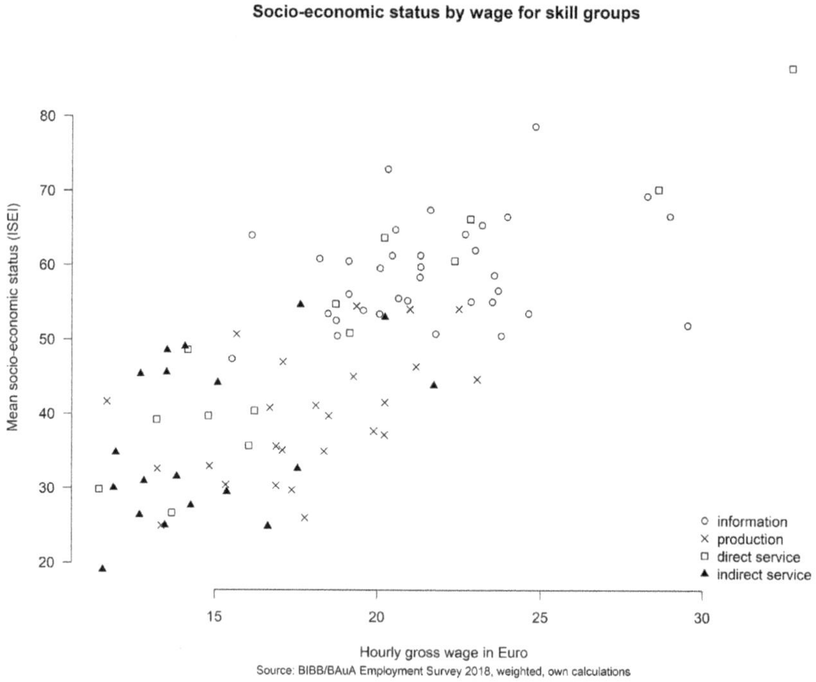

FIGURE 15.4 Socio-economic status by wage for skill groups (BIBB/BAuA Employment Survey 2018, weighted, own calculations)

valuable from a social standpoint. Thus emerge two interesting findings. For one, there are occupations dominated by direct-service skills that are both regarded as less valuable and pay less than other occupations, while some occupations with the highest values for wages and ISEI also belong to this group, reflecting the underlying problem of professional skills as elaborated earlier. The other finding is that occupations dominated by indirect-service skills are also paid less than average while showing lower values for occupational status. These occupations even show lower hourly wages than others with similar ISEI values. In this sense, the lower valuation of specific skills illustrates the cultural construction of a concept like "unskilled" work.

Because just what skilled work is can be more easily agreed upon, we conclude that in the distinction between skilled and unskilled work it makes more sense to speak of varying degrees of skill – with work that ranges in the lower degrees sometimes regarded as unskilled, at least from a social standpoint.

Empirically speaking, it seems that there are no occupations where no skills whatsoever are needed to perform the tasks required. We see this in the definitions of classifications but also in data like the Employment Surveys. Maybe "unskilled work," by definition, needs to be looked for elsewhere? In addition, when low-skilled work requires some kind of learning, then it might be the case that machines – as they cannot learn in the same way as humans do – are the sole entities that could actually perform unskilled work. But even this is a fuzzy area, since there are robots programmed to developing solutions and performing operations that they have not been "shown" beforehand. Besides this, machines and programs are almost exclusively designed to solve specific problems, which means they are designed to perform a specific task or bundle of tasks.

Conclusions and Outlook

Despite the various meanings, there is a core meaning of skills that seems to be of almost universal validity. It refers to an acquired ability to (competently and even cleverly) solve a task that is evaluated as a socially positive one and is attributed to the person and makes him or her a unique personality. This is not only true for such individuals as Anne-Sophie Mutter, Lang Lang, Leonardo da Vinci or Fernando Alonso, but everyone has their own examples that run the gamut of occupations and social milieux. We tend to attribute the quality of a work product directly to the person. This equation with the person, however, can also render the category controversial. It is necessary to contextualize "skill" as a relative concept addressing a certain task within its social environment. Ultimately, we have tried to show here the contingency of evaluations of work and how their content is subject to historical change as well as how little they actually lie within the realm of purely individual skills. It is a constant process of negotiation to define the scope and content of skilled work, and this becomes a particular challenge when different understandings collide. This complexity is not always entailed in policy concepts with global or international relevance, for example, those of international organizations such as the OECD, the ILO or the EU's labor-market and employment policy. A current societal challenge where these categorizations become highly relevant is in the painful experience of many migrants when they realize that their (certified or uncertified) skills are not recognized in another social context. Often the identified "skill-mismatch" might be the result of other processes of social closure than the actual skills possessed by a certain person.

Moreover, skill gaps cannot only be filled by hiring (non-existent) staff but the organization of work must be adapted to the supply of labor. In the long term, this can also contribute to a change in society's understanding of skilled work. Such changes have led to the assumption that a technological change could render obsolete certain aspects of those tasks which people perform at work (e.g., Autor et al., 2003; Goos and Manning, 2007). Programmable machines or automatons could replace specific tasks and entire occupations. But due to differences in work organization, the effects will vary across labor-market traditions. While machines are now called "intelligent," we think it unlikely that in the future they or their work will be called "skilled" on a larger scale. One day, we might read a newspaper review of a violin-robot that gave a particularly virtuoso interpretation of Mozart's *Eine kleine Nachtmusik*, but we expect that the value of the performance will more likely be attributed to the "skilled" developers of the machine . . . but who knows for certain.

Notes

1 PISA is the acronym for "Programme for International Student Assessment" (www.oecd.org/pisa/) and PIAAC stands for "Programme for the International Assessment of Adult Competencies" (www.oecd.org/skills/piaac/)
2 Skills are often equated with tasks. The ad hoc classification applied here can be obtained from the authors on request.
3 Anthropocentric views are expressed by such authors as Lebaron (2018), Hirsch-Kreinsen (2018) and Kurz (2018); anthropomorphic views are expressed by Bruno Latour (2018) and Bates (2018).
4 For reasons of space, we cannot here address the fact that these learning processes have an important motivational dimension and that they primarily serve as a source of social identity, as emphasized by Herzog (2011).
5 Established by the ILO; current version ISCO-08.
6 This is also of significance to the great ambiguity entailed in the term "apprenticeship."
7 We can report values for 94 out of the 144 occupational groups because we only selected occupational groups which provided information from at least 30 respondents.

References

Autor, D.H., Levy, F. and Murnane, R.J. (2003) 'The Skill Content of Recent Technological Change: An Empirical Exploration', *The Quarterly Journal of Economics*, 118(4), pp. 1279–1333.

Bates, D. (2018) 'Theory-Interview on the Relationship Between Societal and Technological Change', www.bibb.de/dokumente/pdf/a12_bates_kurz-transkript.pdf.

Billett, S., Harteis, C. and Gruber, H. (2018) 'Developing Occupational Expertise Through Everyday Work Activities and Interactions', in Ericsson, K.E., Charness, N., Feltovitch, P.J. and Hoffman, R.R. (eds.) *The Cambridge Handbook of Expertise and Expert Performance,* 2nd ed. New York: Cambridge University Press, pp. 105–126.

Brockmann, M., Clarke, L. and Winch, C. (2011) *Knowledge Skills and Competence in the European Labour Market: What's in a Vocational Qualification?* London: Routledge.

Carr-Saunders, A.M. and Wilson, P.A. (1964) *The Professions*, 2nd ed. London: Cass.

Ericsson, K.A. and Harwell, K.W. (2019) 'Deliberate Practice and Proposed Limits on the Effects of Practice on the Acquisition of Expert Performance: Why the Original Definition Matters and Recommendations for Future Research', *Frontiers in Psychology*, 10(2396). doi: 10.3389/fpsyg.2019.02396

European Commission (2008) *The European Qualifications Framework for Lifelong Learning (EQF)*. Luxembourg: Office for Official Publ. of the Europ. Communities.

Ganzeboom, B.G. (2010) 'Questions and Answers about ISEI-08', www.harryganzeboom.nl/isco08/qa-isei-08.htm.

Gardner, H., Csikszentmihaly, M. and Damon, W. (2001) *Good Work: When Excellence and Ethics Meet*. New York: Basic Books.

Goos, M. and Manning, A. (2007) 'Lousy and Lovely Jobs: The Rising Polarization of Work in Britain', *The Review of Economics and Statistics*, 89(1), pp. 118–133.

Green, F. (2013) *Skills and Skilled Work: An Economic and Social Analysis*. Oxford: Oxford University Press.

Grollmann, P., Ulbrich, V. and Hugo, F. (2020) 'D2 Betriebliche Kompetenzentwicklung im internationalen Vergleich', in Bundesinstitut für Berufsbildung (ed.) *Datenreport zum Berufsbildungsbericht*. Bonn: Bundesinstitut für Berufsbildung, pp. 433–440.

Hall, A., Hünefeld, L. and Rohrbach-Schmidt, D. (2020) *BIBB/BAuA Employment Survey of the Working Population on Qualification and Working Conditions in Germany 2018 (SUF_1.0; Research Data Center at BIBB (ed.); GESIS Cologne (data access))*. Bonn: Federal Institute for Vocational Education and Training. doi:10.7803/501.18.1.1.10

Hanushek, E.A. et al. (2015) 'Returns to Skills Around the World: Evidence From PIAAC', *European Economic Review*, 73, pp. 103–130.

Hartig, J. and Klieme, E. (2006) 'Kompetenz und Kompetenzdiagnostik', in Schweitzer, K. (ed.) *Leistung und Leistungsdiagnostik*. Heidelberg: Springer, pp. 127–143.

Herzog, L.M. (2011) 'Wer sind wir, wenn wir arbeiten?: Soziale Identität im Markt bei Smith und Hegel', *Deutsche Zeitschrift für Philosophie*, 59(6), 835–852.

Hirsch-Kreinsen, H. (2018) 'Theory-Interview on the Relationship Between Societal and Technological Change', www.bibb.de/dokumente/pdf/a12_en_hirsch-kreinsen_kurz-transkript.pdf.

Kurtz, Th. (2005) *Die Berufsform der Gesellschaft*. Weilerswist: Velbrück Wissenschaft.

Kurz, H.-D. (2018) 'Theory-Interview on the Relationship Between Societal and Technological Change', www.bibb.de/dokumente/pdf/a12_EN-Kurz_kurzTranskript-fin.pdf.

Latour, B. (2018) 'Theory-Interview on the Relationship Between Societal and Technological Change', www.bibb.de/dokumente/pdf/a12_latour_kurz-transkript.pdf.

Lebaron, F. (2018) 'Theory-Interview on the Relationship Between Societal and Technological Change', www.bibb.de/dokumente/pdf/a12_lebaron_kurz-transkript.pdf.

Maier, T. (2021) 'Change in Occupational Tasks and Its Implications: Evidence From a Task Panel From 1973 to 2011 for Western Germany', *Quality & Quantity*, https://doi.org/10.1007/s11135-021-01158-y.

Mieg, H. (2001) *The Social Psychology of Expertise: Case Studies in Research, Professional Domains, and Expert Roles*. Mahwah, NJ: Erlbaum.

Neuweg, G.H. (2000) 'Mehr lernen, als man sagen kann: Konzepte und didaktische Perspektiven impliziten Lernens', *Unterrichtswissenschaft*, 28(3), pp. 197–217.

Nonaka, I. and Takeuchi, H. (1995) *The Knowledge-Creating Company*. New York and Oxford: Oxford University Press.

OECD (2012) 'Organisation for Economic Co-operation and Development "Programme for the International Assessment of Adult Competencies"', *Pulic Use Files*. webfs.oecd.org – /piaac/puf-data/.

Sennett, R. (2008) *The Craftsman*. New Haven, CT: Yale University Press.

Stasz, C. (2001) 'Assessing Skills for Work: Two Perspectives', *Oxford Economic Papers*, 53(3), pp. 385–405.

Sternberg, R.J. and Grigorenko, E.L. (2003) *The Psychology of Abilities, Competencies, and Expertise*. Cambridge: Cambridge University Press.

Streeck, W. (2011) Skills and Politics: General and Specific. Max-Planck-Institut für Gesellschaftsforschung Discussion Paper 11/1. Cologne.

Tiemann, M. (2014) *Homogenität von Berufen: Arbeit und Beruf im Wandel. Ein Blick auf die gesellschaftliche Differenzierung*. Bielefeld: Bertelsmann.

16

ENTREPRENEURSHIP

Moral Categorizations Across Three Countries

Constance Perrin-Joly and Laure de Verdalle

Historically the entrepreneur has been viewed as a person who takes risks or acts rationally (Vérin, 1982). Both of these two conceptions are rooted in the economic sphere, namely the entrepreneur as a creator and manager of a company, which in turn serves as an engine for growth and a catalyst for innovation. Yet given the different types of entrepreneurs that exist, the category remains very broad and heterogeneous. One might ask what traits are shared by a self-employed architect, a self-employed taxi driver, the owner of a small family business and the founder and director of a large traded company, but each of them will nonetheless be referred to as an entrepreneur. Making the picture even fuzzier, "entrepreneurial work" – defined as a way of finding resources, formalizing relationships, promoting a project or shaping a marketplace (Giraudeau, 2007; Cochoy and Dubuisson-Quellier, 2000) – can also be conducted by salaried workers within companies.

The terms "entrepreneurship" and to an even greater degree "entrepreneurial work" are therefore characterized by their ability to embrace a huge variety of situations. The reality for which they serve as a framework is an evolving one. However, the name "entrepreneur" remains stable and constitutes a powerful reference point in the field of public action, academic work and more widely in everyday language.

In this chapter, we will not be questioning the diversity of entrepreneurial situations in time and space. Instead, we will focus on the dominant categorizations of entrepreneurship as promoted by public policies that develop programs to support entrepreneurial activities and in the same time formulate moral judgments to qualify (or disqualify) some of these activities.[1] Interestingly, one might consider these categories of public action themselves to be the object of an "entrepreneurial work," whereby the entrepreneurs identified and encouraged

DOI: 10.4324/9781003341321-20

by these policies may appropriate these categories to enhance their project while improving their access to resources.

In this chapter, we look at how, in a globalized context, international institutions spread certain types of economic and social policies that are more or less faithfully translated into national categories.[2] Endowed with a performative effect (Callon, 1998) the latter turn into instruments for "exercising power" (Strassel, 2013, p. 66). In each country, they influence the dominant representations and the policy options implemented. Policies in favor of entrepreneurship are part of this logic of circulation. Drawing on three different national configurations (Germany, France and Ethiopia), we propose a slightly offbeat view of a core issue in the European social sciences, using the Ethiopian case as a methodological pivot. France and Germany are part of a European space built on a logic of economic liberalization, and the European social project is struggling to find a consensus on the modes for regulating state intervention. While being included in the sphere of international economic relations, Ethiopia offers an interesting point of comparison because of the state's dirigisme and the weight of the ideological discourse on the economy.

First of all, we describe the dominant visions of "entrepreneurship" and "entrepreneurial work" that are nurtured and disseminated by international institutions, and we examine their operationalization through public policies in Ethiopia, France and Germany. Then we argue that this operationalization always implies a moral dimension, contributing to distinguish between "good" and "bad" entrepreneurs, a terminology that can later be reappropriated by the entrepreneurs themselves to defend their position and lend aid and comfort to their activities.

From Global North to Global South: Doing Business for Good?

One can observe two main lines of economic discourse regarding entrepreneurship and notably enforced by international institutions. On the one hand, entrepreneurship is seen as a way to create one's own job; on the other hand, entrepreneurship is regarded as an engine of growth and economic development. Which line of discourse one mobilizes would seem to depend on whether it is being applied to formerly industrial countries or developing ones. As concerns European countries, employment would appear to be the main issue. When entrepreneurship is applied as a category of public action in France or in Germany, it is primarily about defending or generating jobs. With regard to the Global South, the defense and support of entrepreneurship is subordinated to the development paradigm, which goes far beyond the employment issue. Entrepreneurs are supposed to provide employment for a large local workforce, of course, but they also are expected to invest in sectors that build infrastructure and to bring foreign exchange to countries in dire need of it.

Finally, there is a certain watchword uniting countries of the Global North and South: entrepreneurship must be increasingly inclusive and emancipatory. It was in the 1980s and 1990s that international bodies (World Bank, Organization for Economic Co-operation and Development (OECD)), assisted by NGOs, began to revive the homogeneous figure of the heroic entrepreneur, an image that had been inherited from Schumpeter (2021). In the 1990s, with the advent of the UN's Millennium Development Goals, a change in perspective occurred when the social function of entrepreneurship and its capacity for "empowerment" (Chapus et al., 2021) were asserted in the North as well as in the South. Being an entrepreneur is now frequently seen as a way for individuals to sidestep employment discrimination by creating their own jobs in the Global North and as a stepping stone out of poverty in the Global South.

In the first line of economic discourse, to be found more often in European countries, the recurring arguments favor the creation of jobs. This way of understanding entrepreneurship has been strongly supported by international organizations. The OECD, for instance, developed a large project (DynEmp) that posited the supposed central role played by startups and new firms in creating jobs. Their database suggests that "on average across OECD countries and over years, young firms account for about 20% of employment but create almost half of new jobs." Calvino, Criscuolo, Menon (2016) The International Labor Organization (ILO) points out that "entrepreneurship is one of the great management revolutions of the past 30 years, undermining the logic of the old industrial corporation and putting the focus of innovation and growth on the startups, science-parks, incubators, accelerators, etc."[3] In this sense, entrepreneurship is also frequently put forward as a kind of (desirable) future of work, which generally manifests a political will to overcome the supposed constraints of the wage society.

This discourse seems, moreover, to have become so widespread as to permeate current appropriations of the term "entrepreneurship" in European countries. According to a recent survey, 88 percent of French and 93 percent of German respondents associated self-employment and auto-entrepreneurship with the following statement: "self-employment and auto-entrepreneurship is a means of creating one's own job."[4] In France, which is presented as a country where entrepreneurship is still relatively underdeveloped, data from the Eurobarometer (compiled and analyzed by the *Centre d'analyse stratégique*, 2012) nevertheless indicate that 65 percent of the French survey participants agreed that entrepreneurship was a good career choice. The discourse of a "liberation" of work through entrepreneurial initiative has fed into the policies conducted in France in recent years, as evidenced since 2009 by the promotion of the supposed virtues of self-entrepreneurship (Abdelnour, 2014). The above figures indicate that it has also been appropriated and put forward in ordinary discourses about entrepreneurship, whereas in the same period at least some areas of wage labor appeared to be increasingly deregulated and decreasingly protective of individuals.

Public policies implemented in France and Germany, as in most European countries, follow the recommendations made by the United Nations Conference on Trade and Development:[5] actions on the legislative environment and regulations, tax law, labor law, but also broader actions concerning the education system and aiming to increase people's appetite for business creation. The underlying idea is not only to support "necessity entrepreneurship" by encouraging the unemployed to create their own business and therefore their own job, but also to facilitate "opportunity entrepreneurship" by favoring the establishment of an "entrepreneurship ecosystem" (Isenberg, 2010; Isenberg, 2011; Fuerlinger et al., 2015). This is particularly the case in Germany where unemployment stays at fairly low levels (Fuerlinger et al., 2015). The actions taken are designed to reduce the time and administrative formalities required to set up a business, to make it easier to raise funds and develop an "entrepreneurial spirit" among young people by impacting the training courses (especially at the university). These policies also pay attention to specific "sub-categories" of entrepreneurs, linked to their socio-demographic or migratory characteristics, for example, the promotion of entrepreneurship based on "diversity" (women's entrepreneurship, entrepreneurship implemented by people with a migration background, etc.) in both France and Germany. In this latter country, since the mid-2010s, in the context of migratory flows and the increasing number of refugees, specific actions have focused on migrant entrepreneurship. For instance, programs have been set up to support migrant women's initiatives, seen as a way of promoting greater integration into employment.

For the second line of economic discourse, which applies widely in the Global South, international institutions and local governments identify the entrepreneur as a central actor in economic development. Ethiopia is an interesting case in terms of its relations with world governance bodies and the place given to the private sector in its development. Ethiopia certainly has participated in globalization, particularly through classic extraversion strategies (Bayart, 1999), that is, by making its economic dependence an asset for mobilizing international financial investments. But Ethiopia has distinguished itself through certain economic choices, refusing to totally open its market and relying on state dirigisme for its development in contrast to the structural-adjustment model dominant in international economic discourse (Lefort, 2012). The authoritarianism of the regime and the commitment to the developmental policy make the government a central actor. This authoritarianism has been based on the monopolization of power by a sole political party (the EPDRF)[6] since 1991. This party was initially engaged in an economic policy claiming to be based on Maoism and Albanian Marxism (Young, 1997), until the urban population questioned its efficiency during the 2005 elections. This event accelerated the party's orientation toward a state-led economy (Aalen and Tronvoll, 2009). Moving from hard-line communism to state-led capitalism as inspired by Asian models, Ethiopian Prime Minister Meles Zenawi (1991–2012), the architect of this policy, initiated the developmental state

(Johnson, 1982) in which the public sector plays a catalytic role in economic growth. Admittedly, ever since the 2010s, the private sector has continued to develop to the point that the current Prime Minister Abyi Ahmed, in office since 2018, has adopted a resolutely open-minded attitude toward enterprises, claiming to be "a capitalist" (Nallet, 2019). But this opening toward the private sector has not been perceived by the entrepreneurs themselves as a real change in government policy. The state, itself an economic actor, also functions as something of a constraint on the legal, social and professional environment in which entrepreneurial projects are deployed. The entrepreneur is thus considered as an instrument of the government's poverty-reduction policy, which is widely supported by international institutions that promote micro-credit schemes in particular. In this area, international programs generally regard women's entrepreneurial initiatives as "more virtuous" because they are believed to be more beneficial to children's health and education. These programs particularly encourage female entrepreneurship, as evidenced by the Women's Entrepreneurship Development Project, launched in 2012 and funded by the World Bank and considered a lever for women's empowerment. Ethiopia fits into such schemes that offer significant funding, a source of extraversion for the state, but also because women can be integrated into the "development armies" as mediators through which the ruling party can indoctrinate the population to participate in development programs (Villanucci and Fantini, 2016).

"Good" Versus "Bad" Entrepreneurs

Regardless of local contexts and national situations, the "entrepreneurial spirit" is thus widely encouraged and generally has a positive connotation as a result of economic discourses. Yet a certain mistrust persists insofar as entrepreneurs remain associated with the figure of the utilitarian capitalist. In European countries, entrepreneurs are alternately valued as key players in national economic performance and suspected of behaving like predators with little concern for the collective interest. The latter view justifies state intervention and control of their activities. So too in the African context where the specter of the individualistic entrepreneur, driven solely by his quest for profit, appears regularly when the media highlight the land-grabbing of foreign companies (Lavers, 2012) or "sweatshops" (Barraud de Lagerie, 2012) in countries of the Global South where production costs are much lower and social-protection systems hardly exist.

The process of implementing, at a national level, the policies promoted by international institutions thus reveals the value judgments according to which certain entrepreneurial practices should be encouraged or prohibited. What are the yardsticks involved in valuing or disqualifying these practices according to national contexts?

Moreso than in Europe, in Ethiopa the enterprise and the entrepreneur are ambiguous entities that are regarded as "a necessary evil" (Chaponnière, 2018) for implementing developmental policies. What is valued is not the entrepreneurial spirit as such but the fact that entrepreneurial work is placed in service of the community to assist its development (Vaughan, 2011). That is why "the private sector is only encouraged to the extent that it corresponds to the priorities defined by the party-state" (Bach, 2011, p. 469). In the eyes of the Ethiopian government, a "good" entrepreneur is thus an investor who is part of the development projects promoted by the ruling party. The party itself acts as an entrepreneur through companies included in its investment funds. EFFORT (Endowment Fund for the Rehabilitation of Tigray) is the main fund, comprising some 15 companies and belonging to the TPLF (Tigray People's Liberation Front) which is the dominant faction of the coalition (EPRDF) that was in power until 2018 and is now at war with the current government. This conglomerate, which mobilized aid funds during the 1984 famine, is headed by prominent party members who claim to be rebuilding and developing certain regions, in this case Tigray in the north of the country (Milkias, 2001; Vaughan and Gebremichael, 2011). The EPRDF promotes the use of these parastatal investment funds as tools to develop less profitable areas or more remote regions of the country where traditional private investors will not risk going (Oqubay, 2015). The importance of these parastatal investment funds has helped to define the Ethiopian economic policy as "developmental patrimonialism" (Kelsall and Booth, 2013). This notion refers to a country where the ruling elite centrally manages economic rents to increase their own and others' incomes in the long run rather than maximizing them in the short run – a strategy seen by some economists as an effective way of implementing "a long-term development strategy aimed at guiding Ethiopia to middle-income status" (Kelsall, 2011, p. 3). Entrepreneurship is not an end in itself but a means to achieve state-led economic objectives, that is, becoming a middle-income country. It is also a way to control the population, notably an urban youth which is voluntarily or forcibly integrated into training and support programs for entrepreneurship supervised by the state (Chinigo, 2019). In this category of "good" entrepreneur, the government can also integrate foreign investors, such as those from the diaspora. This positive construct is in contrast to a perceived predatory rent-seeking entrepreneur who seeks to maximize his short-term profit through such things as real estate investments that are also popular with domestic investors (Gebreyesus, 2019).

Entrepreneurship in France, though supported by the public authorities, is also the subject of ambivalent representations that depend on different positions in the political spectrum but which are also widely disseminated throughout the population. Associated with job creation and economic growth, entrepreneurs are at the same time perceived as people who exploit the work of others and only pursue their self-interest. Beyond the shared European context, there are probably more critical views of entrepreneurs and entrepreneurial work in French than in German society. According to the authors of a text published by the French *Centre d'analyse stratégique*, which compared France with Germany, Great Britain and the United States, "a French singularity is emerging with an overvaluation of the freedom associated with self-employment and a lower valuation of the estimated spinoffs of an entrepreneurial activity" (Centre d'analyse stratégique, 2012, p. 5). Moreover, the French debates tend to be dominated by the conflicting relationship between employers and employees. Entrepreneurship initiatives are seen as a way of encouraging an entrepreneurship "for all" and can be touted as a way of transcending the opposition between capital and labor – yet social perceptions of entrepreneurship still remain ambivalent. In Germany, by contrast, the principle of co-determination shapes these perceptions and probably makes them less conflictual, thus helping to moderate the expression of critical views toward enterprises and entrepreneurship.

France also cultivates the image of large companies as national champions, even though business creation nowadays is mainly driven by the rise of self-entrepreneurship and current French companies are being set up mainly without employees, a paradox which corresponds to another facet of this ambiguity in the French view of entrepreneurship. It is through the promotion of family entrepreneurship – as expressed through the very positively connoted category of *Mittelstand* – that Germany partly avoids polarization of the debate around these oppositions relating to the size of companies: "The *Mittelstand* concept as such does not include a size or an age restriction of the business. It comprises new and old businesses, solo entrepreneurs, SMEs, and larger family enterprises – all as long as they are owner managed and independent" (Welter, 2018, p. 101). The relative consensus on the role of the *Mittelstand*, as an essential pillar of the social market economy in the German context, also helps to mitigate the negative perceptions of an entrepreneurship that in France might be perceived as primarily driven by its lack of concern for the social consequences of its activities.

Finally, in both France and Germany it is above all predatory firms, often associated with multinational firms, that are denounced as employing "bad" practices (in terms of tax avoidance and location strategies but also the evasion of social and environmental responsibility). This raises the question as to the legal framework of these practices and the content that is given to entrepreneurial responsibility at both the national and European levels (ever since the so-called Lisbon strategy). However, national policies are often ambiguous. On the one hand, they consist in deploying financial and fiscal measures likely to attract these large firms to the national territory by encouraging them to set up subsidiaries to promote local employment. On the other hand, where appropriate, they carry on a critical discourse reflecting the powerlessness of national governments when sites are closed or jobs are threatened by restructuring. The health situation, containment and policies to combat the COVID-19 epidemic have undoubtedly led to a change of policy in the various countries of Europe, which is reflected in the promotion of national – or even local – entrepreneurship (e.g., through debates on relocating certain types of production, masks or medicines).

The Appropriation and Circulation of Categories: The Ethiopian Case

One facet of entrepreneurial work relies on putting one's business project into figures and words in order to enhance its value and gain access to various resources (namely financial, but also in terms of prestige, networks, etc.). This is all the more visible in a region like Ethiopia where the legitimacy of entrepreneurial activities is hardly self-evident. Entrepreneurs thus draw on different conceptions of entrepreneurship to claim a more legitimate expertise, to attract support (from the state or international organizations), to stigmatize competitors and distinguish themselves. In so doing, they help to redefine the state-promoted categories of "good" and "bad" entrepreneurs. There are mainly two ways of defining a "good" entrepreneur in the Ethiopian context: that of the hero and that of the socially responsible entrepreneur, both of which are associated with certain implicit or explicit characteristics.

The valorization of a "heroic" entrepreneurship is supported, on the one hand, by the social-enterprise sector whose owners may be Ethiopians or foreigners, and on the other hand by the promotors of Africapitalism who act on behalf of local entrepreneurs (Amaeshi and Idemudia, 2015). The social enterprises in Ethiopia, which claim to place social goals before any profit objectives, are largely supported by the British Council both financially and in terms of training and management. The support provided by the British Council – an international institution more widely associated with its cultural and linguistic activities (promoting the learning of English) – is in line with its role of spreading "British values." Since 2005 the institution has been developing a program to support social entrepreneurs who are seen "as a response to state failure" (Teasdale, 2011, p. 112) and thus promoting the role of the market (rather than the state) in ensuring the population's well-being (Perrin-Joly, 2021). The social enterprise operating in Ethiopia takes up the discourse of the American social-innovation school, which makes the social entrepreneur not only an economic actor but a hero and an artisan of social change (Dees and Battle Anderson, 2006; Bacq and Janssen, 2011). The heroic discourse reverses the means and ends in relation to the categories mobilized by public policies – being an entrepreneur is seen as a goal in itself, helping to develop the values of responsibility and autonomy, instead of a tool for economic development.

This way of categorizing the entrepreneur as a hero may also meet the expectations of Ethiopian people employed in the private sector. Entrepreneurship there is seen as a sign of success, a possible route to economic accumulation, but also as an expression of independence as opposed to the discipline and submission associated with salaried employment. The very success of this conception of entrepreneurship can also be understood in the context of a strong uncertainty that weighs on people's lives, of a high vulnerability to hazards and of the individual dependence on a social-protection system that still relies on the family and one's local community. The accumulation of economic capital is seen as the best way to escape this vulnerability (while wage-earning and its potentially progressive but limited income is not conceived as a sufficient means of protection). The fantasized "heroic entrepreneur" is perceived as someone able to "control uncertainty," in contrast to the real experiences of small entrepreneurs in Ethiopia who have low incomes and are soon faced with bankruptcy.

The categorization of the "good" versus "bad" entrepreneur is reinterpreted, secondly, by "merchant"[7] entrepreneurs who have come from elsewhere and settled in Ethiopia. They pass judgment on fellow entrepreneurs and competitors and then disseminate these judgments through chambers of commerce and other professional associations. European entrepreneurs in Ethiopia mainly distinguish between "good" and "bad" entrepreneurs by using their level of commitment to CSR (Corporate Social Responsibility) policies as an indicator. CSR is seen as a concrete manifestation of moral commitment to local populations, compensating for the weakness of the local welfare state. This translation of the "good entrepreneur" into "CSR investment" can be linked to the strong involvement of European institutions in the early 2000s in defining a social and exportable model under this same term (Daugareilh, 2009). It is also the result of companies' enthusiasm for measures that provide a framework that is not too constraining. First, corporate social responsibility as defined in the European framework links morality and economics, with CSR measures being understood and presented as beneficial to the financial and economic performance of the company (see the 2008 Report on European Competitiveness). European CSR principles are then disseminated and more or less leaving room for appropriation and redefinition by companies that depend on the measures implemented. For example, Dutch entrepreneurs in Ethiopia can obtain public-investment aid that is contingent on social-performance criteria.

The uses of these different ways to categorize "good" and "bad" entrepreneurs in Ethiopia are thus governed by a graduated hierarchy. The social entrepreneur sees himself as "better" than the "merchant" entrepreneurs who are driven primarily by economic profit. Local entrepreneurs can claim their "natural" concern for the country where they were born. Their local affiliation allows them to escape the suspicion cast on foreigners that they may be practicing a form of economic neo-colonialism and exploitation of local resources (whether human or natural). They can also assume a posture of economic patriotism toward the state. The activity of the foreign and merchant entrepreneur, therefore, lends itself more easily to criticism from both international civil society (NGOs) and the Ethiopian state. By designating other foreign entrepreneurs operating in Ethiopia as "bad," European entrepreneurs can secure their inclusion in the "good" category and will usually mobilize the repulsive figure of the Asian entrepreneur (mostly Chinese) as their maleficent foil. If Chinese firms are also subject to moral injunctions, their moral framework receives less support from those international institutions still dominated by Western countries. The result is that they remain partially unknown and are regarded as less valuable by European entrepreneurs. China's diplomatic and economic strategy in Africa has been called the "Beijing Consensus," as opposed to the "Washington Consensus," and is indeed based on the principle of non-interference and a refusal to subordinate economic development to any respect for civil rights or other "moral" norms. Chinese entrepreneurs who promote philanthropic activities develop a discourse focused on their own background and the need to give back what they have received and/or they explicitly make reference to Confucian virtues (goodness, righteousness, propriety, wisdom, loyalty) without always appreciating the economic impact of the social policies they develop (Guiheux, 2015). The virtues they promote tend also to be more related to Chinese society, which creates an opening for European entrepreneurs to criticize the weak local roots of their Chinese counterparts.

Conclusion

Questioning the moral uses of the categories "entrepreneur," "entrepreneurship" and "entrepreneurial work" is all the more interesting because in Europe, just as in the Global South, the idea predominates that "developing" an "entrepreneurial spirit" among the population is a good thing – this with a view to not only increasing entrepreneurial initiatives but conveying a positive image of entrepreneurship. Beyond the sphere of entrepreneurial activities in the economic realm, to which we have limited ourselves in this chapter, this observation also corresponds to the rise of discourses glorifying entrepreneurial risk-taking and project valorization in all its forms (Boltanski and Chiapello, 1999). As a category "the entrepreneur" is positively connoted by international economic organizations. On a global scale the "entrepreneurial spirit" might even be seen as a highly desirable future of work. This unanimity of discourse, however, hides variations in the definition of the boundaries between "good" and "bad" entrepreneurs. Each national context, illustrated here by Ethiopia, France and Germany, helps in shaping it, even down to the judgment of the entrepreneurs themselves. This variability is the result of a progressive appropriation process that engages different actors at each level (international, national and individual) but also results in the interpenetration of these levels. For example, foreign entrepreneurs may disseminate the norms of the "good" entrepreneur – as defined in their country of origin – in their country of installation. One should add that the representations associated with the category of entrepreneur often clash with the reality of entrepreneurial work. The most common representation of entrepreneurship focuses on freedom and innovation, a picture which is challenged by the requirements of planning, forecasting and supervision that to a large extent characterize the daily experience of entrepreneurs. Comparing different national situations, therefore, encourages us to question the emergence of local categorizations that should be analyzed in a context of the international circulation of concepts and injunctions that help to frame perceptions of the social value of entrepreneurial activities.

Notes

1 In this regard we would also prefer to leave aside the more open and conceptual perspective which transposes the figure of the entrepreneur as an actor of social change (Barth, 1967) or of "moral entrepreneurs" (Becker, 1963) to those fields that lie outside the economy (Saint-Lary, 2009).
2 One must add that the crisis engendered by the COVID-19 epidemic has served as a stimulus in re-articulating the decision-making between these different levels and in modifying the balance between the market and the state (Boyer, 2020).
3 http://archive.today/LitpK.
4 Opinion way survey, "Les Européens, l'entrepreneuriat et le statut d'indépendant", 2019: https://fr.scribd.com/document/602187474/Etude-Opinionway-Janvier19-1.
5 See their "Entrepreneurship Policy Framework and Implementation Guidance" published in 2012.
6 Ethiopian People's Revolutionary Democratic Front; as of 2019 the Prosperity Party (PP) has succeeded it. The dominant party in the coalition was the TPLF (Tigray People's Liberation Front) but it did not join the PP, whose creation it criticized. These political conflicts have led to the civil war that is currently devastating the country.
7 We propose to use the term merchant entrepreneur to designate entrepreneurs whose main objective is to make an economic profit, as opposed to social entrepreneurs for whom this is a secondary objective as compared to their social impact.

References

Aalen, L. and Tronvoll, K. (2009) 'The End of Democracy? Curtailing Political and Civil Rights in Ethiopia', *Review of African Political Economy*, 36(120), pp. 193–207.

Abdelnour, S. (2014) 'L'auto-entrepreneur: une utopie libérale dans la société salariale ?', *Lien social et Politiques*, 72, pp. 151–176.

Amaeshi, K. and Idemudia, U. (2015) 'Africapitalism: A Management Idea for Business in Africa?', *Africa Journal of Management*, 1(2), pp. 210–223.

Bach, J.-N. (2011) 'Centre, périphérie, conflit et formation de l'État depuis Ménélik II: les crises de et dans l'État éthiopien (XIXème – XXIème siècles).' Thèse pour le doctorat: Université de Bordeaux (LAM-IEP).

Bacq, S. and Janssen, F. (2011) 'The Multiple Faces of Social Entrepreneurship: A Review of Definitional Issues Based on Geographical and Thematic Criteria', *Entrepreneurship & Regional Development*, 23(5–6), pp. 373–403.

Barraud de Lagerie, P. (2012) 'Le salaire de la sueur: un éclairage socio-historique sur la lutte anti-sweatshop', *Sociologie du travail*, 54, pp. 45–69.

Barth, F. (1967) 'On the Study of Social Change', *American Anthropologist*, 69(6), pp. 661–669.

Bayart, J.-F. (1999) 'L'Afrique dans le monde: une histoire d'extraversion', *Critique International*, 5, pp. 97–120.

Becker, H.S. (1963) *Outsiders: Studies in the Sociology of Deviance*. Glencoe: Free Press.

Boltanski, L. and Chiapello, E. (1999) *Le nouvel esprit du capitalisme*. Paris: Gallimard.

Boyer, R. (2020) *Les capitalismes à l'épreuve de la pandémie*. Paris: La Découverte.

Callon, M. (1998) 'Introduction: The Embeddedness of Economic Markets in Economics', in Callon, M. (ed.) *The Laws of the Markets*. Oxford: Blackwell, pp. 1–57.

Calvino, F., C. Criscuolo et C. Menon (2016) 'No Country for Young Firms? : Start-up Dynamics and National Policies', OECD Science, Technology and Industry Policy Papers, n° 29, Éditions OCDE, Paris, https://doi.org/10.1787/5jm22p40c8mw-en.

Centre d'analyse stratégique (2012) 'L'entrepreneuriat en France. Volet 1: Mythes et réalités en comparaison internationale', *La note d'analyse*, p. 296.

Chaponnière, J. (2018) 'La mutation de l'économie éthiopienne: Les limites de la stratégie d'invitation', *Afrique contemporaine*, 266(2), pp. 55–74.

Chapus, Q., Berrou, J. and Onibon Doubogan, Y. (2021) 'Le retour du héros: L'entrepreneur, itinéraire d'un concept chez les "développeurs" en Afrique', *Revue internationale des études du développement*, 245, pp. 11–13.

Chinigo, D. (2019) 'The Peri-Urban Space at Work: Micro and Small Enterprises, Collective Participation, and the Developmental State in Ethiopia', *Africa*, 89(1), pp. 79–99.

Cochoy, F. and Dubuisson-Quellier, S. (2000) 'Les professionnels du marché: vers une théorie sociologique du travail marchand', *Sociologie du Travail*, 42, pp. 359–368.

Daugareilh, I. (2009) 'La responsabilité sociale des entreprises, un projet européen en panne', *Sociologie du travail*, 51(4), pp. 499-517.

Dees, G. and Battle Anderson, B. (2006) 'Framing a Theory of Social Entrepreneurship: Building on Two Schools of Practice and Thought', *ARNOVA*. https://centers.fuqua.duke.edu/case/wp-content/uploads/sites/7/2015/02/BookChapter_Dees_FramingTheoryofSE_2006.pdf.

Fuerlinger, G., Fandle, U. and Funke, T. (2015) 'The Role of the State in the Entrepreneurship Ecosystem: Insights from Germany', *Triple Helix*, 2(3).

Gebreyesus, M. (2019) 'The Private Sector in Ethiopia's Transformation', in *The Oxford Handbook of the Ethiopian Economy*. Oxford: Oxford University Press, pp. 686-702.

Giraudeau, M. (2007) 'Le travail entrepreneurial, ou l'entrepreneur schumpetérien performé', *Sociologie du travail*, 49, pp. 330–350.

Guiheux, G. (2015) 'Philanthropie d'entrepreneurs et construction d'un nouveau compromis social en Chine contemporaine', in Séhier, C. and Sobel, R. (eds.) *Travail, luttes sociales et régulation du capitalisme dans la Chine contemporaine*. Paris: Presses Universitaires du Septentrion, pp. 123–142.

Isenberg, D. (2010) 'How to Start an Entrepreneurial Revolution', *Harvard Business Review*. https://hbr.org/2010/06/the-big-idea-how-to-start-an-entrepreneurial-revolution/ar/1

Isenberg, D. (2011) 'The Entrepreneurship Ecosystem Strategy as a New Paradigm for Economic Policy: Principles for Cultivating Entrepreneurship', Presentation at the Institute of International and European Affairs. Dublin, May 12, http://www.innovationamerica.us/images/stories/2011/The-entrepreneurship-ecosystem-strategy-for-economic-growth-policy-20110620183915.pdf.

Johnson, C. (1982) *MITI and the Japanese Miracle: The Growth of Industrial Policy, 1925–1975*. Stanford: Stanford University Press.

Kelsall, T. (2011) 'Developmental Patrimonialism? Rethinking Business and Politics in Africa', APPP Policy Brief 02.

Kelsall, T. and Booth, D. (2013) *Business, Politics, and the State in Africa: Challenging the Orthodoxies on Growth and Transformation*. London: Zed Books.

Lavers, T. (2012) 'Land Grab as Development Strategy? The Political Economy of Agricultural Investment in Ethiopia', *Journal of Peasant Studies*, 39(1), pp. 105–132.

Lefort, R. (2012) 'Free Market Economy, "Developmental State" and Party-State Hegemony in Ethiopia: The Case of "Model Farmers"', *Journal of Modern African Studies*, 50(4), pp. 681–706.

Nallet, C. (2019) 'Les orientations libérales d'Abiy Ahmed. Sauvetage économique ou tournant idéologique?', *Editoriaux de l'IFRI*, 47(6).

Oqubay, A. (2015) *Made in Africa: Industrial Policy in Ethiopia*. New York: Oxford University Press.

Milkias, P. (2001) 'Ethiopia, the TPLF and Roots of the 2001 Political Tremor', *International Conference on African Development Archives*, 4.

Perrin-Joly, C. (2021) 'Les entreprises sociales à la recherche de leur légitimité: Frictions autour du projet de développement éthiopien et tentatives d'extraversion', *Revue internationale des études du développement*, 245, pp. 115–144.

Saint-Lary, M. (2009) 'Introduction: des entrepreneurs entre rhétorique et action sur le monde', *Bulletin de l'APAD*, pp. 29–30.

Schumpeter, J. (2021) *The Theory of Economic Development*. London: Routledge.

Strassel, C. (2013) 'La France, l'Europe et le modèle allemand', *Hérodote*, 151(4), pp. 60–82.

Teasdale, S. (2011) 'What's in a Name? Making Sense of Social Enterprise Discourses', *Public Policy and Administration*, 27(2), pp. 99-119.

Vaughan, S. (2011) 'Revolutionary Democratic State-Building: Party, State and People in the EPRDF's Ethiopia', *Journal of Eastern African Studies*, 5(4), pp. 619–640.

Vaughan, S. and Gebremichael, M. (2011) 'Rethinking Business and Politics in Ethiopia: The Role of EFFORT, the Endowment Fund for the Rehabilitation of Tigray', *Africa Power and Politics*, Research Report 2, August.

Vérin, H. (1982) *Entrepreneurs, entreprise: histoire d'une idée*. Paris: Presses universitaires de France.

Villanucci, A. and Fantini, E. (2016) 'Santé publique, participation communautaire et mobilisation politique en Éthiopie: la Women's Development Army', *Politique africaine*, 142(2), pp. 77–99.

Welter, F. (2018) 'The Mittelstand: A Specific Entrepreneurial Profile of the Social Market Economy', *Journal for Markets and Ethics*, 6(1), pp. 99–106.

Young, J. (1997) *Peasant Revolution in Ethiopia: The Tigray People's Liberation Front, 1975–1991*. Cambridge: Cambridge University Press.

17

ESSENTIAL WORK

A Category in the Making?

Lisa Herzog, Katrin Sold and Bénédicte Zimmermann

Introduction

During the Corona crisis, especially during the first series of lockdowns in 2020, a new category of work seemed to spring up: "essential work" or work that is "systemically relevant." This latter terminology was mainly employed in Germany, where it had first been used during the 2008 Financial Crisis for describing financial institutions, whereas the notion of "essential work" is reminiscent of war time, when decisions had to be taken about which workers could or could not be recruited to the front (Kocka, 1973; Wehler, 2003). In 2020, the discussion instead turned to those workers who kept society going during the lockdowns: medical staff, supermarket employees, street cleaners or individuals working in the production and logistical provision of important goods. In some countries, these workers received certain privileges, for example, prioritized access to childcare or a "corona bonus."

The focus on "essential" or "systemically relevant" jobs suggests a new way of looking at work through the lens of their "social utility," beyond the valuation by markets and at odds with traditional scales of reputation. Beyond the question of what makes certain jobs essential, it raises the broader issue of which goods or functionings are essential for human societies. It seems not surprising that in times of crisis, such questions about what "really matters" come to the fore. But it is not clear whether such re-evaluations are only temporary and tied to specific circumstances, or whether they can lead to permanent shifts in how work is categorized, valued, and organized.

In this chapter, we therefore discuss the category "essential work" as a category in the making. To do so, we draw on two kinds of sources. First, we look at the recent public discourse on "essential work" during the first wave of the

DOI: 10.4324/9781003341321-21

Corona crisis in Europe. For this purpose, we conducted a press analysis of 180 articles published in three widely read newspapers in Germany, France and the United Kingdom between February and November 2020: *Die Zeit*, *Le Monde* and *The Guardian*.[1] This analysis allows us to detect how "essential work" has been linguistically framed in the dominant public discourses and provides the basis for delineating the semantical field of essential work. Second, we explore existing theoretical frameworks that might address the question of what makes work essential, starting from the aspects that are echoed in the press articles. We discuss two established frameworks, which differ fundamentally in their perspectives on work. The first one is the market framework, the dominant yardstick of valuation of work in capitalist societies but challenged by the social utility-based valuation that features in "essential work." The second framework focuses on workers' own valuation of work, which, although not at first sight more informative on questions of social utility, is nevertheless a constitutive dimension of current debates on essential work. Here we discuss approaches dedicated to "bullshit jobs" (Graeber, 2013; 2018), "meaningful work" (Yeoman, 2014b; Veltman, 2016) or workers' "power to act" (Clot, 2008). To mediate these different perspectives on the valuation of work (society-, market- or worker-driven), we introduce a capability framework inspired by the works of Amartya Sen and Martha Nussbaum (Sen, 1993; Nussbaum, 2000). We show that such a framework allows not only to integrate what is essential for society and its different stakeholders, but also to bring together "essential work" and the issue of sustainable development. Doing so can lay the foundations for conceptualizing "essential work" with respect to another, ongoing crisis: the climate crisis.

Semantic Analysis: Three Main Lines of Conceptualization

To get an insight into the semantic field of "essential work" in the selected newspapers, we used specific search terms in each language, including "essential/key/frontline jobs/professions/work(ers)" for the British press, "activités/professions/métiers essentiel-le-s/indispensables/de première ligne" for the French one and "Systemrelevanz/systemrelevante Berufe" for the German one. In doing so, our aim was less to search for the differences between the three countries than to find common lines of problematization and conceptualization.

Our content analysis allows us to distinguish four types of articles according to their take on essential work. First, many articles are rather technical and provide information on administrative regulations related to the classification of jobs as "essential." This includes the presentation of lists of "key professions," "systemrelevante Berufe" or "professions essentielles." These lists prove to be quite similar in the three countries ranging from health and social care workers to workers in education, childcare and key public services, food production and distribution, public safety, transport or certain financial services. This first set of articles also reports about the related measures and regulations, such as access to schools and childcare facilities for the children of key workers. A second group of articles focuses on portraits of essential workers, mostly with the aim of creating emotional connections and raising awareness for the burdens carried by these groups. Most of the portraits present key workers that are directly involved in public life, such as nurses or bus drivers, and describe the challenges and concerns that these people experience during the Corona crisis. A third type of article covers related political debates, in which essential work introduces a new line of argumentation or is used to strengthen existing positions. For instance, the particular role of care workers in the Corona crisis supported the demands of German and French trade unions for improvements in the wages and labor conditions in this sector. In the United Kingdom politicians and activists fighting for a better treatment of migrants point to the large share of migrants among key workers. The fourth group of articles, finally, addresses essential work in socio-political and conceptual terms, linking it to theoretical and academic debates, primarily in the field of social sciences. These articles appeared mainly in the opinion section of the newspapers and were written primarily by external authors from the academic field. They aim to initiate reflections on what makes certain work essential and to link this question to broader socio-political debates.

An in-depth analysis of the articles of this fourth group points to three main answers to the question of what makes work essential. A *first* answer links essential work to its social utility, that is, to the functioning of the existing economic and social system. The work of those who keep the system running – care workers, police officers, supermarket vendors – is considered "essential" because it allows for securing the fundamental functions of society and fulfilling human basic needs. According to this approach, essential work is what contributes to the survival of the human species and its social organization in a period of crisis. Numerous articles point out that in Corona times, the jobs that were previously poorly paid and mischaracterized as "unskilled" are the ones that are now deemed "essential" for the maintenance and functioning of the system. We can thus observe a substantial shift in the framing and valuation of work, away from the traditional yardstick of market income. This raises the general question of which forms of work are essential for a societal system – and how this categorization affects the valuation, legal status and remuneration of work under current (market) conditions. Thus, the (re-)categorization process of work according to its social utility in the wake of the Corona crisis is accompanied by a reconsideration of other issues, such as the categories of skilled and unskilled work, and their relation to the market value of different forms of work.

A *second* interpretation of "essential work" is a subjective one, linking it to personal and social *perceptions* of work *by the workers themselves*. Work is considered "essential" when it is experienced as meaningful by the worker herself and this perception is fostered by the recognition she and her work receives from society. Here, the category "essential work" is closely linked to categories such as "meaningful work," "prestige" or "recognition," which are also undergoing a certain re-evaluation in the context of the Corona crisis. Many previously little recognized, almost "invisible" jobs suddenly receive great meaning and prestige as pillars of the system. The materialization of this recognition in terms of increased salaries for some categories of workers – in France, for instance, nurses in the public sector received a life-long 183 euros monthly salary increase[2] – points toward a performative effect of the categorization process. The articles, however, raise the question of the sustainability of this recognition in a society in which prestige is traditionally linked to high qualifications, high levels of power and high salaries.

A *third* interpretation, finally, builds on the connection between "essential work" and "social utility" but embeds it into broader socio-political issues. Essential work is then placed in relation to the structural fabric of society and to broader social objectives that go beyond the goals of survival and preservation of the system. Here, essential work goes together with concepts such as (in)equality or sustainability. With regard to social inequalities, the articles emphasize, for example, that workers in "key jobs," which have recently come to be regarded as essential but are still poorly paid and poorly secured, are much more affected by the health and financial consequences of the Corona crisis than workers in other occupations. It is the very characteristics of these jobs (little or no possibility for distant work, night shifts, public transport to reach the workplace, low pay, etc.) that make workers in these sectors more vulnerable to the direct and indirect consequences of the Corona crisis.

In sum, the first interpretation of "essential work" orients the discussion toward the pitfalls of a market-based valuation of work, while the second one steers the analysis toward a worker-based perspective. Finally, the third one invites us to search for an alternative framework that would be able to overcome the limits of the former two with regard to social utility issues and the integration of different valuations of work.

The Market- and the Worker-Focused Frameworks and Their Limits

The Market Answer

As a start, it is worth reflecting on why a category such as "essential work" has, hitherto, so rarely been used in public and academic discourse, and why it stands in a tension with the traditional "market answer" to the question of what makes work "essential." In Western societies, a large part of work is organized as paid work, in labor markets. According to the market logic and the economic thought behind it, work is valued according to what is paid for it; neither the quality of work nor the purpose of the work for the worker plays a direct role. This approach is individualistic in the sense that there is no society-wide, political determination of the value of work. Instead, the logic of supply and demand determines wages and working conditions, within the parameters set by the legal framework of a society. In Germany and France, in some sectors with strong unions and mechanisms of collective bargaining, the approach is less individualistic, with jobs being classified into groups with defined pay spans. But these pay spans are defined without any reference to the "essentiality" or "social utility" of jobs.

Thus, from this perspective, the most "essential" jobs are the most highly paid ones.[3] But it is immediately obvious that there is little overlap between the most high-paying jobs and those considered "essential" during the Corona crisis. Two basic facts explain this discrepancy. The first is the difference between usefulness for society and usefulness for specific employers, especially those with a high ability and willingness to pay. The second is the fact that wages in labor markets are determined by demand *and supply*.[4] Supply is determined by how many individuals are willing and able to do a certain job. Many – though certainly not all – jobs that have been described as "essential work" in the sources we have analyzed earlier do not require highly specialized skills – or at least they are not conceptualized as such.[5] Being easily replaceable, workers are in a weak bargaining position, which is often reflected in low wages and bad working conditions.[6]

A deeper reason for the low valuation of "essential work" in labor markets can be found in the notion of utility that is used in many economic theories, which has its roots in utilitarianism, one of the intellectual predecessors of neoclassical economic theory (e.g., Riley, 2016). It is an individualistic notion, which expresses utility in terms of the satisfaction of individuals' preferences. But such a subjective measurement of utility leads to some problems, which, in the philosophical debate, are captured under the name of "sour grapes" or "adaptive preferences" (Elster, 1982).

Poor individuals often adapt their preferences to their living conditions, drawing great utility from small benefits. But it seems clearly unjust to take this high utility, which is a response to dire social circumstances, at face value. The opposite constellation is the "expensive taste" problem, which concerns individuals with a high standard of living whose utility function only reacts positively to very expensive goods. Economists sometimes defend this notion of utility as anti-paternalistic, because it avoids telling individuals what their "real" needs are, or even asking questions about this. And yet, it seems problematic to treat the adapted preferences of rich and poor individuals on a par.

If one moves to the issue of how *work* gets valued in markets, parallel questions arise about tensions between subjective preference satisfaction and some more objective notion of social utility. Labor markets, rather than offering an objective criterion of value, reflect these subjective notions of utility, mediated by purchasing power.[7] They offer jobs for which there is effective demand, not jobs which, according to some independent criterion, offer "social utility." It is noteworthy that many forms of essential work, for example, in health care, are organized either in the public sector or in publicly subsidized systems, because markets would not, on their own, provide a sufficient supply of the goods in question, or at least not make them financially accessible to the whole population. Thus, by thinking through the logic of how markets evaluate work, it becomes clear why the resulting valuation – in terms of wages and working conditions – cannot be taken as an answer to the question of what makes work "essential," as the newspaper articles analyzed earlier had also noted.

The Worker-Focused Answer

If markets do not provide us with a criterion for which jobs are essential, are individual workers in a better position to do so? In recent years, there have been some debates that have drawn attention to the perspectives of workers. One advantage of this approach is epistemic: workers themselves know their own jobs best and might thus be in a better position to judge the extent to which these jobs are "essential." Yet, it is not clear that this perspective is sufficient for fleshing out the notion of "essential work," or so we will argue, because it remains caught in a subjective framework. Another problem is that even when trying to move toward more objective criteria of valuation, it remains focused on workers, to the detriment of the other roles people endorse in society: patients, consumers, etc.

One major debate in recent years was initiated by anthropologist David Graeber, who in 2013 published an essay on "bullshit jobs," which he then turned into a book (Graeber, 2018). Graeber holds that a bullshit job is one for which it is the case that "if the position were eliminated, it would make no discernible difference in the world" (ibid., 2). He takes the perspective of the individual worker as decisive for determining whether or not this is the case, all while acknowledging that in many such cases workers have to *pretend* that their jobs are useful, even though they "cannot justify [their] existence" (ibid., pp. 9–10).

One example of such bullshit jobs can be found in the staff for board-level management. Graeber argues that the status competition between managers, especially in the financial industry, plays out, among other things, in the race for having more staff members than one's competitors. This creates jobs in finance that have no real purpose in terms of tasks that need to be fulfilled, but rather serve as signaling devices for managers that they are more important than other managers. Other examples he discusses are, for example, in logistics. It is worth noting, however, that as an anarchist, Graeber might underestimate the need for coordination and supervision of many processes of divided labor.

Graeber rejects the idea that there could be any objective criterion for the value of jobs (ibid., xvii), even though he admits that "A world without teachers or dockworkers would soon be in trouble," and also lists "nurses, garbage collectors, or mechanics" (ibid.). This subjectivism leads to a risk of ideological distortion: what if an individual is deceived, maybe because of prevailing ideological narratives, about the actual value of his or her job? Some individuals might believe in the usefulness of their jobs because they accept the rationale for that job that was provided by their employer, which might nonetheless be questionable from an outside perspective. And maybe there can also be cases in which individuals think that their jobs are useless, while this is not objectively true. Thus, while Graeber drives a wedge between the market valuation of jobs and the contribution they make, he remains committed to a subjective perspective instead of asking about the possibility of more objective accounts of "social utility" and "essential work."[8]

Another discourse about work tries to go beyond this, in the direction of objective values, but remains subjective in a different way, namely by throwing light exclusively on the situation of the *worker*, not so much on what the work *brings about* and how *others* benefit from it. This is the discourse on "meaningful work," which moves in an interdisciplinary field between philosophy, psychology and management studies (Yeoman et al., 2019; Bailey et al., 2019). Here, the focus is on the "fundamental human need," as Ruth Yeoman puts it, of work to be meaningful for those who perform it (Yeoman, 2014a; see also Yeoman, 2014b). This perspective contrasts with thinkers who see meaningful work as a mere preference that individuals might have. Drawing on Susan Wolff's account of meaningfulness, which contains both a subjective and an objective dimension, authors like Yeoman (2014a; 2014b) and Andrea Veltman (2016) discuss factors such as the possibility of exercising autonomy or developing one's skills.[9]

These ideas are often expressed in terms of human capabilities, drawing on the work by Amartya Sen and Martha Nussbaum (e.g., Nussbaum and Sen, 1993). According to these authors, the capability of a person reflects what she is able to do and be, that is, the various combinations of functionings she can achieve and is able to choose from according to what she values. With this move, one steps out of the purely subjective realm, toward intersubjective or objective determinations of functionings and capabilities. But in the discourse on meaningful work, the focus is on the functionings and capabilities of the *workers* – not on how workers contribute to ensuring the functionings and capabilities of *others* (as one can understand the notion of essential work). A reference to the needs of others can come in through the back door, as it were, because the *experience* of meaningfulness can contain an element of "purpose" or of attaining certain objective values, including "social utility." But the focus remains nonetheless on the working individual, and without his or her *perception* of such an objective value, it would not count as contributing to meaningfulness. Arguably, one of the risks here is that notions of "meaningfulness" might end up being used as ideological tools in order to elicit a higher work motivation from individuals (see, e.g., Harding, 2019). One proposal that can counter this risk is to ensure that workers themselves are involved in the processes of defining "meaning," as suggested by Yeoman (2014b), who connects meaningful work and workplace democracy – a point to which we come back below. But on a theoretical level, there is still a gap between meaning as (intersubjectively) defined by workers and an objective notion of "essential work."

The approach developed by the French clinical psychologist Yves Clot (2010) goes in the same direction. His concept of "deliberated professionalism" focuses on workers' "power to act" (*pouvoir d'agir*) and participation in the decisions that pertain to the quality of work (Clot, 2008). According to Clot, the gap between how employees think good work should be done and what the organizational environment actually allows them to do fuels "hindered work" (*travail empêché*), a breeding ground for bullshit jobs and feelings of meaninglessness and uselessness. Like Yeoman's, Clot's approach introduces thus a third answer to the question of the valuation of work: neither market-based nor worker-based in an individualistic sense, but driven by collective deliberative practices that involve all workers in defining what good work means and how it should be done.

Drawing on recent industrial disasters and the COVID-19 pandemic Clot (2021) reminds us that the quality of work does not only impact workers' health and quality of life. By impeding the quality of services and goods that are produced, it also affects consumers' quality of health and life. Moreover, by enacting a certain relationship to natural resources and their use, it impacts the quality of the environment. For these reasons, the debate on the quality of work can no longer be confined to the boundaries of the firm and the means for carrying out good work. Instead, it must be expanded into a public debate about the purposes of work.

When addressed through the lens of the purposes of work, the question of the quality of work meets that of its social utility, inviting us to extend the conceptualization of essential work toward its social and ecological sustainability. Under such premises, essential work can lead to a questioning of the existing social and economic system, rather than being implicitly at the service of its perpetuation, as it was during the pandemics.

From Essential Work to Sustainable Work

Delineating the contours of work, while considering its purposes, requires a shift of perspective from the issue of work to the broader one of the goods and functionings it is meant to provide. While there was a broad consensus about the essentiality of access to health care and food during the pandemic, other functionings, like access to education and culture, were more controversial. A key factor here is not only the nature of the functionings but also their temporalities. Health care and food supply fulfill basic needs that cannot be delayed without putting humans' lives at risk, whereas education and culture involve longer time frames. While "essential" refers to what is needed for human survival here and now, according to the specificities of a crisis expected to be relatively short-termed, "sustainable" points toward what is deemed necessary for longer-term, intergenerational flourishing. The differences in temporal emphasis thus provide insights for the road ahead. The aim would be to bridge the gap between the category of essential work as it has been implemented in public policies during the COVID-19 pandemics and the kind of work that is required for addressing the ongoing and long-lasting climate crisis: essential and sustainable at once, targeting not only short-term survival but long-term well-being.

This makes the issue of identifying what functioning matter all the trickier. Addressing human functionings through a capability lens, Nussbaum and Sen (1993) offer a framework for integrating potential conflicting valuations into one and a same approach together with the diverse stakeholders that may defend them: employers, shareholders and workers, consumers, users and citizens, public actors, etc. However, such an approach can and should also go beyond *paid* work, to take into account a much broader picture of work that includes, in particular, the role of care work and unpaid work for the reproduction of society (e.g., Fraser, 2016).

From Needs to Capabilities

Dedicated to human development and people's well-being, the capability approach offers an alternative to the utilitarian theories that we addressed in the second section. One of its starting points is the fact that the satisfaction of desires cannot set the standards for the measurement of well-being, since desires are matters of adaptive preferences. When people suffer from enduring privations, they may resign and lose the ability to express other desires than those they can actually fulfill in their situation (Sen, 1992). For this reason, the capability approach cares, beyond valuable achievements, about the agency-freedom people have to conceive valuable goals and achieve them (Sen, 1987). Another of its features is the shift it initiates from basic needs (Max-Neef et al., 1991) to capabilities in order to conceptualize well-being. Whereas needs put the accent on human beings' dependencies and vulnerabilities, capabilities emphasize people's freedom to choose and to act, the related responsibilities and the means available to them in order to fulfill them. From a capability perspective, human beings are not just passive recipients of goods, but active agents; they are receivers (with respect to their dependences and vulnerabilities), doers (under consideration of their agency) and judges (able of valuations) all at once (Bonvin and Laruffa, 2018). Considering all these different facets of human beings together offers a fertile ground for conceptualizing sustainable essential work.

Despite its focus on individual freedom, the capability approach develops a holistic framework that further offers a way to overcome the shortcomings of the worker-based answer to the question of what essential work means. The basic distinction between resources and functionings and the emphasis on the factors – individual, as well as social and environmental (Robeyns, 2017) – that allow or impede the conversion of those resources and commodities into concrete functionings, make capabilities the result of the interactions between a person and her environment, and their fulfillment a matter of social justice (Sen, 2009). This demand for social justice makes the identification of the functionings that are essential to human flourishing an important issue. Basic functionings in turn raise the question of the kind of work that is required to sustain them (Prainsack and Buyx, 2018).

However, Sen and Nussbaum diverge on the method for identifying basic functionings and capabilities. Nussbaum draws up a list of ten central capabilities related to functionings such as "bodily health," "bodily integrity," "control over one's environment," "play," etc., that should be given the status of universal rights (Nussbaum, 2000). Sen, on the other side, favors a context-dependent determination, built on collective deliberation within democratic bodies. His situated and participative approach seems better suited for capturing the differentiated role of contexts, but also for drawing the line back from basic functionings to work.

Sen's deliberative capability approach here meets Yeoman's workplace democracy and Clot's deliberated professionalism. All three make a plea in favor of enhancing the individual and collective power of those who are directly concerned – employers, workers, consumers, clients, patients, citizens (and all of us endorse several of these positions at once) – to voice what they take to matter. It is by involving individuals in the processes of defining the goals of work, that the challenge of coming to an agreement on "social utility," and hence on "essential work," can best be met.

Essential Work and Sustainable Development

Disentangling essential work from short-term emergency situations, to make it a robust long-term-oriented and potentially critical category, requires revisiting the issue of development. In today's dominant conception of development guided by the objective of endless economic growth, essential work can only be circumstantial. Outside periods of crisis that endanger the system, there is no place for such a category; on the contrary, all work that contributes to economic growth, no matter what its social utility and its human and ecological impact are, is considered equally legitimate. Amartya Sen's definition of development as "a process of expanding substantive freedoms that people have" (Sen, 1999, p. 297) allows a shift in perspective that makes human capabilities the means and purposes of development. While it has inspired the definition of sustainable development and sustainable work by the UNO (Anan and Sen, 2000; UNDP, 2015, 2020), the approach requires further refinement to go from economic and human development, which was its original focus, to social and ecological sustainability (Rauschmayer et al., 2011).

With respect to such a capability-based conceptualization of sustainable development, "essential work" could be understood as involving activities that contribute to the realization of collectively defined basic functionings and capabilities, while being sustainable from the perspectives of the workers, society, and the planet at large. Formulated in these terms, the challenge becomes to reach an agreement on the nature of these functionings and on the balance that can be reached between them. Ideally, deliberators can align human, social and ecological sustainability, or find reasonable compromises between them. As such, the role of nature and the role of care work and social reproduction, including its implication for gender justice, need to be integrated into our understanding of work that is "essential" for society (Littig, 2018).

However, this raises the question of whether local, situated deliberation is best suited for defining and caring about essential functionings at a global scale, as is urgently required by the challenges of climate change and environmental degradation. In addition to situated and local deliberation, we are thus led to questions about democracy at a larger scale, in order to deliberate about the functionings and capabilities that human beings really need for a flourishing life that does not destroy the planet and impede next generations' life.

Conclusion

In this chapter, we have addressed some of the challenges raised by "essential work" as a category in the making. Based on a semantic analysis of newspaper articles during the Corona pandemic, we have argued that it deviates from the way in which markets evaluate work, and also cannot be captured by purely worker-focused approaches. Instead, we have suggested that it could be spelled out in terms of the capability approach, understood in a procedural way that emphasizes the voice of those doing the work and those who are served by it. Involving all the persons who are concerned in the categorization process could make sense of many intuitions about the "essentiality" of certain forms of work, but this does not mean that it would be uncontroversial. Nonetheless, it offers a potential pathway for re-evaluating work by challenging a purely market-based valuation.

One potential of such a category is that it could be helpful in discussions about the ecological transformation of the economy and the need for "sustainable work." This requires however to uproot the concept of essential work from the short-term survival logic it has been associated with during the pandemic, and to combine it with long-term considerations of human flourishing under conditions of social and ecological sustainability.

Notes

1 These three newspapers offer good points of comparison because they occupy a similar position (center-left) in the political landscape of the countries. While a fuller analysis including a broader range of newspapers would have been interesting, our aim in this chapter was just to gain a first insight into the dominant public discourse.

2 https://solidarites-sante.gouv.fr/actualites/presse/communiques-de-presse/article/segur-de-la-sante-le-gouvernement-accelere-la-revalorisation-de-tous-les.

3 For now, we bracket the question of "essential work" done outside of "jobs," that is, in families or through volunteering. The capability approach we suggest below can, however, integrate such work, which is one of its strengths.

4 To be sure, we do not assume that there would be "laws" of supply and demand that would resemble "natural" laws. Labor markets are highly artificial institutions that depend on a plethora of legal, social and cultural norms (Polanyi, 1944), and factors such

as minimum wage legislation, degree of unionization, etc. can have a massive impact on their functioning and outcomes. This is one of the reasons for why it could be interesting to have an independent notion of "essential work," which could serve as a measuring rod for institutional reforms with regard to these legal, social and cultural frameworks.

5 One might well ask whether care work does not require high social and interpersonal skills – but these are not credentialed in the same way as other qualifications, and are often given less weight than, for example, formal degree qualifications.

6 At least this holds for capitalist societies without an unconditional basic income, in which individuals without private means *have* to work in order to generate an income.

7 Note that the more unequal a society, the less these two categories – subjective utility mediated by purchasing power on the one hand, and some objective notion of needs satisfaction or social utility, on the other hand, will overlap.

8 Criticizing the weak empirical foundations Graebers's account, Soffia et al. (2021) in fact debunk his claim that millions of workers are engaged in bullshit jobs. Based on the results of the European Working Conditions survey, they also show that Graeber's choice of examples does not cohere with the occupational groups showing the highest rates of feelings of uselessness. Instead, they argue that alienated and toxic work relations offer a better explanation of workers' feeling of uselessness.

9 Note that while Veltman writes more from a *moral* perspective, Yeoman also takes *political* questions, for example, about the organization of firms and the opportunity for workers to have their voices heard, into account (see also Yeoman's review of Veltman's book, Yeoman, 2018).

References

Anan, S. and Sen, A. (2000) 'Human Development and Economic Sustainability', *World Development*, 28(12), pp. 2029–2049.

Bailey, C. et al. (2019) 'Meaningful Work: Prospects for the 21st Century', *Journal of Management Studies*, 56(3), pp. 481–499.

Bonvin, J.-M. and Laruffa, F. (2018) 'Human Beings as Receivers, Doers and Judges. The Anthropological Foundations of Sustainable Public Action in the Capability Approach', *Community, Work and Family*, 21(5), pp. 502–518.

Clot, Y. (2008) *Travail et pouvoir d'agir*. Paris: Presses universitaires de France.

Clot, Y. (2010) *Le travail à cœur. Pour en finir avec les risques psychosociaux*. Paris: La Découverte.

Clot, Y. (2021) *Le prix du travail bien fait. La coopération conflictuelle dans les organisations*. Paris: La Découverte.

Elster, J. (1982) 'Sour Grapes – Utilitarianism and the Genesis of Wants', in Sen, A. and Williams, B. (eds.) *Utilitarianism and Beyond*. Cambridge: Cambridge University Press, pp. 219–238.

Fraser, N. (2016) 'Contradictions of Capital and Care', *New Left Review*, 100, pp. 99–117.

Graeber, D. (2013) 'On the Phenomenon of Bullshit Jobs: A Work Rant', *Strike Magazine*. www.strike.coop/bullshit-jobs/

Graeber, D. (2018) *Bullshit Jobs. A Theory*. London: Allen Lane.

Harding, N. (2019) 'Identity and Meaningful/Meaningless Work', in Yeoman, R., Bailey, C., Madden, A. and Thompson, M. (eds.) *The Oxford Handbook of Meaningful Work*. Oxford: Oxford University Press, pp. 133–147.

Kocka, J. (1973) *Klassengesellschaft im Krieg. Deutsche Sozialgeschichte 1914–1918*. Göttingen: Vandenhoeck & Ruprecht.

Littig, B. (2018) 'Good Work? Sustainable Work and Sustainable Development: A Critical Gender Perspective from the Global North', *Globalizations*, 15(4), pp. 565–579.

Max-Neef, M., Elizalde, A. and Hopenhayn, M. (1991) 'Development and Human Needs' in Max-Neef, M. (ed.) *Human Scale Development: Conception, Application and further Reflections*. New York: The Apex Press, pp. 13–54.

Nussbaum, M. (2000) *Women and Human Development: The Capabilities Approach*. Cambridge: Cambridge University Press.

Nussbaum, M. and Sen, A. (1993) (eds.) *The Quality of Life*. Oxford: Oxford University Press.

Polanyi, K. (1944) *The Great Transformation*. New York: Farrar & Rinehart.

Prainsack, B. and Buyx, A. (2018) 'The Value of Work: Addressing the Future of Work Through the Lens of Solidarity', *Bioethics*, 32, pp. 585–592.

Rauschmayer, F., Omman, I. and Frühmann, J. (eds.) (2011) *Sustainable Development. Capabilities, Needs and Well-being*. London, New York: Routledge.

Riley, J. (2016) 'Utilitarianism and Economic Theory', in Vernengo, M., Caldentey, E.P. and Barkley, B.J. (eds.) *The New Palgrave Dictionary of Economics*. https://doi.org/10.1057/978-1-349-95121-5_2052-1

Robeyns, I. (2017) *Well-Being, Freedom and Social Justice. The Capability Approach Re-examined*. Cambridge: Open Book Publishers. http://dx.doi.org/10.11647/OBP.0130

Sen, A. (1987) *On Ethics and Economics*. Oxford and New York: Blackwell Publishers.

Sen, A. (1992) *Inequality Reexamined*. Cambridge, MA: Harvard University Press.

Sen, A. (1993) 'Capability and Well-being' in Nussbaum, M. and Sen, A. (eds.) *The Quality of Life*. Oxford: Oxford University Press, pp. 30–53.

Sen, A. (1999) *Development as Freedom*. Oxford: Oxford University Press.

Sen, A. (2009) *The Idea of Justice*. London: Penguin Books Ltd.

Soffia, M., Wood, A.J. and Brendan, B. (2021) 'Alienation is Not 'Bullshit': An Empirical Critique of Graeber's Theory of BS Jobs', *Work, Employment and Society*, https://doi.org/10.1177/09500170211015067

UNDP (2015) *Human Development Report*. United Nations. www.undp.org/publications/human-development-report-2015

UNDP (2020) *Human Development Report*. United Nations. http://hdr.undp.org/en/2020-report.

Veltman, A. (2016) *Meaningful Work*. New York: Oxford University Press.

Wehler, H.-U. (2003) *Deutsche Gesellschaftsgeschichte. Vol. 4: 1914–1949*. Munich: C.H. Beck.

Yeoman, R. (2014a) 'Conceptualizing Meaningful Work as a Fundamental Human Need', *Journal of Business Ethics*, 125, pp. 235–251.

Yeoman, R. (2014b) *Meaningful Work and Workplace Democracy. A Philosophy of Work and a Politics of Meaningfulness*. London: Palgrave Macmillan.

Yeoman, R. (2018) '*Meaningful Work* by Andrea Veltman', *Australasian Journal of Philosophy*, 96(4), pp. 831–834.

Yeoman, R., Bailey, C., Madden, A. and Thompson, M. (eds.) (2019) *The Oxford Handbook of Meaningful Work*. Oxford: Oxford University Press.

18

SUSTAINABLE WORK

Foundations and Challenges of a Contested Category

Maja Hoffmann

Introduction

The global ecological crisis poses existential threats to life on Earth for timespans beyond human imagination. In particular, the intensifying climate crisis requires rapid and fundamental changes to modern societies and economies so as to ensure sustainable living conditions in the long term (IPCC, 2021). Modern-day work[1] plays a central role in this context: it is a main driver of the ecological crisis and structurally inapt to support life and provide for social needs in a sustainable way, and thus has to be transformed to become sustainable (Hoffmann and Paulsen, 2020).

This chapter argues for conceptualizing "sustainable work" as a matter of recognizing that all human activity is embedded within and dependent on the Earth's ecosystems, natural environment and fundamental laws of physics. In the philosophy of science, this corresponds to the position of ontological realism, which assumes a world or reality existing independently of human cognition, beliefs and discourses (Sayer, 2000).[2] This implies an understanding of "sustainability" that focuses primarily on the biophysical environment as the fundamental condition and necessary basis of all life and all human undertakings, and therefore regards ecological concerns as ultimately decisive for sustainability. Assuming Earth's biosphere and its biophysical limits as the necessary, non-negotiable foundation of all existence also implies that "sustainability" cannot be divided into distinct, ontologically separate spheres or "pillars" (as in the notion of sustainable development; see Purvis et al., 2019) or certain degrees of realization (as in the notion of "weak/strong sustainability"; see Neumayer, 2003). Rather, "social" (as well as "economic") and "ecological" conditions are in principle indivisible, and therefore "sustainable" is a fundamental condition that is either fulfilled as a

DOI: 10.4324/9781003341321-22

whole or not at all (Carton, 2009) – something is "able to be sustained" into the indefinite future or it is not.

Taking the embeddedness of all human activity within biophysical reality as the starting point for a discussion of sustainable work means putting the ecological (material and energy)[3] basis of work at the center of our analysis, which allows us to assess which work is ecologically sustainable or not. A sound categorization of sustainable work, however, needs to go further and also take into account the – currently potentially nonexistent – kinds of work that are necessary to provide for social needs and sustain life in general. This requires going beyond solely biophysical criteria and taking the social value of work in relation to human and ecological needs into consideration – which in turn is still dependent on and indivisible from ecological concerns and therefore also grounded in a realist account of ecological necessities.

This is what my chapter aims to investigate. The next section reviews existing notions of sustainable work and related concepts, including their respective underlying conceptions of sustainability. Then I develop criteria for assessing un/sustainable work by analyzing the main biophysical prerequisites of climate change mitigation, illustrated by empirical data on the Austrian national economy. Further, I discuss the social value of work as well as the political implications and institutional challenges of a structural transformation of modern work society, before drawing conclusions.

Work and Sustainability

Research on work and sustainability is overall fragmented and insufficiently developed (Hoffmann and Paulsen, 2020). Sustainable work as a category is thus ill-defined – there are few existing notions of sustainable work, and they differ quite substantially in their approaches.

One strand is focused on the "development in personal resources leading to sustainable work ability" (Kira et al., 2010) or the living and working conditions which ensure that people remain part of the workforce throughout an extended working life (Eurofound, 2021). This narrow understanding of sustainable work does not include environmental or broader societal concerns and is thus devoid of any substantial conception of sustainability. The approach of "environmentally sustainable work behavior" has an equally narrow focus at the individual level, meaning the workplace behavior of individual workers that either benefits the environment or limits the harm inflicted on it (Davis and Challenger, 2015). While this at least incorporates ecological issues, it means neither the actual content or purpose of work (just the behavior it entails) nor an elaborated understanding of sustainability. The concept of "sustainable work systems" (Docherty et al., 2009) likewise focuses on the workplace/organizations, yet then is of very unspecific scope, including a broad variety of aspects and goals. Its conception of sustainability follows the "three pillar" or "triple bottom line" rationale of sustainable development ("people, planet, profit") where "economic, ecological, human, and social resources" should all be able to grow and develop in equal measure. Recognizing anything as sustainable that addresses one of these aspects (or a range of other things) thus implies a broad and arbitrary notion of sustainability.[4]

In a similar manner, the UNDP (2015) emphasizes that sustainable work "is critical not only for sustaining the planet, but also for ensuring work for future generations." Moreover it "promotes human development while reducing and eliminating negative side effects and unintended consequences" (ibid., p. 14). For sustainable work to be realized, three parallel developments are needed: the creation of new work, the transformation of some existing work in order to preserve it, and the termination of work in certain resource-intensive or polluting fields. This notion thus explicitly acknowledges that different kinds of work have to be distinguished so as to assess their sustainability and that some need to be phased out. Its conception of sustainability takes biophysical concerns into consideration, but otherwise, it remains within the parameters of the conventional sustainable development and SDG framework ("people, planet, prosperity") including a commitment to economic growth, modern development, and "progress." Accordingly, it not only takes for granted the modern notion of work as an end in itself but seeks to universalize it.

By contrast, a second elaborated approach to sustainable work, developed by Littig (2002; 2018) and Barth et al. (2016; 2019), draws on a critical research tradition including feminist, Marxist and Polanyian thought as well as critiques of growth and market-based development. It argues for a fundamental social-ecological transformation beyond conventional "green economy" proposals, and for work to be at the center of this transformation. Yet the aim remains to create a "sustainable work society." As in the UNDP's notion, part of the purpose of environmental protection is that work itself must be sustained as a vital source for the development of "human potential." For work to be sustainable it needs to be reorganized as well as redefined, adopting an extended notion of work that comprises all kinds of purposeful activity beyond paid work only (which the UNDP's notion also stresses). This corresponds to the Marxist notion of work as the essentially human interaction with nature, whereby a separate "inner" and "external" nature are assumed (Littig, 2018; Barth et al., 2016; 2019). Not only does this peculiar distinction represent a stark version of the modern ontological separation between human beings and nature but it also naturalizes work by obscuring its specific modern cultural and institutional form and by presupposing the typically modern elevated moral status of work as intrinsically good and an end in itself.

In addition to these notions of sustainable work, there are a number of related concepts. Most prominent among them is the notion of "green jobs," sometimes also "climate jobs," as opposed to "brown jobs" or "(high-)carbon jobs," and often part of debates on "just transition" or "Green New Deal." Green jobs help preserve or restore environmental quality (UNEP et al., 2008), that is, comprise jobs in those specific sectors concerned with environmental protection and management or other "green" products and services. Though under a different heading, the EU's recently adopted "EU taxonomy" also provides a classification of "environmentally sustainable economic activities" (European Commission, 2021). Depending on the definition, green jobs are overall either quite marginal (as statistically recorded in the "environmental goods and services sector"; Eurostat, 2021) or understood so broadly as to include jobs in problematic, energy-intensive and high-carbon industries such as gas, steel and cement production, and other "shades of green" in conventional jobs (UNEP et al., 2008; European Commission, 2021). Green-jobs discourses focus primarily on selected sectors and their "green growth" potential which implies a preoccupation with job gains and job creation, usually within the confines of the modern industrial-capitalist economy. As in the notion of "decent work" there is practically no consideration of indecent and outright harmful, unsustainable work and the need to discontinue such occupations (e.g., Bowen, 2012).

Another strand is based on the theoretical traditions of (eco-)feminism, Marxism, political ecology and post-development, thus broadening the perspective to include the manifold forms of labor and livelihood provisioning prevalent in the Global South. It comprises a number of concepts focused on reproductive labor or care and caring as the basis of all life. Examples include "meta-industrial labor" (Salleh, 2010, p. 212) which "denotes workers, nominally outside of capitalism, whose labor . . . is relational, flow oriented, and regenerative of biotic chains"; "hybrid labor" (Battistoni, 2017, pp. 6, 14) meaning the "collective, distributed undertaking of humans and nonhumans acting to reproduce, regenerate, and renew a common world" while "recognizing nonhumans as co-laborers in the project of building our livable planet"; and "earthcare labour" or "forces of reproduction" (Barca, 2020, p. iii) emphasizing "the historical agency of reproductive and subsistence workers as those subjects that . . . take care of the biophysical conditions for human reproduction, thus keeping the world alive." These concepts share an extended notion of work, even including the "productivity" of nature, which, as noted earlier, tends to generalize and naturalize work despite its historically and culturally specific and vastly different forms. A further commonality is an explicit recognition of ecological concerns and all forms of life as integral parts of all conceptualizations. All of them also address systemic reasons for persistent unsustainability. However, the concepts remain rather abstract and mostly sketch out broad visions and political projects of alternative worlds as imagined by the many "life-making struggles across the world, based on an emerging awareness that keeping the world alive requires dismantling the master's house" (Barca, 2020, p. 7; see also von Redecker, 2020). Yet they remain unspecific about work in a concrete sense and in its predominant capitalist form, and about the ways in which different kinds of work need to be reorganized or abandoned.

This is precisely the focus of another approach inspired by the debate on "bullshit jobs," which in their original definition already contain an element of being detrimental to the world, besides being blatantly meaningless (Graeber, 2018). Taking this further by explicitly including the ecological variable, the concept of "batshit jobs" denotes work "that contributes to destroying the climate and environment" as part of "a kind of systemic madness" where "making a living is also a part of unmaking life on many scales" (Rübner Hansen, 2019). This in turn is close to the notion of "noxious work" or "noxiousness" as developed by the Italian "(post-)operaismo" movements of the late 1960s and 1970s, which were explicitly critical of work and its environmentally harmful impacts and argued for fundamentally questioning the organization, scale and purpose of production (Feltrin and Sacchetto, 2021). While these notions do address core relevancies in any discussion of sustainable work, so far they have remained quite marginal.

To summarize, most of the approaches to sustainable work and related concepts discussed here raise important points, while being limited in certain aspects. In the following, I will both draw on the useful contributions they make and add new elements for constructing a different approach to categorizing sustainable work.

Unsustainable Work

Starting from the premise of biophysical realism means acknowledging that all human activity is embedded in planetary ecosystems and based on material and energy throughputs. Accordingly, all productive activity impacts the biophysical environment – and currently at clearly unsustainable levels (Hoffmann and Paulsen, 2020). To develop a category of sustainable work that is thoroughly grounded in biophysical reality, including criteria that will allow one to assess which kinds of work are un/sustainable, ecological considerations need to be placed at the center of any analysis. Note again that "work" means work *as such*, that is, concrete activities, their content and purpose, according to which different kinds of work can be distinguished. Moreover "work" denotes its (in the Global North) predominant social form as gainful employment within the structures, norms and institutions of modern industrial society.[5]

Environmental concerns are countless. Here the climate crisis is taken as an illustration; it is one of the most existential global ecological problems and clearly decisive in whether or not there is an imminent collapse of stable, life-supporting environmental conditions on Earth in the short term, and thus crucial for any discussion of sustainability. At the same time, climate change as a physical phenomenon is well understood, specifically concerning its drivers and what is required to mitigate it (IPCC, 2021). Taking climate change mitigation seriously, in line with the best available science and international legal obligations under the Paris Agreement, means for industrialized countries to undertake profound, rapid and sustained reductions in greenhouse gas emissions to *absolute zero*, to phase out the use of fossil fuels and to achieve a structural transformation toward a post-fossil economy based entirely on renewable energy, all within the short timeframe of approximately 15 years (Anderson et al., 2020; Jackson et al., 2019; Allwood et al., 2019).

From a physical science perspective, therefore, these basic requirements of climate change mitigation suggest an analytic focus on CO_2 emissions (and their reduction toward zero), fossil fuel use and the potential for transitioning to renewable energy, that is, full substitution of fossil fuels through renewable energy (assuming the current state of technology that is decisive for the relevant timeframe of less than two decades, which rules out speculative so-called negative emissions technologies; Nemet et al., 2018; Allwood et al., 2019). These aspects allow one to assess whether a concrete kind of work is un/sustainable with regard to climate change mitigation.[6] In other words, *CO_2 emissions, fossil fuel use, and renewable energy potential* are necessary (but not sufficient) conditions for work to be un/sustainable and therefore constitute concrete practical criteria for assessing the category of un/sustainable work. More precisely, if CO_2 emissions and fossil fuel usage in a particular work activity tend toward zero and there is potential for reorganization based on renewable energy, then this particular activity is in principle sustainable (unless other severe ecological harm is inflicted); otherwise, it is unsustainable. These criteria thus allow us to demarcate both what is sustainable and unsustainable work in terms of climate change.

By way of illustration, these criteria can be applied to the Austrian national economy as an example of a modern industrial economy and "developed country" signatory to the Paris Agreement. Drawing on empirical data on employment, CO_2 emissions, fossil fuel use and renewable energy potential across all NACE/ISIC-classified branches of economic activity (for the years 2016 and 2017) the Austrian case provides a comprehensive picture of the un/sustainability of work with regard to climate change mitigation (Hoffmann and Spash, 2021).

Key findings include the fact that the overall implications for work are far more substantial and involve considerably more work in more sectors than the literature usually suggests. There is no field of work that is unproblematic in terms of CO_2 emissions and fossil fuel use; almost all sectors of the economy have emitted more than 10,000 tons of CO_2 per year, and many much more than that. Those sectors typically associated with low environmental impact exhibit considerable climate impacts (e.g., "education" with 409,605 tons of CO_2 or "human health and social work activities" with 154,126 tons of CO_2 in 2016). Moreover, existing renewable energy technologies cannot be deployed across a whole range of economic activities that are dependent on the specific properties of fossil fuels (e.g., in "air transport" or "manufacture of basic metals"). This means that these kinds of work currently cannot be reorganized on the basis of renewable energy – especially at the present scale of energy consumption; this amounts to nearly 30 percent of the total Austrian workforce in 2017 (Hoffmann and Spash, 2021). This approach allows us to conclude that based on the criteria of CO_2 emissions and fossil fuel use, almost all work in an average modern industrialized economy such as Austria is currently unsustainable and in need of reduction and reorganization. In terms of renewable energy potential, between a quarter and a third of all work in Austria is structurally dependent on fossil fuels and thus unsustainable, that is, it is work that cannot be sustained given the urgent imperative of climate change mitigation and hence needs to be discontinued, at least temporarily.

The Social Value of Work

As described, biophysical criteria are ultimately decisive for assessing the kinds of work that are (in)compatible with serious climate change mitigation and thus (un)sustainable. Where identified as unsustainable, work needs to be reduced or entirely phased out. However, there are certain kinds of work that cannot simply be reduced across the board and would need to be prioritized for reorganization due to their essential importance for the functioning of society (such as health care in the example given earlier). Moreover, there are vital social and ecological needs that are currently unfulfilled, which would require the creation of new kinds of work (e.g., for the provisioning of small-scale renewable energy or ecosystem restoration). Thus, while certain kinds of work have to be reduced or abandoned, others need to be transformed/reorganized on the basis of renewable energy, and still others need to be created (UNDP, 2015).

Therefore, besides the issue of which kinds of work can or cannot be sustained from an ecological point of view, for a comprehensive categorization of sustainable work it is required to also take into account what is (not) necessary in terms of work to support and sustain both societal life and life in general. In addition to biophysical criteria, it is therefore relevant to consider the *social value and purpose of work*, differentiating whether concrete kinds of work are necessary or essential, meaningful, pointless, harmful – or simply lacking – in relation to the fulfillment of fundamental human and ecological needs (Graeber, 2018; Feltrin and Sacchetto, 2021; Hoffmann and Paulsen, 2020; see also Herzog et al. in this volume).

Taking into consideration the kinds of work that are essential, dispensable, conducive or detrimental to fulfilling societal needs in a sustainable way and to upholding or restoring sustainable environmental conditions means broadening the scope beyond biophysical aspects; however, it still implies an essentially realist approach focused on ecological necessities. Incorporating "social" concerns such as fundamental human needs (Rauschmayer and Omann, 2017) and related claims to human rights, freedom, as well as intergenerational and global justice should, and often does, acknowledge the fact that these are fully dependent on and thus indivisible from ecological concerns. Both present and future living conditions and livelihoods vitally depend on sound environmental conditions, especially in an increasingly climate-constrained world – something addressed by the notions of environmental justice and climate justice or the latest developments in climate litigation. These issues are inherently global in scope with a distinct colonial dimension and as such concern the Global South and North alike.

Yet despite being grounded in biophysical reality – which provides guidance as to what is possible and required to sustain social life and all life on Earth – incorporating a focus on the social value of work in relation to needs evidently requires a different approach. It is not as straightforward as establishing a set of relatively unambiguous criteria based on physical laws (such as the concentration of carbon dioxide in the atmosphere compatible with habitable living conditions on Earth). Instead, it requires a novel kind of assessment as well as institutionalized deliberation and valuation processes at various levels. A general, scientifically informed basis for this is currently lacking (Graeber, 2018), despite recent experience with a coronavirus pandemic which has made abundantly clear that there is substantial variation in different kinds of work with regard to their social value and importance in providing the necessities of life – a theme which has been discussed in some strands of critical social science for decades (e.g., Gorz, 1989).

The coronavirus pandemic has also proven instructive in a related way. Drawing on the lists of essential work that governments have issued as part of the pandemic containment measures, we can see that criteria for assessing the social value or necessity of work depend on the specific aims and purposes of a given society, which then determine its vital needs and functions. The aim of upholding the functioning of modern capitalist societies – with their fossil-fuel-based, growth-dependent, financialized, militarized and competitive nation-states and economies – evidently differs substantially from the aim of creating a sustainable society oriented toward sustaining life on Earth and the fulfillment of fundamental human and ecological needs (Hoffmann and Spash, 2021). Decisive in the effort to carve out criteria for the social value of work must therefore be the question "valuable for what" – what kind of society and which social functions are to be maintained (or created), what is the goal or ultimate vision against which this is being judged? Thus, not only should different kinds of work be distinguished to determine the social value of work, but also different aims that a society might pursue.

The Politics of Sustainable Work

A range of implications and complications arise from this proposal – partly clearly defined, partly only problematized – to assess sustainable work. Evidently, a number of fundamental structural changes are necessary for work to become sustainable. Among the many implications and challenges, only a few can be highlighted here:

A substantial reduction (and partial phase-out) of work is needed according to the criteria of un/sustainability as introduced here, that is, starting with the most harmful sectors in terms of CO_2 emissions and fossil fuel use that presently cannot be reorganized on the basis of renewable energy (Hoffmann and Spash, 2021). The body of research on working time reduction contributes valuable insights on the politics of transformation involved here (e.g., Liebig, 2021).

As discussed, such reduction and reorganization also need to take into account the social value and purpose of work – in order to prioritize essential work, discontinue bullshit and batshit work (Rübner Hansen, 2019) and create work where it is beneficial for society and the biosphere. Many of these decisions can be expected to be very controversial. Besides the qualitative aspects (differentiating concrete kinds of work) there are also quantitative issues to consider, for instance, *how much* work (of a certain kind) is required for the fulfillment of a given set of needs. Moreover, the energy and resource basis of production has to be taken into account, which effectively means economic planning based on (very small) remaining carbon budgets. Such questions, deliberation processes and planning will remain contested and vary over time and space, and thus need to be institutionalized – yet institutions that would be capable of organizing this in a democratic way do not currently exist. This relates to debates on economic democracy, which refers to new institutions of democratic control over the economy (Johanisova and Wolf, 2012; Gorz, 1989).[7]

Related to this latter aspect, it is evident that the labor market as an organizing principle for the allocation of work is not only undemocratic but structurally inapt for distributing or discontinuing work according to criteria of sustainability and societal necessity, let alone for creating new kinds of work which may be socially necessary but unprofitable in terms of market imperatives. The labor market organizes and allocates work only according to the availability of money and motives of gain on the part of employers (Hoffmann and Paulsen, 2020).

Institutionalizing sustainable work implies abandoning the market principle (at least temporarily) in certain sectors, continuing to organize work in markets where it is found meaningful (e.g., for some kinds of production on larger scales) and otherwise establishing structures and institutions beyond market and state (Barth et al., 2019) so as to reorganize work in de-commodified ways. Practical examples that may serve as an inspiration for this are often found in concepts and practices subsumed under the commons (Bollier and Helfrich, 2019) as for instance in community-supported economic practices.[8] In the Global South in particular, countless heterogenous, often commons-based and non-commodified – and potentially sustainable – forms of livelihood provisioning clearly prevail. However, such forms of labor are generally regarded as precarious, deficient remnants of a backward, undeveloped past that need to be overcome on the universal road to development and progress, as for example promoted in SDG 8, instead of taking them seriously (Ferguson and Li, 2018; Hoffmann and Paulsen, 2020; Monteith et al., 2021).

Overall this illustrates that there is a structural problem with the way in which work is organized in modern industrial work societies and that this problem needs to be addressed in a very substantial sense, which makes sustainable work a highly contested category. In particular, a recurring source of controversy is the jobs-versus-environment issue, that is, the tensions between the severe ecological impacts of work and efforts to mitigate them on the one hand, and the structural constitution of modern industrial society as work-centered and work-dependent on the other, which aligns with strong organized interests in favor of the economic status quo. There is a broad consensus across the whole political spectrum – well into the ranks of environmentalism, which would otherwise oppose capitalist economic development – that jobs have to be preserved and new ones created, often regardless of their actual purpose or adverse impact (Hoffmann and Paulsen, 2020).

To resolve this recurring conflict, the various structural dependencies on work in modern society need to be overcome so that work may be reduced without causing major societal and economic crises. One key challenge is therefore to subject central welfare-state institutions to structural reforms so as to gain more independence from work. To this end, a whole bundle of policies to organize social provisioning in alternative ways is being discussed under the rubric of "sustainable welfare" (Koch and Mont, 2016) which would however need to address the issue of the organization of work in greater detail.

Yet this alone will not suffice, given that the social centrality of work is deeply ingrained not only in structures and institutions but in cultural attitudes. The modern work ethic, a peculiar commitment to work as an end in itself and as a general moral obligation (Weeks, 2011), is certainly one of the main factors that nurture the controversy outlined earlier and which prevents more profound changes from transpiring by rendering work sacrosanct and impervious to any critique. Without questioning work more fundamentally, including its specific modern conception and underlying norms and morality, modern societies remain in the structural impasse of growth, job creation and full employment at any cost as main political goals. The ecological crisis requires detaching ourselves from work and productivist mentalities and rethinking commonly held aversions to inaction and idleness – given that the latter are not only very environmentally friendly ways of being but also promise to be more sustainable sources of life satisfaction and well-being in a context where work is growing increasingly problematic and in need of substantial change (Sage, 2019; Hoffmann and Paulsen, 2020).

Conclusions

In reviewing existing notions of sustainable work we can see that these are scarce and quite incoherent. While some notions are clearly insufficient, others offer valuable elements to build on. Taking a novel approach beyond them, this chapter has argued that a reasonable category of sustainable work needs to start from its biophysical basis, that is, its foundation in the physical reality of matter and energy. This approach allows one to derive fairly exact biophysical criteria for assessment of the un/sustainability of work (which have been developed by using climate change mitigation as an example of a necessary condition of ecological sustainability). Yet it is further relevant to take into consideration the social value of work as related to fundamental human and ecological needs. While the question of "what is sustainable work" is therefore relatively easy to answer from a biophysical point of view, taking needs and value considerations into account no longer allows for a straightforward answer because these are contextual, political and clearly non-universal factors (as opposed to the laws of physics). Still, the indivisible ecological foundation of work can provide guidance as to what is needed and overall possible in terms of work to sustain life, which may be taken as a basis for deliberation. However, democratic institutions for deliberating such issues including the amount, means and ends of work that a given society wishes to pursue for a given aim are currently lacking.

Taking these findings seriously implies profound political changes that will effect structures and institutions of a novel kind for deliberating, organizing and allocating sustainable work. This outlook is highly contested, especially given the specific constitution of modern industrial society as centered and structurally dependent on work as well as culturally biased toward work as a glorified end in itself, which restricts critical thinking and any imagination regarding possible alternatives.

Accordingly, there is a considerable gap between the definition of sustainable work as a category and its realization. It would certainly be desirable for sustainable work to become an "emerging category" and a "field in the making"; however, as a category it has hitherto performed rather weakly. While the notions of "just transition" and "decent work" have made it into the preamble of the Paris Agreement (UNFCCC, 2015, p. 2) and the equivalent of "green jobs" into recent EU legislation (European Commission, 2021), sustainable work has thus far remained marginal in both public policy and social science. This corresponds to the general problem that, despite its significance for the ecological crisis, work in a more substantial sense occupies a very marginal position in sustainability research and debates (Barth et al., 2016).

The overall scale of the challenge is therefore huge; far-reaching changes are necessary within a very short timeframe in view of the tight remaining carbon budget. At the same time, ecological urgency is only surpassed by a general lack of awareness and understanding of the magnitude of the problem posed by exacerbating environmental destruction on a planetary scale, especially in consideration of the very low levels of basic ecological literacy in the general population. It is thus uncertain and increasingly unrealistic that "sustainable work" will become a reality, despite hopeful tendencies in the progressive spectrum of academic and public debate.

Notes

1 Understood in the specific modern sense as commodified gainful employment, including its norms, structures and institutions. In this predominant social form, work is a peculiarly modern cultural phenomenon and one of the main social relations of modern industrial society.

2 Assuming ontological realism as a basis does not mean simple positivism but the position of Critical Realism (which cannot be discussed within the parameters of this chapter).

3 "Ecological" here means phenomena, conditions and dynamics pertaining to the natural environment, including their underlying biophysical processes. Fundamentally, this refers to the tenets of thermodynamics according to which "all transformation processes are, at bottom, processes of energy and material transformation" (Mayumi, 2017, p. 91).

4 Representative of this strand of literature – which adopts such a broad meaning of the term that it becomes vacuous, and where ecological issues are at best a sideshow – is also the special double issue on "European Approaches to Sustainable Work" in the *European Journal of Workplace Innovation,* 6(2), 2021.

5 This "narrow" definition of work is contested, and only partly for sound reasons. For a critique of extended notions of work, see Hoffmann (2021).

6 These aspects are central to efforts at climate change mitigation, but other necessary measures include the halting of land use changes, and the restoration of ecosystems. Moreover, emissions of all other greenhouse gases besides carbon dioxide (especially methane) need to be quickly reduced as well. Yet CO_2 can be regarded as the most relevant greenhouse gas due to the near-linear relationship between CO_2 emissions and global warming (IPCC, 2021, p. 36).

7 Note that economic democracy as introduced here aims at democratizing the economy as a whole and thus goes beyond "workplace democracy" which is limited in scope and excludes large parts of the population.

8 In community-supported production systems or networks, producers and consumers coalesce directly to plan the production and provisioning process of certain goods and services. They do this autonomously and democratically, sharing costs, benefits, resources, risks and responsibilities, thus building new kinds of social relationships. A popular and widespread example is community supported agriculture (CSA). The basic organizing principles of CSA are increasingly being transferred to other economic sectors (CSX or CSI). See, for example, https://gemeinschaftsgetragen.de/en/.

References

Allwood, J.M., Dunant, C.F, Lupton, R.C, Cleaver, C.J, Serrenho, A.C.H, Azevedo, J.M.C, Horton, P.M. and Hawkins, W. (2019) *Absolute Zero: Delivering the UK's Climate Change Commitment with Incremental Changes to Today's Technologies*. Cambridge: UK FIRES. DOI: 10.17863/CAM.46075

Anderson, K., Broderick, J.F. and Stoddard, I. (2020) 'A Factor of Two: How the Mitigation Plans of "Climate Progressive" Nations Fall Far Short of Paris-Compliant Pathways', *Climate Policy*, 20(10), pp. 1290–1304. DOI: 10.1080/14693062.2020.1728209

Barca, S. (2020) *Forces of Reproduction: Notes for a Counter-Hegemonic Anthropocene*. Cambridge: Cambridge University Press. DOI: 10.1017/9781108878371

Barth, T., Jochum, G. and Littig, B. (2016) *Nachhaltige Arbeit. Soziologische Beiträge zur Neubestimmung der gesellschaftlichen Naturverhältnisse*. Frankfurt: Campus.

Barth, T., Jochum, G. and Littig, B. (2019) *Transformation of What? Or: The Socio-Ecological Transformation of Working Society*, IHS Working Paper, No. 1. Institute for Advanced Studies (IHS), Vienna.

Battistoni, A. (2017) 'Bringing in the Work of Nature: From Natural Capital to Hybrid Labor', *Political Theory*, 45(1), pp. 5–31. DOI: 10.1177/0090591716638389.

Bollier, D. and Helfrich, S. (2019) *Free, Fair, and Alive: The Insurgent Power of the Commons*. Gabriola Island: New Society Publishers.

Bowen, A. (2012) *"Green" Growth, "Green" Jobs and Labor Markets, Policy Research Working Paper 5990*. Washington, DC: World Bank. DOI: 10.1596/1813–9450–5990

Carton, W. (2009) *Nature and the Myth of a Sustainable Capitalism*, Master's thesis, Aalborg University.

Davis, M.C. and Challenger, R. (2015) 'Environmentally Sustainable Work Behavior', in Flood, P.C. and Freeney, Y. (eds.) *Wiley Encyclopedia of Management. Volume 11: Organizational Behavior*. DOI: 10.1002/9781118785317.weom110022

Docherty, P., Kira, M. and Shani, A.B. (2009) 'What the World Needs Now Is Sustainable Work Systems', in Docherty, P., Kira, M. and Shani, A.B. (eds.) *Creating Sustainable Work Systems*. London and New York: Routledge, pp. 1–21.

Eurofound (2021) 'Sustainable Work', www.eurofound.europa.eu/topic/sustainable-work.

European Commission (2021) 'EU Taxonomy, Corporate Sustainability Reporting, Sustainability Preferences and Fiduciary Duties: Directing Finance Towards the European Green Deal', https://eur-lex.europa.eu/legal-content/EN/TXT/PDF/?uri=CELEX:52021DC0188&from=EN.

Eurostat (2021) 'Environmental Economy – Statistics by Member State', https://ec.europa.eu/eurostat/statistics-explained/index.php?title=Environmental_economy_–_statistics_by_Member_State#Employment.

Feltrin, L. and Sacchetto, D. (2021) 'The Work-Technology Nexus and Working-Class Environmentalism: Workerism Versus Capitalist Noxiousness in Italy's Long 1968', *Theory and Society*, 50, pp. 815–835. DOI: 10.1007/s11186-021-09441-5

Ferguson, J. and Li, T.M. (2018) *Beyond the "Proper Job:" Political-Economic Analysis After the Century of Labouring Man*, Working paper 51. PLAAS, UWC, Cape Town.

Gorz, A. (1989) *Critique of Economic Reason*. London: Verso.

Graeber, D. (2018) *Bullshit Jobs: A Theory*. London: Allen Lane.

Hoffmann, M. (2021) 'Die Problematik eines erweiterten Arbeitsbegriffs', *Blog Postwachstum*. www.postwachstum.de/die-problematik-eines-erweiterten-arbeitsbegriffs-20210623.

Hoffmann, M. and Paulsen, R. (2020) 'Resolving the "Jobs-Environment-Dilemma"? The Case for Critiques of Work in Sustainability Research', *Environmental Sociology*, 6(4), pp. 343–354. DOI: 10.1080/23251042.2020.1790718

Hoffmann, M. and Spash, C.L. (2021) *The Impacts of Climate Change Mitigation on Work for the Austrian Economy*. Social-ecological Research in Economics (SRE) Discussion Paper, Vienna University of Economics and Business. https://econpapers.repec.org/paper/wiwwiwsre/sre-disc-2021_5f10.htm.

IPCC (2021) 'Summary for Policymakers', in *Climate Change 2021: The Physical Science Basis: Contribution of Working Group I to the Sixth Assessment Report of the Intergovernmental Panel on Climate Change*. Cambridge: Cambridge University Press.

Jackson, R.B., Friedlingstein, P, Andrew, R.M, Canadell, J.G, Le Quéré, C. and Peter, G.P. (2019) 'Persistent Fossil Fuel Growth Threatens the Paris Agreement and Planetary Health', *Environmental Research Letters*, 14. DOI: 10.1088/1748–9326/ab57b3

Johanisova, N. and Wolf, S. (2012) 'Economic Democracy: A Path for the Future?', *Futures*, 44(6), pp. 562–570. DOI: 10.1016/j.futures.2012.03.017

Kira, M., van Eijnatten, F.M. and Balkin, D.B. (2010) 'Crafting Sustainable Work: Development of Personal Resources', *Journal of Organizational Change Management*, 23(5), pp. 616–632. DOI: 10.1108/09534811011071315

Koch, M. and Mont, O. (eds.) (2016) *Sustainability and the Political Economy of Welfare*. Abingdon: Routledge.

Liebig, S. (2021) *Arbeitszeitverkürzung als Konvergenzpunkt? Sozial-ökologische Arbeitskonzepte, Wachstumskritik und gewerkschaftliche Tarifpolitik*. Frankfurt and New York: Campus.

Littig, B. (2002) 'The Case for Gender-Sensitive Socio-Ecological Research', *Work, Employment & Society*, 16(1), pp. 111–132. DOI: 10.1177/09500170222119272

Littig, B. (2018) 'Good Work? Sustainable Work and Sustainable Development: A Critical Gender Perspective From the Global North', *Globalizations*, 15(4), pp. 565–579. DOI: 10.1080/14747731.2018.1454676

Mayumi, K.T. (2017) 'Thermodynamics: Relevance, Implications, Misuse and Ways Forward', in Spash, C.L. (ed.) *Routledge Handbook of Ecological Economics: Nature and Society*. Abingdon: Routledge, pp. 89–98.

Monteith, W., Vicol, D.-O. and Williams, P. (eds.) (2021) *Beyond the Wage: Ordinary Work in Diverse Economies*. Bristol: Bristol University Press.

Nemet, G.F., Callaghan, M.W, Creutzig, F, Fuss, S, Hartmann, J, Hilaire, J, Lamb, W.F, Minx, J.C, Rogers, S. and Smith, P. (2018) 'Negative Emissions – Part 3: Innovation and Upscaling', *Environmental Research Letters*, 13(6). DOI: 10.1088/1748–9326/aabff4

Neumayer, E. (2003) *Weak versus Strong Sustainability: Exploring the Limits of Two Opposing Paradigms*. Northampton, MA: Edward Elgar Publishing.

Purvis, B., Mao, Y. and Robinson, D. (2019) 'Three Pillars of Sustainability: In Search of Conceptual Origins', *Sustainability Science*, 14, pp. 681–695. DOI: 10.1007/s11625-018-0627-5.2

Rauschmayer, F. and Omann, I. (2017) 'Needs as a Central Element of Sustainable Development', in Spash, C.L. (ed.) *Routledge Handbook of Ecological Economics: Nature and Society*. Abingdon: Routledge, pp. 246–255.

Rübner Hansen, B. (2019) ' "Batshit Jobs" – No One Should Have to Destroy the Planet to Make a Living', *OpenDemocracy UK*. www.opendemocracy.net/en/opendemocracyuk/batshit-jobs-no-one-should-have-to-destroy-the-planet-to-make-a-living/

Sage, D. (2019) 'Unemployment, Wellbeing and the Power of the Work Ethic: Implications for Social Policy', *Critical Social Policy*, 39(2), pp. 205–228. DOI: 10.1177/0261018318780910

Salleh, A. (2010) 'From Metabolic Rift to "Metabolic Value": Reflections on Environmental Sociology and the Alternative Globalization Movement', *Organization & Environment*, 23(2), pp. 205–219. DOI: 10.1177/1086026610372134

Sayer, A. (2000) *Realism and Social Science*. London: Sage Publications.

UNDP (2015) *Work for Human Development: Human Development Report 2015*. New York: United Nations Development Programme.

UNEP, ILO, IOE and ITUC (2008) 'Green Jobs: Towards Decent Work in a Sustainable, Low-Carbon World', www.unep.org/labour_environment/features/greenjobs.asp.

UNFCCC (2015) 'Paris Agreement', https://unfccc.int/sites/default/files/english_paris_agreement.pdf.

von Redecker, E. (2020) *Revolution für das Leben: Philosophie der neuen Protestformen*. Frankfurt am Main: S. Fischer.

Weeks, K. (2011) *The Problem with Work: Feminism, Marxism, Antiwork Politics, and Postwork Imaginaries*. Durham, NC: Duke University Press.

INDEX

For Product Safety Concerns and Information please contact our EU representative GPSR@taylorandfrancis.com
Taylor & Francis Verlag GmbH, Kaufingerstraße 24, 80331 München, Germany

www.ingramcontent.com/pod-product-compliance
Ingram Content Group UK Ltd.
Pitfield, Milton Keynes, MK11 3LW, UK
UKHW022017180926
475701UK00005B/881
9781032376622